Blending Human Intelligence With Technology in the Classroom

Mohammed H. Alaqad
University of Malaya, Malaysia

Ghadah Al Murshidi
UAE University, UAE

Abdesselam Bougdira
Université Sidi Mohamed Ben Abdellah de Fès, Morocco

Badria Almurshidi
University of South Carolina, USA

Ahmed Al Zaabi
Universiti Utara Malaysia, Malaysia

IGI Global
Scientific Publishing
Publishing Tomorrow's Research Today

Vice President of Editorial Melissa Wagner
Managing Editor of Acquisitions Mikaela Felty
Managing Editor of Book Development Jocelynn Hessler
Production Manager Mike Brehm
Cover Design Phillip Shickler

Published in the United States of America by
IGI Global Scientific Publishing
701 East Chocolate Avenue
Hershey, PA, 17033, USA
Tel: 717-533-8845
Fax: 717-533-8661
Website: https://www.igi-global.com E-mail: cust@igi-global.com

Library of Congress Cataloging-in-Publication Data

Names: Al Aqad, Mohammed, 1985- editor. | Al Murshidi, Ghadah, 1985- editor. | Bougdira, Abdesselam, 1985- editor. | Almurshidi, Badria, 1979- editor. | Alzaabi, Ahmed, 1978- editor.
Title: Blending human intelligence with technology in the classroom / edited by Mohammed Al Aqad, Ghadah Al Murshidi, Abdesselam Bougdira, Badria Almurshidi, Ahmed Alzaabi.
Description: Herhsey, PA : IGI Global Scientific Publishing, [2025] | Includes bibliographical references and index. | Summary: "This book explores the transformative potential of artificial intelligence in the realm of education, offering a comprehensive understanding of how the strategic integration of emerging technologies, such as AI-powered adaptive learning platforms, intelligent tutoring systems, and automated grading tools, can empower educators to redefine teaching and learning paradigms by enabling personalized instruction, real-time performance insights, and enhanced student engagement and outcomes"-- Provided by publisher.
Identifiers: LCCN 2024060409 (print) | LCCN 2024060410 (ebook) | ISBN 9798337307718 (hardcover) | ISBN 9798337307725 (paperback) | ISBN 9798337307732 (ebook)
Subjects: LCSH: Artificial intelligence--Educational applications--Case studies. | Educational technology--Case studies.
Classification: LCC LB1028.43 .B5945 2025 (print) | LCC LB1028.43 (ebook) | DDC 371.33/463--dc23/eng/20250304
LC record available at https://lccn.loc.gov/2024060409
LC ebook record available at https://lccn.loc.gov/2024060410

British Cataloguing in Publication Data
A Cataloguing in Publication record for this book is available from the British Library.

Table of Contents

Detailed Table of Contents

Preface

INTRODUCTION

The integration of technology in education has dramatically reshaped the learning environment, merging traditional teaching methods with cutting-edge technological innovations. As we venture further into the era of Education 4.0, driven by advancements such as Artificial Intelligence (AI), Virtual Reality (VR), and the Internet of Things (IoT), it is crucial to understand how these innovations can be harmoniously blended with human intelligence to enhance teaching and learning.

"Blending Human Intelligence with Technology in the Classroom" explores the profound potential of AI in the educational landscape, offering a comprehensive analysis of how AI-powered tools, such as adaptive learning platforms, intelligent tutoring systems, and automated grading solutions, can empower educators to redefine the educational experience. This book delves into the transformative impact of AI, focusing on its capacity to enable personalized instruction, provide real-time performance feedback, and foster deeper student engagement.

While the promises of AI in education are immense, challenges remain. Teachers' trust in AI-based technologies often hinges on perceptions of their benefits, concerns over the lack of human interaction, and the anxiety surrounding its adoption. The goal of this book is to strike a balance between technological advancements and the enhancement of pedagogical approaches. As we incorporate these new tools into the classroom, it is essential to ensure that the voices of students, teachers, and educational institutions are always at the heart of this transformation.

The content of this book is based on recent empirical research and offers a thorough exploration of AI's potential to improve education. Topics covered include the integration of personalized learning algorithms, the role of intelligent tutoring systems in improving student outcomes, and the implications of automated grading in shaping education. As we look to the future, this book emphasizes the importance of incorporating innovative educational practices, such as Indigenous Pedagogies, into AI system design and development, ensuring that all educational systems remain inclusive and culturally relevant.

Our primary objective in this work is to provide a resource that offers actionable insights and practical strategies for educators at all levels, from K-12 teachers to university lecturers. We also aim to provide academic researchers, policymakers, EdTech developers, and students with a deep understanding of the opportunities and challenges associated with AI in education.

We invite you to explore the chapters of this book with a critical yet open mind, as we navigate the evolving landscape of education in the age of AI. Through careful consideration of both the potential and the challenges, we hope to inspire thoughtful dialogue and meaningful action towards an inclusive, innovative, and equitable future for all learners.

ORGANIZATION OF THE BOOK

Chapter 1: Impact of AI in Education Sector

In this chapter, we explore the growing role of artificial intelligence in addressing the persistent challenges faced in the education sector. As technology continues to advance, educators are increasingly turning to AI tools for their potential to enhance teaching and learning. AI-powered features such as speech recognition offer opportunities to provide tailored support to diverse student populations, including multilingual learners and those with disabilities. This chapter highlights how AI is already being integrated into classrooms and examines the potential of these tools to improve lesson planning, content selection, and overall educational outcomes. The findings underscore the transformative impact of AI in creating a more adaptable and personalized learning experience for students.

Chapter 2: Artificial Intelligence and Machine Learning Methods in the Field of Learning and Development with Focus on Gamification

This chapter delves into the intersection of AI, machine learning, and gamification within the context of learning and development. With the shift toward hybrid and gig-based work environments, the need for personalized learning solutions has become more pressing. The introduction of gamification, where learning modules and assessments are integrated into complex games, has revolutionized the delivery of training programs. The chapter examines the impact of gamification on employee learning experiences, particularly for those newly onboarded, and explores the broader implications of AI and machine learning across various fields of learning and development. It emphasizes the need for cost-effective, scalable solutions that align with the needs of a global workforce.

Chapter 3: Incorporating Artificial Intelligence as a Tool in Teaching Writing Skills

In this chapter, the authors investigate the role of AI tools in transforming the teaching of writing skills, particularly in English composition classes. While AI's ability to speed up the writing process has undeniable advantages, there are concerns regarding overreliance on technology, which may hinder critical thinking and creativity. The chapter reviews traditional pedagogical approaches and explores how AI can both support and challenge existing methods. By analyzing case studies, the chapter offers strategies for integrating AI in a way that fosters creativity and critical thinking, ensuring that educational outcomes are aligned with human cognitive development.

Chapter 4: Enhancing Students' Reading Comprehension Skills through the Use of Epic: A Comparative Study

This chapter focuses on the use of the Epic reading application to enhance reading comprehension among English as a Foreign Language (EFL) students in the United Arab Emirates. Through a mixed-methods study involving 45 Grade 1 Arab students, the chapter assesses the effectiveness of digital reading tools in improving student engagement and learning outcomes. The findings reveal a significant increase in reading motivation, vocabulary acquisition, and overall reading fluency among students. The chapter also highlights the role of digital platforms in fostering gender-specific learning patterns and encouraging greater parental involvement, demonstrating the potential of technology in transforming language learning environments.

Chapter 5: Humanizing the Digital Classroom: The Educator's Role in Fostering Connection Amidst Technology

In this chapter, the authors discuss the crucial role of educators in maintaining human connections within digital classrooms. As technology continues to shape education, the need for social-emotional learning (SEL) and inclusion becomes more pronounced. This chapter provides practical strategies for educators to foster meaningful relationships with students, emphasizing the importance of empathy, communication, and collaboration. By integrating SEL principles into the curriculum and utilizing digital tools to enhance cooperation, educators can create engaging and inclusive learning environments that support student well-being and academic success.

Chapter 6: Balancing Screen Time and Human Interaction in Blended Learning

This chapter addresses the challenges of balancing digital learning with face-to-face interaction in blended learning environments. While digital tools provide unparalleled access to information and enhance student-centered learning, excessive screen time can detract from the social and emotional development of students. The chapter advocates for a balanced approach that integrates technology in a way that complements human interaction rather than replacing it. By examining the cognitive, social, and emotional impacts of screen overuse, the chapter offers practical frameworks for educators to design blended learning experiences that foster both technological literacy and meaningful human connections.

Chapter 7: ChatGPT: The End of Critical Thinking as We Know It

This chapter critically examines the potential impact of ChatGPT on critical thinking skills in educational settings. A systematic review of existing studies highlights both the benefits and risks associated with the use of AI in the classroom. While ChatGPT can enhance lower-order cognitive skills such as knowledge acquisition, its overuse may hinder higher-order thinking, including analysis and problem-solving. The chapter calls for careful management of AI tools in education to ensure they complement, rather than replace, critical thinking and independent learning. The authors emphasize the importance of educator involvement in guiding students to use AI responsibly, ensuring it enhances cognitive efforts without diminishing intellectual autonomy.

Chapter 8: Integrating Classkick in TEFL Instruction: Enhancing Classroom Engagement and Learning Outcomes

This chapter explores how the Classkick platform has been integrated into English as a Foreign Language (EFL) classes for primary school students, specifically focusing on grade five learners in public schools. Through a mixed-methods approach, the study reveals that Classkick significantly enhances academic participation and engagement. Interactive features, real-time responses, and an easy-to-use interface were pivotal in boosting students' motivation and self-confidence. Teachers also observed increased cooperative learning, as the platform fostered a student-centered environment. The findings underscore the potential of Classkick to transform traditional EFL teaching and learning, making it a valuable tool for future language acquisition initiatives in computer-assisted learning contexts.

Chapter 9: The Role of Assistive Technology in Supporting Special Education Needs

Focusing on inclusive education, this chapter addresses the critical role technology plays in supporting students with special education needs. It aligns with the UN Convention on the Rights of Persons with Disabilities, which advocates for equal access to education. The chapter emphasizes how technology, when appropriately implemented, enables access to education for all learners, regardless of their abilities. Assistive technology offers personalized learning experiences, ensuring that students with disabilities are not left behind. By highlighting various assistive tools, the chapter presents technology as a powerful enabler in creating inclusive educational environments where every student has an opportunity to succeed.

Chapter 10: Revolutionizing Classroom Learning with Advanced Technology: Harnessing Augmented Reality (AR) and Virtual Reality (VR) for Immersive Education

This chapter introduces Augmented Reality (AR) and Virtual Reality (VR) as transformative technologies in the classroom. It outlines how these immersive tools blend digital and physical environments to engage students in new ways, enhancing their motivation and accommodating diverse learning styles. The chapter draws from global case studies, showcasing how AR and VR have been used successfully in educational settings. While the technologies provide rich learning experiences, the chapter also addresses challenges like accessibility and teacher readiness. Actionable strategies are proposed to integrate AR and VR into curricula effectively, maximizing their educational potential and ensuring sustainable implementation.

Chapter 11: Teacher Preparation and Professional Development Programs with Technology-Enhanced Learning

In this chapter, the importance of integrating technology into teacher preparation and professional development programs is explored. With the increasing reliance on digital tools in teaching, this chapter emphasizes the need for teachers to enhance their digital literacy. It examines the evolving role of Professional Development Programs (PDPs) in equipping teachers with the necessary skills to use technology effectively in the classroom. The chapter identifies key challenges in integrating technology into teacher preparation and offers practical solutions to overcome them. Additionally, it provides guiding principles for developing comprehensive PDPs that support teachers in adopting technology-enhanced learning methods to improve teaching outcomes.

Chapter 12: Building Teacher Skills for Effective Integration of Technology in the Classroom

As the integration of technology into classrooms continues to reshape education, this chapter focuses on developing teachers' skills to leverage technology for effective learning outcomes. It highlights frameworks such as SAMR and TPACK, which guide teachers in aligning technology with curriculum goals and assessing its impact on students' learning. The chapter explores blended and flipped classroom models, underlining how these innovative approaches enhance student engagement and comprehension. By fostering a culture of continuous professional development, the chapter offers a roadmap for educators and school leaders to integrate technology meaningfully into the learning process, ensuring that classrooms are equipped for the digital age.

Chapter 13: Teachers in Blended Learning Environment: Mapping Their Evolving Roles

Blended learning, which combines traditional teaching with digital tools, is reshaping the role of teachers. This chapter delves into the evolving responsibilities of educators in blended learning environments, offering an in-depth analysis based on recent research. By examining various studies, the chapter outlines the potential roles that teachers can adopt to drive deeper changes in educational practices. It emphasizes the need for targeted professional development programs that equip educators with the skills to navigate this shift. The chapter also provides insights into policy implications for teacher education, suggesting strategies to enhance teacher readiness in adapting to blended learning models.

Chapter 14: Future Trends in Blended Learning and the Evolving Role of Teachers

Looking ahead, this chapter explores the future of blended learning and its impact on teachers' roles in education. Blended learning, which combines face-to-face and online learning, is increasingly being adopted due to its flexibility and ability to cater to individual student needs. The chapter outlines various blended learning models, such as flipped classrooms and rotation models, while highlighting the benefits of personalized instruction and increased student engagement. However, it also discusses challenges like the digital divide and the need for proper teacher training. The chapter concludes by examining emerging trends, such as gamification and immersive learning through VR and AR, which will continue to shape the future of blended learning and educators' roles in these dynamic learning environments.

CONCLUSION

In conclusion, this collection of chapters provides a comprehensive exploration of the transformative role technology plays in modern education. From enhancing classroom engagement with platforms like Classkick to revolutionizing learning experiences through AR and VR, the contributions highlight the immense potential of digital tools to shape the future of teaching and learning. The chapters also emphasize the critical need for educators to continuously develop their digital skills through professional development programs and the integration of technology in their teaching practices. As we look to the future, the evolving role of teachers in blended learning environments and the advancement of assistive technologies further underscore the importance of inclusivity and adaptability in educational settings. Together, these insights offer a roadmap for educators, institutions, and policymakers striving to create more dynamic, engaging, and equitable learning experiences for all students. We hope this book serves as a valuable resource for educators and leaders committed to harnessing the power of technology to enhance educational outcomes worldwide.

Mohammed H. Alaqad
University of Malaya, Malaysia

Ghadah Al Murshidi
UAE University, UAE

Abdesselam Bougdira
Université Sidi Mohamed Ben Abdellah de Fès, Morocco

Badria Almurshidi
University of South Carolina, USA

Ahmed Al Zaabi
Universiti Utara Malaysia, Malaysia

Chapter 1
Impact of AI in Education Sector

Deepa Sharma
https://orcid.org/0000-0003-4374-917X
Maharishi Markandeshwar University, India

ABSTRACT

Many of the goals set to improve teaching and learning are not being achieved today. Educators are looking for scalable, safe, and effective ways to meet these concerns with the help of technology. Educators naturally wonder if the rapid advances in technology can be beneficial in daily life. Like everyone else, teachers use AI-powered services in their daily lives. Examples include automated travel planning on their phones, voice assistants in their homes, and tools that can create essays, correct grammar, and finish sentences. AI tools have just been made available to the public, and many instructors are eagerly investigating them. Educators see the potential to leverage AI-powered features like speech recognition to improve the support they provide to multilingual children, students with disabilities, and other learners who could use more customization and adaptability from digital learning tools. They are investigating how AI can help them write or enhance classes, as well as how they find, select, and modify content for their lessons.

BACKGROUND

The branch of computer science known as artificial intelligence (AI) focuses on building intelligent machines that can replicate human intellect (Amponsah et al., 2022). AI has permeated every aspect of our lives, from the snarky replies you get from Siri on your smartphones to the self-driving cars that seem like they belong in a science fiction film.AI helps physicians diagnose illnesses in the healthcare

DOI: 10.4018/979-8-3373-0771-8.ch001

industry, and also analyzes financial data to identify fraudulent activity (Wilkens et al., 2020). As you can see, artificial intelligence is more than just a fancy word used by techies. It has already arrived and is improving the efficiency and ease of our lives. AI saves teachers time by helping with administrative duties like assessment and grading. AI-powered automated grading systems simplify repetitive duties, freeing up teachers to concentrate on mentorship, interactive teaching strategies, and focused interventions for underachieving students (Felix et al., 2020).

The advent of devices like mobile phones and calculators, as well as their possible effects on education and learning, are frequently the subject of intense controversy, generating discussions about both the advantages and disadvantages (Stone et al., 2020). No matter where you are, it is essential for you and your pupils to grasp the fundamentals and adjust to ever changing technology. Although many of us may be unfamiliar with the AI issue, it has existed for decades. In order to train a computer to play checkers, the first artificial intelligence software was created in 1951. The computer was able to play checkers at a respectable pace by the next year. The need to comprehend and assess AI grew as it started to develop. In the 1930s, Alan Turing, a British logician and computer pioneer, started researching machine intelligence. He proposed key ideas of artificial intelligence in the 1950s and questioned if a computer could think. The Turing test is still used to assess computer intelligence, and Turing is now regarded as the founder of artificial intelligence and contemporary cognitive science. As technology developed across the world in the next decades, it entered classrooms (Vartiainen et al., 2024). Unprecedented possibilities arose with every new tool, if the technology was applied properly. More recently, the educational environment has been irrevocably changed by cell phones and the internet. AI is expected to follow suit. In other words, In fact, the phrase "artificial intelligence" was first used in 1956. The phrase "artificial intelligence" was first used in that year at a crucial workshop led by John Mc Carthy, a professor at Dartmouth College, with the goal of building robots that could reason and speak like humans. One Research interest in artificial intelligence (AI) waned for a few decades after a rapid start, but improvements in machine learning and neural networks in the 1990s sparked a comeback. An important turning point was reached in 2022 with the public release of Chat GPT, which demonstrated previously unheard-of powers in natural language synthesis and comprehension and fueled other AI developments. AI now has a big influence on a lot of industries, including manufacturing, transportation, healthcare, and finance. Many believe it has the potential to transform education as well.

Education: The process of transmitting information, skills, and character qualities is called education, and the wide spectrum of activities pertaining to learning and knowledge distribution is known as the education sector. Formal, informal, and non-formal education are only a few of the various modes of education.

Education Sector: A wide range of learning and knowledge-dissemination-related activities are included in the educational sector. It is essential in forming people, communities, and countries. In order to increase knowledge and develop skills, it refers to the teaching, training, and learning process, particularly in schools and universities (Giuggioli et al., 2023).The education sectors include both public and private educational institutions that offer instruction at different levels, ranging from kindergarten to higher education. The field of education has a significant role in forming people, communities, and countries (Singh, E. et al., 2024). It is essential for preparing children's and teens for the tasks and responsibilities of adulthood.

AI in Education: One of the most significant instruments influencing education and preparing students for the workforce of the future is artificial intelligence. In order to increase standards, accessibility, and creativity in the field and improve teaching and learning globally, education has embraced the introduction of artificial intelligence. The application of AI in education has transformed the field and is driving changes in the way that education is provided, just like it has in many other fields. The advent of AI has altered people's perceptions of education and given the education industry a whole new character. AI now has a significant impact on education and has created a wealth of new prospects for institutions, instructors, and students. Artificial intelligence has the ability to improve learning, support educators, and promote more successful customized learning in the classroom. This is both exciting and a little intimidating (Paschen et al., 2019). One must first go past fantastical science-fiction visions of computers and robots educating our kids in place of teachers and eliminating the human element from what is really a human activity if one hopes to have a meaningful discussion about AI in education. AI improves classroom education in many ways rather than diminishing it. Artificial Intelligence (AI) in Education AI is the brain behind chatbots like Siri and Alexa. AI ensures that every student gets the same level of direction and attention. AI is drastically changing the way students learn in the digital age. Data on student's learning patterns can be analyzed by artificial intelligence, which gives timely feedback. It is slowly making its way into our classrooms, bringing with it a variety of benefits and challenges (Satratzemi et al., 2019). Below we describe the importance of AI in education and how students benefit from it.

1. **Personalization:** Determining how to address the requirements of each children's in one's classroom may be extremely challenging for a single instructor (Okunlaya et al., 2022). AI systems may tailor training according to each student's strengths and shortcomings and readily adjust to their unique learning demands.
2. **Tutoring:** AI programs are able to provide tailored support and instruction by gauging a student's learning style and prior knowledge.

3. **Grading:** AI can compile data about how students performed and even grade more abstract assessments such as essays, in addition to assisting with test grading using an answer key (Amponsah et al., 2022).
4. **Course quality feedback:** For instance, AI can zero in on the specific information or concepts that students are missing, so educators can deliver targeted improvements in materials and methods if a large number of students are giving erroneous answers to a topic.
5. **Giving student's timely and meaningful feedback:** While some students might be afraid to take chances or get critical comments in the classroom, with AI, students can feel comfortable to make the mistakes necessary for learning and receive the feedback they need for improvement (Felix et al., 2020). The main goal of AI's potential in education is to free up teachers' time from boring activities so they may focus on more important ones.

Examples of AI in Education

a. **Offer AI learning assistants and tutors:** AI in education isn't meant to take the place of educators. Indeed, chatbots and AI tutors may help teachers and offer individualized learning support to students. These virtual aides increase the effectiveness and concentration of the learning process while also making education more enjoyable (Kong et al., 2024).

A tutor will help you solve problems step-by-step. For topics where students frequently struggle, schools can implement one. As an alternative, AI chatbots provide 24/7 answers to frequently asked inquiries, cutting down on response times.

b. **Use instructional games and simulations to teach:** These methods make learning difficult without feeling like learning. With this specific use of AI, learning may really become a fun experience. Adaptive learning environments are produced by advanced AI systems. To put it another way, they adjust the study materials to the unique learning preferences and speeds of each learner. Additionally, AI data give teachers insight into students' performance and learning styles.
c. **Automate grading and give immediate feedback:** Continuous feedback is essential for student achievement, and quick grading makes assessments easier. AI makes both feasible, allowing teachers to concentrate less on paperwork and more on knowledge exchange. Both parties benefit: teachers get to actively educate and help kids develop their abilities, while young learners gain assistance in learning more quickly. Flashcards, games, and quizzes with immediate feedback are used in teaching on platforms such as Quizlet. There are several feedback

mechanisms available in Turnitin Feedback Studio. Gradescop was created to make it easier for teachers to grade assessments that were completed on paper. The sidekicks that identify pupils' errors are artificial intelligence algorithms. However, they whisper advice to get better rather than yelling them out. They are able to provide each student with tailored, practical advice on how to get better.

d. **Automate administrative duties:** A magic assistant robot can be used by teachers. A tool or platform that manages all the tedious paperwork and schoolwork not a real robot. Teachers now have more time and mental energy to spend with their kids and instruct thanks to automation (Klaus et al., 2020). Additionally, having all of the learning resources in one place makes the schools smarter. Google for Education offers a full range of tools to automate communication and classroom administration. Additionally, School Mint automates key administrative procedures including school choice and enrollment. Teachers may better manage their classrooms and recover control of their time with the aid of AI-driven technologies.

INTRODUCTION

Artificial Intelligence is a technology that is revolutionizing all aspects of life, despite its general lack of familiarity. It is a versatile tool that helps individuals to reconsider how we combine data, evaluate information, and use the insights that are obtained to make better decisions. We believe that this thorough review will help policymakers, opinion leaders, and interested observers understand artificial intelligence (AI) and show how it is already changing the world and posing significant issues for government, the economy, and society. In order to make choices, artificial intelligence systems frequently need real-time data. They differ from passive machines, which can only react mechanically or according to preset patterns. Through the use of sensors, digital data, or remote inputs, they aggregate data from several sources, do real-time analysis, and take action based on the insights gained. They are capable of extremely sophisticated analysis and decision-making thanks to significant advancements in storage systems, computing rates, and analytical methodologies. In today era, Artificial Intelligence (AI) can improve consistency in our complex decision-making processes and eliminate thoughtless human errors. AI has the potential to greatly benefit people, as it takes away the boring and tedious tasks that no one likes to do. AI in education is used for many purposes, including data-driven curriculum creation insights, intelligent learning systems, automated grading, and personalized learning (Chen et al., 2024). By drastically cutting down on grading time and providing immediate, in-depth feedback, AI can improve grading efficiency, accuracy, and fairness. It enables teachers to provide students with more writing tasks and quick, helpful feedback, which help students, develop their writing abilities (Ivanov et al., 2023). It enables teachers to provide students with more writing tasks and quick, helpful feedback, which help students, develop their writing abilities. By drastically cutting down on grading time and providing immediate, in-depth feedback, AI can improve grading efficiency, accuracy, and fairness. This enables teachers to provide students with more writing assignments and quick, helpful feedback, which help students, develop their writing abilities. Among the many technologies revolutionizing the world, artificial intelligence (AI) is now ubiquitous and has transformative pedagogical potential (Amponsah et al., 2022).

AI enables teachers to customize lessons to meet each unique student's needs, thereby increasing learning effectiveness and engagement. Additionally, AI-enabled technology helps with administrative duties, streamlining processes and allowing teachers to focus on instruction. With the current uses of AI-powered technologies by teachers and school administrators, it won't be wrong to say that AI in education will be very useful in the future as well. Education is the sector where AI is expected to have a significant impact. Platforms with AI capabilities can help in this by offering real-time communication and teamwork capabilities. Standardized exams that only help assess a limited range of student skills should be eliminated with the help of AI assessment techniques. AI gives customized feedback keeping in mind the unique learning preferences of each student. AI has the ability to completely transform a wide range of sectors, including healthcare, banking, education, and more, it has grown in significance in the modern world. In a number of industries, the application of AI has already raised accuracy, decreased expenses, and boosted efficiency (Leelavathi et al., 2024) . AI has the ability to completely transform education by providing more specialized and personalized instruction as well as better learning results. AI can evaluate student data and give teachers and students immediate feedback so they may modify their methods of instruction and learning. The potential to deliver specialized and personalized instruction is one of the main advantages of AI in education. AI is able to evaluate student data and provide a customized learning plan for every student, accounting for their learning preferences, areas of strength, and shortcomings (Benuyenah et al., 2023) . Learning results and engagement might be significantly enhanced by this strategy. AI has huge educational potential and is predicted to completely change how we approach degree and certificate programs in the future. AI has huge educational potential and is predicted to completely change how we approach degree and certificate programs in the future (Felix et al., 2020). AI-powered tools may provide students immediate feedback, assist them in maintaining their academic progress, and deliver a more interesting and customized learning environment.

LITERATURE REVIEW

Many reviews have been studied regarding the impact of AI in the field of education. According to Ivanov (2023) the purpose of the paper was to assess how ChatGPT will affect tourism research and education. The findings suggest that due to its ability to create assignments and research papers, ChatGPT has the potential to completely transform tourism education and research. According to Giuggioli (2023) this study shows how artificial intelligence (AI) has a significant impact on entrepreneurship and how AI affects entrepreneurship as a facilitator for entrepreneurs. The findings show AI particularly benefits entrepreneurs in four areas such as opportunities, performance, decision making, and education and research. Although there is growing consensus about the disruptive potential of artificial intelligence (AI) and its beneficial effects on entrepreneurship, there is a distinct lack of knowledge of AI on this relationship in organizations. According to Elbanna (2024), the purpose of this paper is to examine the benefits of using an innovative generative artificial intelligence (AI) technology in the classroom. It was to see how ChatGPT can be used for content creation, assessment, and personalized learning. According to the findings of the study, ChatGPT can be successfully incorporated in the classroom to automate repetitive work and improve students' learning experiences, which will ultimately boost output and efficiency and promote adaptive learning. Even with the updates, it is important to note the shortcomings of ChatGPT, which include factual errors, the potential to promote bias, lack of complete understanding, and security issues. Nevertheless, the study emphasizes the benefits of incorporating ChatGPT in a responsible manner in the educational sector. According to Hussain (2023) how artificial intelligence (AI) is a technology that is often used in libraries and has the potential to revolutionize one of the greatest services available in the information age. Also the purpose of this study was to demonstrate how AI is used in library operations. According to the results of this study, artificial intelligence (AI) is a promising technology that can be used in library services. However, there are several barriers that prevent AI from being fully implemented in library operations, including lack of funding, librarians' attitude, and technical expertise. The results also show that libraries will move more quickly in the right direction if AI is used in library operations. This study also identifies several applications that can be implemented without spending money. According to Felix (2020) this chapter examines the advantages and disadvantages of AI in higher education. Teachers are no longer the sole source of information due to the development of artificial intelligence (AI) and new technologies in general. The findings show that AI has enhanced teachers' uniquely human skills to ensure high-quality education. According to Satratzemi (2019) the purpose of this paper was to provide the results of earlier research and investigate the potential of voice assistants in the classroom. The findings show that artificial intelligence (AI) has progressed significantly in recent years, and its potential is only increasing. Natural language processing (NLP) is an application area of artificial intelligence. Voice assistants can interact with consumers in natural language and integrate AI through cloud computing. These days, voice assistants are found in millions of gadgets in homes because they are simple to use. Smart speakers are the most popular gadgets with voice assistants, and their use in colleges and universities is relatively new. According to Chen (2024) this study investigated how students use and engage with generative artificial intelligence (AI) technologies in their course. The purpose of this study was to see how students use these resources. The findings show that in addition to using AI to help come up with new ideas, most respondents used generative AI to generate ideas for papers, projects, or assignments. According to respondents, course syllabi and university regulations provide clear direction on the appropriate and ethical application of generative AI. According to Halgatti (2023), the goal of the study was to understand the function of AI in student performance assessment and to investigate its potential future role in educational performance assessment. The findings suggest that the application of AI in student performance assessment has assisted in early prediction of actions to be implemented by teachers. The data obtained from AI assessment can be combined and interpreted to create graphics. According to Wilkens (2020) the goal of this paper was to describe the ways in which artificial intelligence (AI) can enhance learning in the workplace. The findings suggest that AI has the potential to improve workplace learning and development for individuals. AI complements human intelligence, which can result in improvements, especially in terms of quality, accuracy, and precision. In addition, AI can help with organizational learning and the development of individual competence. However, artificial intelligence (AI) in the workplace has a dual impact as it easily exhibits reward effects in both individual and organizational learning, which can have unexpected consequences. According to Stone (2020) the goal of this paper was to analyze the literature on the use of artificial intelligence (AI) in strategic contexts and to point out research gaps in the area of using AI to inform strategic marketing choices. The findings suggest that the use of AI in strategic marketing decision making has not received much attention and it is time to focus on using AI for marketing decision making due to the lessons learned from the use of AI. According to Paschen (2019) the purpose of this study is to explain artificial intelligence (AI), a technological phenomenon, and how it can support B2B knowledge-based marketing. The findings explain the fundamental components of an artificial intelligence system and how they interact with each other. According to Klaus (2020) the purpose of this study was to describe how artificial intelligence (AI) has changed the consumer decision-making process and suggest how this change affects service management, service research, and service marketing. The results show that AI has taken consumer convenience to a new level.

Customers who use bots as their preferred service delegate their decision-making to algorithms and, as a result, pay little attention to traditional consumer decision-making models and brand focus. This is now especially true for low-involvement decisions, but high-involvement decisions are increasingly being handed over to AI. As a result, managers must change their approach to how customers make decisions and how services are run.

ROLE OF ARTIFICIAL INTELLIGENCE IN EDUCATION SYSTEM

The use or study of computer systems or machines that have some of the qualities that the human brain has is the definition of artificial intelligence. The ability to interpret and produce language in a way that seems human, recognize or create images, solve problems, and learn from data supplied to them is a few examples of these attributes. The ultimate goal of artificial intelligence is to optimize normal tasks by increasing their typical speed and efficiency (Amponsah et al., 2022). AI is already being used to reduce administrative duties in many schools, colleges, and institutions. AI is a relatively new technology, requiring further study and advancement to determine its optimal applications in education. Artificial intelligence can bring a positive change to teaching (Chen et al., 2024). It has many applications in education, and as AI progresses, new features are always being found. This can be implemented for the benefit of instructors and students. Here are some examples of how AI can be used in the classroom:

a. AI has been helpful in automating administrative duties such as marking and grading work.
b. AI can be used by teachers to create personalized learning programs for each student, taking into account the student's learning preferences, strong points, and areas of improvement.
c. Education experts can give students personalized feedback and explain to students how they can improve their work, but this can take a lot of time. Feedback generated by AI is more effective and can be a useful format for students who find it difficult to react to constructive criticism.
d. In online education, teachers can quickly design educational games, quizzes, or other activities that test and instruct students using AI. By tracking student answers and modifying the work to make it easier or more difficult, whether they get something right or wrong, this virtual learning can produce a personalized learning experience.
e. By entering the content to be covered in a syllabus or lesson, plans generated by AI can be tailored specifically to a class, student, or course.

f. AI can discover knowledge and skill gaps by analyzing data, including student assessments.
g. AI provides chatbots to answer inquiries. Chatbots are useful in universities, where students can ask questions and get the knowledge they need immediately. They can include details about courses, admissions, or student services.
h. AI can lighten the workload of teachers by taking over computer-based duties.
i. AI will be completely tailored to the individual's needs and also provide them with additional support beyond their teacher.

BENEFITS AND CHALLENGES OF AI IN EDUCATION

As artificial intelligence (AI) quickly advances both within and outside of education system, it has the potential to impact almost every facet of society and education.AI will be used more in curriculum building, education personalization, and promoting the testing of novel teaching and learning approaches as education rapidly changes (Halagatti et al., 2023). The potential of AI must be cautiously embraced, as is the case with the introduction of any new technology. Education professionals are eager to discover how AI will affect students and educators. It is their duty to harness AI's potential for good while actively avoiding pitfalls like bias, plagiarism, erroneous material, and cyber safety issues. Below we describe the benefits and challenges of AI in education. **AI's benefits for Education**: Despite being a relatively young technology, artificial intelligence is already having a significant and disruptive impact on education (Al-Mamary et al., 2024) .

1. **AI Personalizes Education:** Using data patterns, AI can understand a student's academic past and present carefully chosen information. You just need to ask!
2. **AI Automates Teacher and Administrator Tasks:** Teachers in a variety of school positions can save time by delegating administrative duties including posting assignments, sending emails, assessing student proficiency, and identifying patterns (Benuyenah et al., 2023).
3. **AI Provides Intelligent Educational material:** Asking AI to provide interesting and educational material may help both teachers and students. In a lot less time than it would typically take to construct a new curriculum unit, teachers may produce complete lesson or unit plans.
4. **AI Enhances Educational Equity and Accessibility:** Learners may get top-notch instruction and even have it translated, which enhances educational equity, no matter where they are in the globe. AI-driven conversion technologies can be used to transform the information into a more accessible format for those who are blind or hard of hearing.

5. **AI Fills Skill Gaps in Education:** Students can use AI to improve their skills without having to ask their teachers to create additional practice materials.
6. **AI Provides Students with Data-Based Feedback**: Teachers, families, and children can communicate openly thanks to AI's data-based feedback system. It can decrease or eliminate prejudice, raise student happiness, and pinpoint which students are still falling short of content standards (Giuggioli et al., 2023). All members of the school community may stay informed about trends for individuals or the district as a whole by swiftly synthesizing its data.
7. **AI Enhancements Instructors:** Teachers are indispensable, and AI in education is a useful adjunct to this fundamentally human profession. Based on the observations of instructional coaches, AI can assist with student tutoring or recommend professional development to instructors in understaffed schools.
8. **AI Tutors around-the-Clock:** Study buddies and tutor bots are two popular uses of AI in education. When students are alone and in need of one-on-one attention, conversational AI aides can provide it. Compared to earlier times, chatbots are now far more advanced (Halagatti et al., 2023). They may respond to inquiries from students, check the quality of their responses, and even recommend changes based on each student's historical performance statistics.
9. **AI Offers Secure Learning Systems for Data protection:** All educational institutions have student data protection as one of their top priorities. Decentralized AI-based solutions enhance data security and protection (Chen et al., 2024).
10. **AI Provides Education Assessment Integrity:** AI for education can keep an eye on students during online tests by tracking their web browser usage and using their camera and microphone to ward against questionable activity. It can exchange information on patterns seen with specific students and promptly alert teachers or proctors about problems.

AI'S CHALLENGES FOR EDUCATION

It's crucial to remember that AI in education is still very new. There will be restrictions that must be addressed when the education industry adjusts and gains a greater understanding of AI. Accessibility is one of the key issues. Learners who are unable to use AI-powered tools and platforms are denied opportunities that AI offers. AI in education has countless advantages, but it also raises concerns about educational equity and the potential for a growing divide between those who have access to it and those who do not, depending on financial class and geographic location, among other factors. The ethical and privacy issues around the use of AI in education provide another obstacle to overcome. One significant barrier to the use of AI in education that has to be overcome is the concern about privacy violations and inadequate data protection. Discrimination and bias are also seen as limitations, referring to the algorithms that run the platforms and may exploit societal biases (Hussain et al., 2023). All students, teachers, administrators, and institutions wishing to use AI in the education field should be aware of these difficulties, which stand in the way of the use of AI in education.

1. **AI in Education:** While there are many benefits to using AI in education, there are also some drawbacks that should be considered.
2. **Privacy:** Complete defense against a cyber attack is not guaranteed, even when cybersecurity best practices are followed. To guarantee that data and content processed by AI technology are used appropriately, companies that produce AI products must adhere to industry security requirements.
3. **Equity:** Although AI may provide educational materials to every location in the globe, using the technology requires internet connectivity. Communities that already lack resources are burdened further by this, which may cause them to fall farther behind.
4. **Teaching roles:** AI will alter the function of the teacher as we presently understand it, but it will never completely replace human instructors. Some people are concerned about what it will be like to teach in an AI-powered classroom.
5. **Ethics:** There are issues with algorithmic prejudice and other ethical applications of AI. This happens when erroneous assumptions made throughout the machine learning process cause the algorithm to provide results that are consistently biased.

CHALLENGES OF AI TO SOCIETY

a. **Job Losses:** The possibility that AI would supplant human labor is one of the primary worries surrounding this technology. The ability of more sophisticated AI systems to carry out activities that were previously completed by humans might result in employment losses in some industries.
b. **Bias and Discrimination:** AI systems' level of objectivity is determined on the data they are trained on. AI systems have the potential to reinforce preexisting prejudice and discrimination if they are trained on biased or insufficient data. Biased AI systems have the potential to reinforce current disparities, which can have major repercussions, especially in fields like hiring and criminal justice.

c. **Lack of Transparency:** Another issue with AI is that certain systems are opaque. It might be difficult to identify biases or errors in AI systems due to their complexity and difficulty in understanding. This lack of transparency may make it challenging to hold AI systems accountable for their actions.
d. **Cyber security Risks:** As artificial intelligence becomes more integrated into our daily lives, new cyber security threats also arise. Systems with AI capabilities may be susceptible to hacking and other online assaults, which might result in data breaches and other security risks.

IMPACT OF AI IN EDUCATION

In order to enhance the entire educational experience, higher education has been increasingly embracing contemporary technology and methods in recent years. Examples of how technology has enhanced student engagement and educational planning include learning management systems, gamification, video-assisted learning, and virtual and augmented reality. Let's discuss AI in the classroom (Elbanna et al., 2024) . Students could instantaneously participate in real-time conversations and respond to multiple-choice questions using the classroom response system. Even while technology has greatly improved education, there are still worries about how it may affect universities. Many conventional universities and colleges are concerned about their institutions futures due to the growth of online education and the expansion of educational resources available online (Chen et al., 2024). Unquestionably, AI is revolutionizing every aspect of education institutions. It is crucial that we use AI responsibly going ahead in order to take advantage of its potential to build a progressive and inclusive educational environment that benefits all students. Beyond conventional bounds, artificial intelligence (AI) has become a transformative force that is changing industries all over the world. The way we teach and learn is being drastically altered by the widespread use of technology in the educational field. AI is revolutionizing the education industry by bringing about major improvements in teaching strategies, individualized learning, and general student engagement. By fusing the best qualities of instructors and technology, artificial intelligence (AI) in education seeks to maximize student results. A new age of innovation and change is being ushered in by artificial intelligence, which is changing the face of education. Traditional educational methods are being transformed by AI technologies, which offer cutting-edge solutions that adjust to the demands of each individual student, expedite administrative duties, and yield insightful data through data analytics (Hussain et al., 2023). AI is revolutionizing the way that knowledge is taught and learned, from sophisticated tutoring programs to engaging virtual reality experiences. Even while there are a ton of potential advantages, there are also problems with equal access, data privacy, and ethical issues. The importance of comprehending and utilizing AI' s influence to establish a more flexible, inclusive and productive learning environment is highlighted by the dynamic interaction between technology development and educational growth. Artificial intelligence (AI) is a powerful catalyst for improving teaching efficacy in various ways. By evaluating individual student data, AI makes personalized learning experiences possible, allowing teachers to tailor their lessons to students' varying learning styles and paces. This flexibility results in students having a better understanding of things. AI saves teachers time by helping with administrative duties such as assessment and grading. AI-powered automated grading systems simplify repetitive duties, allowing teachers to focus on mentorship, interactive teaching strategies, and focused interventions for low-achieving students. This makes it possible for teachers to quickly spot learning gaps and proactively fix them. Additionally, AI provides data-driven analytics, giving teachers critical information about students' growth and areas that need improvement. AI helps teachers grow professionally by giving them access to cutting-edge information and technologies (Amponsah et al., 2022). It helps teachers keep up to speed on changing teaching approaches by facilitating ongoing learning and updates on best practices. Essentially, AI enhances the efficacy of instruction by offering individualized assistance, automating repetitive activities, delivering real-time insights, and promoting continuous professional growth. AI is a cooperative partner that enables educators to design dynamic and captivating learning environments, which eventually helps students and instructors in their educational journey. AI makes it easier to transition from a one-size-fits-all strategy to customized lesson plans. Real-time feedback is provided by intelligent teaching systems, which pinpoint problem areas and provide focused support. In addition to addressing individual learning gaps, this encourages a mastery-based, self-paced educational approach. AI also brings data-driven insights into instructional strategies. In order to maximize learning outcomes, educators may use analytics to evaluate student development, pinpoint successful teaching methods, and make well-informed judgments (Al-Mamary et al., 2024). Teachers will move into positions that prioritize mentoring, creativity, and individualized instruction as AI becomes more incorporated into the classroom. Education will continue to be a collaborative and enjoyable experience thanks to the symbiotic link that will be created between the human touch in teaching and AI's capabilities. By adopting these innovations, teachers will be able to support students' individualized learning paths and set them up for success in a world that is always changing due to technology.

USE OF AI FOR TEACHERS IN EDUCATION SYSTEM

To improve learning outcomes, educators are utilizing AI in a variety of ways. With a variety of tools and capabilities that improve teaching efficacy and expedite different parts of the educational process, artificial intelligence (AI) is a useful partner for educators. Here is one example of how AI for educators might enhance teaching strategies:

a. **Personalized learning:** AI uses data about each individual student to create instructional materials that are tailored to their various learning preferences. Teachers can meet each student's specific requirements with this individualized approach, which promotes a better comprehension of the material.
b. **Real-time feedback and interventions:** AI-powered intelligent tutoring solutions provide real-time performance feedback to students. By using this data, educators can quickly detect learning gaps and provide focused assistance and interventions.
c. **Professional development:** AI offers instructors options for ongoing professional development. Teachers may keep up to date on changing educational techniques and improve their teaching practices by having access to cutting-edge teaching resources, data-driven insights, and collaborative platforms.
d. **Improved teaching techniques:** AI-powered analytics provide information on the best ways to instruct individual pupils or entire classes. Teachers may improve their techniques and adjust to the changing demands of their pupils thanks to this data-driven approach. AI facilitates inclusive education by delivering instruments for the early detection of learning difficulties and providing focused treatments (Hussain et al., 2023). All students, including those with a range of learning disabilities, will get the assistance they need thanks to this proactive approach. Personalized learning experiences, administrative work automation, real-time feedback, professional development, improved teaching methods, and inclusion in education are just a few of the ways AI helps instructors (Al-Mamary et al., 2024). As a cooperative partner, AI makes the classroom more dynamic and productive while enabling teachers to design individualized and significant learning experiences for their students.
e. **Collaboration between teachers and AI:** AI has previously been used in education, mostly in assessment systems and technologies that aid in skill development. It is hoped that when AI educational solutions develop further, they will be able to assist close gaps in teaching and learning and provide educators and schools more capabilities than ever before (Giuggioli et al., 2023). In areas where machines would struggle, AI may boost productivity, customization, and administrative work, giving teachers more time and flexibility to impart

knowledge and flexibility. Our educational institutions must expose students to and encourage their usage of AI as today's students will need to work in a world where it is a reality (Chen et al., 2024).

f. **Individualized and differentiated learning:** Teachers have long prioritized adapting instruction to each student's unique requirements, but AI will provide a degree of differentiation that is not feasible for educators who must oversee 30 childrens in each class. A number of businesses, including Content Technologies and Carnegie Learning, are now creating digital platforms and intelligent instruction design that use artificial intelligence (AI) to give students from pre-K through college the learning, testing, and feedback they need. These platforms identify knowledge gaps, give students the challenges they are prepared for, and, when necessary, reroute them to new subjects (Duong et al., 2024). As artificial intelligence (AI) advances, it may eventually be able to recognize the facial expressions of students who are having difficulty understanding a subject and adjust a course accordingly (Elbanna et al., 2024). Although it is not feasible to tailor the curriculum to each student's needs today, AI-powered computers will be able to do so.

g. **Automate administrative tasks:** Grading assignments and tests takes a lot of time for teachers. AI can take over and quickly complete these jobs while also making suggestions on how to fill up the knowledge gaps. While robots are currently capable of grading multiple-choice exams, they are almost ready to evaluate written replies as well. Teachers have more time to interact with each pupil as AI takes over administrative duties. AI has a lot of promise to improve admissions and enrolling procedures.

h. **Help teach vocabulary:** Using AI, an instructional designer helps instructors create graphics for a wide range of subjects and grade levels. Determine which vocabulary words will be difficult for the next courses. Choose an AI tool that is convenient to use and meets your demands. Create targeted prompts to create visuals representing vocabulary words. Show students the visuals generated by the AI and give them credit for helping them understand the concept.

i. **Using Artificial Intelligence to Plan Math Lessons**: Teachers and high school math teachers explain how generative AI can help instructors create engaging math classes by:

- Use AI to connect mathematical concepts to students' interests and real-world applications.
- Create projects, performance assignments, and word puzzles that follow curriculum guidelines.
- Create detailed lesson plans that include practice problems, critical questions, and opportunities for extension.

- Use AI to design inquiry-based learning exercises that promote mathematical literacy and critical thinking.
- Use your favorite AI-enabled search engine to find other teacher-generated content.

USE OF AI FOR STUDENTS IN EDUCATION SYSTEM

A Guide for Learners In the digital era, artificial intelligence (AI) has become a vital part of our lives and is revolutionizing numerous sectors. Education is another area where this shift is evident. It is impossible to overstate the value of AI in education for kids today. AI's capacity to customize the educational process is one of its main advantages. AI-enabled learning platforms can analyze vast volumes of data to determine which subject's students struggle with the most. This ensures that no learner is left behind. This allows teachers to intervene when necessary, ensuring that no student is left behind. It's like having a personal coach that pushes you to succeed in the classroom. The field of artificial intelligence (AI) is developing quickly and has the potential to significantly boost a number of sectors. Artificial Intelligence (AI) has enormous potential to change the educational process for students. Discussed below are the potential benefits that Artificial Intelligence (AI) will provide to students in the future that will transform student learning, engagement, and academic performance:

1. **Personalized learning:** AI is able to deliver resources and information based on a student's academic past.
2. **Better evaluation:** AI may assist in spotting learning trends that administrators and teachers would otherwise overlook. AI may, for instance, design examinations that begin with conventional questions and modify them in response to student performance.
3. **Data-based feedback:** Students may stay motivated by receiving quick feedback on their learning via AI.
4. **Better critical thinking:** AI may assist students in honing their critical thinking abilities, which are highly sought after in the labor market.
5. **Greater accessibility:** No matter where they are in the globe, AI can assist students in accessing and translating top-notch teaching.
6. **Less work for teachers:** Teachers may devote more time to other duties by using AI to automate chores like sending emails, publishing assignments, and monitoring trends.
7. **Better digital literacy:** AI can assist students in acquiring digital literacy abilities, which are highly sought after in the labor market.

8. **Enhanced creativity:** AI can assist students in initiating brainstorming sessions and generating an unrestricted flow of ideas.
9. **Better problem-solving:** AI may assist students in honing their problem-solving abilities, which are highly valued in the workforce.
10. **Universally accessed by Students:** All students can have universal access to global classrooms thanks to artificial intelligence capabilities, even those who may have visual or hearing disabilities or speak different languages. A free PowerPoint add-on called Presentation Translator generates subtitles for the instructor's words in real time. Additionally, this creates opportunities for children who may be unable to attend school because of illness or who need to learn a topic or at a different level that isn't offered at their current school and colleges.
11. **Outside of the classroom, tutoring and assistance:** If you ask any parent who has had difficulty helping their adolescent with mathematics, they will be thrilled about the possibility of using AI to help their kids with homework or test preparation at home. Artificial intelligence is helping to develop tutoring and study programs, which will soon be more accessible and adaptable to different learning styles (Elbanna et al., 2024). Numerous further AI applications for education are being explored, such as AI mentors for students, additional intelligent material production, and a novel approach to instructor's personal growth through virtual international conferences. Although the adoption of AI and machine learning in education may be a little delayed, the changes are already happening and will continue.
12. **Increased Student Engagement:** Artificial intelligence is taking over with new study techniques like gamification, interactive simulations, and customized learning programs that are specifically targeted at the university level when the human brain is unable to process additional information. Students may communicate with one another in an entertaining and captivating fashion via the use of technologies like interactive classrooms and platforms with hyper-real characteristics, which enhances learning and motivates them to investigate new ideas.
13. **Data-Driven Decision Making:** Finally, by evaluating enormous amounts of data, AI is able to sort through mountains of student test results, learning patterns, and possible curricular changes. This provides educators and school administrators with the resources they need to make data-driven choices that increase the effectiveness of education. Concerns over an over-reliance on AI and whether it may compromise their own creative faculties have been voiced by some students, nevertheless.

USE OF AI FOR SOCIETY IN EDUCATION SYSTEM

a. **Enhanced Productivity and Efficiency:** The speed and accuracy with which AI can do jobs is one of its primary advantages. AI systems have the ability to evaluate vast amounts of data in real time (Giuggioli et al., 2023) . This will enable companies to make informed decisions more quickly than ever before, and both enterprises and people can achieve cost savings and better results as a result of this increased productivity and efficiency.
b. **Improved consumer Experience:** By offering immediate assistance and tailored suggestions, chatbots and virtual assistants driven by AI are revolutionizing the consumer experience. Businesses may use AI to evaluate consumer data and offer specialized services and goods that cater to each individual's requirements and preferences.
c. **Healthcare Advancements:** By improving patient outcomes and reducing costs, AI has the potential to totally revolutionize the healthcare sector. Doctors may detect illnesses more rapidly and precisely with AI-powered diagnostic tools, which results in earlier treatment and better results. Healthcare professionals may create individualized treatment regimens that are more successful than conventional one-size-fits-all methods by using AI to assist them find patterns and trends in patient data.
d. **Better Safety and Security:** From public areas to private residences, AI-powered surveillance systems may enhance safety and security in a number of contexts. AI can detect possible dangers and take prompt action to stop incidents from happening via real-time monitoring and analysis.

AI'S CURRENT APPLICATIONS IN EDUCATION SECTOR

AI applications in education can help professors and students create and curate information more easily and promote interactive collaboration. These resources assist educators in creating curriculum-aligned content, guaranteeing that learning resources successfully address the various requirements of students. Students are engaged by interactive resources like instructional games and virtual labs, and peer learning is facilitated via collaborative platforms (Al-Mamary et al., 2024). By offering adaptive feedback and personalizing learning routes, teachers may improve the overall learning experience by utilizing these technologies and the data-driven insights they give. By providing cutting-edge solutions in the areas of intelligent tutoring systems, adaptive learning platforms, automated grading and feedback, customized learning, and administrative duties, artificial intelligence is revolutionizing K-12 education (Duong et al., 2024).

a. **Personalized education:** AI in education helps students, instructors, and resource-constrained institutions by customizing educational materials to meet the requirements of each individual student. With this method, students may work at their own speed, participate in activities that suit their learning preferences, and take charge of their own education. With little addition to the teacher's burden, using AI assistants to differentiate assignments and provide a data-driven, adaptive practice improves the learning process overall (Elbanna et al., 2024).
b. **Systems for intelligent tutoring:** AI tutoring programs can give flexible, easily available learning opportunities with real-time feedback and remedial direction according to student performance (Hussain et al., 2023). By managing common instructional duties and offering comprehensive data on the student's learning process, these uses of contemporary educational technology are assisting in the closure of learning gaps, enhancing conceptual comprehension, and freeing up instructor time.
c. **Automated feedback and grading**: Because teachers' assessments can be impacted by their own inclinations, emotions, and unconscious biases, traditional grading for written work frequently contains subjectivity and biases. This lack of objectivity may lead to biased and inconsistent evaluations. Furthermore, teachers' ability to give comprehensive feedback is limited by the time-consuming aspect of evaluating a high number of assignments, which may impede student's learning. Traditional methods of assessing student achievement are being revolutionized by the incorporation of AI into the grading process. By drastically cutting down on grading time and offering immediate, thorough feedback, AI can improve grading efficiency, accuracy, and fairness. This enables educators to provide students more writing assignments and prompt, helpful feedback, which helps students develop their writing abilities. To make sure AI-generated feedback meets the requirements of each individual student and is in line with educational objectives, teachers must critically evaluate it. While AI helps instructors with more objective measures like grammar and structure, it should be viewed as assistance rather than a substitute, allowing teachers to concentrate on evaluating creativity and critical thinking. Teachers may preserve the integrity of tests and guarantee students' learning by being involved in the grading process and spot-checking AI output.
d. **Applications for administration:** Teachers may save a great deal of time by using artificial intelligence technologies to automate the process of creating material and organizing lessons. Under strict time limitations, these AI technologies

may provide targeted research materials, personalized content and high-quality photographs. Teachers may improve the quality of their lessons without adding to their burden by utilizing AI for effective research and content creation, which will eventually help students and schools with limited resources. AI technology can also be used by school principals to lessen their heavy administrative workloads. AI chatbots help automate administrative duties including creating professional development sessions, scheduling appointments, and writing emails. Large datasets may be analyzed by AI algorithms to help make decisions, such as allocating summer classes according to parent preferences. Administrators are able to concentrate more on strategic projects, interpersonal communication, and relationship development as a result.

INFLUENCE AI TO EDUCATION IN THE FUTURE

Reactions to AI's broad acceptance in recent years, especially its increasing usage in schools, have ranged from enthusiastic endorsement to outright restriction. Teachers and educational administrators must confront a number of ethical issues about AI in education as the technologies will only advance and alter how we live in every aspect of our lives. Artificial intelligence has a profound effect on education, influencing K–12 education in the future by bringing about revolutionary innovations that increase efficiency, promote individualized learning, and improve learning experiences:

a. **Personalized learning:** To accommodate a range of learning styles and speeds, AI-powered adaptive learning platforms examine personal student data to tailor instructional materials. Students will receive training that is specifically customized to them thanks to this customization, which fosters a better comprehension of the material.
b. **Data-driven insights:** AI gives teachers insightful information on the performance and learning styles of their students. Making educated judgments, improving instructional techniques, and identifying areas that might need more focus are all made easier with the use of this information.
c. **Global accessibility:** AI makes online learning possible, allowing students to access courses and learning materials from any location in the globe. Opportunities for education are increased by this inclusion, particularly for pupils who live in rural or underdeveloped locations.

d. **Future skill preparation:** AI-powered educational resources, such as gamified learning environments and virtual tutors, encourage the growth of students' critical thinking, problem-solving, and digital literacy abilities, therefore equipping them for the changing needs of the labor market.
e. **Privacy, prejudice, and equality concerns:** One of the main issues with artificial intelligence in education is privacy. Large volumes of data are frequently gathered and processed by AI systems, which raises concerns regarding its usage and security (Hussain et al., 2023). In order to solve this, educators should make sure that there is openness by telling parents and kids about the data that is gathered and obtaining their consent before utilizing AI tools. Another major problem with AI is bias, which can result in unfair or discriminating outputs since AI systems might inherit biases from their training data. Teachers ought to be conscious of these biases and want to employ AI technologies that have undergone extensive testing to ensure impartiality (Elbanna et al., 2024). Additionally, issues may be lessened by periodically testing for bias and integrating a variety of viewpoints into AI development. When thinking about access to AI technologies, equity issues come up. The digital gap may deepen as a result of unequal access to technology among pupils. To guarantee that everyone can take advantage of these technologies, schools should work to ensure that everyone has fair access to AI resources and provide training for both teachers and students (Al-Mamary et al., 2024).
f. **Concerns regarding the usage of AI by Students:** Teachers are concerned about students abusing AI technology to get around learning, including utilizing it to finish homework. Creating assignments that need critical thinking and human interaction. It is essential to teach AI literacy. Pupils should be aware of both the advantages and disadvantages of AI, including the possibility that biased or incorrect information may be produced by AI systems (Giuggioli et al., 2023). Academic integrity may be preserved by encouraging students to use AI tools for learning instead of rushing through homework. Teachers and administrators may capitalize on AI's advantages while mitigating its possible disadvantages by taking these worries into account and putting deliberate plans into action.

RECOMMANDATIONS

The study suggests that all higher education institutions make the use of AI a prerequisite. Academic staff members should receive intensive training in AI to provide students with the tools they need to deal with future care difficulties. Since AI poses a threat to humanity, the researchers recommend emphasizing ethics and humanity first when educating about it. Furthermore, since AI can be used without restriction and may violate human rights, privacy and dignity should be upheld and protected by rules and international laws. Finally, universities should regulate AI so that it benefits humanity rather than endangers it.

CONCLUSION

AI is essential to education because it helps instructors, makes learning more accessible, and personalizes instruction. It is a useful tool for improving the educational experience and preparing pupils for the future because of its capacity to adjust to individual needs and expedite administrative procedures. By working together to create a learning environment that is prepared for the future, educators can embrace the revolutionary potential of AI in education. Parents, stakeholders, legislators, and educators may work together to promote appropriate AI integration to fully utilize AI's potential; give instructors continuous professional development a priority. Encourage fair access to AI-powered materials so that every student may take advantage of this advancement in technology. Leaders in the industry can fund cooperative projects to create cutting-edge AI resources that complement educational objectives. By working together, educators and stakeholders can fully utilize AI to create inclusive, impactful, and customized learning experiences. An educational environment where AI empowers students, fosters innovation, and equips them for the challenges of a changing world will be shaped by a shared commitment. AI has the potential to revolutionize education by improving teaching quality, customizing learning and expediting administrative duties. Ethical issues including prejudice, privacy, and equity, however, continue to be major obstacles. Educators may capitalize on AI's advantages while upholding academic integrity and equality by tackling these problems and putting best practices into effect. AI in education has the power to completely transform how we teach and learn. Students can benefit from customized learning experiences and individualized coaching using AI-powered learning systems. AI also helps to improve the processes of assessment and collaboration. AI has the potential to make education more interesting and successful for students all around the world with further development and innovation.

FUTURE IMPLICATIONS

In future the impact of the use of AI in other sectors like marketing, banking sector, tourism and hospitality can also be investigated.

REFERENCES

Al-Mamary, Y.H. and Abubakar, A.A. (2024). Artificial intelligence powering education: ChatGPT's impact on students' academic performance through the lens of technology-to-performance chain theory, *Journal of Applied Research in Higher Education*, Vol. ahead-of-print No. ahead-of-print. DOI: 10.1108/JARHE-04-2024-0179

Amponsah, R., Budu, J., & Farinloye, T. (2022). Rethinking the Implementation of Artificial Intelligence for a Sustainable Education in Africa: Challenges and Solutions, *Management and Information Technology in the Digital Era* (*Advanced Series in Management, Vol. 29*), Emerald Publishing Limited, Leeds, pp. 27-46. DOI: 10.1108/S1877-636120220000029003

Benuyenah, V. (2023). Commentary: ChatGPT use in higher education assessment: Prospects and epistemic threats. *Journal of Research in Innovative Teaching & Learning*, *16*(1), 134–135. DOI: 10.1108/JRIT-03-2023-097

Chen, K., Tallant, A. C., & Selig, I. (2024). Exploring generative AI literacy in higher education: student adoption, interaction, evaluation and ethical perceptions, *Information and Learning Sciences*, Vol. ahead-of-print No. ahead-of-print. DOI: 10.1108/ILS-10-2023-0160

Duong, C. D., & Nguyen, V. H. (2024). How effort expectancy and performance expectancy interact to trigger higher education students' uses of ChatGPT for learning. *Interactive Technology and Smart Education*, *21*(3), 356–380. DOI: 10.1108/ITSE-05-2023-0096

Elbanna, S., & Armstrong, L. (2024). Exploring the integration of ChatGPT in education: Adapting for the future. *Management & Sustainability: An Arab Review*, *3*(1), 16–29. DOI: 10.1108/MSAR-03-2023-0016

Felix, C. V. (2020). The Role of the Teacher and AI in Education, *International Perspectives on the Role of Technology in Humanizing Higher Education* (*Innovations in Higher Education Teaching and Learning, Vol. 33*), Emerald Publishing Limited, Leeds, pp. 33-48. DOI: 10.1108/S2055-364120200000033003

Giuggioli, G., & Pellegrini, M. M. (2023). Artificial intelligence as an enabler for entrepreneurs: A systematic literature review and an agenda for future research. *International Journal of Entrepreneurial Behaviour & Research*, *29*(4), 816–837. DOI: 10.1108/IJEBR-05-2021-0426

Halagatti, M., & Banakar, V. (2023). *Artificial Intelligence: The New Tool of Disruption in Educational Performance Assessment, Artificial Intelligence and Sustainable Performance Management in a Global Digitalized Economy (Contemporary Studies in Economic and Financial Analysis, Vol. 110A)*. Emerald Publishing Limited., DOI: 10.1108/S1569-37592023000110A014

Hussain, A. (2023). Use of artificial intelligence in the library services: Prospects and challenges. *Library Hi Tech News, 40*(2), 15–17. DOI: 10.1108/LHTN-11-2022-0125

Ivanov, S., & Soliman, M. (2023). Game of algorithms: ChatGPT implications for the future of tourism education and research. *Journal of Tourism Futures, 9*(2), 214–221. DOI: 10.1108/JTF-02-2023-0038

Klaus, P., & Zaichkowsky, J. (2020). AI voice bots: A services marketing research agenda. *Journal of Services Marketing, 34*(3), 389–398. DOI: 10.1108/JSM-01-2019-0043

Kong, H., & Yu, J. (2024). Influence of artificial intelligence (AI) perception on career resilience and informal learning. *Tourism Review, 79*(1), 219–233. DOI: 10.1108/TR-10-2022-0521

Leelavathi, R. and Surendhranatha, R.C. (2024). ChatGPT in the classroom: navigating the generative AI wave in management education, *Journal of Research in Innovative Teaching & Learning*, Vol. ahead-of-print No. ahead-of-print. DOI: 10.1108/JRIT-01-2024-0017

Okunlaya, R. O., & Alias, R. A. (2022). Artificial intelligence (AI) library services innovative conceptual framework for the digital transformation of university education. *Library Hi Tech, 40*(6), 1869–1892. DOI: 10.1108/LHT-07-2021-0242

Paschen, J., Kietzmann, T. C., & Kietzmann, T. C. (2019). Artificial intelligence (AI) and its implications for market knowledge in B2B marketing. *Journal of Business and Industrial Marketing, 34*(7), 1410–1419. DOI: 10.1108/JBIM-10-2018-0295

Satratzemi, M. (2019). Voice Assistants and Artificial Intelligence in Education. BCI'19: Proceedings of the 9th Balkan Conference on Informatics. Article No.: 34, Pages 1 - 6. DOI: 10.1145/3351556.3351588

Singh, E., Vasishta, P., & Singla, A. (2024). AI-enhanced education: Exploring the impact of AI literacy on generation Z's academic performance in Northern India. *Quality Assurance in Education*. Advance online publication. DOI: 10.1108/QAE-02-2024-0037

Stone, M., & Machtynger, L. (2020). Artificial intelligence (AI) in strategic marketing decision-making: A research agenda. *The Bottom Line (New York, N.Y.)*, *33*(2), 183–200. DOI: 10.1108/BL-03-2020-0022

Vartiainen, H., & Tedre, M. (2024). "ChatGPT and imaginaries of the future of education: insights of Finnish teacher educators, *Information and Learning Sciences*, Vol. ahead-of-print No. ahead-of-print. DOI: 10.1108/ILS-10-2023-0146

Wilkens, U. (2020). Artificial intelligence in the workplace - A double-edged sword. *International Journal of Information and Learning Technology*, *37*(5), 253–265. DOI: 10.1108/IJILT-02-2020-0022

Chapter 2
Artificial Intelligence and Machine Learning Methods in the Field of Learning and Development With a Focus on Gamification

Sameer Kumar Sinha
https://orcid.org/0009-0007-9403-6221
IBM India Pvt. Ltd., India

ABSTRACT

With the pandemic confining most of the global workforce to their homes, delivery and optimisation of formal learning and development modules delivery and optimisation have taken centre stage. Personalisation of learning & development module holds immense importance today when gig economy is on the rise, and workplace culture has turned hybrid. The introduction of Gamification – the delivery of learning modules and assessment of key performance indicators through complex computerised games – has streamlined this process. This research project aims to understand the impact gamification has had on the learning experience of both newly onboarded and existing employees. It also aims to study other fields of L&D where AI and machine learning modules have been implemented and gauge their impacts as well, to provide a basis for these systems to be developed and implemented globally, with cost-effectiveness in mind.

DOI: 10.4018/979-8-3373-0771-8.ch002

INTRODUCTION

"Training programmes can contain critical content, but participants will feel uninspired if it is not given in the right way. It is critical to create programmes that help people grow and develop (even if the information is dry) and entertain and engage them while learning. Fun-filled training is not only more entertaining for the student – or the facilitator – but it is also more successful and powerful, resulting in fewer resources being committed to retraining programmes and a higher likelihood of application and retention. In the past few years, Gamification has become a key tool to increase the enjoyment of training as well as accelerate the participant's learning and application of information."

"Gamification is the process of introducing gaming aspects into an eLearning environment in order to create a more effective and interesting learning environment. To encourage participants to invest in the training, Gamification is usually accompanied by scores, badges or ribbons, and leader boards. The student receives rapid feedback in the form of scores or points and gratification or a sense of accomplishment. By linking learning with the fun of playing games and competing, Gamification specifically targets learners who may lack an inner motivation to participate actively."

"When implemented properly, it can also inspire learners to apply what they have learned in the classroom to their current job by putting them in real-world circumstances in a safe atmosphere. Gamification also functions as a feedback loop when employees practise skills in a real-world setting. For example, if a student is unable to acquire a badge, increase his or her score, or go to the next level, this indicates that there is room for improvement in that particular learning module."

"Learners are especially motivated to improve their skill sets in order to contribute to the organisation's knowledge base. The capacity of gamified solutions to actively target learner motivation boosts learner participation. Gamification keeps employees interested, which leads to improved retention and behavioural changes. These features encourage employees to compete in order to enhance their talents. Gamification tactics are still in the early stages of development. Many advanced gamified systems go beyond ribbons and points to focus on each learner, tailoring their eLearning experience to their strongest motivators — for example, competitiveness amongst co-workers, recognition, rewards, collecting badges, etc. Employees are confronted with settings that are as near as possible to normal duties and problems that they can meet in their work routines when a gamification strategy is successful. The immersive aspects provided by blended learning to get the most out of what Gamification offers should be used. Employees are less likely to forget what they have learned because they are not under the strain of a regular training session."

This chapter thus aims to understand the various cases where gamified setups have been used, study the works of various authors in this field, and establish the degree of importance this technology holds specifically for learning and development today, among all other advancements of artificial intelligence and machine learning.

LITERATURE REVIEW

"The concepts of artificial intelligence and machine learning have been around for quite some time now and have been used in human resources very often. Multiple authors worldwide have worked on these topics and have published articles regarding various aspects of the same. Each author or each paper tries to shed light on a particular angle of the matter to provide a wholesome picture to the next reader. Multiple authors have welcomed the idea of Gamification and its related innovations, stating the need to work faster and more efficiently in today's world. Many other authors are against introducing technology into a field traditionally governed by human interaction only."

Papers Reviewed

Armstrong, M. B., & Landers, R. N. in "**Gamification of employee training and development**" "talk about Gamification becoming more popular in employee training. Their study aims to discuss the current scientific understanding of Gamification and how it might be utilised to improve web-based employee training realistically. They define Gamification in the context of training because it is frequently misinterpreted. Because Gamification is frequently misunderstood, research on the effectiveness of gamified learning concerning training design is examined. Finally, in order to give a clear roadmap for training design, they describe a formal process for statistically supported Gamification of web-based training."

Untung Rahardja et al. in "**Gamification Framework Design of Management Education and Development in Industrial Revolution 4.0**" "talk of technological advancements, as a result of which the education sector is being compelled to embark on a technological revolution, focused on educational innovation and agility, and ultimately replacing traditional learning techniques. Many works of literature have examined educational innovation to improve student motivation and alter the classroom atmosphere. According to a literature review on Gamification, it promotes student achievement and motivation at the college level. According to the findings, individual points, badges, achievements leader boards, and levels are the most often used forms of Gamification."

Sridevi Nair and Jain Mathew, in "**A Theoretical Framework for Gamified Learning**", "say that the term 'gamified' has been applied to a wide range of business activities. Human resource managers have attempted to gamify personnel procedures such as recruitment and onboarding, while marketing experts have attempted to gamify customer interactions. Gamification can revolutionise how people work, interact, and develop by acting as a powerful engine for goal-oriented behavioural change. The use of Gamification, on the other hand, has had mixed results in the company. The lack of success has been linked to a lack of grasp of the notion by researchers. Their study examines the literature in the field of Gamification in order to develop a conceptual model that explains how gamification influences learning. The approach provided in this study is straightforward and is based on major learning and technology theories. The review's goal is to give a foundation for future studies as well as a fundamental understanding for practitioners who are striving to implement gamified learning."

Robert Mitchell, Lisa Schuster, Hyun Seung Jin in "**Gamification and the impact of extrinsic motivation on needs satisfaction: Making work fun**?" "write that despite the widespread use of Gamification in the workplace, little is known about the context elements that influence its effectiveness and impact on employee engagement and productivity. The impact of extrinsic incentives, such as social pressure or internalised guilt, on employees' psychological needs, satisfaction and behavioural intention is investigated using self-determination theory. As the first study to empirically evaluate the function of extrinsic motivation, this lays the groundwork for a better understanding of how Gamification works."

Penny Simpson and Pete Jenkins in "**Gamification and Human Resources: an overview**" "talk of how the usage of game principles to aid learning and development shifts our focus away from typically obsolete views of knowledge acquisition and toward thoughts of pushing employees' learning capabilities and capacities. Learning and development that is gamified can assist employees in their quest for mastery. Gamification, when done right, may assist an employee to enhance their skills while also allowing them to take risks and fail in a safe environment. Health and safety training, as well as leadership development, are examples of learning and training that have already proven to be quite successful when applying gamification techniques."

J. Hamari, J. Koivisto and H. Sarsa in "**Does Gamification Work? -- A Literature Review of Empirical Studies on Gamification**" "examine peer-reviewed gamification research. They use the definitions of Gamification and the debate on motivational affordances to construct a framework for studying the effects of Gamification. The results, independent variables (studied motivational affordances), dependent variables (examined psychological/behavioural effects from Gamification), gamification contexts, and types of studies performed on gamified systems are all included in the literature review. The report assesses the current status of research on the subject and identifies gaps in the existing literature. According to the study, Gamification has beneficial impacts; however, the results are very reliant on the context in which it is applied and the users that utilise it. The review's conclusions can be used to guide future research and the development of gamified systems."

Katie Seaborn, Deborah I. Fels in "**Gamification in theory and action: A survey**" "present a comprehensive study of Gamification in action, with an emphasis on empirical findings related to purpose and context, system design, methodologies and techniques, and user impact. The survey's findings reveal that a standard definition of Gamification is forming against a backdrop of empirical participant-based research. However, definitional subjectivity, various or unexplained theoretical assumptions, inconsistencies among empirical findings, and poor experimental design continue to be issues. They address how Gamification might be presented more effectively as part of a bigger effort to improve the user experience of interactive technologies through gameful design. Finally, they offer some points of departure for future empirical studies of gamified practise and its impacts."

Data Collection

Primary Data

Primary data for this project has been collected to a target group through a Google Form.

Secondary Data

With reference to the papers listed under literature, secondary data was collected.

Data Analysis

The data collected gave us the following insights:

Figure 1. Please select your age band

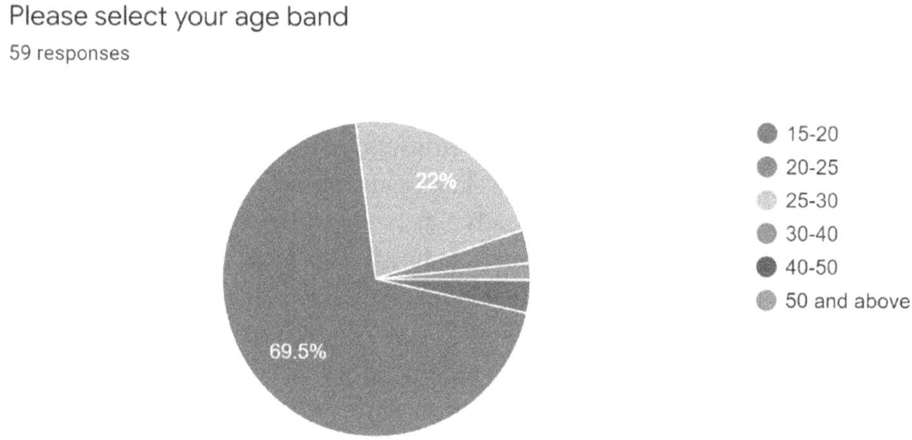

Figure 2. Please state your gender

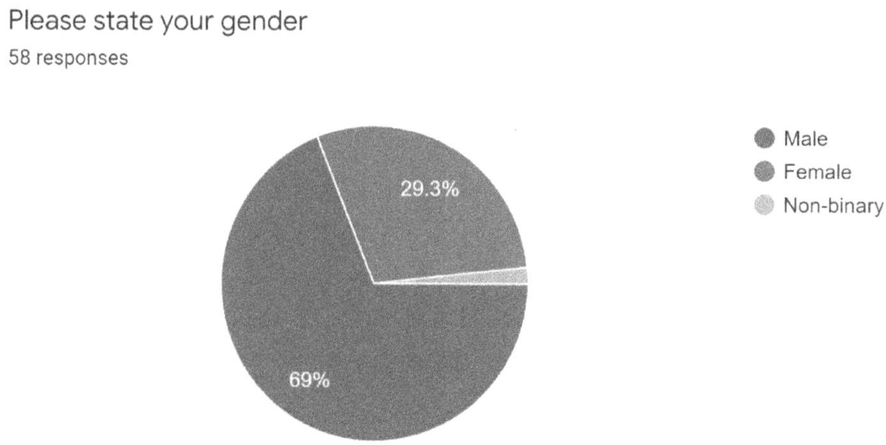

Figure 3. Do you have any work experience?

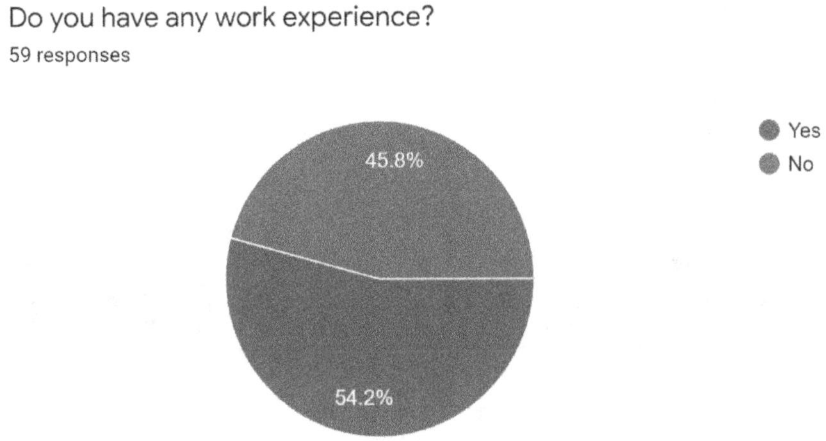

Figure 4. Were virtual systems of training (learning management systems etc) used in your previous organization?

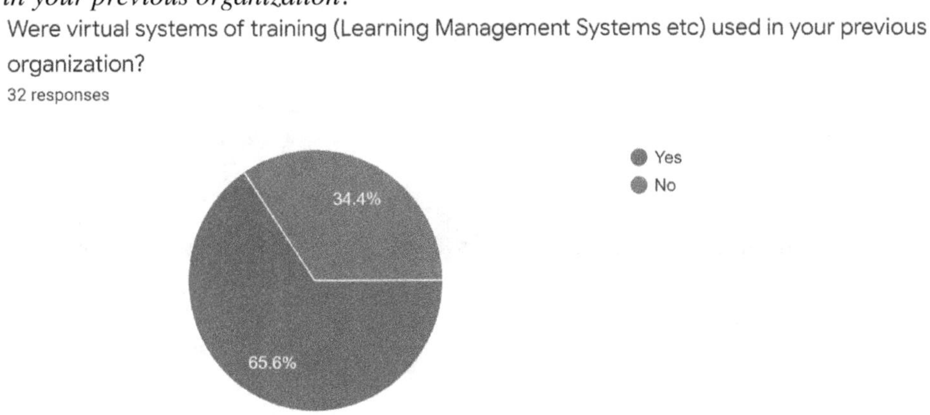

Figure 5. Please state which training system was used in your organization

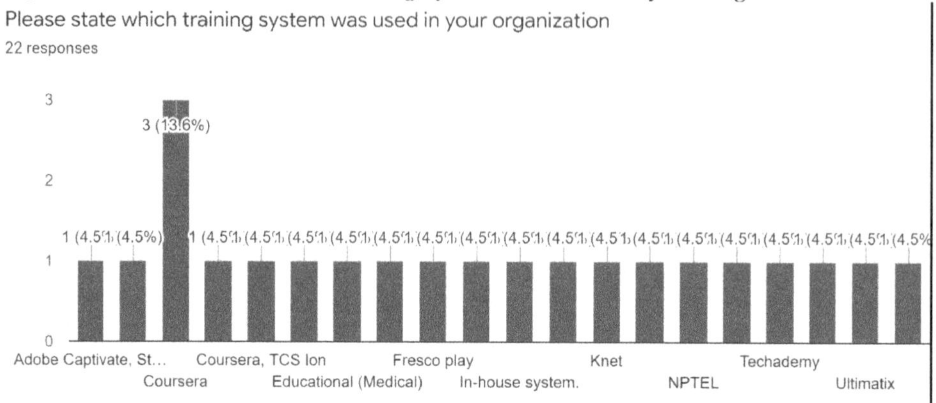

Figure 6. How was your experience with the virtual LMS?

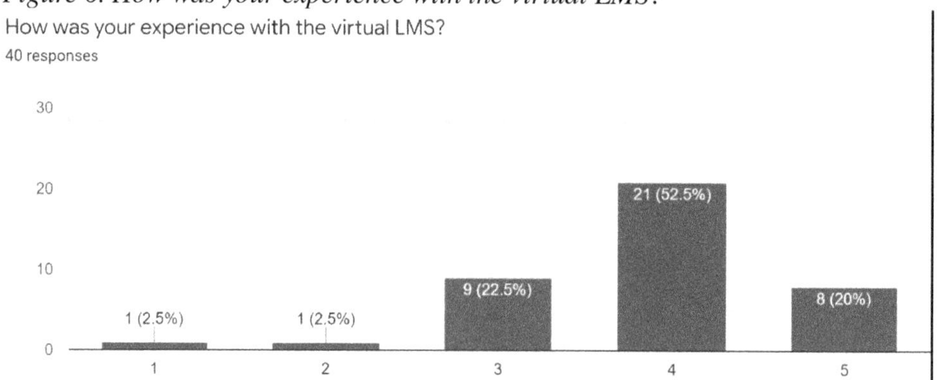

Figure 7. Was the LMS designed in a way to incorporate your feedback and evaluation results into the next module?

Was the LMS designed in a way to incorporate your feedback and evaluation results into the next module?

40 responses

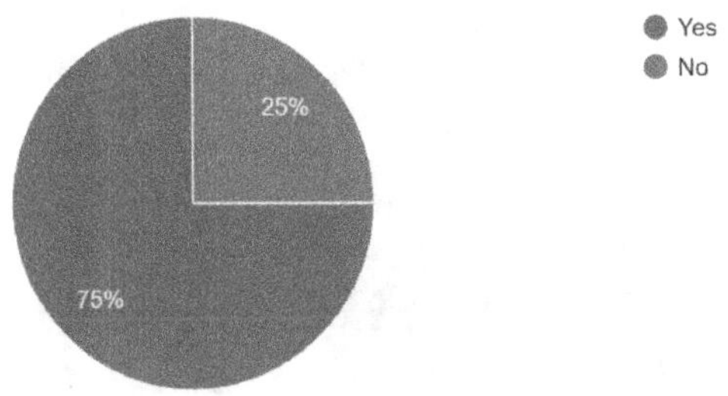

Figure 8. Please rate your virtual training system under the following parameters

Please rate your virtual training system under the following parameters

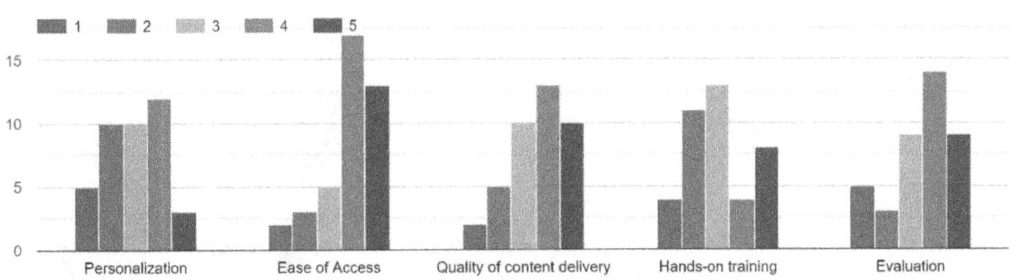

Figure 9. Would an LMS (with hanmds-on pracical projects) be your first preference over physical training, if offered a choice?

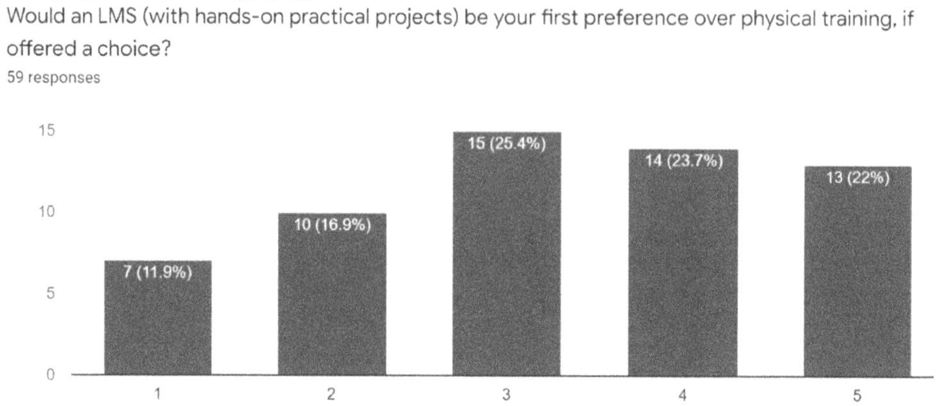

Figure 10. Do you think a virftual system could match up to the quality of training provided by the instructors?

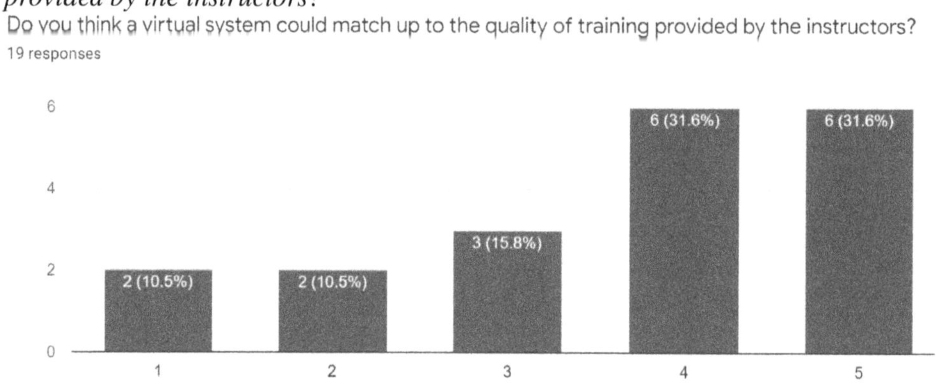

Figure 11. Have you come across virtual learning systems used in school/college/ coaching?

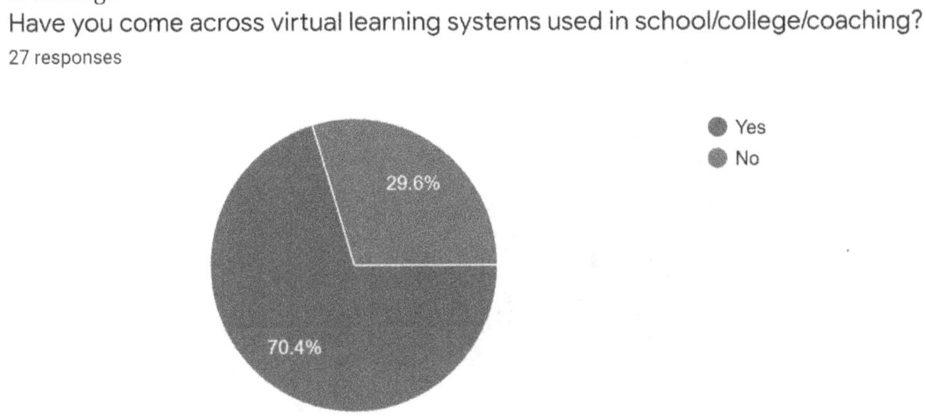

CONCLUSION

Reading through the relevant works of these authors brings to light the various pros and cons that Gamification poses in the field of learning and development. While the advancements of technology are always sought after to aid convenience, some trade-offs have to be taken care of to provide a well-rounded picture. This study shall further aim to analyse the effect Gamification has on the learning and development of employees in the Indian scenario, with primary and secondary data collection.

Figure 12. Do you think feedback-based virtual games would be good learning tools?

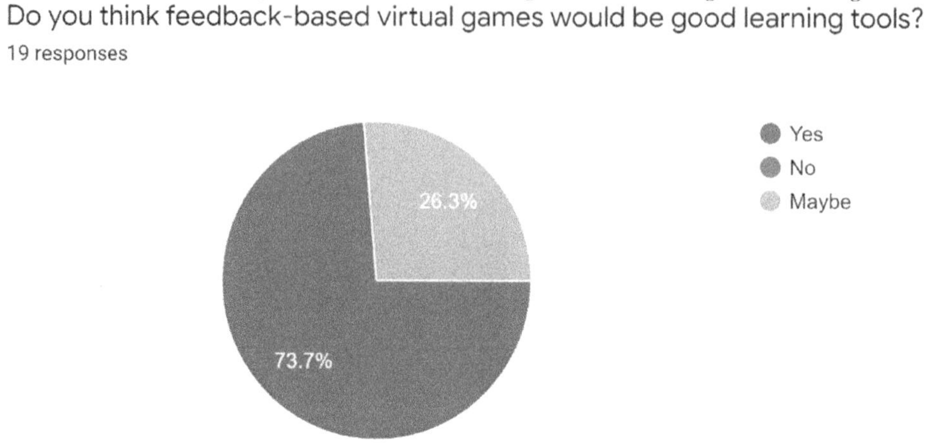

REFERENCES

Armstrong, M. B., & Landers, R. N. (2018). *Gamification of employee training and development*. Wiley Online Library. DOI: 10.1111/ijtd.12124

Hamari, J., Koivisto, J., & Sarsa, H. (2014). *Does Gamification Work? —A Literature Review of Empirical Studies on Gamification*. IEEE. DOI: 10.1109/HICSS.2014.377

Mitchell, R., Schuster, L., & Jin, H. S. (2020). Gamification and the impact of extrinsic motivation on needs satisfaction: Making work fun? *Journal of Business Research, 106*, 323–330. DOI: 10.1016/j.jbusres.2018.11.022

Nair, S., & Matthew, J. (2019). A Theoretical Framework for Gamified Learning. *International Journal of Innovative Technology and Exploring Engineering, 8*(12), 2846–2851. DOI: 10.35940/ijitee.L3032.1081219

Rahardja, U., Aini, Q., Graha, Y. I., & Tangkaw, M. R. (2019). *Gamification Framework Design of Management Education and Development in Industrial Revolution 4.0*. ResearchGate. DOI: 10.1088/1742-6596/1364/1/012035

Seaborn, K., & Fels, D. I. (2015). Gamification in theory and action: A survey. *International Journal of Human-Computer Studies, 74*, 14–31. DOI: 10.1016/j.ijhcs.2014.09.006

Simpson, P., & Jenkins, P. (2019). Gamification and Human Resources: an overview.

Chapter 3
Incorporating Artificial Intelligence as a Tool in Teaching Writing Skills

Sheren Khalid Alhiti
https://orcid.org/0009-0002-7853-7994
Al-Buraimi University College, Oman

ABSTRACT

This chapter argues that AI tools have revolutionized the educational domain. The accessibility of these tools and the incredible speed of composition have encouraged learners' overdependence. This has threatened the individual's ability to think critically and compose creatively and raises concerns over the possible discrepancy between the module's learning outcomes and the actual learning process. This is especially evident in the English writing composition classes, as confirmed by past literature. Therefore, revising traditional pedagogical strategies has become crucial. The chapter first addresses the challenges traditional pedagogical strategies face in teaching essay writing composition in the AI era. Then, it offers a comparative essay analysis. Then, it explains empowering critical thinking to maintain creativity. Then, it rigorously analyzes the pedagogical frameworks for incorporating AI and critical thinking supported by a case study analysis. The chapter concludes with suggestions for the efficient implications of AI tools while preserving human creativity.

INTRODUCTION

Artificial intelligence (AI) has revolutionized all aspects of knowledge and created drastic changes in all walks of life. Domains that exclude AI are labeled traditionalists and would neither cope with modern societies nor attract younger generations.

DOI: 10.4018/979-8-3373-0771-8.ch003

Education is no exception. AI has transformed the learner's experience and teachers' methods of generating engagement and transferring knowledge. However, the drastic increase in mobile apps and AI-generated texts, their availability, and accessibility in generating quick solutions to school assignments raise concerns over learners' overdependence and a drastic decrease in learning levels.

Moreover, experts argue that as digital natives constitute the majority of learners in schools, pedagogical approaches must evolve to align with the advancements of the digital era (Aljuaid, 2024). Technology and artificial intelligence (AI) in education concentrate on writing instruction. Technology companies have created numerous solutions to enhance the writing education process. Thus, learners' written production in writing class can be enhanced, yet there is no guarantee that the composition skills have been learned.

A challenge in writing instruction is that individual feedback on learners' writing difficulties is often diminished as class sizes increase; however, online AI-driven writing tools may solve this issue. Therefore, it is necessary to transform teaching methods to incorporate AI, utilizing its benefits and guiding learners to use it as a tool to enhance their academic skills, especially academic writing. This chapter explores how AI can effectively teach English writing, highlighting its benefits, challenges, and best practices. The chapter examines how educators may utilize AI to improve learner engagement, maintain critical thinking, and enhance creativity.

This chapter will first set the rationale and objectives and will provide an overview of methodologies and successful practices of incorporating AI in teaching academic writing. Then, it will offer a practical pedagogical framework that addresses the issues of AL literacy among instructors and students and the issue of fostering creativity and critical thinking. Subsequently, the chapter will discuss a set of ethical considerations and suggest solutions and insights for further research and practices for how various educators in academia may integrate AI into their writing education.

1.1 Background and Rationale

The instruction of writing skills has a rich history and is of paramount importance in education. For centuries, writing instruction has included traditional pedagogical methods, including drill-and-practice activities, individual or peer writing discussions, and rubric-based evaluation of written assignments. However, many researchers have observed that the gap between writing pedagogical methods and advancements in writing theory, technology, and cognitive research is widening (Amirjalili et al., 2024). The utilization of artificial intelligence (AI) in writing instruction is expected to rectify shortcomings. AI systems provide learners with immediate, context-relevant, and customized learning assistance, highlighting advanced educational methodologies while also improving outcomes that are difficult to achieve with traditional writing instruction and assessment methods. The fundamental assumptions of the utilization of AI in writing instruction were implicitly challenged as early as the 1970s when metaphors emerged to illustrate the mind and cognition within a socio-technological framework of networked computers. The employment of AI as a writing mentor will be considered a distinct facet of overarching concerns regarding the evolution of educational methodologies as education adjusts to rapidly progressing forms of "educational" computing. This arena is marked by considerable conflict as huge investments intersect with powerful theories of education and technologies (Mahyoob et al., 2023).

The common methodologies of teaching academic writing often depend on traditional lectures and instructor-led sessions, demonstrating a conventional, teacher-centered approach prevalent in many educational institutions. This analysis does not seek to criticize or praise this established practice; instead, it opens an essential discussion about the importance of interactive strategies within the extensive field of writing pedagogy (Ahmed, Siddique, & Yasmin, 2024).

This section examines many strategies that might significantly enhance learners' abilities as academic writers. While lectures continue to be the primary method of instruction, our initial emphasis will be on evaluating their efficacy compared to conventional writing courses. Upon examining the deficiencies of passive pedagogical methods relative to more interactive techniques—such as workshops, peer reviews, and conferences—we can discern a broader spectrum of effective strategies for cultivating exceptional writing skills in learners (Amirjalili et al., 2024; Kelly & Smith, 2014).

Many writing teachers make online resources available, such as instructional videos or writing software, that allow additional support at different stages of the writing process. This approach allows for the enhancement of the writing workshop environment outside of the classroom, without which valuable class time is wasted reiterating concepts that could otherwise be better addressed through focused, specialized, or more personal attention (Adam & Chowdhury, 2024). On the other hand, technology has also been considered for its potential to provide instant feedback, for example, through digital comments or rubrics. Some examples include using feedback studio features and multiple classes and drawing learners' attention to common misconceptions or mistakes through a summary comment feature (Van et al., 2025; Pytash et al., 2015). It is argued that digital comments lead to more precise learner responses since they can access library resources and dictionaries. Furthermore, technology has the potential to offer learners equal standing regarding access to resource materials (Hsu, 22023). It is widely agreed that despite still being new to writing learners, this feature could partially level the playing field for all learners, especially regarding resources equipping them to define and execute complex writing tasks.

1.2 Scope and Objectives

This chapter involves several disciplines and dimensions, comprising four separate sectors, each prioritizing writing as a central exploration theme. A psychological perspective of the writing process has profoundly influenced the pursuit of enhanced instructional strategies in the classroom. Subsequently, these basic origins developed into a broader undertaking in educational psychology; presently, approaches are considered inefficient due to the inefficiency, insufficiency, or obsolescence of cognitive and experimental psychology findings. Although recognizing the variety of genres and forms of writing, the emphasis is on *Governor-Military* writing and the *teacher-learner task dynamic* established. The focus will be on three dimensions. The writing process is considered a cognitive invention that includes but is not confined to, a linear model. Secondly, product attributes, including the linguistic structure of drafts and the final submission. Finally, learner attributes that are associated with or expected to affect the process or the resultant outcomes. Since the 1980s, there has been a substantial proliferation of computer applications utilized as instructional tools (Aljuaid, 2024).

1.3 Popular AI Applications for Teaching Writing Skills

Applications can be considered customized AI-driven instruments that improve the learning experience by catering to the distinct requirements of learners. They noted that AI is profoundly transforming writing instruction through the development of interactive grammar and style-checking tools, concluding that as these tools progress from isolated applications to more extensive, collaborative AI systems, there will be increased opportunities for peer learning among both educators and learners. Writing pedagogy has increasingly integrated technology into educational settings, transforming it into a holistic educational and psychological framework that promotes the creation of dynamic and interactive learning environments. Process writing arises from the amalgamation of technology, yielding numerous specialized systems. Many deep learning models have been applied to innovative linguistic challenges, and these technologies are currently utilized in various digital applications, including chatbots, image recognition, and game artificial intelligence. These have potential applications in secondary creative writing. In this setting, AI can act as a spark for learner creativity by providing access to vast resources available online, while educators serve as tutors or facilitators in the learning process (Al-Sofi, 2024).

In addition, essay writing is a fundamental component of academic education, requiring the development of critical thinking, coherence, and argumentation skills in pupils. Traditional assessment methods rely heavily on manual review by educators, which can be arduous and subjective. The basis for AI applications originate in the study of Natural language processing (NLP), which is essential for AI applications centered on language development, as it enables automatic speech recognition and interpretation. The efficacy of AI-generated writing includes educational settings designed to provide writing assistance. Artificial Intelligence can support educators and educational institutions via commercial AI products that enhance teaching, particularly in managing multiple writing assignments, especially when instructors must meticulously identify and rectify errors in written work (Mudawy, 2024). A plethora of AI writing technology is presently accessible for free online. Alongside enhanced mechanization, numerous AI solutions feature algorithms that purport to understand how learners structure, create, and deliver texts. Thus, these AI products can go beyond simple writing correction by offering tailored feedback highlighting the organization of ideas, grammatical precision, and the caliber of reasoning (Shen et al., 2023).

Figure 1. Popular AI tools

Figure 1 highlights the most popular AI applications used as tools in writing assignments. To summarize the role of Artificial Intelligence in aiding teaching instructions, a focus is driven to the delivery of immediate corrections and suggestions on a list of aspects:

1. **Grammar and Style Correction** – AI applications such as Grammarly, ProWritingAid, and Hemingway Editor assess learners' writing for grammatical, punctuation, and stylistic inaccuracies, aiding them in improving their compositions.
2. **Enhanced Learner Engagement** AI-generated recommendations and interactive tasks enhance writing engagement, hence maintaining learner motivation. AI-Enhanced Writing Prompts – Tools such as ChatGPT and Quillbot generate prompts and suggest ideas, aiding learners in overcoming writer's block and cultivating creativity.
    2. **Essay Evaluation and Prompt Feedback** – Platforms like Turnitin's Revision Assistant and WriteLab evaluate learner essays and offer suggestions to improve coherence, organization, and arguing efficacy. AI tools provide immediate feedback, allowing learners to correct mistakes and gain knowledge in real time, rather of waiting for a teacher's response.
        4. **Customized Learning Pathways**—AI analyzes learner writing patterns and tailors lessons to rectify specific deficiencies, offering a more targeted educational experience.
        5. **Personalized Education:** AI's ability to analyze writing patterns allows learners to receive customized courses that address their specific needs.
        6. **Plagiarism Detection** AI driven plagiarism detection systems, such Copyscape and Turnitin, maintain academic integrity by identifying unoriginal content.

Many technical and commercial factors contribute to the popularity of these tools. Nonetheless, they have proven to be user-friendly. The chapter builds on research conducted on these tools.

1.4 Challenges and Concerns

Despite the advantages of AI in writing education, educators may be resistant to its adoption. Both educators and learners may favor the personal aspect of writing training and regard it as vital. Additionally, there is apprehension surrounding excessively polished writing resulting from AI-driven writing education. The AI-generated comments also disclosed prompts for successful essays, raising concerns regarding the fairness of providing the tool in conjunction with an examination. Additional problems exist surrounding the privacy of feedback; several students relied only on it, which may diminish the quality of student-generated content and enable inferences about the author due to current advancements in AI. Literature demonstrates predominantly valuable benefits for both educators and learners, while the study also uncovers significant disparities. Literature revealed a set of challenges facing writing instructors (Shofiah et al., 2023). Firstly, excessive dependence on Artificial Intelligence. Learners might foster an undue dependence on AI technologies for revisions, hindering their ability to nurture vital editing skills. Secondly, there are limitations on accuracy. Artificial intelligence is not without its flaws and may, at times, misinterpret context or provide inaccurate recommendations. It is imperative for educators to encourage learners to engage in a thorough analysis of feedback generated by artificial intelligence. Thirdly, moral considerations. Learner's improper utilization of AI-generated content could result in significant risks of plagiarism and violations of academic integrity, thereby compromising the essence of the original creation. Fourthly, lack of human creativity. While AI tools can assist in writing, they cannot replace the essential human component in storytelling, creative expression, and the formulation of sophisticated arguments.

These challenges encapsulate broader concerns about learners' writing abilities in particular and the goal of education as a whole.

PEDAGOGICAL STRATEGIES FOR INCORPORATING AI IN WRITING INSTRUCTIONS

The impact of incorporating AI tools into writing pedagogy is not only a pressing concern for researchers in Writing Studies but also a valuable opportunity for education officials and teacher educators. By embracing AI as part of their teaching strategies, they can influence policy changes by recognizing this technology as an essential component of teacher education programs. In this light, educators should consider stepping into the role of practitioner-researchers. By doing so, they can deepen their understanding of melding AI technology effectively with traditional writing methods, ultimately crafting more impactful writing instruction (Aljuaid, 2024).

One compelling strategy is to thoughtfully design writing assignments that utilize the unique strengths of various AI tools to assist learners in their tasks (Pytash et al., 2015). By integrating these assignments into a dynamic mix of collaborative and creative writing instruction alongside digital resources particularly those enhanced by Artificial Intelligence—learning outcomes can be significantly bolstered.

Another effective tactic involves creating assignments across multiple genres. Given the modern imperative to merge the rhetorical demands of both print and multimodal media, each learner should engage with AI-powered writing and design tools. This facilitates efficient teamwork, fostering trust in each other's abilities as learners share responsibilities (Mahyoob et al., 2023). In this framework, learner groups can reflect on their experiences in completing assignments, offering valuable insights for refining existing applications or inspiring the development of innovative tools. Through a collaborative synthesis of their findings, educators will be assisted in designing methodologies that incorporate AI, thereby enriching their pedagogical approaches.

The framework developed in this chapter compresses the aims of writing pedagogy of empowering learners to be able to compose academic essays that are logical, coherent, and linguistically rich. It goes into several stages, starting with setting the aims and objectives of the teaching practice, designing the materials and tasks, setting the assessments and feedback methods, encouraging interaction and collaborative work, designing personalized feedback, and assessing the process.

1.5 Designing Writing Tasks for AI Support

Writing tasks are vital for both learners of writing at different linguistic literacy levels. Educators can struggle with developing creative, educational assignments that are supported by AI tools, and the criteria for effective and engagement tasks can be addressed. Since writing tasks may differ in level (elementary, middle, and high school learners), and writing skills (story writing, opinion writing, and argument writing), the criteria for the design of tasks are illustrated using general writing skills for targeted language proficiency levels, closely aligned with 10 educational objectives for further opportunities. The tasks can involve learners' engagement with AI tools by integrating their generated texts through several types of possible interactions — input, modification, verification, and choice (Köpeczi-Bócz, 2025). Tasks examples illustrate how AI objects can enhance writing tasks' engagement and education capability. The examples can increase writing quality, creativity, and critical thinking, although the use of AI in writing tasks can face potential problems with access to technology and the necessity of learners' familiarity with AI tools. Some practices and strategies to design effective writing tasks are also offered to support learners with diverse writing and literacy needs. The next subsections can also address the design of AI objects to support effective and influential writing tasks and how educators can be trained to make AI to make educational writing tasks effective, engaging, and supporting improved writing performance.

1.6 Setting Goals for Academic Writing Lessons

Several pedagogical issues beyond the classroom need to be considered before deploying AI writing tools with learners: the choice of tool(s) that can meet the goals of a given writing task, the decision on the extent to which learners can benefit from the chosen tool's functionality, how to integrate/tailor the tool in a possible writing routine throughout the course, and what kinds of training or a set of instructions need to be provided to learners prior to and during the use of the AI writing software (Cui, 2025). Hence, equal time should be devoted to fostering learners' critical thinking about their work and the AI suggestions, and a careful balance is needed between the use of tool-led and teacher-led instruction during the writing lessons.

IDENTIFYING THE KEY AREAS IN ACADEMIC WRITING WHERE AI TOOLS CAN BE BENEFICIAL

The first step in this comprehensive pedagogical plan is to provide lectures and will consist of the principles and best practices of academic writing. These principles and best practices will introduce learners to the formal, stylistic, and organizational expectations of academic writing. Lectures will cover the literary review process, argumentation, plagiarism and citation, academic tone, writing from sources, cohesion and coherence, and proper referencing. The second step in the comprehensive pedagogical process will cover hands-on training and practice sessions. Hands-on training and practice sessions are based on academic writing software and involve a set of grammar and style exercises. This is to enhance their academic writing skills by providing just-in-time grammatical reviews and alternative style suggestions of the text, ideally prior to their actual writing. This process supports the alignment of the approach to the writing tasks and evaluation parameters and to better clarify interpretations of expectations among learners. Hands-on training and practice sessions include mechanisms and introduced tools such as paraphrasing with vocabulary check, grammar and cited-text review, target-format training with downloadable publication templates and live examples, novel style exercises, and general paper preparation guidelines. On completion, learners write four extra drafts that are reviewed by the teacher and the software concurrently. Building Learners' Understanding of AI Tools

There is a common concern that AI tools can substitute human teachers in higher education, especially for grammar lessons in extensive writing tasks as AI tools are increasingly applied in school instruction, teaching can be removed from humans. In particular, AI can be utilized in the vivid enhancement of expressive writing skills. In addition, there is a discourse that AI cannot evaluate actual writing completions. Grammar and style are some of the primary focuses in academic writing, and these aspects are easy to assess by AI tools. These tools can provide writing suggestions to enhance grammar and style, making writing cleaner and polished (Amirjalili et al., 2024). This learning approach may promote faster writing improvement with cost efficiency for online workshops wherein the AI is streamlined. However, there are concerns regarding the new tools' accuracy in real-time grammatical and style assessment. Introducing specific AI tools used in academic writing.

Academic writing is a skill often found difficult to teach due to its complex nature influenced by multiple variables. The interaction of English scholars with technological tools support academic writing in the predominant foreign language of communication, English, on which major publication standards, academic articles, books, and theses rely. Therefore, assessing academic writing should integrate the merits of human and Artificial intelligence. The educational method seeks to evaluate learners' capacity to utilize AI tools judiciously, enhancing their creativity and critical thinking rather than depending on the tools. Furthermore, human observation and the assessment of student performance remain incongruous. Teachers may augment the process with awareness of specific objectives of the lesson tailored to accommodate elements unique to the educational process, such as observations of learners' individual abilities, cognitive variations, and psychological aspects of education.

1.7 Designing Assessment Rubrics that Align with AI Tools

As assignments and exams are key drivers for learners to grow, change, improve, therefore designing relevant, challenging academic tasks can improve their learning goal. For writing courses, both formative assessment strategies and summative assessment strategies are essential, as frequent formative feedback tasks can help learners meet the requirements of writing assignments and progress step by step toward course goals. At the same time, assessments should be designed as realistically as possible so that learners' learning process will align with the skills topic they are taught. The assessment design process should actively consider learners' use of AI tools (Cheng et al., 2024).

Moreover, it is crucial to design rubrics for assessing writing tasks that clearly show to what extent learners can use AI tools. When research project-based writing tasks, which involve attribute reasoning and special topics, are scheduled, assessment rubrics must include different factors and criteria to align with writing quality and academic norms for learners (Cheng et al., 2024). Regular discussions between teachers and AI tool representatives can be organized before and after assessments are implemented to meet these goals. In these meetings, teachers and AI tool representatives can clarify the abuse or overuse of an AI tool, what kind of feedback AI tools could give learners to enhance the quality of their writing, and alignment between evaluation rubrics and the use of AI tools. Creating a rubric to evaluate writing composition in an AI-enhanced class entails assessing conventional writing abilities in conjunction with learners' proficient utilization of AI resources. Presented herein is a sample rubric that incorporates these elements:

Table 1. Criteria for evaluating writing composition in an AI-incorporated lesson

Criteria	Excellent	Good	Average	Below expectations
Thought Development	Ideas are original,, thoroughly developed. AI tools are utilized to enhance depth, creativity.	Ideas are clear, well-developed. AI tools are used effectively to support content development.	Ideas are basic, lack depth. Limited use of AI tools in developing content.	Ideas are unclear or undeveloped—no evidence of AI tool utilization.
Organization	Writing is logically organized with clear transitions. AI tools are used to refine structure, flow.	Writing has a clear structure with appropriate transitions. AI tools assist in organizing content.	Organization is attempted but inconsistent. Minimal use of AI tools for structural improvement.	Lack of clear organization. No use of AI tools to assist with structure.
Word choice	Demonstrates sophisticated vocabulary, varied sentence structures. AI tools enhance word choice, fluency.	Uses appropriate vocabulary, sentence structures. AI tools are used to improve language use.	Language is simple with limited sentence variety. Some use of AI tools for language enhancement.	Language is unclear with frequent errors—no use of AI tools for language improvement.
Grammar,	Writing is free from grammatical, punctuation,, spelling errors. AI tools are effectively used for proofreading, editing.	Minor errors in grammar, punctuation, or spelling. AI tools are used to correct most mistakes.	Frequent errors that distract from meaning. Limited use of AI tools for error correction.	Persistent errors that hinder underst,ing. No evidence of AI-assisted proofreading.
Ethical AI Use	Skillfully integrates AI-generated content, maintaining academic integrity and originality. Clearly distinguishes between own ideas AI suggestions.	Appropriately uses AI tools, ensuring originality—some distinction between personal ideas, AI-generated content.	Relies heavily on AI-generated content with minimal personal input. Lacks clear distinction between own ideas, AI suggestions.	Inappropriately uses AI tools, leading to issues with academic integrity. No distinction between personal work, AI-generated content.
Reflection on AI Use	Provides a thoughtful reflection including benefits, limitations.	Reflects mentioning some benefits, challenges.	Briefly mentions with little insight into its impact on writing.	No reflection in the writing process.

Table (1) combines the scale of evaluating academic writing and the scale of evaluating AI literacy. This rubric aims to test the learners' ability to use the AI tools wisely, improving their creativity and critical thinking instead of relying on the tools. Moreover, human observation and student performance evaluation are still incompatible. That is, the instructors may add details to the rubrics based on the customized goals of the lessons to address variables peculiar to the educational process.

1.8 Providing Feedback and Assessment with AI Tools

This section aims to provide rich feedback to learners, which is essential for supporting learner learning. Recent advances in generative AI provide the opportunity to deliver repeatable, scalable, and instant automatically generated feedback to learners. This approach is feasible from a technical perspective due to recent advances in AI and NLP, though it introduces several potential ethical issues (Lindsay et al., 2023). The attractiveness of AI systems to developers is that they can be trained to execute tasks in a way that is effective enough to replace humans (or offload significant burdens of labour), and to do so much more efficiently in terms of both time taken and scale. These efficiencies can potentially significantly improve the scalability of a given teacher or cohort. However, these decisions often lead to overlooking the needs of specific minorities within a population. Automated systems, trained on a given corpus, tend to and by design to push all output towards the formation of the corpus, making small but meaningful linguistic and pedagogical tweaks hard to enforce. This is particularly important for the UG L2 grammar where small tweaks can greatly affect the validity of a given sentence. Central to PapagAI's design is a selection of AI capabilities combined to deliver this kind of tool. Due to detecting essay length limitations, the solution can be divided between LanguageTool and creating a few simpler token-based machine learning models that can catch and automatically generate notes based on simple mistakes. All annotations are then sent through to the core as a list of human-readable reasons, and a tokenizer is used to preserve the index values of words in the tokenized original document (Solopova et al., 2023).

AI-augmented writing instruction can provide educators feedback and insights on their learners' writing fluency, grammar, support, and structure through automated scoring, human ratified scoring, and comment code suggestions. Automated feedback can flag where learners are having trouble and provide suggestions to improve. Educators can use these results to modify their teaching materials and activities. However, challenges remain as educators calibrate assessments. Many educators may struggle with how to teach writing skills effectively given the vast quantity of text that learners produce. As a result, there is a need for tools that automatically analyze learners' text and provide them with relevant and timely feedback. To be useful, such feedback must be both actionable and reliable (Adam & Chowdhury, 2024; Lindsay et al., 2023).

On the other hand, having access to overly detailed feedback may distract learners from more substantive issues. When learners receive a remarkable amount of feedback, they spend too much time reviewing it instead of dedicating their efforts to refining their paper as a whole. Limiting the number of comments and suggestions or focusing on those that address thematic issues is a useful approach to balancing quantity and depth in the feedback.

1.9 Case Studies and Successful Implementations

As digital writing pedagogy proliferates, a plethora of technological advances have emerged. Among these, Artificial Intelligence (AI) provides an innovative solution to enrich writing instruction and practice. With recent attention paid to integrating AI tools within writing instruction, this section will focus on case studies illustrating best practices for AI integration during the teaching of writing. Several successful implementations of AI tools within diverse educational settings and curricula are detailed. By examining unique strategies used in practice, key insights are available for uptake to inform their own teaching practice (Maphoto et al., 2024; Rowland, 2023).

In higher education, researchers design an AI system that provides individuals with instant, fine-grained feedback on the grammatical, stylistic, and adaptability dimensions of an essay (Seufert et al., 2021). A comprehensive investigation of the effectiveness and implications of AI learning tools within academic writing instruction is conducted. Not only do scholars design AI tools that provide personalized feedback in different linguistic aspects of academic English, but they also demonstrate the impact of these AI learning tools on academic writing performance improvements in terms of grammatical accuracy, text coherence, and high-quality wording. Throughout this review, a surge of mixed-expertise software tools combining AI algorithms has made it possible to automate essential parts of written language processing, which gives rise to more complex feedback on not only surface structures but also on coherence, word selection, and style. Analysis proved that these new AI tools positively impacted ESL and L1 writing practices. In writing classrooms, children are growingly diagnosing practice with intelligent technologies, imitating what teaching experts do amid paper-based exercises (Cui, 2025; Guo & Zaini, 2024).

A case study at a university in the United States exhibits how both learners and instructors engaged with an AI software tool that features grammar checking, plagiarism detection, and text-to-speech functions. Another institution in Canada adopted an AI grading system in a post-entry language assessment and found that AI scores were similar to human raters. The next case highlights a writing course that investigated using Lexile measures with an AI tool to scaffold vocabulary in computer-based lessons. In another instance, UK institutions administered My Access, an online writing program, and examined how AI tools impacted learner writing proficiency. In a writing center at an Australian university, adaptive scaffolding in Turnitin feedback was used to assist nursing learners with the academic writing genre. Finally, a description and mentor training at an institution in the USA is provided. Findings from each case study suggest that integrating AI technologies in education can have both positive and negative outcomes. Positive impacts include the enhancement of learner learning, improvement in writing proficiency, increase in teacher compliance, and engaging learners in the learning process, particularly those who struggle in writing. AI-generated feedback was perceived as helpful by learners and more revisions were made in subsequent essays (Cui, 2025). The challenges include learner resistance toward AI technologies, technical problems, concerns about the authenticity of an AI score, and additional workload for teachers. However, educators can analyze these successful implementations to develop tactics to overcome these challenges when integrating AI technologies into their own classrooms. A larger view is provided on these cases to appreciate how educators successfully adapted and implemented AI technologies despite constraints such as time, lack of training, and limited resources from institutions.

FOSTERING CRITICAL THINKING AND CREATIVITY IN ACADEMIC WRITING

Educators have the important responsibility of enabling learners to develop a strong set of academic writing skills. Besides syntactic, semantic, and pragmatic abilities, one who can write well is also creative, skillful, and knowledgeable about academic discourses. Therefore, both the teaching and learning of academic writing should have multifaceted characteristics. Due to the increasing use of AI academic writing tools, it is also important to discuss AI's capabilities and limitations in fostering critical thinking, creativity, and other higher-order skills.

Understanding the audience's expectations and purposes, the writer selects materials to write to convey information and to be critiqued, analyzed, and improved by readers. This ability is already enhanced using blogs in some AI workspace where critiques of fellow learners are elicited. More such activities provide training in questioning and actively analyzing texts and ideas. The wider focus on form, exemplified in precision studies, aims to contribute to the large body of understandings whereby those who write admirably exercise a continuous drive for retouching. The rare, the stylish, the structurally elegant, the challenging, and twisted are all aspects usually appearing for multiple refinements (Cui, 2025). However, this picture of what might seem almost obsessive text management is balanced by evidence of initial draft structures and commenting upon engaging with content at composition points where rethinking and reshaping are clearly in progress. This stage might be perceived to demonstrate awareness of the strictures of some writing pedagogy approaches but also encourage these learners to develop a concern for principled craft and effect (Arteaga & Peirats, 2024).

Critical Thinking in academic writing refers to the skill of analyzing, evaluating, and synthesizing information in a logical, objective, and well-structured manner. It involves challenging assumptions, considering multiple perspectives, and developing well-reasoned arguments based on evidence. The importance of critical thinking in academic writing is highlighted here. In addition to ensuring that arguments are comprehensive, accurate, and credible, it also assists in developing autonomous thought and original viewpoints. Furthermore, it enhances the capacity to participate in intellectual debates and conversations.

Critical thinking transforms academic writing from a simple summation into an insightful, well-reasoned, and convincing discourse. Furthermore, important aspects of Critical Thinking in the Context of academic writing lie in six main areas. First, *analytical thinking* is the process of dissecting complicated ideas, recognizing patterns, and comprehending the connections between different ideas. Evaluating evidence involves determining the sources' credibility, relevance, and dependability for the purpose of providing support for arguments. Secondly, logical reasoning refers to the ability to construct coherent arguments with clear claims, evidence to support those claims, and solid reasoning. Thirdly, objectivity is the practice of avoiding one's own personal prejudices and considering a variety of perspectives before arriving at a conclusion. Another important aspect is a problem-solving approach, which involves identifying problems, challenging preconceived notions, and proposing solutions that are supported by sound reasoning. In addition, clarity and precision refer to the ability to communicate ideas through plain language effectively. structured reasoning, and logical flow. Finally, critical reflection refers to the practice of continually examining ideas, assumptions, and interpretations rather than taking information at face value. If these aspects are reflected in the learner's academic essays, one goal of the educational process is met.

1.10 Encouraging Learners to Critically Evaluate AI-Generated Suggestions

Many studies find that some learners, depending on their educational background and discipline, can benefit from AI-generated writing feedback, while many studies suggest that the use of such software may not improve the overall writing quality skills. Instead, it may only help fix minor writing mistakes. Due to the mixed findings on the use of artificial intelligence tools in academic writing instruction, educators and researchers in the field of education are encouraged to critically evaluate the use of such technology in academic writing instruction. Critical evaluation can be made by discussing the limitations and advantages of AI tools in academic writing instruction based on the findings of the studies that are included in this 2024 systematic review. It may trigger further discussion among educators and researchers in the field of second language writing and the higher education sector at large in order to develop more effective pedagogies (Johnson & Paulus, 2024).

1.11 Promoting Creativity in Writing While Using AI Tools

Using AI tools for academic writing instruction in higher education is a complex matter when considering educators' and learners' diverse needs and preferences. Important concerns revolve around how to use AI -- as prompting or detection tools -- and minimize its negative side effects, such as depriving learners of learning opportunities, blurring the boundary between plagiarism and collaboration, or objectifying writing too much. Besides, there is the need to decide what to expect from AI tools -their complementarity to existing writing centers, their ability to accelerate the feedback process, or simply their cheaper provision of grammar correction. A comprehensive set of mostly context-specific recommendations is developed, grouped under ten major pedagogical considerations (Hsu, 22023; Pytash et al., 2015).

Essential elements of creativity in writing encompass linguistic flexibility and the liberty of expressing different aspects of conventional issues. This set of attributes encapsulates creativity in writing. Firstly, originality is the main concern. It refers to formulating novel ideas, viewpoints, and methodologies. It also refers to formulating a distinct perspective and robust tone. That is achieved by offering an innovative viewpoint or an unconventional interpretation of a subject and enthusiasm or wit while preserving clarity and intent deviating from conventional norms when required to improve narrative effectiveness. In addition, linguistic capabilities and Aesthetics are sharpened by literary techniques such as metaphors, similes, alliteration, and rhythm, reflecting expressive and engaging language utilizing vivid descriptions, impactful word selections, and rhetorical devices. The linguistic aspect is to be well-structured in a diverse Sentence Structure, preventing boredom by combining concise, impactful sentences with extended, fluid ones. Also. Creative organization is another attribute of creativity in writing that explores structural variations, such as commencing with a personal narrative prior to analysis or employing a circular format. Learners need to be trained to escape the conventional views and think of unaddressed variables. Re-organizing knowledge can be encouraged and reinforced by the instructors' enthusiasm to address conventional issues from new perspectives. In sum, creativity can be fostered by the joint efforts of the instructor and learner.

COLLABORATIVE WRITING AND PEER REVIEW WITH AI TOOLS

In response to the debates on the efficacy of AI-infused writing instruction, research findings show that most learners have positive attitudes toward the instructed AI tool-supported writing learning (Nguyen et al., 2024). They perceived that AI tools can facilitate the checking of academic writing quality, reduce grammatical errors, prevent plagiarism effectively, and enhance peer learning and peer teaching experience. Even most learners hold a positive view on the potentiality of the instructed AI tool for boosting academic writing performance. In learners' writing output, those learners employing AI tool support produced more cohesive writing than those of the learner group without AI tool support (Fathi & Rahimi, 2024; Fathi & Rahimi, 2024).

This study proposes a pedagogical plan that integrates collaborative writing projects with various AI tools to help learners learn to write academic English. Its teaching model comprises three stages: *modeling, practice*, and *project-based collaborative writing*. The model enables learners to become well acquainted with activities under eLearning settings and empowers them to acquire academic writing skills. In the first stage, learners are invited to read academic essays, discuss the patterns and key features of academic writing, create an analytical list report, and use descriptive language. In the second stage, learners try to improve cohesion and coherence, paraphrase, and avoid the use of inappropriate conjunctions by using Lextutor, AntConc, GATES191, Mendeley, and SCI-HUB. A successful collaborative approach was connected to learners who improved their reading comprehension and writing abilities by analyzing texts using Sip-and-Puff.

The quality by which learners engage in peer review processes could be variable and heavily influenced by their assessment literacy. As such, the pedagogical features in the AI tools can be used to help coach the learners to be more expert-like reviewers, i.e. as an innovative way to scaffold the learning process—initiate a discussion of an article by: First, reviewing and identifying the summarizer's inference. Second, reviewing five learners' responses for: a) whether or not it acknowledges the inferences of the article, and b) the overall quality of the review. Third, drafting a critique of the five responses and summating the discussion.

1.12 Encouraging Learners to Adapt and Learn New Writing Tools

In both research and day-to-day life, assumptions about the potential impact, benefits, and adoption of AI-based academic writing tools have been made. There is an expectation that academia is heading towards a future where such tools facilitate the academic writing process. Therefore, it is important for the field to understand better how users, especially learners, can be encouraged to adapt to and learn from these tools most effectively, and what broader impacts a more widespread use of AI-based academic writing tools might have on individuals and systems (Aljuaid, 2024). AI tools can help cultivate better writing behaviours and habits. These tools can prompt the learners to "learn by doing,", offer an abundance of tailored learning opportunities, and elaborate on feedback and suggestions to increase language awareness and focus attention on meaningful language features. In addition, AI tools can cognitively ease the writing process, potentially leading to higher-quality texts by redirecting cognitive resources and allowing writers to invest more time in thinking about higher-level linguistic and argumentative features of their texts. All that said, it is critical that learners are encouraged to attend and learn from the feedback and suggestions that the tools generate (Omodan & Marongwe, 2024).

ETHICAL AND PRIVACY CONSIDERATIONS IN AI-ENHANCED WRITING INSTRUCTION

This study examines critical ethical, privacy, and pedagogical considerations in AI-enhanced writing instruction. Privacy and ethical configurations are crucial for writing instructors and AI tool developers to ensure the education sector has guidelines that protect learners and teachers and prevent malfeasance. Data collection and processing are significant threats, and risks in harms and barriers to individuals' freedom. To learn to write better, information is collected and saved on each portion of the writing procedure. Much of this information can be employed to create profiles on how a learner composes. Educators, algorithm users, AI businesses, and information processors are urged to safeguard this information against future uses (Hysaj, Freeman & Hamam, 2024).

A clear view of AI technology is revealed in order to be conscious individuals about the AI tool they are utilizing if they are learners or utilizing as a technique to defend against bias in AI algorithms. When familiarity and use are low, AI might only maintain existing inequalities within obscure practices. Knowledge of AI relationships has increased cautiously and has been intertwined with privacy issues for quite some time (Pereira et al., 2024). The ideas discussed are applicable to AI developers, teachers, and makers of syllabi for schools and colleges, and for additional configurations in writing and educational technology.

SUMMARIZING THE PEDAGOGICAL PLAN

A Comprehensive Pedagogical Plan for teaching academic writing with AI tools was developed following a review of the current literature on the subject. Instructors may be interested in utilizing AI tools in academic writing instruction. The first inclination might be to choose from the resources available without necessarily considering pedagogical approaches that make the best use of them. This chapter houses a pedagogical plan designed to maximize learner improvement in academic writing while minimizing the chance of learners becoming over-reliant on AI algorithms. Offered within are approaches to teaching the writing process, classroom activities, assignments, comments, grading, and strategies for addressing common learner concerns that will enhance learners' argumentation, organization, language use, writing formats, and lessening the odds of academic dishonesty.

Although AI is revolutionizing English writing instruction by providing instant feedback, personalized learning, and enhanced engagement, but it should be used thoughtfully to ensure it complements human instruction rather than replaces it. By effectively employing AI, instructors can empower learners to become more creative and proficient writers while maintaining the integrity of traditional writing skills. AI can be a powerful tool for teaching writing skills in various ways. Here are some ways AI can assist both instructors and learners in various aspects following the stages of preparing the lesson to achieve the goals as in the following figure:

Figure 2. Writing lessons enhanced by AI tools

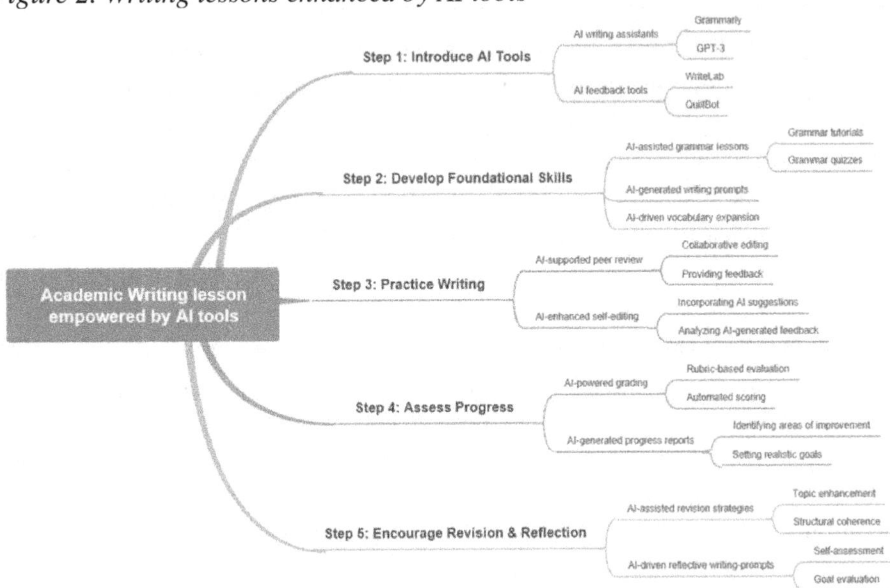

Figure 2 shows the AI implementation process in teaching writing skills. In the first step, "Introduce AI tool," instructors are familiar with the avenues offered by these tools. The aim of this step is to ensure that the tools are utilized to their fullest potential, especially given the cost of these software applications. Once instructors are familiar with the use of these applications, the learners are directed to the wise use of the applications. It is important to note that instructors must indicate the difference between human intelligence and artificial intelligence. The importance of this step is to minimize the issue of overreliance. The instructor may also consider the mixed-abilities classes where learners may be not only in their cognitive capabilities but also in their technical skills. In addition, the psychological and social factors of accepting or rejecting technology intervention and the deviation from traditional writing instructions are also points to consider.

The second stage is developing the fundamentals of academic writing. The instructor needs to identify the lesson's goals or series of lessons and the expected outcomes. The instructor may develop certain goals to be achieved from each section of the lesson, considering that the nature, speed, and quality of the learning process might differ from conventional classes.

Furthermore, the selected AI tools should be empowered with the selected grammar and vocabulary lessons, such as quizzes, rules, and other related effects that enhance learning. The third stage is writing practice. AI-driven grammar checkers such as Grammarly or ProWritingAid assist learners by detecting inaccuracies in spelling, grammar, punctuation, and stylistic elements. They can provide recommendations to enhance sentence structure, vocabulary, and clarity. These solutions offer instantaneous feedback, particularly beneficial for learners who may not obtain prompt responses from an instructor. AI can assist learners in rephrasing words or articulating their views in alternative ways, fostering the enhancement of style and creativity in writing. Usually, a writing lesson would involve brainstorming and generating a logical sequence of events, topics, and relationships between variables. Depending on the learner's familiarity with the given topic, instructors may use various AI tools that enhance learners' knowledge of the subject matter. AI systems such as ChatGPT or Jasper can produce writing prompts or concepts for students who may find it challenging to initiate an essay or creative writing project. AI can assist learners in brainstorming, structuring their ideas, and developing outlines before initiating their drafts. AI can produce sample essays or other works responding to certain prompts or subjects. This provides learners with a framework for analysis and comprehension. Educators may utilize AI-generated examples to demonstrate effective writing strategies, structure, and stylistic elements. AI-driven speech recognition solutions can aid learners who favor verbal expression over written communication by transcribing their spoken ideas into text. This is particularly beneficial for individuals with disabilities or those who encounter difficulties with handwriting or typing.

In addition, peer review and editing tools may sharpen the learners' observations and logical reasoning and refine thought structures. It may also encourage creativity by sharing drafts with AI. Learners may utilize suggestions and feedback from AI to enhance their original thoughts rather than replace them. The next stage involves generating progress reports and assessments of outcomes by identifying key strengths and areas of improvement. This will enable the learner to direct their attention to the important aspects. The last stage is revision. The learners may utilize the tools to polish their work and may accept or reject suggestions from AI. Revisions may involve coherence, cohesion devices, vocabulary, logical sequence, essay structures, etc.

Finally, learners and instructors must evaluate the process of learning based on the written outcome, prompt results, and personal reflections. AI-powered paraphrasing tools demonstrate how varying vocabulary, and syntax can alter the tone or focus of a written work. By linking sentences and concepts, AI can evaluate the coherence of a student's writing. It can assess logical progression, pinpoint areas requiring transitions, or identify paragraphs that lack a definitive topic sentence.

AI tools can also assist learners in organizing their essays to enhance readability and engagement, enhance vocabulary, and foster creativity in Writing. Certain AI tools can propose alternative vocabulary or generate imaginative prose, assisting learners in broadening their lexical repertoire and enhancing expressiveness in their writing. AI can aid in creating fictional narratives by proposing plot advancements or character attributes. AI can propose synonyms, enhance word selection, and assist learners in acquiring new vocabulary. This can particularly advantage individuals aiming to enhance their linguistic abilities or those acquiring English as a second language. Thus, AI-driven technologies may assess students' writing according to multiple criteria, including grammar, style, tone, diction, and coherence. This aids learners in identifying the precise elements of their work that want enhancement. Additionally, certain AI programs offer a task score or grade, enabling educators to concentrate on overarching input.

Furthermore, AI can facilitate collaborative writing endeavors by offering a platform that enables numerous learners to compose simultaneously in real-time. It can monitor modifications, offer recommendations, and enhance the overall quality of collaborative efforts. In addition, AI systems can identify plagiarism by juxtaposing learners' inputs with extensive databases, thereby safeguarding academic integrity and assisting learners in producing original writing.

Educators can incorporate AI by generating automated assessments of objective writing components (grammar, spelling) and synchronous collaborative writing in which students utilize AI technologies for joint composition and editing during class.

Targeted courses utilizing AI to address specific deficiencies in learners' writing, including clarity and coherence. In short, instructors need to design lessons tailored perfectly to the selected AI tools in order to fully utilize their potential and achieve the desired lesson outcomes.

CONCLUSION AND FUTURE DIRECTIONS

Most higher education institutions are expected to embrace AI-based writing editors and implement them in their writing courses. This plan sets forth a general pedagogical plan for educators teaching academic writing while using AI tools. The proposed plan considers the different stages of writing a research paper: planning, pre-writing, drafting, revising, and proofreading. Each step includes specific tasks learners undertake, often using AI writing tools (Guo & Zaini, 2024). In response to these tasks, learners submit portions of their writing, such as a research question, outline, or first draft, in progress to the teacher for formative feedback. Top of Form

1.13 Future Directions in AI and Writing Instruction and Research

In the near future, Artificial Intelligence (AI) is expected to become more sophisticated, especially in the areas of natural language processing and user data analysis. Although this advancement has much potential to influence every aspect of life, educational settings and instructional strategies—writing instructors will remain crucial to learners' literacy development. As technology evolves, education professionals must learn how to implement and maintain AI-driven writing pedagogy. They need to understand how this technology works and how many aspects of the writing process it targets. It could furnish learners with resources to develop ideas, assist in translating texts, or revise drafts. In addition, it empowers self-paced learning by providing real-time feedback and instant guidance for writing exercises. Nevertheless, tutoring should involve human feedback, and AI should enhance—not replace—teacher instruction. Despite apprehensions that automated systems might replace educators, a blend of human and machine feedback is considered the most favored model of instruction. However, the pressure to additionally teach AI technology or to always keep abreast of innovative educative AI developments may prove challenging amidst the myriad changes already occurring in education. This may explain why, despite the anticipation that AI use in education will expand, many educators hold a modest attitude regarding AI applications (Song & Song, 2023). To inspire more teachers to leverage AI in writing education, it is suggested that information on technology-enhanced writing pedagogy be disseminated across educational sectors.

Common problems that users might encounter with AI-supported academic writing assignments can be identified for informing future users and developers. Along with the qualitative data, a quantitative data set can be amassed from analyzing user-commands and the actual operation of the software. While the development and applications of natural language processing and AI tools keep prospering, education curators, linguists, and AI engineers can team up for conducting interdisciplinary R&D work on this emerging area. After examining the following research genres and challenges, a focus is drawn on the future research directions. There are keyword searches of matched the publication title or abstract of articles. A focused review is then annotated. Next, a trend analysis is made based on the examined articles. The rationale for conducting the present research is to examine a gap between pioneering research and oncoming tasks. Given the diverse demands and readiness levels, it is valuable to match the tasks to satisfactory tools. Educational innovators and AI toolmakers can be involved in seeking an optimal match between the tools and tasks.

1.14 Recommendations

Several lessons have been learned, and worthwhile outcomes emerged from synthesizing case studies on integrating artificial intelligence tools into teaching writing skills. Reliable guidance is offered to educators who are considering integrating AI tools into their writing instruction. They can be inspired to develop teaching strategies that allow them to improve their writing individually while safely monitoring the ongoing process. However, there are things to avoid making errors commonly committed by early adopters. Such insights were gleaned by identifying patterns of positive results and challenges described in case studies of early adopters. Results were split into lessons learned and recommendations that serve as a roadmap for educators aiming to capitalize on the advantages of AI-supported writing instruction.

While being inspired by the outcomes of other teachers' studies on AI-supported writing instruction, it is critical to consider the broader settings in which they took place. A fair proportion of the case studies reported were placed in resource-rich settings. Everything else, especially the technological choice faced by the early adopters in less advantaged settings, is unprecedented turbulence for those standing at the frontier of writing education and wondering how to avail themselves of smart digital technologies to help learners become proficient writers (Amirjalili et al., 2024).

Therefore, this critical reflection looks behind the scenes of the early implementations of AI-supported writing instruction. The purpose is to contemplate these practices, which while seemingly accidental or obvious, concern decisions that were deliberated most thoroughly. In addition, papers also analyzed recurring challenges hamper the adoption of AI-supported strategies. Case studies on the less successful launches of artificial intelligence in writing classes are reported. It thus shed light on the less evident dangers in hopes that readers may learn to avoid the pitfalls before embarking on AI-enhanced writing instruction operations. These are discussed to provide a fuller picture of the newest and most innovative educational practices. Considering AI-based tools are about to revolutionize writing instruction, an awareness of the width of the landscape is desirable for educators about to undertake their first exploratory steps.

Furthermore, when considering the introduction of AI-based tools into writing instruction, schools cannot underestimate setting up a high-tech infrastructure ready to handle heavy loads, notably in terms of storage and processing power. Schools also need a communications infrastructure capable of delivering and uploading large files rapidly. In other words, to effectively take advantage of AI-enhanced writing instruction, investing in the digital realm is crucial, ideally with the capacity to handle big data.

Another factor that cannot be overlooked is the resistance to change. Case studies present various problems that resist the implantation of AI-enhanced writing instruction. It becomes evident that the instructor may, from the outset, manifest reservations, skepticism, or even hostility towards the new technologies rushing into their classroom. It is thus necessary to foster broad engagement around the oncoming changes by creating well-elaborated debates, inviting guest speakers who advocate AI-based writing instruction, and advertising its benefits. Finally, it is crucial to engage parents in a discussion surrounding the AI-enhanced education to ensure the concerted implementation of innovative practices.

Therefore, it is important to set clear objectives and foresight. Be very clear about the reasons for using a particular AI tool in a given classroom. Ask oneself what is expected from AI use and what is the desired outcome of its application. Then, it is pivotal to follow up on these considerations to establish whether proposed solutions produce the expected effects. Regularly audit the progress in using the AI-enhanced writing instruction. If no improvement is identified, question the rationale for this particular AI setup.

REFERENCES

Adam, K., & Chowdhury, M. (2024). From Prompt to Paper: A Case Analysis of AI and Academic Writing. In *Proceedings of the 18th International Conference of the Learning Sciences-ICLS 2024, pp.* 2241-2242. International Society of the Learning Sciences. DOI: 10.22318/icls2024.268898

Ahmed, M., Siddique, M., & Yasmin, T. (2024). Impact of artificial intelligence-based writing assistant on the academic writing skills of university faculty in Pakistan. [IJHS]. *International Journal of Human Sciences*, *4*(1), 539–545.

Al-Sofi, B. B. M. A. (2024). Artificial intelligence-powered tools and academic writing: To use or not to use ChatGPT. *Saudi Journal of Language Studies*, *4*(3), 145–161. DOI: 10.1108/SJLS-06-2024-0029

. Aljuaid, H. (2024). The impact of artificial intelligence tools on academic writing instruction in higher education: A systematic review. *Arab World English Journal (AWEJ) Special Issue on ChatGPT.*

Amirjalili, F., Neysani, M., & Nikbakht, A. (2024, March). Exploring the boundaries of authorship: A comparative analysis of AI-generated text and human academic writing in English literature. [). Frontiers Media SA.]. *Frontiers in Education*, *9*, 1347421. DOI: 10.3389/feduc.2024.1347421

Arteaga, F., & Peirats, A. (2024). ACADEMIC WRITING AND INNOVATION: FOR AN EFFECTIVE MANAGEMENT IN THE DIRECTION OF ACADEMIC PAPERS. In *INTED2024 Proceedings* (pp. 5509-5517). IATED.

Cheng, Y., Lyons, K., Chen, G., Gašević, D., & Swiecki, Z. (2024, March). Evidence-centered assessment for writing with generative AI. In *Proceedings of the 14th Learning Analytics and Knowledge Conference* (pp. 178-188). DOI: 10.1145/3636555.3636866

. Cui, Y. (2025). What Influences College Learners Using AI for Academic Writing?-A Quantitative Analysis Based on HISAM and TRI Theory. Computers and Education: Artificial Intelligence, 100391.

Fathi, J., & Rahimi, M. (2024). Utilising artificial intelligence-enhanced writing mediation to develop academic writing skills in EFL learners: A qualitative study. *Computer Assisted Language Learning*, •••, 1–40. DOI: 10.1080/09588221.2024.2374772

Guo, H., & Zaini, S. H. (2024). Artificial Intelligence in Academic Writing: A Literature Review. *Asian Pendidikan*, *4*(2), 46–55. DOI: 10.53797/aspen.v4i2.6.2024

Hsu, H. P. (2023). Can generative artificial intelligence write an academic journal article? Opportunities, challenges, and implications. *The Irish Journal of Technology Enhanced Learning*, *7*(2), 158–171. DOI: 10.22554/ijtel.v7i2.152

Hysaj, A., Freeman, M., & Hamam, D. (2024, June). Using AI tools to enhance academic writing and maintain academic integrity. In *International conference on human-computer interaction* (pp. 57-66). Cham: Springer Nature Switzerland. DOI: 10.1007/978-3-031-61305-0_4

Johnson, C. W., & Paulus, T. (2024). Generating a Reflexive AI-Assisted Workflow for Academic Writing. *The Qualitative Report*, *29*(10), 2772–2792. DOI: 10.46743/2160-3715/2024.7634

Kelly, E., & Smith, S. (2014). *Workshop: Teaching, Technology, and Theory, Oh My!* Teaching with Technology for Learning's Sake.

Köpeczi-Bócz, T. (2025). A Multidisciplinary Theoretical Framework for Enhancing Scientific Writing: A Validated Model for Supporting Young Researchers. bioRxiv, 2025-01.

. Lindsay, E., Johri, A., & Bjerva, J. (2023). A framework for responsible development of automated learner feedback with generative AI.

Mahyoob, M., Al-Garaady, J., & Alblwi, A. (2023). A proposed framework for human-like language processing of ChatGPT in academic writing. [iJET]. *International Journal of Emerging Technologies in Learning*, *18*(14), 282–293. DOI: 10.3991/ijet.v18i14.41725

Maphoto, K. B., Sevnarayan, K., Mohale, N. E., Suliman, Z., Ntsopi, T. J., & Mokoena, D. (2024). Advancing learners' academic excellence in distance education: Exploring the potential of generative AI integration to improve academic writing skills. *Open Praxis*, *16*(2), 142–159. DOI: 10.55982/openpraxis.16.2.649

Mudawy, A., & Mohammed, A. (2024). Investigating EFL faculty members' perceptions of integrating artificial intelligence applications to improve the research writing process: A case study at Majmaah University. *Arab World English Journal (AWEJ) Special Issue on ChatGPT*.

Nguyen, A., Hong, Y., Dang, B., & Huang, X. (2024). Human-AI collaboration patterns in AI-assisted academic writing. *Studies in Higher Education*, *49*(5), 847–864. DOI: 10.1080/03075079.2024.2323593

Omodan, B. I., & Marongwe, N. (2024). The role of artificial intelligence in decolonizing academic writing for inclusive knowledge production. *Interdisciplinary Journal of Education Research*, *6*(s1), 1–14. DOI: 10.38140/ijer-2024.vol6.s1.06

Pereira, R., Reis, I. W., Ulbricht, V., & Santos, N. D. (2024). Generative artificial intelligence and academic writing: An analysis of the perceptions of researchers in training. *Management Research: Journal of the Iberoamerican Academy of Management, 22*(4), 429–450. DOI: 10.1108/MRJIAM-01-2024-1501

Pytash, K. E., Testa, E., & Nigh, J. (2015). Writing the world: Preservice teachers' perceptions of 21st century writing instruction. Teaching/Writing. *The Journal of Writing Teacher Education, 4*(1), 8.

Rahimi, M., Fathi, J., & Zou, D. (2024). Exploring the impact of automated written corrective feedback on the academic writing skills of EFL learners: An activity theory perspective. *Education and Information Technologies*, •••, 1–45.

Rowland, D. R. (2023). Two frameworks to guide discussions around levels of acceptable use of generative AI in learner academic research and writing. *Journal of Academic Language and Learning, 17*(1), T31–T69.

Seufert, S., Burkhard, M., & Handschuh, S. (2021, November). Fostering Learners' Academic Writing Skills: Feedback Model for an AI-enabled Support Environment. In *Innovate Learning Summit* (pp. 49-58). Association for the Advancement of Computing in Education (AACE).

. Shen, C., Shi, P., Guo, J., Xu, S., & Tian, J. (2023). From process to product: writing engagement and performance of EFL learners under computer-generated feedback instruction.

Shofiah, N., Putera, Z. F., & Solichah, N. (2023, December). Challenges and opportunities in the use of artificial intelligence in education for academic writing: A scoping review. In *Conference Psychology and Flourishing Humanity (PFH 2023)* (pp. 174-193). Atlantis Press. DOI: 10.2991/978-2-38476-188-3_20

. Song, C. & Song, Y. (2023). Enhancing academic writing skills and motivation: assessing the efficacy of ChatGPT in AI-assisted language learning for EFL learners.

Van Niekerk, J., Delport, P. M., & Sutherland, I. (2025). Addressing the use of generative AI in academic writing. *Computers and Education: Artificial Intelligence, 8*, 100342. DOI: 10.1016/j.caeai.2024.100342

Chapter 4
Enhancing Students' Reading Comprehension Skills Through the Use of Epic:
A Comparative Study

Fatema Jameel Khalaf
https://orcid.org/0009-0005-5181-6127
Arab Open University, Bahrain

Fatema Ahmed Wali
https://orcid.org/0000-0003-4600-8238
Bahrain Polytechnic, Bahrain

ABSTRACT

This chapter examines the impact of Epic reading application on English as Foreign Language (EFL) Grade 1 Arab students in classroom settings. Through a mixed-methods investigation of 45 students at a private school in the United Arab Emirates, the chapter analyzes student perceptions and learning outcomes related to digital reading integration. The research employs structured questionnaires, classroom observations, and feedback sessions to evaluate the application's effectiveness across learning, peer interaction, usability, and student preferences. The findings demonstrate that 87% of participants exhibited increased reading motivation, while 92% benefited from interactive features for vocabulary acquisition. The chapter highlights gender-specific usage patterns, improved classroom management capabilities, and enhanced parent involvement through home access features. The analysis reveals significant benefits in phonemic awareness, sight word recognition, and reading

DOI: 10.4018/979-8-3373-0771-8.ch004

fluency, suggesting the vital role of digital platforms in EFL instruction.

INTRODUCTION

The remarkable rise of e-book digital platforms has transformed worldwide access to written materials. One such platform that has gained widespread use in recent years is *Epic*, an online library providing learners with high-quality e-books across various genres. Epic has established itself as a significant element in the online reading space by offering a remarkable e-book experience to its users. In spite of this advantage, the use of e-books has some drawbacks, including overdependence on them while neglecting traditional paper books, which can cause eye problems and the unavailability of mobile phones and computers for some students to access these e-book platforms. In addition, e-books lack tangibility that early year students would be able to benefit from and potentially make these books less effective in satisfying their needs.

This paper examines the development of reading abilities among Arab male and female students in Grade 1 providing an insightful case study of *Epic*. This case study specifically investigates whether E-book tools, including *Epic*, can markedly enhance the reading abilities of Grade 1 EFL Arab students. Furthermore, the current study reveals that Epic platform has improved EFL students' learning experiences, providing early education practitioners more insight into the efficacy of e-reading tools.

LITERATURE REVIEW

Learning using reading platforms and applications is a growing area in research. While online reading applications and platforms are increasingly significant in English as Foreign Language (EFL) instruction to facilitate students' reading development, few studies have discussed these applications and platforms for reading comprehension, such as Epic's built-in feature which are read to me feature, in-built dictionaries, interactive quizzes, and tracking the progress of reading. Most of the research papers published discussed the impact of online reading mediums (e.g., PDF, Gamified, and Flip HTML5). Epic reading platform is an online reading application that contains a variety of interactive e-books that allow EFL students to improve their reading fluency and accuracy through the online books and to check their reading comprehension through the application's post-reading quizzes. Studies discussed Epic platform including, Porath and Unruh (2021), who investigated how Epic is used in EFL classrooms by instructors and how primary level students engage with the platform. The result of the study shows EFL teachers appreciated Epic's in-built features. Furthermore, primary students enjoyed the platform's range of genres, being able to customise their own reading profile, variety of videos, and flipping the e-book's pages feature.

Several studies have analyzed the impact of e-books on students' levels of motivation. Liman, Kaban & Karadeniz (2021), for instance, analyzed 96 sixth-grade Turkish students' perception regarding their e-reading experiences in the English as Foreign Language (EFL) classroom according to Raz Kids personalised, gamified using program (see Figure 1), and PDF reading forms and their influence on their motivation during their 5-week study. The study concluded that the participants who experienced the e-books reported a high level of motivation compared to the control group which received traditional printed books.

Figure 1. Razkids (www.raz-kids.com)

Raz-Kids Read Aloud E-Books Program

Another study by Moutsinas et al. (2023) examined the impact of a variety of e-book formats (e.g., PDF, customized, gamified using RazKids program (see figure 1) on 84 fifth-grade students in Greek schools on their reading comprehension, attitudes, and motivation levels. Moutsinas et al. (2023) concluded that the experimental group who used e-books reported a positive and enjoyable experience compared to the control group who received traditional printed books.

A variety of studies have analyzed the impact of e-books on EFL students' vocabulary acquisition. Lee & Choi (2022), for example, studied the influence of e-books on 19 Korean students' vocabulary acquisition levels. The participants read eight books (e.g., independent e-books and shared printed books) and were assigned pre- and post-tests. The analysis of the tests concluded that both forms of books showed positive results on students' vocabulary learning. However, the reading level of the e-books group was more effective than that of the shared printed book group. Another study by Ali et al. (2021) aimed to analyze the role of e-books in building EFL students' vocabulary and their perceptions regarding the use of e-books to enhance their vocabulary acquisition levels. The participants consisted of 45 undergraduate students at the National University of Modern Languages (NUML). The study revealed that e-books played a crucial role in students' vocabulary building, and students reported a positive attitude regarding the e-books' role in enhancing their vocabulary.

Moreover, very few studies have discussed the role of e-books in enhancing students' critical thinking abilities. Pratiwi et al. (2022), for instance, explored the effect of Html5 e-books on improving 30 high school students' critical thinking abilities in economics subjects (see Figure 2). The results of the study showed that there is a vital difference in the analyzed average result between the experimental and control groups' critical thinking skills after leveraging e-books. The experimental group reported a high level of scores above the KBM value, while the control group reported scores below the KBM value. Also, e-books were used significantly as a tool during learning to enhance students' critical thinking skills.

Figure 2. Flipgrid HTML5 (www.fliphtml5.com)

Flipgrid Program Page Turning Book

Collaboration is another facet that is reinforced in reading comprehension tools or platforms. A study conducted by Al-Jarf (2021) on 72 Saudi females Arab EFL freshman students at King Saud University. The study consisted of an experimental group that was assigned to read collaborative e-books libraries downloaded from Google Play and iPhone App Stores (see Figure 3) while the control group received traditional instructions using printed books. Moreover, the researcher selected self-help books for the participants as shown in Figure 4. The researcher reported remarkable differences between the post-test results between the experimental and control groups. Moreover, the experimental group showed an increase in their reading abilities. While the post-survey reported several reasons that led to students' improvement in reading including, activities revolved around student-centeredness, students' participation, active interaction between peers, a safe and non-judgmental environment to make mistakes, and teachers' support.

Figure 3. Variety of E-book Libraries on Google Play (Al-Jarf, 2021)

Online E-Books Downloaded Programs on Google Play Used in the Study

Figure 4. A sample of self-help e-book assigned to students (Al-Jarf, 2021)

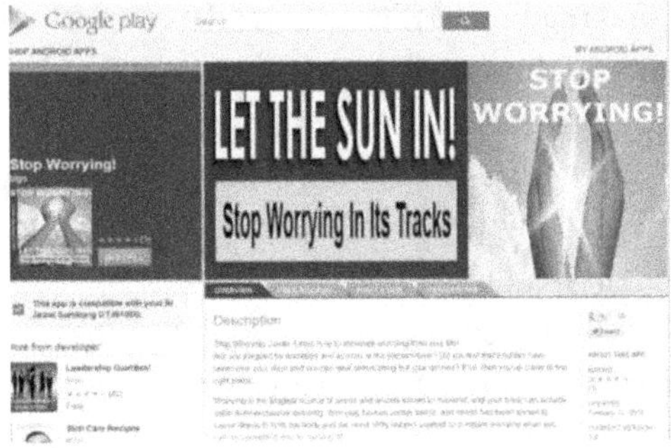

Stop Worrying Guidebook in E-Book Format Read by EFL Students Al-Jarf (2021)

A few studies explored the impact of e-books as a means of reading using tablets versus printed books on students' reading comprehension skills. For example, Park & Lee (2021) studied the role of tablets using Reading Gate application (see Figure 5) and traditional teaching instructions. They examined Korean students who received extensive reading instruction using tablets, printed books, and traditional teaching instruction. The researchers concluded that e-books can be very beneficial for shallow reading, while traditional printed books are significant for deeper understanding.

Figure 5. ReadingGate (www.readingq.readinggate.com)

Reading Gate Platform User-friendly Interface

Recently, a study by Medjahed and Yahiaoui (2023) investigated twenty-seven third-year EFL Arab students' preferences at Mascara's university regarding the use of tablets to read. The study concluded that students prefer e-books and hold a positive attitude towards them during their language learning. Also, it enhances students' strategy use and reading abilities. Some features of e-books include availability, variety of modes, and improving reading strategies, which is why students prefer e-books. In study on students' perceptions of the effectiveness of e-books by Merentika Arianda et al. (2023), the study led to students' positive perceptions of e-books as an effective tool in their second language acquisition process as they enhance their independent reading skills.

The current research studies emphasize the varied gains of online reading applications and platforms in EFL instruction. However, a notable gap in investigating detailed characteristics and their influences on reading comprehension exists. The reviewed studies disclose that e-books and related online tools and resources have largely improved students' motivation, vocabulary acquisition, and critical thinking skills. However, there is a clear demand for more studies investigating the effectiveness of specific features within these applications, such as Epic's built-in features for reading comprehension.

METHODOLOGY

The Tool

The Epic platform is an online reading tool launched in 2013. It contains a variety of e-books, videos, and quizzes. English as Foreign Language (EFL) students can enjoy reading books that are related to a variety of genres and their sub-titles including English books, science and arts books, social emotional studies books, social studies books, and math books (see Figure 6).

Figure 6. Epic platform 1st grade genres

Epic Platform with Its Genres Including English Language Arts, Science & Arts, Social Emotional Learning, Social Studies, and Math

Furthermore, students can access the platform using their tablets, computers, and mobile devices. The books are arranged according to their level of difficulty using the Accelerated Reading (AR) levels and grade levels, starting with Pre-K to the seventh grade. English as Foreign Language (EFL) teachers can choose the suitable level for their students (see Figure 7). These levels allow teachers to help high- and low-achieving students improve their reading fluency as they are personalized, and students will be able to know their current level and work out to reach the higher level.

Figure 7. Explore the stories by grade and reading level

Categorizing Epic Online Books Based on Students' AR and Grade Levels

The Epic Platform includes a variety of features that can improve EFL students' reading abilities including read to me feature and reading comprehension quizzes assigned as post reading activities. The read to me feature allows students to listen to the story with appropriate pronunciation, stress, and rhyme, which can all contribute to their reading fluency. Students will be able to recognize the sounds of the letters by clicking on each word in the story, and it will be readable to them. Moreover, by clicking on the word itself, students will be able to recognize the part of speech as well as the meaning of it, which can help them to be autonomous students as they depend on themselves. It also helps students to be vocabulary detectives and use these new vocabulary items in their writing and speaking. The class will revolve around the student-centered approach, with the teacher monitoring students' progress while reading.

The reading comprehension quizzes contain different levels of higher- and lower-order thinking skills. It improves students' critical thinking abilities through open-ended questions. For instance, students can create meaningful sentences using the words learned in the story, which develops their creativity (see Figure 8). Furthermore, these questions cater to the students' learning styles; kinesthetic students can create a puppet show, visual students can draw their favorite characters, and auditory students can listen to the story using the read to me feature.

Figure 8. Open-and closed-ended post-reading activities

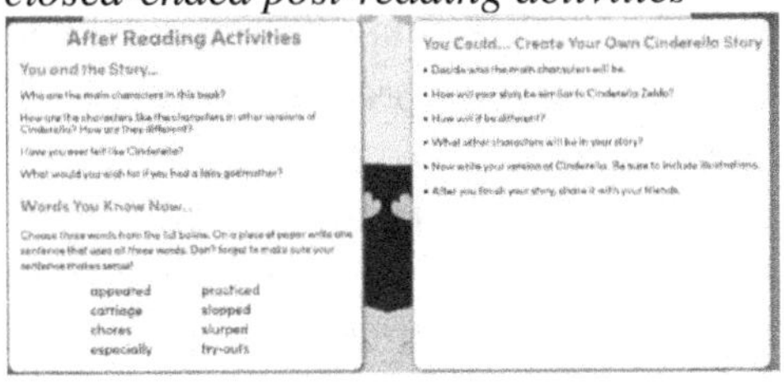

After Reading Activities for Cinderella Story on Epic Platform, Catering All Learning Styles

Basic questions are displayed through multiple choice questions which are close-ended questions which can improve the lower order thinking skills. It balances both the higher and lower order thinking skills of students as teachers can assign stories with each type.

Figure 9. Post-reading multiple choice questions

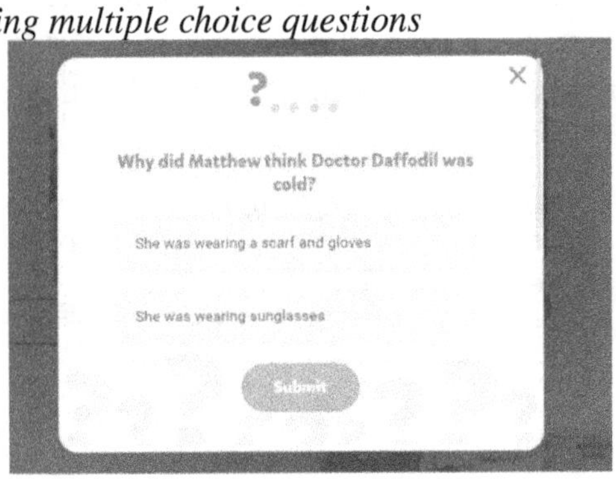

Two-Options Multiple-Choice Questions Assigned to Students After Reading the Story

The other types of questions are basic multiple-choice questions based on the story events at the end of the book (see Figure 9). It has two options, and students get immediate feedback on their answers as well as rewards once they finish all the questions they are required to answer. This feature enhances students' reading comprehension skills and engagement as they focus on the events of the story while reading, not shadow reading. Furthermore, students can access the website at school or home, which is a vital way to continuous reading progress outside the classroom. Also, it contains video tutorials containing tips for teachers that showcase ways to create school accounts and steps on how to find and assign books to students. These tutorial videos can be found on YouTube on the Epic channel. The videos allow EFL teachers to explore the key features of Epic and make use of them in an easy and understandable way. Furthermore, for the books that require quizzes, teachers can assign various books with quizzes to students as homework and track their progress using the platform. Once the story is assigned, the student will get a notification in their mailbox.

Once students are done with the multiple-choice quiz, they will receive their earned points and the amount of time spent reading the story, which motivate them to set their own goals regarding how many books they want to read. Also, it helps students recognise their fluency level, as they can challenge themselves and try again to read the story with more time. For those who answered incorrectly, they have the option to retake the quiz, as this gives students an opportunity to try again and increase their confidence regarding their reading comprehension abilities.

The platform records the students' scores, the amount of time spent on taking the quiz, and attempt numbers, as shown in Figure 10. It is a time-consuming feature, as EFL teachers are not required to correct the quizzes by themselves or use traditional paper assignments. Also, it allows EFL teachers to keep a permanent record of students' progress and compare it to the end of the semester's progress.

Figure 10. Analysis of the quiz assigned to students

The Summary of the Assigned Quiz Shows How Many Students Took It, the Average Scores, and the Assigned Date

Subjects and Context

The study involved 21 first-grade students aged between 6 and 7 years old at a private school in the Kingdom of Bahrain. The participants consist of 10 female students and 11 male students. All the students are Bahraini and have a variety of English language proficiency.

Data Collection

The first semester of the academic year 2023-2024 lasted for five months, and the study was over six weeks. The students had daily English classes for 40 minutes, five days a week. The participants were asked to answer a paper-based questionnaire regarding their perceptions toward the use of the Epic platform in the English classes. The Likert questionnaire contains seven questions related to students' motivation and attitudes regarding the use of Epic during English classes. It consists of graded options (e.g. strongly agree, agree, disagree, and neutral) and it has emojis to suit students' level of understanding. The questionnaire aims to target how students perceive Epic as a learning tool to enhance their motivation to read. Table 1 below showcases the weekly lesson objectives, and the expected outcomes attached to the Epic activities. The table shows each lesson's objective for five weeks, as each objective contains objectives for the story genres the students will read to be able to answer reading comprehension questions. Furthermore, Epic activities are the post-reading quiz assigned after each story, while the expected outcomes for each lesson are related to the anticipated results of reading a particular e-book story and engaging in Epic activities.

Table 1. Weekly objectives and outcomes of Epic activities

Weekly Lesson Objective	Epic Activity	Expected Outcomes
By the end of the lesson, students will be able to read a fiction story and answer reading comprehension questions.	The students will read the story assigned to them and answer the post-reading quiz.	Students will get a deep understanding of the details of the story and improve their fluency skills.
By the end of the lesson, students will be able to read a non-fiction story and answer reading comprehension questions.	The students will read the story assigned to them and answer the post-reading quiz.	Students will familiarize themselves with non-fiction stories.
By the end of the lesson, students will be able to read a fairy tale story and answer reading comprehension questions.	The students will read the assigned story to them and answer the post-reading quiz.	Students will take note of details from the story and improve their fluency skills.
By the end of the lesson, students will be able to read a story about bullying and answer reading comprehension questions.	The students will read the story assigned to them and answer the post-reading quiz.	Students will identify the meaning of bullying and improve their fluency skills.
By the end of the lesson, students will be able to read a story about kindness and answer reading comprehension questions.	The students will read the story assigned to them and answer the post-reading quiz.	Students will identify the meaning of kindness and improve their fluency skills.

FINDINGS AND DISCUSSION

The aim of the survey is to evaluate the effectiveness and students' perceptions of Epic platform as a learning tool that leads to improve their language learning. The survey consisted of several questions regarding students' interaction using Epic. The researcher conducted a well analysis of the results, focusing on students' age, gender, and several questions assessing Epic's impact on learning, peer interaction, usability, and general preference (see Figure 11 as it shows the students' response distribution).

Figure 11. Students' response distribution

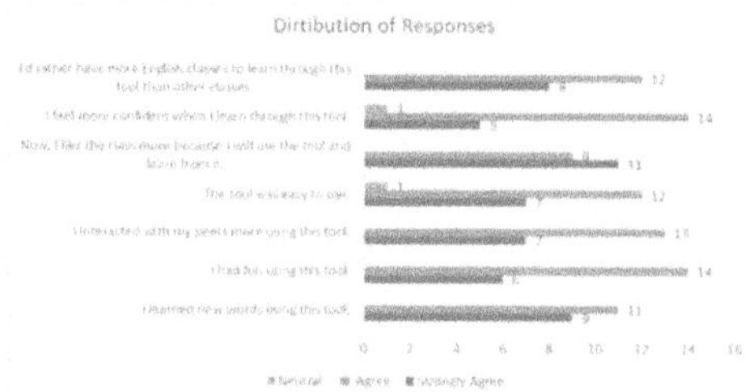

The students' age distribution shows that almost all the participants are in the six-year-old group. Moreover, there is an equal gender representation of both male and female students, and this balance is vital to make sure that the tool is comprehensive and enjoyable for both genders. The responses of the survey indicate that Epic can improve vocabulary learning, which is evident in the students' high replies with "Strongly Agree," which shows that they are benefiting a lot from the tool in this aspect. This result emphasizes the usefulness of the tool to engage students and provide vital educational content as an additional language-learning tool. As the results of the survey show, all students enjoyed using the tool as an effective educational resource in their English classes. Furthermore, the survey assessed peer engagement, competition, and collaboration learning that the tool offered through its' discussion and the diverse genres (see Figure 6). Also, all the students reported that the tool was easy to use, as Epic has a user-friendly design that aims to meet students' needs and expectations. Regarding the interactivity of the tool, the participants showed a positive attitude regarding the usefulness of the tool to share ideas and express their opinions freely, as well as enhancing their critical thinking abilities and creativity. Another aspect of the tool was students' feelings towards utilizing it in their classes. The responses indicate that the tool raised students' enjoyment and engagement in the classes, and it encouraged competition among students. Moreover, the survey's results demonstrated students'

The results of the survey provide crucial insights on the effectiveness and students' experiences with utilizing Epic. The positive feedback suggests that students enjoyed using the tool and that it remarkably enhanced their learning experiences. The tool provided significant benefits, including enhanced second language acquisition, boosted confidence, user friendliness, and collaborative learning. These results emphasize the role of Epic in improving learning objectives and providing students with a delightful and appealing learning experience. The long-term benefits of using the tool on students' level and engagement might be explored in a more detailed manner.

The case study's findings go in line with the existing literature, stressing the positive effect of online and electronic reading tools on distinct EFL instruction aspects. The implementation of Epic as an online reading platform exhibited substantial gains in vocabulary acquisition improvement, reading comprehension, critical thinking capacities, and general language learning use. These results corroborate the findings of Liman, Kaban, and Karadeniz (2021) and Moutsinas et al. (2023), which demonstrated how e-books and gamified reading platforms can considerably motivate learners and develop conclusive reading experiences.

The survey results revealing prominent levels of agreement on Epic's effectiveness in vocabulary learning align with the findings of Lee and Choi's (2022) indicating that vocabulary acquisition can be more effectively achieved through e-books than traditional printed books. Along the same lines, Wang (2016) developed an adaptive computer-assisted reading system and assessed its influence on English as a foreign language Taiwanese college learners' contextual vocabulary learning. Results showed substantially better vocabulary gain and retention and concluded that the reading system efficiently supports vocabulary development. Nevertheless, Soracco, Hasenohr and Orellana (2020) indicated that vocabulary pertains to word comprehension and employing them in different contexts which was negatively perceived by the participants in their study using Leer+. Another aspect that was indicated in their study was that using the reading apps improved reading comprehension skills which was not highlighted in this case study. This was due to the use of technology and the lack of motivation for reading in general. Chen-Worley (2021) reports the same findings using vocabulary e-gaming platforms and stated that phonological awareness linked to vocabulary is crucial for developing literacy skills including spelling and reading comprehension.

The Epic tool's ease of use and its user-friendly design positive findings support Medjahed and Yahiaoui's (2023) findings, which highlighted the benefits of e-books' accessibility and diversity of methods in improving reading approaches and students' preferences. Likewise, the reported peer engagement, competition, and collaboration developments by Epic mirror those of Al-Jarf's (2021) on the merits of e-book libraries in improving reading skills and student collaboration. Epic's adoptive feature availing a secure and interactional learning environment that supports critical thinking and creativity reinforces Pratiwi et al.'s (2022) relevant findings on how e-books develop critical thinking skills.

The current study emphasizes the need for more focused research on the specific features within online reading applications that support these educational objectives. Despite the general encouraging influence of Epic, knowing which elements (e.g. interaction, comprehension, gamification) are most adequate can assist in enhancing the implementation of these platforms in EFL contexts. Moreover, considering the gender and age range of the case study, it is indicative that Epic is equally useful and entertaining for both genders. This is essential for the wide implementation of the tool across distinct learner populations. Despite the positive students' perceptions and effects of reading tools as indicated in the case study and others, Robles, Burden and Villalba (2021) state that there is limited understanding of the pedagogical considerations and decisions educators make when selecting reading comprehension tools. It is challenging for teachers to choose reading apps or tools that raise engagement, foster self-confidence, and develop reading approaches.

CONCLUSION

This study has provided constructive insights into the effectiveness of the Epic platform in developing the reading comprehension skills of Grade 1 EFL students in the Arab context. The findings highlighted overwhelming results that Bahraini EFL learners exposed to the Epic reading tool have positive perceptions on how the tool could enhance their learning experiences and language skills including reading fluency and vocabulary acquisition.

The results revealed evidence that online or gamified reading comprehension apps have positive impacts on learners. Students reported improved motivation and collaboration as well as increased confidence in handling texts in English as a Foreign Language which aligns with current and previous research in the same field. Moreover, the user-friendly design of Epic was highlighted as a fundamental contributing factor to its efficacy, making it available and engaging for young learners. The platform's capability to provide several learning techniques fosters its well-developed functionality in different classroom environments.

Future research should investigate Epic's long-term impacts on language proficiency and continuous engagement over long periods. Furthermore, exploring certain elements within Epic that contribute most significantly to learning outcomes would provide useful insights into heightening its implementation in educational environments.

In sum, Epic emerges as a promising tool for educators seeking to enhance students' reading comprehension skills through engaging and interactive digital platforms. Continued exploration and refinement of such tools are essential for advancing educational practices that foster literacy development in EFL contexts.

REFERENCES

Al-Jarf, R. (2021). Collaborative mobile eBook reading for struggling EFL college readers. *IOSR Journal of Research & Method in Education*, *11*(6), 32–42. DOI: 10.9790/7388-1106023242

Ali, S. S., Ullah, H., Amin, T., Hayat, Q., & Hussain, M. (2021). Analyzing the role of E-Books in vocabulary development and language learning and students' perspectives about it: A case study at NUML, Pakistan. *Psychology and Education*, *58*(3), 4415–4459.

Chen-Worley, S. (2021, October). Vocabulary Learning Through Games on the e-Platform. In *SITE Interactive Conference* (pp. 115-117). Association for the Advancement of Computing in Education (AACE).

Lee, S., & Choi, Y. (2022). The effect of E-books on young EFL learners' vocabulary acquisition and parents' perceptions of E-books. *Korean Journal of English Language and Linguistics*, *22*, 593–617. DOI: 10.15738/kjell.22.202206.593

Liman Kaban, A., & Karadeniz, S. (2021). Children's reading comprehension and motivation on screen versus on paper. *SAGE Open*, *11*(1), 215824402098884. DOI: 10.1177/2158244020988849

Medjahed, M. R., & Yahiaoui, H. (2023). Using E-books as reading material to enhance EFL learners' strategy use and reading skill. *Literatures and languages Journal, 23*(1), 66-82.

Merentika Arianda, S., Jaya, A., & Theriana, A. (2023). Efl (English as a foreign language) students' perception about the effectiveness of learning reading by using electronic books. *Esteem Journal of English Education Study Programme*, *6*(2), 246–256. DOI: 10.31851/esteem.v6i2.12322

Moutsinas, G. A., Orosco Gavilán, J. C., Cubas Ramirez, C. E., Panduro, B. C., Aníbal, O. G., Ngoc Dieu, D. L., & Naz, S. (2023). Reading comprehension and behavior in children using E-books vs. printed books. *World Journal of English Language*, *13*(3), 172. DOI: 10.5430/wjel.v13n3p172

Park, J., & Lee, J. (2021). Effects of E-books and printed books on EFL learners' reading comprehension and grammatical knowledge. *English Teaching*, *76*(3), 35–61. DOI: 10.15858/engtea.76.3.202109.35

Porath, S., & Unruh, H. (2021). Poster: Teacher use of the multimedia book app - Epic. *Society for Information Technology & Teacher Education International Conference*, 679-683. https://www.learntechlib.org/p/219200

Pratiwi, A. D., Kristiani, K., & Noviani, L. (2022). The effectiveness of using E-Book to improve student's critical thinking skill. *International Journal of Multicultural and Multireligious Understanding*, *9*(10), 196–201.

Robles, H., Burden, K., & Villalba, K. (2021). A socio-cultural approach to evaluating and designing reading comprehension apps for language learning. [IJMBL]. *International Journal of Mobile and Blended Learning*, *13*(1), 1–21. DOI: 10.4018/IJMBL.2021010102

Roth Soracco, C. I., Valenzuela Hasenohr, F., & Orellana, P. (2020). Experience in the Use of a Digital Platform for the Practice of Reading Comprehension and Vocabulary: Perception of Elementary School Students.

Wang, Y. H. (2016). Promoting contextual vocabulary learning through an adaptive computer-assisted EFL reading system. *Journal of Computer Assisted Learning*, *32*(4), 291–303. DOI: 10.1111/jcal.12132

Chapter 5
Humanizing the Digital Classroom:
The Educator's Role in Fostering Connection Amidst Technology

Andi Asrifan
https://orcid.org/0000-0002-9934-6129
Universitas Negeri Makassar, Indonesia

Fathullah Wajdi
Universitas Negeri Makassar, Indonesia

Suryadi Ishak
Universitas Negeri Makassar, Indonesia

Alimin Alwi
Universitas Negeri Makassar, Indonesia

ABSTRACT

This chapter examines the essential function of educators in cultivating human relationships in digital classrooms, highlighting the significance of social-emotional learning (SEL) and inclusion. As technology progressively influences educational settings, preserving significant relationships between educators and students is crucial for improving engagement and academic achievement. The chapter delineates effective ways for cultivating supportive digital environments, encompassing the establishment of explicit communication standards, the incorporation of social-emotional learning principles into the curriculum, and the employment of digital tools to enhance cooperation. Furthermore, it underscores the importance of comprehending varied learner requirements and resolving equity concerns to guarantee

DOI: 10.4018/979-8-3373-0771-8.ch005

that all pupils may prosper in a digital environment. By emphasizing connection, empathy, and inclusivity, educators may cultivate engaging learning experiences that enable students to confront the challenges of a technology-driven environment.

UNDERSTANDING THE DIGITAL CLASSROOM

1.1 The Evolution of Education Technology

The advancement of educational technology has significantly altered conventional classrooms into vibrant digital environments, redefining instructional methods and learning experiences (Haleem et al., 2022). This transition has been propelled by swift technological breakthroughs, which have offered novel instruments and approaches that enrich the educational experience.

Initially, the incorporation of technology in education was confined to rudimentary instruments like overhead projectors and videotapes, which complemented conventional teaching methods (Vetrivel et al., 2024). The integration of computers in the classroom was a pivotal moment, granting pupils access to knowledge and tools that were once inaccessible. With the proliferation of the internet, the possibilities for digital education have increased significantly. Online research, instructional websites, and digital libraries have equipped students with an abundance of knowledge, radically transforming the information landscape (Panda & Kaur, 2024).

The emergence of Learning Management Systems (LMS) significantly transformed the educational experience by optimizing course delivery and enhancing communication between instructors and students (Namada, 2021). These systems facilitated the organizing of course materials, assignments, and evaluations inside a centralized digital environment, thereby enhancing student engagement with content and progress monitoring. This transition improved organizational efficiency and promoted a more engaging learning methodology.

The advancement of technology, particularly the proliferation of mobile devices and applications, has facilitated education accessibility for students, allowing learning to take place at any time and location (Haleem et al., 2022). This accessibility has significantly aided non-traditional learners, enabling them to reconcile schooling with other life obligations. The incorporation of social media and collaborative technologies has cultivated a sense of community among students in online settings, alleviating feelings of isolation frequently linked to digital learning (Agrawal et al., 2024; Smith et al., 2021).

In recent years, the advent of artificial intelligence (AI) and immersive technologies, including virtual and augmented reality, has significantly altered the educational landscape. AI-driven personalized learning systems adjust to the specific needs of each student, offering customized resources and support that improve engagement and comprehension (Strielkowski et al., 2024; Ellikkal & Rajamohan, 2024). Simultaneously, immersive technologies facilitate experiential learning, enabling students to investigate intricate concepts inside interactive settings.

Notwithstanding these achievements, the difficulty persists for educators to personalize the digital classroom (Edwards & Magill, 2023; Sidhu et al., 2024). With the growing integration of technology in education, the educator's role is vital in cultivating connections and establishing relationships that enrich the learning experience (Heilporn et al., 2021). The subsequent chapters will examine techniques for educators to traverse the digital realm while emphasizing human connection, ensuring that technology functions as a means of engagement rather than an impediment to meaningful contact.

1.2 The Benefits and Challenges of Digital Learning

Digital learning has transformed education, providing various advantages that improve accessibility and engagement (Haleem et al., 2022). Nonetheless, technology also poses considerable hurdles that educators must address to cultivate a substantive learning experience. Comprehending these benefits and challenges is essential for developing a human-centered digital classroom.

A significant advantage of digital learning is its accessibility (Gherhe et al., 2021; Maatuk et al., 2022). Digital platforms facilitate students' access to educational resources globally, dismantling geographical constraints that formerly restricted learning opportunities. This adaptability enables learners to interact with course content at their own speed, catering to various schedules and learning preferences. Students with impairments can employ assistive technologies to obtain content that may have been difficult in conventional environments. Furthermore, digital learning offers chances for non-traditional students, including working professionals and parents, to engage in education without the limitations of a rigid classroom timetable.

Engagement represents a significant benefit of digital learning (Salas-Pilco et al., 2022). Interactive instruments, including multimedia presentations, discussion forums, and gamified learning experiences, engage students' attention and foster active engagement. These tools can augment motivation and cultivate a sense of community among learners, even in digital surroundings. When students experience engagement, they are more inclined to commit to their study, resulting in enhanced academic performance (Amerstorfer & Freiin, 2021; Huang et al., 2022).

Nevertheless, the transition to digital learning presents problems that may impede the educational experience. A notable apprehension is the possibility of solitude. Although internet platforms enhance communication, they may also foster a sense of isolation among students. The absence of in-person interaction may result in feelings of isolation and disconnection, adversely affecting motivation and educational results (Kaufmann & Vallade, 2022; Juntunen et al., 2022). Educators must employ tactics that foster social engagement and collaboration, enabling students to establish relationships and support networks.

Distraction constitutes an additional challenge inherent in digital learning contexts (Skulmowski & Xu, 2022; Pattermann et al., 2022). The prevalence of many internet distractions, including social media and entertainment platforms, hinders students' ability to concentrate on their academic pursuits. The multitasking capabilities of digital gadgets exacerbate this issue by fragmenting attention and diminishing the quality of learning. Educators must devise methods to establish organized, distraction-free settings that promote prolonged focus and concentration (Fensie et al., 2024; Brady et al., 2022).

1.3 The Role of the Educator in a Digital Environment

In a swiftly changing digital environment, the educator's position is increasingly vital (Mohamed et al., 2022; Akour & Alenezi, 2022). As technology revolutionizes conventional pedagogical practices, instructors must modify their strategies to enhance connection and participation among students. This adaptation is crucial for establishing a human-centered digital classroom that prioritizes connections and collaboration.

Educators can enhance connection in a digital context by emphasizing communication (McCarthy et al., 2023; Imran, 2023). Establishing transparent communication is essential for fostering trust and connection with kids. Educators can employ many digital platforms, like discussion forums, chat applications, and video conferencing, to promote consistent connections. By promoting student expressions of views, inquiries, and experiences, educators can cultivate a supportive community that enriches learning (Abbas et al., 2022). Regular evaluations and feedback sessions enable educators to assess student well-being and engagement, facilitating prompt responses when necessary.

Another efficacious technique is to include collaborative learning activities. Collaborative projects, peer evaluations, and online study groups can enhance teamwork and social engagement among students, alleviating feelings of isolation. Utilizing digital tools that facilitate collaboration, such as shared documents and project management platforms, educators can foster chances for students to collaborate, exchange ideas, and learn collectively (Javaid et al., 2023). This cooperative method not only cultivates relationships but also improves analytical thinking and problem-solving abilities.

Educators might modify their pedagogical approaches by incorporating interactive and stimulating content (El-Sabagh, 2021). Employing multimedia tools, like films, podcasts, and interactive simulations, can engage students and enhance the dynamism of learning. Gamification components, such quizzes and challenges, might augment engagement by introducing an aspect of enjoyment and competition (Chans & Portuguez Castro, 2021; Anunpattana et al., 2021). By rendering learning engaging and pertinent, instructors can inspire students to actively engage and relate to the content.

Furthermore, acknowledging and accommodating the varied requirements of students is essential in a digital context. Educators must endeavor to develop inclusive educational experiences that accommodate diverse learning styles and backgrounds (Shorey et al., 2021). This may entail supplying several formats for knowledge dissemination, delivering individualized assistance, and promoting autonomous learning. By cultivating an inclusive environment, educators can guarantee that all students feel esteemed and included within the learning community.

Ultimately, educators must exemplify digital citizenship and appropriate technology utilization. Educators can assist students in navigating the complexity of the digital realm by exemplifying ethical conduct and promoting courteous online interactions (Harrison & Laco, 2022). This counsel is crucial for cultivating a secure and supportive educational atmosphere in which kids can flourish.

BUILDING RELATIONSHIPS IN A DIGITAL SPACE

2.1 The Importance of Connection in Learning

The need of connection in schooling is paramount. The relationships between educators and students, as well as among peers, are essential for improving learning outcomes and fostering student well-being (Lera et al., 2023). In a digital realm, where in-person contacts may be constrained, cultivating these connections is essential for establishing an effective and supportive learning atmosphere.

Research repeatedly indicates that robust interactions in school environments enhance academic success (Edgerton & McKechnie, 2023; Xu, 2024). Students who sense a connection with their professors are more inclined to engage in the subject, participate in conversations, and request assistance when necessary. A supportive teacher-student connection cultivates a sense of belonging, hence augmenting motivation and resilience. In a digital environment, educators can foster this relationship through consistent contact, tailored feedback, and by demonstrating authentic interest in students' lives and academic progress.

Furthermore, peer interactions are of comparable significance in the learning process. Collaborative learning experiences, including group projects and discussion forums, promote student interaction, idea exchange, and mutual learning (Sugino, 2021; Herrera-Pavo, 2024). These interactions enhance comprehension and cultivate a sense of community among pupils. In a digital classroom, where isolation is a difficulty, fostering possibilities for peer involvement is crucial. Educators can do this by creating collaborative activities, encouraging group discussions, and employing technology to link students with their peers (Tang & Hew, 2022; Ng et al., 2022).

The emotional and social aspects of learning are essential to student well-being. Constructive connections foster a supportive environment in which students feel secure to articulate their thoughts, embrace challenges, and investigate novel concepts (Sugino, 2021; Amerstorfer & Freiin, 2021). This emotional security is especially crucial in a digital context, where pupils may experience vulnerability or disconnection. Educators can enhance their well-being by being accessible, empathic, and attentive to students' needs. Through attentive listening and addressing issues, instructors can assist children in overcoming problems and fostering resilience.

Moreover, cultivating relationships in a digital environment can significantly influence students' social competencies and emotional intelligence. Participating in significant encounters with classmates and educators facilitates the development of crucial interpersonal skills in kids, including communication, empathy, and collaboration (Amerstorfer & Freiin, 2021). These skills are essential for academic achievement as well as for future career and personal interactions.

2.2 Strategies for Fostering Student-Teacher Connections

Fostering robust relationships between educators and students in a digital context is crucial for cultivating a supportive and engaging educational experience (Haleem et al., 2022; Engeness, 2021; Cavinato et al., 2021). Although virtual environments may pose difficulties in establishing rapport and trust, educators can employ several effective ways to cultivate meaningful interactions.

1. Consistent Communication: Regular and transparent communication is essential for establishing rapport. Educators ought to implement a regular plan for check-ins, utilizing emails, virtual office hours, or discussion boards. This accessibility indicates to pupils that their instructor is approachable and committed to their achievement. Promoting student expression of their opinions and inquiries can foster a discussion that strengthens connections.
2. Personalization: Dedicating time to understanding students' interests, backgrounds, and unique learning styles can markedly improve the educator-student interaction. Instructors may implement icebreaker activities at the course's

commencement to obtain information regarding their pupils. Customizing assignments and discussions to align with students' interests enhances the relevance of learning and demonstrates that educators appreciate their students as unique people.

3. Utilization of Video: In a digital classroom, video conferencing solutions help mitigate the separation imposed by physical distance. Instructors ought to employ video conferencing for lectures and discussions, as visual interaction enhances a sense of connection. Moreover, instructors may produce concise introductory movies to convey their teaching philosophy, personal interests, and expectations, so fostering a sense of familiarity and connection among students.
4. Fostering Collaboration: Advocating on collaborative projects and group discussions can enhance relationships among students and between students and educators. By giving collaborative tasks that necessitate interaction, educators can foster peer relationships while simultaneously demonstrating collaboration and communication competencies. Utilizing breakout rooms in virtual meetings can offer students a more personal environment to interact with each other and their instructor.
5. Delivering Constructive Feedback: Prompt and constructive feedback is essential for fostering trust. When educators offer individualized feedback on tasks, it demonstrates to pupils that their efforts are acknowledged and esteemed. This approach enhances students' academic performance while strengthening the bond between the instructor and the learner.
6. Establishing a Secure Environment: Creating a safe and inclusive digital space is crucial for cultivating trust. Educators must establish explicit standards for polite speech and conduct in online debates. Fostering an environment where students may articulate their views and emotions without fear of criticism enhances transparency and fortifies connections.
7. Acknowledging Achievements: Recognizing and commemorating student accomplishments—whether substantial or minor—can greatly improve relationships. Acknowledging students' efforts through class shout-outs, personalized remarks, or virtual certificates cultivates a pleasant environment and strengthens their bond with the educator.

2.3 Encouraging Peer Interactions and Collaboration

In a digital classroom, promoting peer interactions and collaboration is crucial for cultivating a feeling of community among students (Zengilowski et al., 2023; Gopinathan et al., 2022; Li, 2022; Cavinato et al., 2021). When learners interact, they cultivate social skills, deepen their comprehension of the subject matter, and forge enduring relationships. Educators can implement several techniques to foster teamwork and social interaction among pupils using digital media.

1. Collaborative Initiatives: Designating group initiatives is among the most efficacious methods to promote teamwork. Educators can employ digital systems like Google Workspace or Microsoft Teams, enabling students to collaborate in real-time on shared documents, presentations, or spreadsheets. By designating responsibilities within the group, students can assume responsibility for particular duties while cultivating an appreciation for their colleagues' contributions. This cooperative method not only improves learning but also promotes responsibility and collaboration.
2. Discussion Forums: Online discussion boards or forums provide a venue for students to exchange ideas, pose inquiries, and participate in substantive dialogues. Educators can develop prompts that stimulate student interaction, promoting a discussion that transcends individual responses. By promoting discourse on course material or pertinent subjects, educators can assist students in establishing connections and acquiring knowledge from varied viewpoints.
3. Peer Review Activities: The implementation of peer review processes enables students to offer constructive criticism on one another's work. This not only augments their critical thinking and analytical abilities but also motivates them to interact with their peers' concepts. Educators can establish rules and rubrics to guarantee that feedback is courteous and constructive, fostering a secure environment for sharing and learning.
4. Virtual Study Groups: Promoting the formation of virtual study groups among students can enhance collaboration and companionship. Educators can enable this by offering platforms for student interaction, such as specialized chat rooms or video conferencing applications. Facilitating collaborative study for examinations or assignments enables students to academically assist one another while fostering friendships.
5. Gamification: Incorporating gamification into the educational experience can markedly improve peer engagement. Educators can design team-oriented challenges or competitions utilizing platforms such as Kahoot or Quizizz, enabling students to collaborate in answering questions or resolving problems. This method not only renders learning enjoyable but also fosters collaboration, as students are required to communicate and devise strategies to achieve success.
6. Social Media Integration: Utilizing social media platforms can enhance peer relationships. Educators can establish private groups on platforms such as Facebook or Discord, enabling students to exchange materials, pose inquiries, and engage with one another beyond formal class hours. This informal envi-

ronment might enhance students' ease in communicating with each other, so it is fortifying their ties.

7. Icebreaker Activities: At the commencement of a course or during virtual sessions, educators may use icebreaker activities that prompt students to introduce themselves and disclose personal interests. These activities facilitate the dismantling of barriers and foster a more relaxed environment, hence enhancing student engagement with one another.

CREATING AN INCLUSIVE DIGITAL ENVIRONMENT

3.1 Understanding Diverse Learner Needs

In the digital classroom, acknowledging and comprehending varied learner requirements is essential for cultivating an inclusive educational environment (Tariq, 2024; Markey et al., 2021). Students originate from diverse origins, exhibit individual learning styles, and encounter specific problems that can affect their educational experiences. By recognizing these disparities, educators can customize their methodologies to guarantee that all kids feel esteemed, supported, and engaged.

A major aspect affecting learning is the cultural backgrounds of students. Students may originate from diverse ethnic backgrounds, socioeconomic conditions, and localities, each contributing unique ideas and experiences to the classroom. Educators must exhibit cultural responsiveness by including diverse perspectives and resources into the curriculum (Kondo, 2022; Berlian & Huda, 2022). This may involve integrating literature, case studies, and examples that represent the diverse backgrounds of all pupils, so affirming their experiences and fostering a sense of belonging.

Learning styles significantly influence student engagement with content. Certain learners may be visual, assimilating information via visuals and videos, whereas others may be aural, gaining advantages from discussions and lectures. Kinesthetic learners excel in experiential activities and physical engagement. Comprehending these diverse learning styles enables instructors to deliver information in various formats, accommodating the preferences of all pupils (Haleem et al., 2022; Szymkowiak et al., 2021). Incorporating movies, interactive simulations, and group discussions can effectively accommodate various learning styles.

Furthermore, it is crucial to acknowledge the distinct problems encountered by students with disabilities. In a digital context, accessibility is a key concern. Educators must guarantee that all digital resources adhere to accessibility requirements, offering alternate forms for pupils who may need them (Beyene et al., 2023; Kocdar & Bozkurt, 2024). This encompasses the utilization of captions for videos, offering text-to-speech functionalities, and guaranteeing that online platforms are accessible for pupils with visual or movement disabilities. By proactively addressing these requirements, educators may cultivate an atmosphere in which all children possess equal possibilities for success.

Additionally, the emotional and social needs of pupils must be acknowledged. Numerous learners may encounter anxiety, particularly in a digital environment where they could feel lonely or detached. Establishing a supportive environment in which students feel secure to articulate their issues and request assistance is essential. Educators can foster this environment by facilitating open communication, increasing peer support, and being vigilant regarding students' emotional well-being (Zheng, 2022).

Ultimately, acknowledging the diverse degrees of digital literacy among pupils is crucial. Certain learners may possess technological proficiency, whereas others may encounter difficulties in utilizing digital technologies. Offering training and tools for efficient technological use can enable all students to fully engage in the learning process (Haleem et al., 2022).

3.2 Implementing Universal Design for Learning (UDL)

Universal Design for Learning (UDL) is an educational paradigm designed to enhance teaching and learning for all people by offering diverse methods of interaction, representation, and action/expression (Roski et al., 2024; Yaqoubi et al., 2022; Bray et al., 2024). In a digital classroom, the implementation of UDL principles is crucial for developing accessible and engaging learning experiences that address the varied requirements of all students. Implementing UDL criteria allows instructors to personalize the digital classroom and guarantee that each learner has the potential to thrive (Fovet, 2021; Brzezinska, 2022).

1. Diverse Engagement Strategies: A fundamental premise of UDL is to offer many methods for engaging students in the learning process. This can be accomplished by integrating a variety of activities that cater to diverse interests and incentives. Educators can employ gamification to establish interactive and competitive components that incentivize students. Furthermore, providing options for assignments—such as enabling students to produce films, presentations, or written reports—can empower them to interact with the subject in a manner that aligns with their own preferences.
2. Multiple Means of Representation: To cater to varying learning styles and preferences, instructors ought to deliver knowledge in several formats. This may encompass the utilization of text, photos, videos, infographics, and audio materials to communicate content. A lecture on a historical event could be

enhanced with a video, an interactive timeline, and primary source materials. By delivering knowledge through several modalities, instructors can guarantee that all students access the subject in the most effective manner for them.

3. Multiple Means of Action and Expression: UDL underscores the significance of enabling students to exhibit their comprehension through many methods. Educators can provide other techniques for pupils to demonstrate their learning, rather than depending exclusively on standard exams. This may encompass project-based evaluations, portfolios, or digital presentations. By offering avenues for expression, educators may cater to diverse abilities and preferences, enabling students to interact with the content more profoundly.
4. Accessibility Considerations: The implementation of UDL necessitates a robust emphasis on accessibility. Educators must guarantee that all digital information adheres to accessibility standards, including the Web information Accessibility Guidelines (WCAG). This entails utilizing legible fonts, supplying alternate text for photographs, and guaranteeing that videos are captioned. Furthermore, educators must contemplate the implementation of assistive technologies, including screen readers or speech-to-text software, to aid students with disabilities.
5. Ongoing input and Enhancement: UDL is a cyclical process that motivates instructors to solicit input from students about their learning experiences. Consistently seeking feedback enables educators to see obstacles and implement essential modifications to enhance accessibility and engagement. This collaborative method not only improves the educational atmosphere but also empowers students by granting them a say in their learning.

3.3 Addressing Equity and Access Issues

In the digital classroom, it is essential to address equity and access challenges to ensure that all students may succeed (Tate & Warschauer, 2022; Farley & Burbules, 2022). Disparities in access to technology, internet connectivity, and educational resources can pose substantial obstacles to learning. Educators must adopt measures to close these disparities, cultivating an inclusive environment that enables every kid to succeed (Tariq, 2024; Farley & Burbules, 2022; Eden et al., 2024).

1. Evaluating Technology Accessibility: The initial step in tackling equality concerns is to evaluate kids' access to technology and the internet. Educators may administer questionnaires or informal assessments to collect data regarding students' devices, connectivity, and any obstacles they encounter. Comprehending these criteria allows instructors to recognize students requiring supplementary assistance and resources.

2. Allocating Resources: After educators ascertain their pupils' needs, they can proactively supply the requisite resources. This may involve providing gadgets, such as computers or tablets, to pupils who do not have access at home. Educational institutions may collaborate with local organizations or enterprises to obtain donations of technology or financial resources for acquiring devices. Furthermore, supplying printed materials or offline resources can assist pupils lacking dependable internet access.
3. Ensuring Internet Connectivity: To resolve connectivity concerns, educators may investigate methods to provide internet access to pupils. This may entail partnering with local internet service providers to provide cheap or complimentary services for economically disadvantaged families. Educational institutions may also create Wi-Fi hotspots in community centers or libraries, enabling students to access the internet for academic purposes.
4. Providing Flexible Learning Alternatives: Acknowledging that not all students can access digital content concurrently is essential. Educators must provide adaptable learning alternatives, including recorded lectures and asynchronous assignments, enabling students to access resources at their convenience. This adaptability caters to diverse schedules and obligations, especially for students with employment or familial duties.
5. Delivering Focused Assistance: To guarantee that all kids can proficiently traverse the digital landscape, educators must provide focused support and instruction. This may encompass digital literacy workshops that instruct pupils in the utilization of diverse technologies and platforms, alongside the provision of continuous technical support. By providing students with essential skills, educators enable them to fully participate in the learning experience.
6. Cultivating a Supportive Community: Establishing a feeling of community is crucial for tackling equality concerns. Educators can foster peer support by implementing mentorship programs or study groups that link students with varying degrees of access and experience. This collaborative method not only cultivates relationships but also facilitates peer learning among students.
7. Ongoing Reflection and Enhancement: Ultimately, educators must participate in ongoing reflection of their methodologies and the resources accessible to students. Consistently obtaining feedback from students and family can reveal persistent access challenges and guide essential modifications to promote equity in the digital classroom.

LEVERAGING TECHNOLOGY TO ENHANCE HUMAN CONNECTION

4.1 Choosing the Right Tools for Engagement

In the digital classroom, the selection of appropriate tools and platforms is essential for promoting engagement and cultivating significant relationships between students and instructors (Heilporn et al., 2021; Selfa-Sastre et al., 2022; Haleem et al., 2022; Moorhouse et al., 2023). The proficient application of technology can augment engagement, foster cooperation, and establish a conducive learning atmosphere (El-Sabagh, 2021; Su & Zou, 2022; Haleem et al., 2022). This document examines diverse digital tools that instructors might utilize to augment interpersonal connections within their classrooms.

1. Video Conferencing Tools: Platforms such as Zoom, Microsoft Teams, and Google Meet have become indispensable for virtual classrooms. These tools facilitate real-time, direct contacts, enabling instructors to deliver live lectures, engage in conversations, and conduct group activities. The capacity to see and hear one another cultivates a sense of presence and community, facilitating active engagement and participation among students. Breakout rooms facilitate small group talk, enhancing cooperation and peer engagement.
2. Learning Management Systems (LMS): A Learning Management System (LMS), including platforms like Canvas, Moodle, or Blackboard, functions as a centralized repository for course materials, assignments, and communication. These platforms provide engagement via discussion boards, announcements, and direct messaging. Utilizing a Learning Management System (LMS) enables educators to establish an organized environment that facilitates students' access to resources and interaction with peers and instructors. The capacity to monitor engagement and deliver feedback strengthens the relationship between educators and students.
3. Collaborative Document Tools: Applications such as Google Docs, Microsoft OneNote, and Padlet enable students to work together on projects and exchange ideas instantaneously. These platforms provide concurrent collaboration among numerous users on a same document, enhancing teamwork and communication. Educators may assign group assignments that facilitate brainstorming, editing, and feedback among students, so developing their collaboration skills and fostering relationships.
4. Interactive Presentation Tools: Platforms like Nearpod, Pear Deck, and Prezi enable educators to develop interactive presentations that actively engage students. These instruments provide real-time quizzes, polls, and conversations during

lectures, promoting engagement and involvement. By integrating interactive components, instructors can enhance the dynamism of learning and cultivate a sense of connection among students.

5. Social Media and Communication Applications: Employing social media platforms or communication applications such as Edmodo, Flipgrid, or Discord can facilitate casual environments for engagement and collaboration. These platforms enable students to exchange information, engage in discussions, and connect with their peers in a more informal environment. By cultivating a sense of community beyond the conventional classroom, educators may augment student engagement and connection.
6. Gamification Tools: Integrating gamification features via platforms such as Kahoot, Quizizz, or Classcraft can enhance engagement and enjoyment in the learning process. These tools enable educators to design quizzes and challenges that promote amicable rivalry among pupils. The participatory aspect of gamified learning promotes collaboration and camaraderie, strengthening relationships among students.
7. Virtual Reality (VR) and Augmented Reality (AR): These nascent technologies offer immersive experiences that can augment education and foster interaction. Platforms such as Nearpod VR and Google Expeditions enable students to collectively explore virtual settings, promoting cooperation and shared experiences that enhance comprehension and engagement.

4.2 Incorporating Social-Emotional Learning (SEL) in Digital Spaces

Integrating Social-Emotional Learning (SEL) into digital environments is crucial for enhancing students' emotional well-being and cultivating a constructive learning atmosphere (Demirdis, 2025; Kazanjian, 2023; Philibert & Slade, 2022). Social and Emotional Learning (SEL) emphasizes the cultivation of competencies like self-awareness, self-regulation, social awareness, interpersonal skills, and responsible decision-making. Integrating SEL approaches into online education enables instructors to improve student engagement, foster resilience, and cultivate significant connections among learners (Yang, 2021; Levine et al., 2023; Philibert & Slade, 2022).

1. Establishing a Secure and Supportive Environment: Cultivating a safe digital space is essential for good Social and Emotional Learning (SEL). Educators should establish explicit expectations for polite communication and conduct in online interactions. This entails fostering active listening, empathy, and constructive feedback in conversations. Establishing rules and guidelines fosters a

sense of security and value among students, promoting the open expression of their views and emotions.

2. Integrating Check-Ins and Reflective Activities: Consistent check-ins enable educators to assess students' emotional well-being and cultivate connections. Educators may utilize technologies such as Google Forms or Padlet to develop rapid surveys or reflection prompts inquiring about students' emotional states or the challenges they encounter. This approach aids educators in identifying kids requiring further assistance and promotes students' reflection on their feelings and experiences.
3. Integrating SEL Content into Curriculum: Educators can integrate SEL principles into the curriculum by including courses that emphasize emotional intelligence, conflict resolution, and empathy. Literature conversations can examine characters' feelings and motivations, encouraging students to contemplate many views. Furthermore, offering pupils opportunities for role-playing or simulations can facilitate the development of empathy and social skills within a secure atmosphere.
4. Employing Digital Tools for SEL Activities: Various digital tools can enhance SEL activities. Platforms such as Flipgrid enable students to articulate their opinions and experiences via video reflections, promoting a sense of community and connection. Likewise, applications like ClassDojo assist educators in identifying and reinforcing positive behaviors, promoting student support and the celebration of achievements.
5. Fostering Mindfulness and Self-Regulation: Incorporating mindfulness techniques into the digital classroom can markedly improve students' emotional well-being. Educators may conduct guided meditation sessions or mindfulness activities at the commencement or conclusion of class utilizing platforms such as Headspace or Calm. These techniques facilitate the development of self-regulation skills in students, thereby alleviating stress and enhancing concentration.
6. Promoting Peer Support and Collaboration: Cultivating peer relationships is essential for social-emotional learning (SEL). Educators can facilitate chances for students to cooperate on projects or engage in group discussions, promoting mutual emotional and academic support. Implementing mentorship programs or buddy systems can augment peer interactions, enabling students to exchange experiences and cultivate connections.
7. Ensuring Access to Emotional Support services: Ultimately, educators must guarantee that children may access services for emotional support. This may involve disseminating information regarding counseling services, mental health resources, or virtual support groups. By offering these tools, educators exhibit their dedication to students' emotional well and promote the pursuit of assistance when necessary.

4.3 Feedback and Communication in a Digital Context

In a digital classroom, effective feedback and transparent communication are vital elements for cultivating significant relationships between instructors and students (Haleem et al., 2022; Cavinato et al., 2021; Archambault et al., 2022; Heilporn et al., 2021). These techniques not only improve learning results but also foster a supportive environment in which students feel appreciated and included. Here are optimal strategies for delivering constructive feedback and ensuring transparent communication in a digital environment.

1. Prompt and Specific Feedback: Delivering prompt feedback is essential for student development. Educators ought to immediately return tasks and assessments, enabling students to contemplate their performance while the material remains salient. Targeted feedback that emphasizes strengths and identifies areas for enhancement aids students in comprehending their advancement and establishes explicit expectations for subsequent tasks. For example, rather than stating, "Good job," educators can articulate what was especially effective, such as, "Your analysis of the character's motivations was perceptive and well-substantiated by evidence."
2. Employ Digital Tools for Feedback: Numerous digital tools can optimize the feedback process. Platforms such as Google Classroom and Turnitin enable professors to annotate student responses directly, facilitating contextual comprehension of feedback for students. Voice feedback solutions, such as Mote or Vocaroo, allow educators to deliver personalized audio remarks, which may be more interesting and accessible for students than textual feedback.
3. Promote Self-Assessment and Reflection: Integrating self-assessment opportunities fosters student accountability in their learning process. Educators may offer rubrics or reflective prompts to assist students in assessing their work prior to submission. This practice cultivates critical thinking and assists students in developing a growth mindset by enabling them to recognize their strengths and areas for enhancement.
4. Encourage Transparent Communication: Sustaining transparent communication is essential for establishing trust and rapport. Educators ought to motivate students to communicate inquiries, problems, or feedback regarding the course. Employing communication technologies like as Slack, Microsoft Teams, or specialized channels inside a Learning Management System helps promote continuous discourse. Regularly planned virtual office hours offer students a chance to discuss their work and seek help in a supportive setting.

5. Establish a Secure Environment for Feedback: Cultivating a culture of constructive criticism is vital for motivating kids to articulate their thoughts and emotions. Educators ought to exemplify the provision and reception of feedback in a polite and constructive manner. Facilitating structured peer feedback can enhance student learning through mutual exchange and cultivate a sense of community.
6. Employ Surveys and Polls for Ongoing Enhancement: Consistently gathering input from students regarding the course and instructional techniques can yield significant insights for educators. Platforms such as Google Forms or SurveyMonkey enable educators to design anonymous surveys that assess student satisfaction and identify areas for enhancement. This approach illustrates that instructors appreciate student feedback and aid in the adaptation of teaching tactics to more effectively address learner requirements.
7. Acknowledge Progress and Accomplishments: Recognizing and applauding student successes, regardless of their magnitude, can bolster motivation and foster connection. Educators might utilize digital channels to showcase student work, generate commendation posts, or disseminate success narratives during class discussions. Commemorating advancement cultivates a constructive atmosphere in which students feel valued and motivated to persist in their endeavors.

THE FUTURE OF HUMANIZING EDUCATION

5.1 Trends in Educational Technology

As the educational landscape evolves, emerging technologies are transforming teaching and learning methodologies (McDiarmid & Zhao, 2023; Hashim et al., 2022; Alam & Mohanty, 2023; Almufarreh & Arshad, 2023). These developments not only improve educational methods but also have the potential to humanize the digital classroom, promoting closer ties between students and educators. Comprehending these technologies and their ramifications is essential for educators aiming to establish engaging and inclusive learning settings (Molina et al., 2021; Haleem et al., 2022; Mhlongo et al., 2023).

1. Artificial Intelligence (AI): AI is progressively being incorporated into educational environments, providing customized learning experiences designed to meet the specific needs of individual students. Intelligent tutoring systems can evaluate student performance instantaneously, offering tailored resources and assistance. This degree of customization facilitates student advancement at their individual rate, hence augmenting engagement and comprehension.

Furthermore, AI-powered chatbots can enhance communication by delivering immediate responses to student questions and assistance beyond standard class hours.

2. Virtual and Augmented Reality (VR/AR): VR and AR technologies are transforming experience learning by immersing students in dynamic settings. These tools enable learners to investigate intricate concepts through practical engagement, such as performing virtual science experiments or exploring historical places. Through immersive encounters, VR and AR cultivate curiosity and engagement, rendering learning more pertinent and memorable. As these technologies become increasingly available, they possess the capacity to bridge gaps in comprehension and foster shared experiences among students.
3. Gamification: The integration of gamification aspects into education is increasingly recognized as a method to augment motivation and engagement. By using gamified elements, including points, badges, and leaderboards, educators can cultivate a more dynamic educational atmosphere. Gamification promotes collaboration and amicable competition, enhancing relationships among students and encouraging active engagement in the learning process. This tendency enhances the enjoyment of learning while fostering a sense of community and belonging.
4. Learning Analytics: The utilization of learning analytics is becoming progressively widespread in educational environments. Through the collection and analysis of data regarding student performance and engagement, educators can get significant insights into both individual and collective learning processes. This data-centric methodology allows educators to recognize at-risk pupils, customize interventions, and improve educational tactics. Utilizing analytics, educators may make educated decisions that enhance student success and promote a more individualized learning environment.
5. Mobile Learning: The proliferation of mobile technologies has revolutionized student access to instructional content. Smartphones and tablets enable learners to access resources at any time and location, providing more flexibility and convenience. Mobile learning applications promote cooperation and communication, allowing students to engage with peers and educators beyond conventional classroom environments. This tendency encourages ongoing education and cultivates a sense of community, enabling students to exchange materials and provide mutual support instantaneously.
6. Collaborative Online Learning Platforms: The proliferation of collaborative online learning platforms, such as Google Classroom and Microsoft Teams, has facilitated enhanced interaction among students and educators. These platforms enable communication, resource sharing, and joint endeavors, fostering cooperation and social interaction. Utilizing these tools, instructors can establish

a more interconnected and interactive learning environment, so augmenting student engagement and cultivating partnerships.

5.2 The Ongoing Role of Educators in a Tech-Driven World

As technology progresses and transforms the educational environment, the function of educators is undergoing substantial change (Yu, 2024; Haleem et al., 2022). Digital tools and platforms provide promising prospects for improving teaching and learning, although they also introduce new obstacles that necessitate educators to adjust and redefine their roles. In this technology-oriented society, educators are crucial in navigating students through their academic paths, cultivating relationships, and guaranteeing that technology functions as an instrument for development rather than an obstacle to significant engagement (Sandoval et al., 2021; Malik et al., 2023; Alqahtani et al., 2023; Wang et al., 2023).

1. Learning Facilitators: In a digital context, educators evolve from conventional knowledge disseminators to facilitators of learning. They must develop captivating and inclusive educational experiences that utilize technology efficiently. This entails curating digital content, devising interactive exercises, and promoting collaborative projects that empower students to assume responsibility for their learning. By promoting inquiry-based learning and critical thinking, educators enable students to cultivate vital abilities for navigating a complicated world.
2. Mentors and Supporters: As students increasingly depend on technology for knowledge and engagement, educators assume a crucial role as mentors and supporters. They must be responsive to the emotional and social needs of their students, offering direction and support. This encompasses identifying indicators of stress or disengagement, providing tailored feedback, and establishing a secure environment for transparent communication. By cultivating robust relationships, instructors can enable students to feel esteemed and interconnected, so promoting a sense of belonging in the digital classroom.
3. Proponents of Equity and Inclusion: In a technology-oriented society, educators are urged to champion equity and inclusion in education. They must guarantee that all students have access to essential tools and support to excel in a digital environment. This entails recognizing and rectifying inequalities in technology access, fostering digital literacy, and applying Universal Design for Learning (UDL) principles. By emphasizing equality, educators may foster an inclusive environment in which every kid has the opportunity to thrive.
4. Lifelong Learners: Given the rapid evolution of technology, instructors must adopt a lifelong learning perspective. Remaining knowledgeable about evolving technologies, instructional methodologies, and optimal practices is crucial

for the efficient integration of technology in the classroom. Opportunities for professional development, communication with peers, and involvement in educational communities can assist educators in perpetually refining their skills and knowledge. This dedication to development not only advantages educators but also favorably influences their students.

5. Ethical Guidelines for Technology Utilization: As technology becomes more prevalent in school, educators must instruct students on ethical technology use and digital citizenship. This encompasses advocating appropriate online conduct, comprehending privacy and security concerns, and acknowledging the significance of critical thinking in assessing information sources. By imparting these values, educators equip students to traverse the digital landscape ethically and make judicious choices.

5.3 Creating a Vision for a Human-Centered Digital Classroom

In the digital era, it is imperative to establish a vision for a human-centered digital classroom (Yang et al., 2021; Zort et al., 2023; Mercan and Köseoğlu, 2023). This vision emphasizes human connection, emotional wellness, and collaborative learning, ensuring that technology functions as a conduit rather than an impediment. Educators are essential in promoting and executing activities that cultivate these values (Chan, 2023; Alam & Mohanty, 2023; Wei, 2022). Here are some techniques to assist educators in establishing a more human-centered digital learning environment.

1. Prioritize Relationship Development: Central to a human-centered classroom is the focus on interpersonal connections. Educators ought to proactively establish connection with their students through consistent check-ins, demonstrating authentic interest in their lives, and facilitating informal contacts. Elementary activities, such as commencing courses with personal narratives or prompting students to share their experiences, can foster a sense of community and belonging.
2. Promote Collaborative Learning: Encouraging student participation is essential for strengthening interpersonal connections. Educators might construct group projects, peer review sessions, and collaborative conversations that necessitate student cooperation and idea exchange. Employing digital tools like collaborative papers and discussion boards can enhance teamwork and foster social engagement, enabling students to cultivate relationships while learning from each other.
3. Integrate Social-Emotional Learning (SEL): Implementing SEL practices in the digital classroom is essential for fostering students' emotional well-being. Educators can execute exercises that foster self-awareness, empathy, and inter-

personal skills. This may encompass mindfulness practices, reflective journaling, or dialogues around emotional management. By emphasizing social-emotional learning, educators cultivate an environment in which children feel secure to articulate their emotions and engage with their peers.

4. Utilize Technology Judiciously: Although technology can augment learning, it is essential to employ it with discernment to prioritize human interaction. Educators ought to choose tools that enhance interaction and engagement instead of supplanting real encounters. Utilizing video conferencing for live conversations, interactive platforms for collaborative work, and social media for casual communication can foster a sense of presence and connection among students.
5. Promote Equity and Access: Establishing a human-centered digital classroom necessitates the resolution of equity and access challenges. Educators must champion resources and support that guarantee all students possess the requisite tools for full engagement in digital learning. This may involve partnering with school administration to obtain technology for underprivileged kids or offering training in digital literacy to enhance the capabilities of all learners.
6. Promote Student Voice and Agency: Enabling students to engage actively in their learning cultivates a sense of ownership and connection. Educators can facilitate chances for students to express their thoughts, provide feedback, and engage in decision-making processes related to classroom activities. This approach improves involvement and fosters a sense of value and respect among pupils.
7. Foster a Feedback Culture: Creating an environment of open and constructive feedback is crucial for enhancing connection in a digital classroom. Educators should consistently seek feedback from students regarding their learning experiences and be prepared to modify their practices accordingly. This collaborative method enhances relationships and displays dedication to ongoing enhancement and student-focused education.

CONCLUSION

In the changing realm of education, especially in digital classrooms, the role of educators in cultivating significant connections is essential. As technology becomes more integrated into educational settings, the difficulty is to preserve the human factor crucial for optimal learning. This publication underscores the significance of cultivating robust relationships between educators and students, as well as among peers, to augment engagement and foster well-being. Effective methods for fostering these relationships encompass creating a secure and friendly atmosphere, promoting collaboration, and delivering prompt, constructive feedback. Through the use of digital tools and the promotion of peer connections, educators can cultivate a community that alleviates the isolation frequently encountered in online environments. Furthermore, including social-emotional learning (SEL) principles into the curriculum enhances students' emotional well-being and augens their academic experience. The application of Universal Design for Learning (UDL) principles guarantees the accommodation of varied learning demands, enabling all students to excel in a digital environment. By providing many methods of interaction, representation, and expression, educators may accommodate different learning styles and preferences, therefore improving overall educational results. The dedication to humanizing the digital classroom is a collective obligation of educators, students, and the wider educational community. By emphasizing connection, empathy, and diversity, we may develop meaningful educational experiences that enable kids to thrive in a progressively digital landscape.

REFERENCES

Abbas, N., Whitfield, J., Atwell, E., Bowman, H., Pickard, T., & Walker, A. (2022). Online chat and chatbots to enhance mature student engagement in higher education. [tandfonline.com]. *International Journal of Lifelong Education, 41*(3), 308–326. DOI: 10.1080/02601370.2022.2066213

Agrawal, S., Agrawal, N., Bansal, R., & Rawat, A. (2024). Online Social Networking: Navigating the Myth and Reality of Friendship in the Era of Zero Trust. Online Social Networks in Business Frameworks, 523-549. [HTML]

Akour, M. & Alenezi, M. (2022). Higher education future in the era of digital transformation. Education Sciences. mdpi.com

Alam, A., & Mohanty, A. (2023). Educational technology: Exploring the convergence of technology and pedagogy through mobility, interactivity, AI, and learning tools. Cogent Engineering. tandfonline.com

Alam, A., & Mohanty, A. (2023). Cultural beliefs and equity in educational institutions: Exploring the social and philosophical notions of ability groupings in teaching and learning of mathematics. [tandfonline.com]. *International Journal of Adolescence and Youth, 28*(1), 2270662. DOI: 10.1080/02673843.2023.2270662

Almufarreh, A. & Arshad, M. (2023). Promising emerging technologies for teaching and learning: Recent developments and future challenges. Sustainability. mdpi.com

Alqahtani, T., Badreldin, H. A., Alrashed, M., Alshaya, A. I., Alghamdi, S. S., bin Saleh, K., Alowais, S. A., Alshaya, O. A., Rahman, I., Al Yami, M. S., & Albekairy, A. M. (2023). The emergent role of artificial intelligence, natural learning processing, and large language models in higher education and research. [sciencedirect.com]. *Research in Social & Administrative Pharmacy, 19*(8), 1236–1242. DOI: 10.1016/j.sapharm.2023.05.016 PMID: 37321925

Amerstorfer, C. M., & Freiin von Münster-Kistner, C. (2021). Student perceptions of academic engagement and student-teacher relationships in problem-based learning. [frontiersin.org]. *Frontiers in Psychology, 12*, 713057. PMID: 34777094

Anunpattana, P., Khalid, M. N. A., Iida, H., & Inchamnan, W. (2021). Capturing potential impact of challenge-based gamification on gamified quizzing in the classroom. Heliyon. cell.com

Archambault, L., Leary, H., & Rice, K. (2022). Pillars of online pedagogy: A framework for teaching in online learning environments. [HTML]. *Educational Psychologist, 57*(3), 178–191. DOI: 10.1080/00461520.2022.2051513

Berlian, Z. & Huda, M. (2022). Reflecting culturally responsive and communicative teaching (CRCT) through partnership commitment. Education sciences. mdpi.com

Beyene, W. M., Mekonnen, A. T., & Giannoumis, G. A. (2023). Inclusion, access, and accessibility of educational resources in higher education institutions: Exploring the Ethiopian context. [tandfonline.com]. *International Journal of Inclusive Education*, *27*(1), 18–34. DOI: 10.1080/13603116.2020.1817580

Brady, A. C., Kim, Y. E., & von Spiegel, J. (2022). Learning in the face of digital distractions: empowering students to practice self-regulated learning. In *Digital distractions in the College Classroom* (pp. 120–142). IGI Global. [HTML] DOI: 10.4018/978-1-7998-9243-4.ch006

Bray, A., Devitt, A., Banks, J., Sanchez Fuentes, S., Sandoval, M., Riviou, K., Byrne, D., Flood, M., Reale, J., & Terrenzio, S. (2024). What next for Universal Design for Learning? A systematic literature review of technology in UDL implementations at second level. [wiley.com]. *British Journal of Educational Technology*, *55*(1), 113–138. DOI: 10.1111/bjet.13328

Brzezinska, M. (2022). Global skills in the global pandemic: how to create an effective bichronous learning experience during an emergency shift to remote instruction. In *Learning with Technologies and Technologies in Learning: Experience, Trends and Challenges in Higher Education* (pp. 679–706). Springer International Publishing. [HTML] DOI: 10.1007/978-3-031-04286-7_32

Cavinato, A. G., Hunter, R. A., Ott, L. S., & Robinson, J. K. (2021). Promoting student interaction, engagement, and success in an online environment. springer.com

Chan, C. K. Y. (2023). A comprehensive AI policy education framework for university teaching and learning. [springer.com]. *International Journal of Educational Technology in Higher Education*, *20*(1), 38. DOI: 10.1186/s41239-023-00408-3

Chans, G. M. & Portuguez Castro, M. (2021). Gamification as a strategy to increase motivation and engagement in higher education chemistry students. Computers. mdpi.com

Demirdis, B. (2025). Integrating Digital Literacy to Enhance Emotional and Social Skills in Education. In Innovative Educational Frameworks for Future Skills and Competencies (pp. 1-38). IGI Global Scientific Publishing. [HTML]

Eden, C. A., Chisom, O. N., & Adeniyi, I. S. (2024). Cultural competence in education: Strategies for fostering inclusivity and diversity awareness. [fepbl.com]. *International Journal of Applied Research in Social Sciences*, *6*(3), 383–392. DOI: 10.51594/ijarss.v6i3.895

Edgerton, E. & McKechnie, J. (2023). The relationship between student's perceptions of their school environment and academic achievement. Frontiers in Psychology. frontiersin.org

Edwards, W. & Magill, K. R. (2023). Rethinking the educational ecology in the wake of COVID: Intellectual solidarity, teacher prestige, and educational humanization. Policy Futures in Education. sagepub.com

El-Sabagh, H. A. (2021). Adaptive e-learning environment based on learning styles and its impact on development students' engagement. [springer.com]. *International Journal of Educational Technology in Higher Education, 18*(1), 53. DOI: 10.1186/s41239-021-00289-4

Ellikkal, A. & Rajamohan, S. (2024). AI-enabled personalized learning: empowering management students for improving engagement and academic performance. Vilakshan-XIMB Journal of Management. emerald.com

Engeness, I. (2021). Developing teachers' digital identity: towards the pedagogic design principles of digital environments to enhance students' learning in the 21st century. European Journal of Teacher Education. tandfonline.com

Farley, I. A. & Burbules, N. C. (2022). Online education viewed through an equity lens: Promoting engagement and success for all learners. Review of Education. wiley.com

Fensie, A., Pierre, T. S., Jain, J., & Sezen-Barrie, A. (2024). Engaged learning during distraction: A case study of successful working moms in distance education. [springer.com]. *Journal of Computing in Higher Education, 36*(2), 389–434. DOI: 10.1007/s12528-023-09359-0 PMID: 37359045

Fovet, F. (2021). Exploring the Use of Universal Design for Learning to Support In-Service Teachers in the Design of Socially-Just Blended Teaching Practices. In Re-Envisioning and Restructuring Blended Learning for Underprivileged Communities (pp. 143-164). IGI Global. [HTML] DOI: 10.4018/978-1-7998-6940-5.ch008

Gherhe , V., Stoian, C. E., Fărca iu, M. A., & Stanici, M. (2021). E-learning vs. face-to-face learning: Analyzing students' preferences and behaviors. Sustainability. mdpi.com

Gopinathan, S., Kaur, A. H., Veeraya, S., & Raman, M. (2022). The role of digital collaboration in student engagement towards enhancing student participation during [Sustainability. mdpi.com]. *COVID*, •••, 19.

Haleem, A., Javaid, M., Qadri, M. A., & Suman, R. (2022). Understanding the role of digital technologies in education: A review. Sustainable operations and computers, 3, 275-285. sciencedirect.com

Harrison, T. & Laco, D. (2022). Where's the character education in online higher education? Constructivism, virtue ethics and roles of online educators. E-Learning and Digital Media. sagepub.com

Hashim, M. A. M., Tlemsani, I., Matthews, R., Mason-Jones, R., & Ndrecaj, V. (2022). Emergent strategy in higher education: Postmodern digital and the future? [mdpi.com]. *Administrative Sciences*, *12*(4), 196. DOI: 10.3390/admsci12040196

Heilporn, G., Lakhal, S., & Bélisle, M. (2021). An examination of teachers' strategies to foster student engagement in blended learning in higher education. [springer.com]. *International Journal of Educational Technology in Higher Education*, *18*(1), 25. DOI: 10.1186/s41239-021-00260-3 PMID: 34805484

Herrera-Pavo, M. (). Collaborative learning for virtual higher education. Learning. [HTML]

Huang, Y. M., Silitonga, L. M., & Wu, T. T. (2022). Applying a business simulation game in a flipped classroom to enhance engagement, learning achievement, and higher-order thinking skills. [HTML]. *Computers & Education*, *183*, 104494. DOI: 10.1016/j.compedu.2022.104494

Imran, A. (2023). Why addressing digital inequality should be a priority. [wiley.com]. *The Electronic Journal on Information Systems in Developing Countries*, *89*(3), e12255. DOI: 10.1002/isd2.12255

Javaid, M., Haleem, A., Singh, R. P., Khan, S., & Khan, I. H. (2023). Unlocking the opportunities through ChatGPT Tool towards ameliorating the education system. BenchCouncil Transactions on Benchmarks [sciencedirect.com]. *Standards and Evaluations*, *3*(2), 100115.

Juntunen, H., Tuominen, H., Viljaranta, J., Hirvonen, R., Toom, A., & Niemivirta, M. (2022). Feeling exhausted and isolated? The connections between university students' remote teaching and learning experiences, motivation, and psychological well-being during the COVID-19 pandemic. [tandfonline.com]. *Educational Psychology*, *42*(10), 1241–1262. DOI: 10.1080/01443410.2022.2135686

Kaufmann, R., & Vallade, J. I. (2022). Exploring connections in the online learning environment: Student perceptions of rapport, climate, and loneliness. [HTML]. *Interactive Learning Environments*, *30*(10), 1794–1808. DOI: 10.1080/10494820.2020.1749670

Kazanjian, C. J. (2023). The Social-Emotional Learning Upgrade: Merging SEL and Technology Curricula to Support Young Learners. [HTML]

Kocdar, S., & Bozkurt, A. (2023). Supporting learners with special needs in open, distance, and digital education. In *Handbook of open, distance and digital education* (pp. 881–895). Springer Nature Singapore.

Kondo, C. S. (2022). Walking the talk: Employing culturally relevant pedagogy in teacher education. [HTML]. *Teachers College Record, 124*(4), 65–94. DOI: 10.1177/01614681221096797

Lera, M. J., Leon-Perez, J. M., & Ruiz-Zorrilla, P. (2023). Effective educational practices and students' well-being: the mediating role of students' self-efficacy. Current Psychology. springer.com

Levine, R. S., Lim, R. J., & Bintliff, A. V. (2023). Social and Emotional Learning during Pandemic-Related Remote and Hybrid Instruction: Teacher Strategies in Response to Trauma. Education Sciences. mdpi.com

Li, L. (2022). Students' isolation challenges in blended EFL learning during covid-19: how can social presence and interaction help develop sense of community?. Psychology research and behavior management. tandfonline.com

Maatuk, A. M., Elberkawi, E. K., Aljawarneh, S., Rashaideh, H., & Alharbi, H. (2022). The COVID-19 pandemic and E-learning: Challenges and opportunities from the perspective of students and instructors. [springer.com]. *Journal of Computing in Higher Education, 34*(1), 21–38. DOI: 10.1007/s12528-021-09274-2 PMID: 33967563

Malik, A. R., Pratiwi, Y., Andajani, K., Numertayasa, I. W., Suharti, S., Darwis, A., & Marzuki, . (2023). Exploring artificial intelligence in academic essay: Higher education student's perspective. [sciencedirect.com]. *International Journal of Educational Research Open, 5*, 100296. DOI: 10.1016/j.ijedro.2023.100296

Markey, K., O'Brien, B., Kouta, C., Okantey, C., & O'Donnell, C. (2021). Embracing classroom cultural diversity: Innovations for nurturing inclusive intercultural learning and culturally responsive teaching. [HTML]. *Teaching and Learning in Nursing, 16*(3), 258–262. DOI: 10.1016/j.teln.2021.01.008

McCarthy, A. M., Maor, D., McConney, A., & Cavanaugh, C. (2023). Digital transformation in education: Critical components for leaders of system change. [sciencedirect.com]. *Social Sciences & Humanities Open, 8*(1), 100479. DOI: 10.1016/j.ssaho.2023.100479

McDiarmid, G. W. & Zhao, Y. (2023). Time to rethink: educating for a technology-transformed world. ECNU Review of Education. sagepub.com

Mercan, G., & Köseoğlu, P. (2023). Digitalization of Higher Education in the Digital Age: The World's Current Digital Transformation and Its Goals. In Global Perspectives on the Internationalization of Higher Education (pp. 278-299). IGI Global. [HTML]

Mhlongo, S., Mbatha, K., Ramatsetse, B., & Dlamini, R. (2023). Challenges, opportunities, and prospects of adopting and using smart digital technologies in learning environments: An iterative review. Heliyon. cell.com

Mohamed Hashim, M. A., Tlemsani, I., & Matthews, R. (2022). Higher education strategy in digital transformation. [springer.com]. *Education and Information Technologies, 27*(3), 3171–3195. DOI: 10.1007/s10639-021-10739-1 PMID: 34539217

Molina Roldán, S., Marauri, J., Aubert, A., & Flecha, R. (2021). How inclusive interactive learning environments benefit students without special needs. [frontiersin.org]. *Frontiers in Psychology, 12*, 661427. DOI: 10.3389/fpsyg.2021.661427 PMID: 33995221

Moorhouse, B. L., Li, Y., & Walsh, S. (2023). E-classroom interactional competencies: Mediating and assisting language learning during synchronous online lessons. Relc Journal. sagepub.com

Namada, J. M. (2021). Learning management systems in the era of e-learning. In *Machine Learning Approaches for Improvising Modern Learning Systems* (pp. 169–190). IGI global. [HTML] DOI: 10.4018/978-1-7998-5009-0.ch007

Ng, P. M. L., Chan, J. K. Y., & Lit, K. K. (2022). Student learning performance in online collaborative learning. [HTML]. *Education and Information Technologies, 27*(6), 8129–8145. DOI: 10.1007/s10639-022-10923-x

Panda, S., & Kaur, N. (2024). Empowered Minds: Navigating Digital Seas With Emerging Information Literacy Framework. In Examining Information Literacy in Academic Libraries (pp. 48-82). IGI Global. [HTML]

Pattermann, J., Pammer, M., Schlögl, S., & Gstrein, L. (2022). Perceptions of digital device use and accompanying digital interruptions in blended learning. Education Sciences. mdpi.com

Philibert, C. T. & Slade, A. (2022). Everyday SEL in the virtual classroom: Integrating social emotional learning and mindfulness into your remote and hybrid settings. [HTML]

Roski, M., Sebastian, R., Ewerth, R., Hoppe, A., & Nehring, A. (2024). Learning analytics and the Universal Design for Learning (UDL): A clustering approach. [sciencedirect.com]. *Computers & Education, 214*, 105028. DOI: 10.1016/j.compedu.2024.105028

Salas-Pilco, S. Z., Yang, Y., & Zhang, Z. (2022). Student engagement in online learning in Latin American higher education during the COVID-19 pandemic: A systematic review. [wiley.com]. *British Journal of Educational Technology, 53*(3), 593–619. DOI: 10.1111/bjet.13190 PMID: 35600418

Sandoval, M., Muñoz, Y., & Márquez, C. (2021). Supporting schools in their journey to inclusive education: Review of guides and tools. Support for Learning. wiley.com

Selfa-Sastre, M., Pifarré, M., Cujba, A., Cutillas, L., & Falguera, E. (2022). The role of digital technologies to promote collaborative creativity in language education. [frontiersin.org]. *Frontiers in Psychology, 13*, 828981. DOI: 10.3389/fpsyg.2022.828981 PMID: 35222209

Shorey, S., Chan, V., Rajendran, P., & Ang, E. (2021). Learning styles, preferences and needs of generation Z healthcare students: Scoping review. [HTML]. *Nurse Education in Practice, 57*, 103247. DOI: 10.1016/j.nepr.2021.103247 PMID: 34768214

Sidhu, M. S., Mousakhani, S., Lee, C. K., & Sidhu, K. K. (2024). Educational impact of Metaverse learning environment for engineering mechanics dynamics. [HTML]. *Computer Applications in Engineering Education, 32*(5), e22772. DOI: 10.1002/cae.22772

Skulmowski, A. & Xu, K. M. (2022). Understanding cognitive load in digital and online learning: A new perspective on extraneous cognitive load. Educational psychology review. springer.com

Smith, D., Leonis, T., & Anandavalli, S. (2021). Belonging and loneliness in cyberspace: Impacts of social media on adolescents' well-being. [tandfonline.com]. *Australian Journal of Psychology, 73*(1), 12–23. DOI: 10.1080/00049530.2021.1898914

Strielkowski, W., Grebennikova, V., Lisovskiy, A., Rakhimova, G., & Vasileva, T. (2024). AI-driven adaptive learning for sustainable educational transformation. Sustainable Development. wiley.com

Su, F., & Zou, D. (2022). Technology-enhanced collaborative language learning: Theoretical foundations, technologies, and implications. [HTML]. *Computer Assisted Language Learning, 35*(8), 1754–1788. DOI: 10.1080/09588221.2020.1831545

Sugino, C. (2021). Student perceptions of a synchronous online cooperative learning course in a Japanese women's university during the COVID-19 pandemic. Education Sciences. mdpi.com

Szymkowiak, A., Melović, B., Dabić, M., Jeganathan, K., & Kundi, G. S. (2021). Information technology and Gen Z: The role of teachers, the internet, and technology in the education of young people. [HTML]. *Technology in Society*, *65*, 101565. DOI: 10.1016/j.techsoc.2021.101565

Tang, Y., & Hew, K. F. (2022). Effects of using mobile instant messaging on student behavioral, emotional, and cognitive engagement: A quasi-experimental study. [springer.com]. *International Journal of Educational Technology in Higher Education*, *19*(1), 3. DOI: 10.1186/s41239-021-00306-6 PMID: 35036520

Tariq, M. U. (2024). Equity and Inclusion in Learning Ecosystems. In Preparing Students for the Future Educational Paradigm (pp. 155-176). IGI Global. [HTML] DOI: 10.4018/979-8-3693-1536-1.ch007

Tate, T. & Warschauer, M. (2022). Equity in online learning. Educational Psychologist. tandfonline.com

Vetrivel, S. C., Arun, V. P., Maheswari, R., & Saravanan, T. P. (2024). Technology integration in online learning platforms: Blended learning gamification. In Transdisciplinary Teaching and Technological Integration for Improved Learning: Case Studies and Practical Approaches (pp. 219-247). IGI Global. [HTML]

Wang, T., Lund, B. D., Marengo, A., Pagano, A., Mannuru, N. R., Teel, Z. A., & Pange, J. (2023). Exploring the potential impact of artificial intelligence (AI) on international students in higher education: Generative AI, chatbots, analytics, and international student success. [mdpi.com]. *Applied Sciences (Basel, Switzerland)*, *13*(11), 6716. DOI: 10.3390/app13116716

Wei, L. (2022). Translanguaging as a political stance: Implications for English language education. ELT journal. oup.com

Xu, B. (2024). Mediating role of academic self-efficacy and academic emotions in the relationship between teacher support and academic achievement. Scientific Reports. nature.com

Yang, C. (2021). Online teaching self-efficacy, social–emotional learning (SEL) competencies, and compassion fatigue among educators during the COVID-19 pandemic. [HTML]. *School Psychology Review*, *50*(4), 505–518. DOI: 10.1080/2372966X.2021.1903815

Yang, S. J., Ogata, H., Matsui, T., & Chen, N. S. (2021). Human-centered artificial intelligence in education: Seeing the invisible through the visible. [sciencedirect.com]. *Computers and Education: Artificial Intelligence*, *2*, 100008.

Yaqoubi, T., Mohammadi, Z., & Golzar, J. (2022). An analysis of Universal Design for Learning at collegial level: Effective ways to maximise learning outcomes, inclusion, and equity. [HTML]. *Research in Post-Compulsory Education*, *27*(4), 594–621. DOI: 10.1080/13596748.2022.2110775

Yu, H. (2024). The application and challenges of ChatGPT in educational transformation: New demands for teachers' roles. Heliyon. cell.com

Zengilowski, A., Lee, J., Gaines, R. E., Park, H., Choi, E., & Schallert, D. L. (2023). The collective classroom "we": The role of students' sense of belonging on their affective, cognitive, and discourse experiences of online and face-to-face discussions. [sciencedirect.com]. *Linguistics and Education*, *73*, 101142. DOI: 10.1016/j.linged.2022.101142

Zheng, F. (2022). Fostering students' well-being: The mediating role of teacher interpersonal behavior and student-teacher relationships. Frontiers in Psychology. frontiersin.org

Zort, Ç, Karabacak, E., Öznur, Ş, & Dağlı, G. (2023). Sharing of cultural values and heritage through storytelling in the digital age. Frontiers in Psychology. frontiersin.org

Chapter 6
Balancing Screen Time and Human Interaction in Blended Learning

Pawan Pant
https://orcid.org/0000-0003-1774-5650
Chandigarh University, India

ABSTRACT

Blended learning has emerged as a teaching method in the age of digital transformation, combining digital learning with face-to-face learning. Though screen tools have never been matched for ready access to information, student-centred learning, or developing digital literacy, over-reliance on them can deprive learners of social exposure, critical thinking, or emotional growth. Thus, equilibrium should be kept between hours of screen-gazing and genuine human connections so as to enliven and sustain education. The discussion of the overuse of screens touches on cognitive, social and emotional impacts. It develops practical frameworks to aid teachers in designing and implementing blended learning with balance and technology to enrich, not replace, human contact. Case studies and action recommendations thus highlight how educators may find a balance between the digital and interpersonal elements of education and pave the way toward resilient and adaptive learning ecosystems.

1. INTRODUCTION: THE EVOLVING CLASSROOM DYNAMIC

The face has completely changed when a technological approach is incorporated into education. A class that was initially a face-to-face experience became a blended learning model, which allows for the extra digital tools to combine human interaction in developing a better learning outcome. This change would be due to

DOI: 10.4018/979-8-3373-0771-8.ch006

the accessible adaptive learning technologies available, which help personalise a path for students and address their different needs of study (Graham, 2006b). Nonetheless, while these progressions offer plenty of opportunities for growth, they also bring various challenges, starting with the likely overuse of screens, as observed to cause problems like cognitive overload, reduced attentiveness, and decreased social competency (Twenge, 2018).

Blended learning fills in the gap between technological efficiency and the irreplaceable value of human connection. Educators today not only give out knowledge but also encourage critical thinking, creativity, and collaboration skills that technology alone cannot help to develop (Johnson et al., 2016). A classroom where such a blended approach is increasingly dominant calls for a more excellent balance between time spent on the screen and that spent engaging with other people. This chapter explores such an evolving dynamic, offering the reader insights and strategy toward harmonising those elements toward effective holistic schooling.

The modern classroom has become so much more than just four walls and a singular teaching methodology. It is defined now by the usage of digital tools to create new methods that allow learning to become dynamic and tailored. The method has come to be called blended learning, whereby online learning has brought along its flexibility and accessibilities combined with face-to-face benefits that come along with a relation and teamwork setting (Garrison & Vaughan, 2008). In this blended model, learners have adaptive technologies that support learning according to requirements, keeping them engaged and improving their academic outcomes (Bonk & Graham, 2012).

However, over-exposure caused by the growing number of screens at school becomes an issue that degrades their cognitive, social, and physical development. High levels of screen time correlate with attentional issues, loss of interpersonal skills, and various health problems, such as eye strain in computer users and sedentary (Twenge, 2018). Also, the reliance on technology may drown out the need for teachers as guides and activators of thought and emotional intelligence (Johnson et al., 2016).

Such limitations mean that educationalists and decision-makers should not simply replace human interaction with the best of technology but find the harmony between both ingredients. Effective, well-crafted, and hybrid learning is more about the virtues of digital mediums intertwined with humanly interactive engagements prepared to achieve educational success in learning at school and also in life, as argued through this chapter of balancing screen-based time with humane interaction by proposing evidence-based strategy in the path towards sustainable education.

2. UNDERSTANDING SCREEN TIME IN EDUCATION

Screen time in schools is one way through which pupils interact with study materials and respond to the curriculum. As more technology is introduced into the class, it will be important to understand the benefits and disadvantages of screen time to ensure a good balance in learning activities.

2.1 Advantages of Screen Time in Schools

a) Variety of Learning Material

One of the significant benefits for students who spend screen time studying is the vast volume of material that is possible to access by digital means. They are offered a wide variety of content, which can range from videos and articles to online courses and simulations meant to make a learning experience even richer (Mayer, 2021). These may supplement texts and lectures by creating different paths for the students to learn complex ideas. For example, video and tutorial resources on the internet can describe concepts engagingly and visually, which may be of particular help to students with a variety of learning preferences (Clark & Mayer, 2016).

b) Personalized Learning

Digital tools enable personalised learning. Adaptive technologies and LMS can identify each student's strengths and weaknesses and deliver content based on their learning pace. Such personalisation ensures that every student has a chance to succeed, regardless of where they begin (Fitzpatrick, 2020). The platforms also track progress, providing instant feedback to students and allowing educators to adjust instruction based on real-time data.

c) Engagement and Motivation

Learning could be made interesting through interactive learning tools, such as games in learning, gamified assessment, and virtual simulations. The incorporation of game-like aspects such as points, levels, or challenges within the lesson plans would make the students want to take part in activities and contribute to their performance (Gee, 2003). Simulations, in this case, are those in science or mathematics that enable the student to see the world in absolute terms and apply concepts to an actual situation.

d) Development of Digital Literacy

In this technological world, digital literacy is one of the crucial competencies required. Learning is the capacity of the student to develop and hone his digital competencies through screens. Educational software, online research, and digital collaboration enable students to master using the right technology required in an increasingly digital economy for their future careers (Van Deursen & Van Dijk, 2014).

2.2 Problems with Too Much Screen Time in School

a) Physical Health Issues

Overuse of screens in school can cause some problems in the physical setup, including eye strain, headache, and poor posture. "Computer vision syndrome" is another name for digital eye strain, a condition that people experience when they spend too much time focusing on screens for an extended period; they experience blurred vision, dryness of eyes, and headaches (Rosenfield, 2016). In addition, screen-based learning is sedentary and causes long-term health problems, including obesity and cardiovascular diseases, because it results in a sedentary lifestyle (LeBlanc et al., 2012).

Excessive screen use in school impacts teachers negatively on their health, leading to physical and emotional stress. A lot of eye strain, headache, and musculoskeletal complications arise due to the improper body posture taken up (Sheppard & Wolffsohn, 2018). The constant compulsion to interact with online materials causes mental strain and stress leading to emotional fatigue and reduced work satisfaction (Klussman et al., 2021). Digital instructional needs, such as managing student motivation and online resources, also increase burnout and chronic exhaustion (Maslach & Leiter, 2016). A balanced approach to technology use is necessary to enhance teachers' well-being and effective teaching.

b) Cognitive Overload and Attention Issues

One of the highest mental challenges presented by screen time is the risk of cognitive overload. It has been proven that students who are excessively multi-tasking and constantly switching between various digital platforms cannot concentrate and forget information (Carr, 2011). This problem is also compounded by constant exposure to the barrage of notifications and digital distractions, making it hard for learners to focus and maintain their concentration in learning activities (Rosen et al., 2013).

c) Social and Emotional Impact

Excessive screen use reduces face-to-face interaction with peers, an interaction factor vital to the development of social and emotional skills. Face-to-face contact in a physical classroom teaches how to cooperate with others, negotiate conflicts, and communicate with their peers and instructors. The more one uses the screen, the less one develops interpersonal skills, and a person may struggle to develop a relationship and work well with colleagues in real-life situations (Twenge, 2018). Overdependence on technology for socialisation also tends to isolate younger students.

d) Reduced Critical Thinking and Problem-Solving Skills

While technology can give students information and resources, it cannot replace the critical thinking and problem-solving skills that are developed through human interaction and guided instruction. It does show that students could easily find information through digital tools but do not go deeply into the critical sense and, hence, might not be able to attain an even greater extent of the skill in the domain of critical thinking for analysis, synthesis, and application of knowledge in reality (Saavedra & Opfer, 2012). Such a statement also implies a sense of balance regarding digital tools versus other activities requiring the active involvement and reflection of students.

3. THE ROLE OF HUMAN INTERACTION IN LEARNING

It is well understood that educational processes cannot do without human interaction, which influences cognitive, social, emotional, and behavioural development. Technology in education undoubtedly offers many benefits, such as personalised learning and broad access to information, but what it supports uniquely are the social and emotional aspects of learning. In this regard, both student-to-teacher and student-to-student relationships are important because they perform specific functions that give additional depth, meaning, and effectiveness to learning.

a) Cognitive Development Through Human Interaction

Dynamic, collaborative human interactions enhance cognitive development. The students are exposed to diverse perspectives through discussions, debates, and problem-solving with teachers and peers, which stimulates critical thinking and deeper understanding. Vygotsky's scaffolding theory focuses on how more knowledgeable persons, like teachers or higher-ability peers, facilitate learning so that students can attain levels that they cannot do by themselves (Vygotsky, 1978). Face-to-face learning environments provide students with instant feedback that will help in the correction, reflection, and consolidation of learning at the moment (Hattie & Timperley, 2007). In addition, the ability to pose questions, clarify confusion, and probe ideas using both verbal and non-verbal responses further increases understanding and retention. Human interaction also permits instruction that is individualised and sensitive to the needs, pace, and capabilities of each learner, thus enabling a more comprehensive learning experience than that provided by technology alone (Piaget, 1952).

b) Emotional and Social Development

Apart from cognitive growth, human interaction in the learning process encourages emotional and social development. Classroom interaction promotes communication skills, empathic feelings, and teamwork through classwork and peer discussions. For instance, group work and peer discussion deal with social problems, how to resolve conflicts, and a sense of community through class works and peer discussions (Johnson & Johnson, 1994). The opportunities developed bring along trust and respect for one's peers, which is positively essential in developing a non-hostile learning environment (Dewey, 1916).

Human interaction also brings along the development of emotions. The teachers guide students through the emotional realms; they support, comfort and allow students to be risk-taking intellectuals in safe settings without the feeling of judgment. Good interactions between the teacher and the student, as well as among the students, help boost the self-esteem and motivation of a student while ensuring belonging in school (Cohen & Sandy, 2007). On the other hand, lack of frequent social interaction results in feelings of isolation, disengagement, and reduced emotional well-being, which negatively impact learning outcomes.

c) Interpersonal Skills Development

Human interaction is also essential for developing interpersonal skills, which are very important in the academic environment and beyond. Through face-to-face communication, students learn to articulate their ideas, listen actively, and adjust their behaviour based on social cues. These are essential to facilitate a collaborative workplace within diverse groups, as well as for working professionally in careers following graduation (Goleman, 1995). Regular interactions with people while learning facilitate the development of high emotional intelligence, an essential predictor of both academic and professional success, Salovey & Mayer (1990).

d) Disadvantages of Reduced Human Interaction

One of the disadvantages of this development will probably be a reduction in meaningful human-to-human interaction. Thus, online education, effective as it might be in almost every other way, lacks this spontaneous, organic interaction that could be present in a more natural classroom. The lack of non-verbal cues in virtual communication might prove to be counterproductive for developing closer relationships between students and teachers and between peers (Baker, 2004). The students will face difficulties in being motivated, engaged, and building social connections when there is a lack of sufficient face-to-face contact (Twenge, 2018). Furthermore, excessive dependence on technology to learn may reduce the development of practical interpersonal skills. A student can become more at ease communicating electronically and less skilful in interpersonal communication, which is the kind of communication needed in academia and in the workforce. The reduced personal classroom contact can also fail to allow a student to gain experience in settling disputes and developing group dynamics in a supportive but guided environment.

e) The Synergy Between Technology and Human Interaction

Human interaction is widely regarded as essential for fostering cognitive, social, and emotional development in learners (Vygotsky, 1978). While technology offers personalised and scalable learning solutions, its effectiveness is maximised when it complements, rather than replaces, face-to-face interactions that support engagement, collaboration, and emotional growth (Johnson et al., 2014). The most effective learning environments integrate the strengths of both technology and human connection, allowing technology to expand learning opportunities while maintaining the essential interpersonal elements that make education a transformative and holistic experience (Greenhow et al., 2020).

4. FRAMEWORK FOR BALANCING SCREEN TIME AND INTERACTION IN BLENDED LEARNING

A good balance of screen time through face-to-face human interaction in a blended environment would, hence, require an approach to the structured application of technologies in a blended nature without eliminating substantial face-to-face interactions. For instance, outlined below is the demonstration of an example of this framework that works to balance learning both on a screen and engaging on campus by complementing these to achieve better outcomes of a student's acquisition of knowledge for their benefit while ensuring overall welfare.

4.1 Setting Clear Educational Objectives

The first step in balancing screen time and interaction in learning is to define proper educational goals with both online learning experiences and direct in-person contacts. These targets should be established in line with course content, the goals of the class, and the particular needs of the students (Wiggins & McTighe, 2005).

Action Steps:

a) Set learning outcomes both online and offline, ensuring technological support for enhanced classroom communication.
b) Determine and outline practices for various delivery modes, for example, using online resources, face-to-face classes on critical thinking, or collaborative problem-solving.
c) Use backward design to plan activities based on the desired outcomes so that every mode of learning addresses particular aspects of the learning process, such as foundational knowledge online and application in class.

4.2 Flexible Learning Activity Design

Blended learning should involve both screen and face-to-face activities. It is a type of instruction in which students work individually and in groups while using flexible learning activities (Graham, 2006a).

Action Steps:

a) Implement asynchronous online modules (e.g., video lectures, readings, and quizzes) that students can view at any time convenient to them.
b) Synchronous web activities, such as discussions over the Internet and Live Q&A Sessions, to give real-time input opportunities.
c) In-class activities such as group discussions, project-based learning, or hands-on workshops where students can apply their learning, interact with peers, and receive immediate feedback.

4.3 Technology as an Enabler

Technology is not meant to replace in-class interactions but should complement them. When adequately embedded, technology enables learning, feedback, and flexibility in resource use (Anderson & Dron, 2011).

Action Items:

a) Technology-based repeated practice and review of the fundamentals (for example, adaptive learning platforms and quizzes).
b) Digital collaboration tools, such as Google Docs, Padlet, or Trello, are to be provided to encourage collaborative work and peer-to-peer engagement in online courses.
c) Provide multimedia resources such as videos, podcasts, and simulations to reach various types of learners and maximise the content's exposure.

4.4 Monitoring and Managing Screen Time

As mentioned by Gazzaley and Rosen (2016), the adverse effect of over-engagement in digital activities can be avoided by monitoring and controlling screen time, such as by setting a conscious time limit for reading the digital screen and encouraging breaks.

Action Steps:

a) Allocate time limits on screen-based learning to ensure students spend enough quality time with content without ever elongating the amount of time devoted to screens.
b) Schedule breaks throughout the screen-intensive sessions to lower eye strain and help the students focus better.
c) Use tools and track screen usage to help the learners understand so that they can manage their time independently.

4.5 Encouragement of Active Learning and Engagement

Engage active learning activities both online and face-to-face to keep learners activated. Active learning is said to retain the content in the brains of students for a longer time and makes a student understand content better (Bonwell & Eison, 1991).

Action Steps:

a) Use Kahoot, Poll Everywhere, etc., in online learning sessions.
b) Project-based or problem-solving-based activities should be assigned in contact classes.
c) Student-centered discussions in virtual and physical environments where students discuss and debate issues of relevance.

4.6 Continuous Feedback and Support

Facilitative mastery: Continuous giving of feedback is part of the whole process that an element can produce for students who go through a particular blended learning. Feedback in these regards should reach individual needs and the need to concentrate on the fact that it was supporting a particular student's face-to-face or digital experience alike (Hattie & Timperley, 2007).

Action steps:

a) Immediate digital feedback through quizzes, assignments, and automated responses in learning management systems (LMS).
b) Provide in-person feedback during office hours, group sessions, or peer reviews to address misunderstandings or deepen discussions.
c) Use peer assessment strategies in both online forums and in-person settings to promote active learning and self-reflection.

4.7 Fostering Collaborative Learning and Peer Interaction

Collaboration mainly facilitates learning according to the situation. Like online learning, in-person learning, which facilitates opportunities for peer interaction, enables students to deepen their knowledge as they discuss, work together, and share experiences (Johnson et al., 1998).

Action Steps

a) Group design projects, in which the work is taken both digitally (through shared documents and virtual meetings) and face-to-face for final presentations or hands-on work.
b) Online forums for discussion and in-class breakouts where smaller groups can work on specific activities.
c) Opportunities for peer review and mentoring, as students provide feedback on each other's work with constructive suggestions and help each other learn.

4.8 Balance in the Learning Environment

This would balance the hours spent in front of the screen with those spent talking with other human beings. In other words, that environment would prioritise students' welfare: give them access to technology but also provide them with access to social support so that they can successfully work (CASEL, 2020).

Action Steps:

a) Set standards of engagement that would help the students utilise screen time appropriately but still leave space for in-person interactions to connect and build community.
b) Including SEL components either in virtual or in vivo formats to allow students to be able to regulate their emotions, build relationships and maintain interest better
c) Technology would be used more as a supplement than a replacement for human connections, keeping things centred on relationship building and interactive participation.

5. EXPLANATION OF BALANCING SCREEN TIME AND INTERACTION

Figure 1. Balancing screen time and interaction

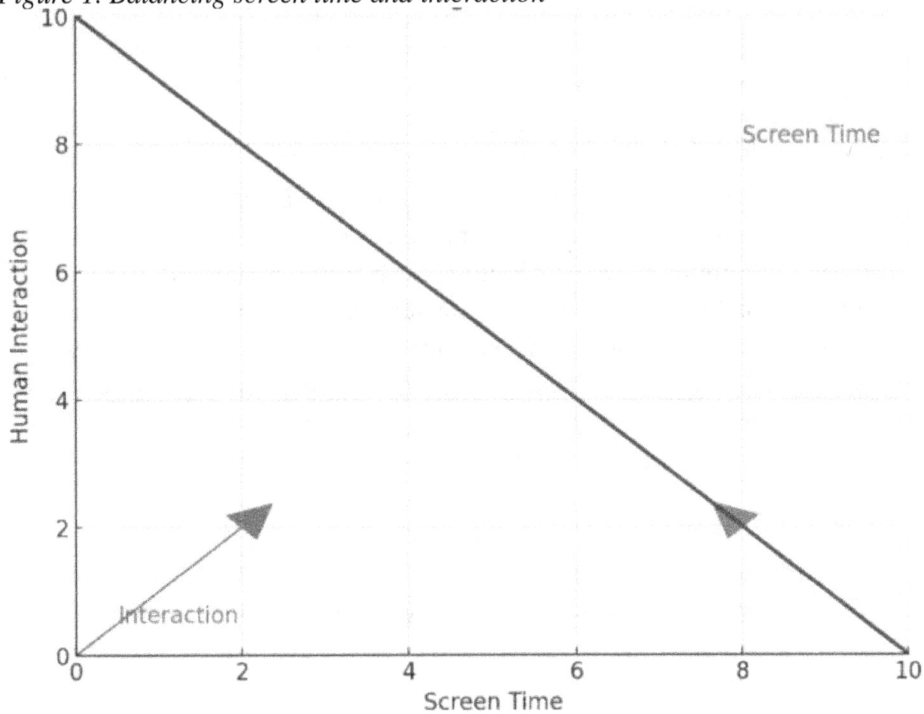

The ray diagram illustrates the connection between screen time, as the red arrow indicates, and human interaction, represented by the green arrow, within the blended learning environment. A balance needs to be achieved between these two aspects to optimise students' engagement, learning outcomes, and well-being.

a) Screen Time: As per this diagram, overuse of time in the form of screen-based learning can also reflect a scenario for adverse impact- digital fatigue, shorter spans of concentration and cognitive overload. This in no way minimises the effect brought about by digital tools but definitely indicates reduced levels of experience among students for engagement with lessons that have excessive amounts of time using screens (Gazzaley & Rosen, 2016). As digital learning tools become increasingly integrated into education, it is essential to monitor and manage screen time to avoid these adverse effects (Wang et al., 2020).
b) Human Interactivity (Green Arrow): Interventions that increase students' motivation, emotional support, and critical thinking are mostly via human interaction (Schunk, Pintrich, & Meece, 2008). Face-to-face interactions that exist within the blended learning model offer avenues of discussion, collaborative learning, and social growth that are not replicable with technology. Human interaction leads to a more engaged presence, better comprehension, and a sense of community for participants in the learning environment. Thus, human interaction should be maintained at a sufficient level to create a balanced and holistic learning experience (Selwyn, 2016).
c) The optimum balance occurs when the diagonal line in the diagram is reached: optimum screen time to human interaction. According to research, blended models of learning are most effective when they combine the best of both worlds: technology for personalised, flexible learning experiences and human interaction for social learning and emotional connection (Garrison & Kanuka, 2004). Educators should strive to design learning experiences that use digital tools to complement face-to-face engagement rather than displace it so that technology supports rather than diminishes the critical role of human interaction in learning.

In blended learning, balancing human interaction and screen time would optimally optimise benefits. That way, one can avail oneself of the benefits of technology without sacrificing the benefits that human interaction will provide for social, emotional, and cognitive support.

6. BLENDED LEARNING MODELS IN ACTION

Blended learning models are becoming popular across all settings of education because they allow the flexibility to merge traditional face-to-face instruction with online learning. The models can be varied in structure and delivery but still aim to combine the best strengths of both the physical and digital learning environments. Flipped classrooms are the most popular among them, wherein students learn a given content at home through videos or modules in advance and, then, with the guidance of the teacher, apply the learning in collaborative activities inside the classroom. According to Bergmann and Sams (2012), this can increase student engagement, foster deeper learning, and enhance critical thinking skills. The next is the station rotation model, where students are divided into smaller groups and rotate within learning stations that provide online learning, group projects, or teacher-led instruction. This model of learning ensures that every learner gets a learning experience tailored to their needs in such a way that teachers can address the needs of each learner as required (Horn & Staker, 2014).

This has made them versatile and in charge of their learning paths. It is very convenient for higher learning as students can control the course schedules as well as the environment in which they learn (Staker & Horn, 2012). Then, sometimes, the combined models integrate both the synchronous and the asynchronous learning elements: students may interact with instructors as well as their peers in real-time for discussion or activities while others learn independently at their own pace from online resources (Garrison & Vaughan, 2008).

These blended learning models have been known to increase students' outcomes by providing tailored learning experiences, increased student control over learning, and a deeper content understanding. Success, however, greatly relies on the quality of technology being used, the readiness of teachers to manage and integrate both modes and the assurance that appropriate support is offered to the learners (Means et al., 2013). When applied mindfully, blended learning provides an exciting and flexible approach to education that honours the many diversities of today's learners.

7. CHALLENGES IN ACHIEVING BALANCE

Challenges of Achieving a Balance between Screen Time and Human Interaction in Blended Learning. This poses a very complex challenge to educators, students, and institutions in balancing screen time with human interaction, technical, pedagogical, and socio-economic. A proper balance can bring ideal improvement to learning outcomes and well-being; however, such an approach needs multi-faceted efforts to resolve the intricacies involved. Next, the significant problems noticed in an effort to achieve a balance between screen time and interactions within a blended learning system are described below.

7.1 Screen Fatigue and Cognitive Overload

Students, as well as teachers, are susceptible to screen fatigue, which is caused by the protracted use of digital devices under a blended learning process. Information overload from screens dilutes the students' ability to concentrate, perceive information, and remember learning under cognitive overload. Too much time spent on screen makes students inattentive and quickly fatigued, hence affecting their efficiency while learning (Gazzaley & Rosen, 2016; Rosen, Lim, Carrier, & Cheever, 2011).

Challenges:

a) Physiological Fatigue: Long working hours in the presence of displays can cause eye strain, a headache, or poor posture, which can make the learner uncomfortable while staying focused over long periods.
b) Mental Fatigue: The brain is overloaded with too much or disorganised information, leading to a failure in knowledge retention and application.
c) Lower Engagement: The more students feel tired, the less they can carry out learning activities, lowering participation and motivation.

7.2 Digital Divide and Access Inequality

This would be one of the significant problems in achieving a balance between screen time and human interaction for students in a blended learning environment. Socio-economic disparities regarding technology access, especially internet connectivity and digital devices, can prevent students from participating fully in online aspects of a blended learning course (Warschauer, 2003; van Dijk, 2020).

Challenges:

a) Technology Access: Children in lower socio-economic backgrounds may not have access to the right machines (for instance, computers or tablet devices) and internet connection or a stable one to use, therefore limiting them to online learning.
b) Digital exclusion results in unequal participation born out of a significant gap between appropriate access to technology for children and those who do not.

c) Teacher flexibility: Teachers may find it challenging to adapt to teaching students without access to technology. This may force teachers to alter their approach or provide alternative means.

7.3 Teacher Preparedness and Training

Technology integration in classrooms remains a central challenge for the majority of teaching staff. These teachers are still not well-trained or conversant with new, more advanced technologies, and their failure to exploit such technology increases the likelihood that it will reduce human interaction potential in blended settings. Teachers lack appropriate pedagogical knowledge on how to achieve a balance between digital and face-to-face learning to avoid overreliance on one modality or ineffective student engagement (Ertmer & Ottenbreit-Leftwich, 2010; Hutchison & Reinking, 2011).

Challenges:

a) Technology skills: Teachers might not be competent enough in using technology or were not prepared to prepare blended learning with engaging activities.
b) Resistance to Change: The teachers have resisted some of the new technologies partly because they are unfamiliar with them or fear that their introduction would disturb traditional teaching methods.
c) To succeed with blended learning, teachers must undergo pedagogical changes. For example, they create active learning experiences specially designed for the online setting and implement technology in the more traditional face-to-face learning model.

7.4 Student Engagement and Motivation

Engaging and motivating students in a high-screen-time blended learning environment is likely to be challenging. When face-to-face interaction with the teacher and fellow students is minimised, there is a likelihood of a lack of motivation in the learning process, especially when depending on digital tools for learning (Schunk, Pintrich & Meece, 2008; Nistor & Lerche, 2020).

Challenges:

a) Social Isolation: Due to the lack of face-to-face interaction, students are socially isolated from their peers and instructors, leading to feelings of isolation and disconnection that decrease motivation.
b) Passive Learning: The online activities do not involve interactive activities. As a passive learner, the student disengages from learning soon.
c) Distractions: Social media, games, and so many more bombard the student during his time online, engaging the mind away from proper learning focus.

7.5 Personalized learning v/s standard curriculum

This is why blended learning provides the doorways for personal learning yet is so well balanced with the constraint of a traditional curriculum. It, therefore, requires teachers to allow the students to attain prescriptive standards and requirements of their learning environment despite every individual's different style and pace while trying to include some screen time besides human interaction (Koller, Harvey, & Magnotta, 2013; Darling-Hammond, & Adamson, 2014).

Challenges:

a) Individual vs. Group Needs: The conflict in designing blended learning experiences stems from the need to meet individual needs while simultaneously ensuring that every student meets the same learning outcomes.
b) Assessment Alignment: A standardised test, along with a more traditional assessment, truly does not represent the more laid-back, individualised environment that will best typify a blended learning classroom, thereby making it difficult to measure the student's knowledge accurately.
c) Curriculum Rigidity: The institutions have rigid curricula that cannot be readily modified to personalise learning. Thus, students might experience an incompatibility between content coverage and the path taken to acquire it.

7.6 Overdependence on Technology

While technology is highly effective, overreliance on digital means may overlook the points that are equally important in human interaction, such as the teacher-student relationship and collaboration among peers. If technology is used more as the primary medium of learning, then the learners will have less social-emotional involvement in classes, which would weaken the quality of education (Sheninger, 2014; Selwyn, 2016).

Challenges:

a) Dehumanization of Learning: With too much emphasis on digital delivery, aspects that involve humans, such as interaction, can lead to emotional support and mentorship or social learning becoming minimal.
b) Loss of Teacher Presence: A teacher's absence in a virtual setting reduces emotional engagement; therefore, learners are not interested in seeking help.
c) Over-Automaton: If technology does too much automation for learning, such as grading and assessments, then students miss the insights that humans provide because of feedback and personal guidance.

8. CASE STUDIES

8.1 Finland's Digital Education Model

8.1.1 Overview

Among the world's most innovative student-centred education systems, Finland uses digital tools alongside classrooms, avoiding the dilution of the human factor. Finnish learning fosters equity, creativity, and critical thinking, which may well serve as a model for striking an equilibrium in screen time versus human interaction in a blended learning environment (Sahlberg, 2011).

8.1.2 Implementation

a) Phenomenon-Based Learning (PhBL): One of the key features of the Finland curriculum is phenomenon-based learning. In PhBL, students learn complex ideas from practical and interdisciplinary perspectives. For instance, a climatic project will take science, social studies, and geography to increase the understanding of interrelated phenomena. This model can be done by using digital tools such as Google Workspace and Eduten, which allow students access to online materials, collaborative work on projects, and data analyses. However, the foundation of this strategy is in-class collaboration and discussion, which guarantees that all learning goes hand in hand with human interaction and critical thinking (Holappa & Soini, 2020).
b) Differentiated Classroom Teacher-Led Technology Integration: Teachers in Finland, overall, show considerable skill in fully integrating the role of technology while maintaining their core pedagogy. Even simple tools, such as Kahoot!

and Minecraft: Education Edition, are used quite popularly alongside teaching methods without attempting to supplant these methodologies entirely. Quizzes online- For instance, the assessment of learning comprehension can be done by conducting an online quiz that simulates what one would undertake when using Kahoot! However, the underlying nature of learning is a group discussion led by the teacher. There, one can explore the concept further, think deeply, and solve problems collaboratively. It makes perfect sense that technology, with this approach, keeps a balance that will enrich learning without losing the main thing about human communication and deep consideration (Kampylis et al., 2015; Voogt et al., 2017).

c) Time Management and Digital Literacy: Finnish educators ensure they maintain a well-balanced curriculum of online and offline activities and do not 'overload the child with screen'. The curriculum thus has been tailored to inter-weave these across the day-to-day activities while providing an excellent blend of new and traditional methods of learning. Moreover, this curriculum is deeply rooted in terms of digital literacy and equips the learner with how to use these tools effectively and responsibly. Other issues, including safe online practices, ethical use of information, and critical evaluation of digital resources, are also involved in ensuring that digital citizenship responsibility is inculcated (Vuorikari et al., 2019). This can be seen to reflect Finland's philosophy of learning, which promotes balance between high-tech and man-to-man, face-to-face relations.

d) Collaborative Learning Environments: Today, Finland classrooms are designed to be pretty fluid settings because there is always room for flexible seating arrangements and instant access to electronic gadgets. This promotes collaboration and experiential learning. Such settings allow the students to work in groups with the help of technology, which allows the utilisation of real-world problems in their hands for experiential learning. This approach has the added impact of enhancing teamwork and interpersonal skills, giving students the competencies to be able to accurately apply digital instruments in solving issues, analysing information, and coming up with ideas. In an attempt to foster collaboration-friendly environments, Finland adopts a creative approach of embedding technology with interactive and problem-based learning to make sure that students are prepared for the complexities of the digital world (Sahlberg, 2011; Hämäläinen & Vähäsantanen, 2011).

8.1.3 Advantages

a) Increased Interaction: Digital tools make lessons more interactive, especially for young students. Techniques involving gamification in learning have been quite effective in motivating students.
b) Equitability in Learning: Finland equalises access to technology for its children, minimising the technological gap. Students are given equal chances to acquire all such devices and proper digital content.
c) Critical Thinking and Collaboration: The approach encourages higher-order thinking skills by applying project-based and collaborative tasks.

8.1.4 Challenges

a) Teacher Workload: It increases the planning and training workload for teachers since using digital tools is a relatively new phenomenon in education.
b) Manages Screen Times: Though managed, the usage needs to be frequently monitored to make sure that there is no harmful welfare to the students because of using the screen.

8.1.5 Outcomes

Studies on Finland's digital education model have been successful and have helped provide creative, cooperative, and critical-thinking students. An OECD report stated that Finnish students were consistent world leaders in problem-solving and collaborative skills. This is because the country balanced the use of technology (OECD, 2021a).

8.1.6 Lessons Learned

Successful blended learning would depend on proper integration, such as in Finland. Technology is being used to support pedagogy, not for its own sake. Human interaction, creativity, and collaborative learning are still the heart of learning.

8.2 Khan Academy in U.S. Schools

8.2.1 Overview

Khan Academy, a non-profit, has transformed the world of education through free, high-quality online learning resources. It has collaborated with many schools in the United States to use blended learning models that combine online learning with teacher-led classroom activities. This personalised learning aims to ensure heightened learning outcomes and critical thinking while still adhering to important human engagement through interactive learning (Murphy et al., 2014).

8.2.2 Implementation

a) Individualized Learning Pathways: The self-paced learning environment by the vast online system supported by the Khan Academy shall provide students with video lessons, exercises, and practice quizzes adjusted to the specific learner's skill levels. Through this, they can learn individually and have an appropriate foundation, such as maths, science, and reading, to understand those concepts. The role of the teachers is to assign modules based on the curriculum that help them in targeted guidance in specific situations. The personalised and flexible model of learning here points to the way technology can be well-implemented in environments of learning for individuals' support towards self-learned practices (Bhagat et al., 2016; McLaughlin et al., 2014).
b) Data-Driven Teaching: Teachers use these real-time analytics of the Khan Academy platform to track each student's improvement, identify places of knowledge gaps, and thereby adjust teaching methodologies according to every learner's individual needs. For example, if a particular math concept causes trouble for the student, that data allows him to pinpoint the point of struggle. This enables the teacher to support students in class. Such support is targeted at helping the student get more assertive about what he or she has learned. Thus, the integration of technology with traditional teaching not only increases the effectiveness of learning by dealing with individual needs but also saves the fundamental human aspects of individualised learning (Anderson & Krathwohl, 2001; McLaughlin et al., 2014).
c) Classroom Activity: The students frequently use Khan Academy videos either during the time set aside outside of scheduled study periods or during the scheduled time for activities, projects, and discussions on solved problems in the classroom. This method is based on the flipped classroom model, in which students learn theoretical concepts at home through videos and online resources.

They will be applied to the class using a variety of activities and class discussions that further cement their learning and retention. Such a model supports active learning and develops critical thinking and problem-solving abilities by providing support from teachers and other peers through feedback in the process of working out problems during the in-class session. It makes use of technology effectively to optimise the outcome of learning by bringing self-paced online learning together with interactive, teacher-guided classroom activities (Tucker, 2012; Bergmann & Sams, 2012).

d) Accessibility and Inclusivity: Khan Academy is device-agnostic. It can be accessed using any technology by the student regardless of the device he has at his disposal. This adaptability ensures that even schools without substantial resources can be helped by the platform in offering shared access to laptops or tablets, therefore reducing the digital divide. Khan Academy offers support for various devices and equates access across schools, meaning that less affluent schools can offer opportunities for inclusive learning environments in which all students get to interact with high-quality education content, notwithstanding their technological barriers (Foley & Lee, 2012; An, 2015).

8.2.3 Advantages

a) Better Academic Results: Recent research conducted by SRI International found a 30% rise in the math test scores of students who used Khan Academy with blended learning compared with other traditional learning methods (Murphy et al., 2014).
b) Personalization: The adaptive learning software personalises learning content for the individual student and allows advanced students to move more rapidly while assisting struggling students through additional support.
c) Teacher Support: This platform reduces bureaucratic tasks such as grading and monitoring, which has been reported to free up their time to conduct teaching and mentorship.
d) Student Engagement: Components such as badges and progress tracks motivate students to engage with active participation in the learning process

8.2.4 Challenges

a) Digital Fatigue: Prolonged screen time can lead to fatigue, necessitating a balance between online and offline activities.

b) Training Needs: Teachers require professional development to effectively integrate Khan Academy into their instruction and maximise its potential.
c) Access Gaps: Although Khan Academy is free, differences in connectivity and access to devices are likely to hinder implementation equitability, more so in less powerful schools.

8.2.5 Outcomes:

Indeed, Khan Academy is an excellent propeller for blended learning. Schools that incorporate the platform record increased student interest, academic attainment, and ability to think. For instance, in the California-based Los Altos School District where this Khan Academy is being piloted, students gained mathematics knowledge, especially those needing more time on task, and performed at an accelerated rate (Darrow, 2012).

8.2.6 Lessons Learned

This is why Khan Academy's success in U.S. schools points to the importance of combining personalised digital resources with meaningful human interaction. Technology, though scalable for individualised learning, still needs teacher involvement to create collaboration, meet emotional needs, and develop students holistically.

8.3 Singapore's "Home-Based Learning" during COVID-19

8.3.1 Overview

To help ensure seamless learning during the COVID-19 pandemic, the Singapore Ministry of Education designed an initiative that went by the name "Home-Based Learning". HBL followed a blended mode, with time being devoted both to synchronous and asynchronous online teaching in addition to face-to-face contact as practicable. Highly digitised infrastructures were the hallmark of Singapore, yet so also was their educational equity imperative; thus, HBL became effective in balancing a period of pandemic lockdown with optimal time on-screen against human interplay (MOE Singapore, 2021).

8.3.2 Implementation

a) Student Learning Space (SLS): The central learning and assignment hub in the national online education platform of Singapore, the SLS provides the students with easy access to hundreds of curriculum-aligned multimedia resources, quizzes, and discussion forums. Such features ensured interactive and engaging learning. Synchronous sessions were done using Zoom or Microsoft Teams, which allowed real-time engagement of the students. To develop active participation during these sessions along with instant feedforward, guaranteeing the maintenance of high qualities of teacher/student interaction even outside the physical boundary, the program used the opportunity to incorporate both technology and dynamism to keep a balance between digital contents and the necessary teacher-student interaction (Chia & Tan, 2020; Korkmaz & Aydın, 2020).

b) Asynchronous Learning Activities: Teachers prepare homework and projects that promote self-directed learning. These offscreen activities were essential, such as doing their experiments at home, reading assignments, and journaling, to reduce screen time while at the same time promoting holistic learning. The tasks helped the students take an ownership role in learning outside of class and entrenched the findings into a holistic approach, balancing practical experiences with academic study. This not only promoted the academic development of the student but also provided skills in self-instruction that are imperative to lifelong success in education (Zimmerman, 2002; Schunk, 2012).

c) Parent Involvement and Support: Parents were empowered to enable well-learned and engaged children at home. Support was rendered to parents through updates and resources. This would then enable them to keep abreast and be involved in this process. To the younger ones, parents took a proactive role and guided them on technology so as to ensure the proper application thereof in their learning activities. Such collaboration between the parents and the teachers provided a supportive, engaging learning atmosphere for the student, with mutual emphasis on personal growth as much as academic gains (Epstein, 2011; Jeynes, 2012).

d) Equity Measures: It addressed the issue of the digital divide by providing needy students with laptops, tablets, and internet connectivity. On the part of the schools, they supported the initiative by making their consultative hours rotate on campus so that those students who may need more support or lack the resources to do so at home will get support from teachers in person. This was to ensure that all students were given equal opportunities for success and had access to resources necessary for growth in the classroom, thereby promoting an inclusive learning environment (Digital Inclusion Coalition, 2020; Warschauer, 2003).

8.3.3 Benefits

a) Learning Continuity: The HBL model ensured learning was not largely disrupted, as pupils could continue in school even when schools were shut down.
b) Learning Flexibility: Combining synchronous and asynchronous approaches guaranteed that students mastered the subject at their own pace yet were simultaneously enjoying live, direct interpersonal relationships with the teachers.
c) Acquisition of Skills: In HBL, learners learn 21st-century skills like digital literacy, time management, and self-learning (OECD, 2021b).
d) Balanced Access: Through proactive policies, the government has enabled all students of any economic class to access HBL effectively.

8.3.4 Challenges

a) Digital Fatigue: Long hours on the screen were tiring; hence, it was essential to plan online and offline activities very carefully.
b) Parental Load: Balancing employment and childcare activities prove a challenge to many home-working parents because children require so much learning.
c) Teacher Adaptation: Teachers had to adapt to a variety of digital tools and sometimes pedagogy, which required much more time in training and preparation.
d) Emotional Wellness: Less face-to-face interaction in the classroom ensures that the learner loses touch. Thus, creating and maintaining a virtual sense of belonging and connection among students must also be considered an issue for discussion.

8.3.5 Outcome

a) Academic Performance: The academic performance of students in Singapore remained relatively higher in HBL. Teachers effectively utilised SLS real-time data to support students.
b) Digital Integration: COVID influenced the acceleration of digital integration with education, with many HBL practices becoming a permanent feature of the Singaporean educational system.
c) Resilience: HBL was totally successful as it showed the strength of Singapore's education system, which has technological prowess that could complement human interaction in times of crisis.

8.3.6 Lessons Learnt

Singapore is another example of how a successful HBL initiative takes place. With strong digital infrastructure, equity measures, and thoughtfully designed pedagogy being important for Singapore's blended learning, the overall success of these measures was mainly ensured by technological support in effortless transitions to distance learning, supplemented by live interactions, personalised feedback, and even parental involvement so that the process of education has a balanced, holistic approach.

8.4 Harvard Business School's HBX Program

8.4.1 Overview

Harvard Business School (HBS) introduced HBX (now Harvard Business School Online) in 2014 with the aim of delivering quality business education to learners worldwide using an innovative blended learning approach. The program combines interactive digital content, case study learning, and real-time collaboration to provide an interactive learning experience. HBX differs from conventional online courses as it focuses on active engagement, peer-to-peer interaction, and practical application of business principles (Christensen et al., 2019).

8.4.2 Implementation

HBX program had the following essential building blocks to interleave screen time and human interactions:

a) HBX Live – HBX Live is Harvard Business School-developed virtual classroom that mimics an interactive lecture hall experience based on high-definition video conferencing.It offers a state-of-the-art studio with a large video wall, where 60 remote users can join live debate with faculty (Porter, 2019). With respect to traditional online learning, HBX Live promotes engagement through face-to-face interaction and Socratic questioning, enhancing engagement and retention (Christensen et al., 2019). By removing location-related limitations, it provides high-quality, scalable learning to global professionals (Kim, 2018).
b) Case-Based Learning – Case-Based Learning in HBX (previous Harvard Business School Online) presents business theory through actual case studies, with the combination of video content, interactive learning, and discussion forums (Kim, 2018).It facilitates decision-making and critical thinking by forcing students to navigate actual business problems, stimulating interest and application of

theory to practice (Christensen et al., 2019). It leverages the use of multimedia with peer-to-peer conversation, enhancing active learning, reinforcing concept clarification, and readying professionals for actual decisions (Porter, 2019).

c) Peer Collaboration in HBX: Peer collaboration is one of the distinguishing aspects of HBX (currently Harvard Business School Online), where students collaborate in virtual teams, discuss, and work on group assignments to promote networking and social learning.This interactive framework mimics the collaborative nature of a typical classroom, with students sharing ideas, debating views, and refining their knowledge of business concepts through peer-to-peer discussion (Kim, 2018). Through discussion forums, live video lectures, and structured group projects, HBX ensures students do not consume course material passively (Porter, 2019). This model not only improves problem-solving and critical thinking but also develops professional networks among international participants, affirming the importance of collaboration in business decision-making (Christensen et al., 2019).
d) Enhancing Engagement Beyond the Online Platform: HBX (currently Harvard Business School Online) combines live webinars and networking sessions to reach beyond its online platform. Faculty-led sessions allow for real-time interactive engagement, allowing students to ask questions, debate case studies, and gain deeper insights into business principles (Kim, 2018). Besides, face-to-face networking socials afford chances for students to interact with peers, business practitioners, and educators, creating professional connections and peer learning (Porter, 2019). Such elements ensure that learners are active learners and not mere receivers of knowledge, mitigating digital fatigue and enhanced knowledge retention (Christensen et al., 2019).

8.4.3 Benefits

The HBX program yielded many significant benefits:

a) Increased Completion and Participation Levels – HBX students achieved approximately 85% completion levels, in contrast to approximately 10–15% completion levels for conventional MOOCs (Baldwin, 2020).
b) Improved Learning Outcomes – The learners displayed improved problem-solving, critical thinking, and application of business concepts. Harvard Business School Online conducted a survey of graduates, and the survey showed 94% of the graduates felt more prepared for careers upon graduation (Kim, 2018).
c) Flexible and Scalable Learning – The program offered first-class education to working professionals all over the world, enabling them to learn at their convenience without necessarily relocating.

d) Extended Peer Networks – Video conferencing and online interactions made it simpler to collaborate, with the students having the opportunity to build international professional networks.sional connections.

8.4.4 Challenges

In spite of its success, HBX encountered some challenges:

a) Digital Fatigue – Although the program promoted active participation, extended screen time and high interactive discussions resulted in mental fatigue for some students.
b) Cost Barrier – The high-end pricing of HBX courses rendered it less accessible than other online learning platforms (Porter, 2019).
c) Time Commitment – The rigors of coursework required enormous time commitment, and it became difficult for professionals to study and conduct professional work simultaneously.

8.4.5 Outcomes

a) The HBX model was successful in demonstrating that blended learning could be leveraged to enhance knowledge retention, interest, and application of business concepts in real-life situations.
b) The high rates of success of the program and positive student reaction validated the efficacy of a blended model that combines digital learning with live engagement.
c) HBX has influenced the design of online executive education globally, inspiring business schools and corporate training facilities to adopt similar trends.

8.4.6 Lessons Learned

The HBX experience teaches several important lessons in online learning. Interactivity is more engaging, as the inclusion of real-time discussions, collaborative exercises, and peer feedback actively engages learners instead of having them passively consume information. Blended learning models are also more effective than fully digital ones, with case-based instruction, virtual collaboration, and live faculty interactions resulting in better learning outcomes. The program also highlights personalization and adaptability, as providing a combination of synchronous and asynchronous learning opportunities allows learners to make their education fit their own calendars, enhancing accessibility. Finally, screen fatigue is important, and future versions of HBX and comparable programs should consider ways to mitigate cognitive overload, such as shorter video classes and the inclusion of more offline activities to help keep students well and engaged.

9. IMPLEMENTATION CHALLENGES

The adoption of blended learning poses a number of challenges, such as technological infrastructure, teacher readiness, student motivation, and digital equity. One of the biggest challenges is the provision of stable internet connectivity and sufficient digital devices, especially in disadvantaged areas, which can lead to inequalities in learning opportunities (Selwyn, 2020). Besides, most teachers are confronted with difficulties in implementing blended learning models because they lack adequate training in instructional technology and digital pedagogy (Redmond, 2019). Studies show that teachers struggle to balance online and offline teaching approaches while ensuring student motivation and engagement (Graham, 2019). The increased screen time involved with blended learning may also lead to cognitive overload and digital fatigue on the well-being of learners and educators (Sheppard & Wolffsohn, 2018). The solution to these drawbacks, however, requires universities to invest in staff development, provide technical support, and implement policies that guarantee digital accessibility and balanced learning strategies. In the absence of such provisions, the effectiveness of blended learning can be compromised, and its potential benefits to teachers and students can be limited.

10. RECOMMENDATIONS FOR EDUCATORS AND STAKEHOLDERS

Educators and stakeholders should strategically find the balancing act in a blended learning environment between the times spent with a screen and times spent interacting face-to-face so that the student has practical well-being, is highly engaged, and learns appropriately. The following recommendations may be considered as a guideline in the balance of the two:

a) Structured Screen Time Guidelines: Educators should establish guidelines on the right amount of screen time per day, which corresponds to research findings on cognitive load and screen fatigue (Gazzaley & Rosen, 2016). To not drown the student in the midst of technological noise, one would need to maintain an appropriate balance of digital content delivery with face-to-face, interactive sessions. In the short run, some techniques, such as controlling passive screen time used merely to consume lectures rather than experiences, can help combat cognitive overload.

b) Better Teacher Training and Support: Teachers must be professionally trained in the usage of technology in the classroom for enhanced efficiency, according to Ertmer & Ottenbreit-Leftwich (2010). The teacher needs to be able to design blended learning activities that involve learners in both digital and human interactivity. There is a need for frequent training for teachers in the LMS, digital tools, and pedagogies of the blended classroom setting in order for teachers to take full advantage of technology in the classroom setting.

c) Bridging the Digital Divide: Stakeholders need to invest in equitable access to technology so that all students can participate fully in blended learning experiences (Warschauer, 2003). This means equipping disadvantaged students with devices, internet access, and digital literacy training. Schools and governments must collaborate in formulating policies that foster digital inclusion so that learners from all walks of life can be treated equitably in the pursuit of learning.

d) Adequate social interaction and peer collaboration; blended learning must allow students the possibility of meeting other peers as well as lecturers face to face or online (Schunk, Pintrich, & Meece, 2008). Instructors should help create socially practical collaborative activities, group discussions, and peer feedback that support a social learning environment that eliminates the tendency to lock oneself inside from screen-based learning. This would balance the online learning process with meaningful interpersonal interaction, thereby influencing the motivation of students and the sense of community.

e) Personalized Learning Path: As stipulated by Koller, Harvey, and Magnotta (2013), a suggested use of blended learning's flexibility is in offering personalised learning experiences to address the learners' varied needs and preferences. This may include giving students options in terms of the type of content used (videos, articles, interactive simulations) or modifying the instruction to reflect student progress. Personalised learning is more effective and takes ownership of educational responsibility.

f) Encourage the Implementation of Formative Assessment Continuous monitoring of student progress through formative assessment should be conducted to enable feedback that can be used both by students and teachers (Darling-Hammond & Adamson, 2014). Real-time digital assessments, along with tailored personal feedback, will be used to ensure that learning objectives are met and teaching strategies improved to achieve better outcomes.

g) Healthy balance between technology and human interaction. Last but not least, the stakeholders should propagate a philosophy of balance whereby technology complements and does not substitute human interactions. This includes realising that face-to-face engagement helps one build relationships, emotional support, and critical thinking skills (Selwyn, 2016). Institutions should promote blended learning designs that carefully blend digital and in-person components in such a way that technology acts as an auxiliary to the human factor in education.

Adapting these strategies will help educators and stakeholders make better use of their budgets in designing blended learning environments that reap the benefits of technology while maintaining human interaction as essential, thereby improving the experiences and outcomes of all students.

11. FUTURE DIRECTIONS IN BLENDED LEARNING

Advancements in digital tools, pedagogical innovation, and the increasing integration of artificial intelligence will determine the future of blended learning. Some of the most important directions include adaptive learning technologies, which adjust content and assessments based on real-time performance to tailor educational experiences to individual learners (Huang et al., 2019). This has the potential to increase engagement and, thus, better learning outcomes as it meets the needs of each student. Moreover, AI and machine learning will be helpful to educators in managing blended learning environments because they will automatically deal with some of the administrative work, present data-driven insights into the performances of students, and provide immediate feedback to educators (Zawacki-Richter et al., 2019). For example, it will identify students at risk, who would then require special attention. In return, this would give teachers an opportunity for more profound learning and human contact.

Another promising trend includes virtual and augmented reality in the blended learning environment. These are immersive technologies that allow a student to get thoroughly engaged with the material in an incredibly interactive and experiential way. For example, VR can build simulated environments: medical students might practice procedures, history students navigate ancient civilisations, and so much more, and make it all more engaging and practical.l (Bailenson et al., 2021). Blended platforms that interconnect students of different backgrounds are going to further provide collaborative and cross-cultural learning opportunities within the more global educational landscape. Students will also be exposed to different perspectives when using digital tools for collaboration. This is what will make the learning experience so much more interactive and prepare the students for the more interconnected world (Sung et al., 2020). Despite these innovations, there is still a strong emphasis on digital equity in any future where blended learning is needed. Without adequate tools and resources, no student will be able to succeed. Tackling the problem of the digital divide would be critical in blending equal opportunities with technology that improves education for all students, regardless of socio-economic background (Warschauer, 2003).

In the near future, the blended learning environment will be significantly characterised by increased personalisation, innovative uses of AI and immersive technologies, and greater attention to inclusivity and collaboration. If these changes can be combined with human interaction, then blending can become an even more effective, engaging, and equitable form of learning.

12. CONCLUSION: TOWARD A BALANCED EDUCATIONAL ECOSYSTEM

Finally, in summary, the future of blended learning lies in that fragile balance of the potential of transformation that may be brought forth through technology with irreplaceable human interaction. Evolving Educational Environments Blending uses of digital and face-to-face interaction to evoke more dynamic, inclusive, personalised learning experiences, careful implementation, and continuity in teacher support and access to the technologies form a key route for this success. The adaptation technologies, AI, and immersive learning experiences promise to make educational outcomes more favourable. Important in all these innovations is that they complement the already critical role played by human interaction in fostering motivation, social learning, and emotional well-being. Going forward, educational stakeholders will make sure that, in designing blended learning models, there will be collaboration, adaptability, and mindfulness of the different needs of all learners so that technology does not appear as a barrier but as an empowerment tool. All will ultimately be focused on the construction of an educational environment that values and celebrates both technology efficiency and the availability of means for human association in profound, meaningful connection, thus the foundation upon which effective learning happens.

REFERENCES

An, H. (2015). Digital inclusion: Bridging the digital divide in education. *Journal of Educational Technology*, *19*(3), 253–270.

Anderson, L. W., & Krathwohl, D. R. (2001). *A taxonomy for learning, teaching, and assessing: A revision of Bloom's taxonomy of educational objectives*. Longman.

Anderson, T., & Dron, J. (2011). Three generations of distance education pedagogy. *International Review of Research in Open and Distance Learning*, *12*(3), 80–97. DOI: 10.19173/irrodl.v12i3.890

Bailenson, J. N., Beall, A. C., Blascovich, J., & Loomis, J. M. (2021). Immersive virtual reality and education. In *Handbook of Research on Educational Communications and Technology* (pp. 1–17). Springer.

Baker, J. D. (2004). The role of face-to-face interaction in distance education. *International Journal of Instructional Technology and Distance Learning*, *1*(5), 3–10.

Baldwin, R. (2020). HBX and the future of online business education. *Harvard Business Review*, *98*(4), 56–64.

Bergmann, J., & Sams, A. (2012). *Flip your classroom: Reach every student in every class every day*. International Society for Technology in Education.

Bhagat, K. K., Chang, C. K., & Chang, C. Y. (2016). A review of research on the impact of Khan Academy on student learning. *Journal of Educational Technology & Society*, *19*(3), 89–99.

Bonk, C. J., & Graham, C. R. (Eds.). (2012). *The Handbook of Blended Learning: Global Perspectives, Local Designs*. Pfeiffer.

Bonwell, C. C., & Eison, J. A. (1991). *Active learning: Creating excitement in the classroom*. ERIC Clearinghouse on Higher Education.

Carr, N. (2011). *The Shallows: What the Internet Is Doing to Our Brains*. W.W. Norton & Company.

CASEL (Collaborative for Academic, Social, and Emotional Learning). (2020). *CASEL framework for social and emotional learning*. CASEL.

Chia, L. S., & Tan, L. S. (2020). *Digital learning in Singapore: Innovations and challenges*. Springer.

Christensen, C. M., Raynor, M. E., & McDonald, R. (2019). *The Innovator's Solution: Creating and Sustaining Successful Growth*. Harvard Business Press.

Clark, R. C., & Mayer, R. E. (2016). *e-Learning and the Science of Instruction: Proven Guidelines for Consumers and Designers of Multimedia Learning* (4th ed.). San Francisco, CA: Wiley.

Cohen, J. J., & Sandy, S. V. (2007). Teacher-student relationships and academic achievement. *Journal of Educational Psychology*, *99*(3), 634–645.

Darling-Hammond, L., & Adamson, F. (2014). Beyond test scores: A broader vision of student success. *American Educator*, *38*(1), 20–29.

Darrow, R. (2012). *Khan Academy pilot program in the Los Altos School District*. EdSurge.

Dewey, J. (1916). *Democracy and Education: An Introduction to the Philosophy of Education*. Macmillan.

Digital Inclusion Coalition. (2020). *Bridging the digital divide: Initiatives for equitable access in education*. United Nations Educational, Scientific and Cultural Organization.

Epstein, J. L. (2011). *School, family, and community partnerships: Preparing educators and improving schools*. Westview Press.

Ertmer, P. A., & Ottenbreit-Leftwich, A. T. (2010). Teacher technology change: How knowledge, confidence, beliefs, and culture intersect. *Journal of Research on Technology in Education*, *42*(3), 255–284. DOI: 10.1080/15391523.2010.10782551

Fitzpatrick, C. (2020). The Role of Adaptive Learning Technologies in Modern Education. *Journal of Educational Technology*, *47*(3), 45–58.

Foley, J., & Lee, L. (2012). *Technology and education: Enhancing learning for all students*. National Education Policy Center.

Garrison, D. R., & Kanuka, H. (2004). Blended learning: Uncovering its transformative potential in higher education. *The Internet and Higher Education*, *7*(2), 95–105. DOI: 10.1016/j.iheduc.2004.02.001

Garrison, D. R., & Vaughan, N. D. (2008). *Blended Learning in Higher Education: Framework, Principles, and Guidelines*. Jossey-Bass.

Gazzaley, A., & Rosen, L. D. (2016). *The distracted mind: Ancient brains in a high-tech world*. MIT Press.

Gee, J. P. (2003). What Video Games Have to Teach Us About Learning and Literacy. [CIE]. *Computers in Entertainment*, *1*(1), 20–20. DOI: 10.1145/950566.950595

Goleman, D. (1995). *Emotional Intelligence: Why It Can Matter More Than IQ*. Bantam Books.

Graham, C. R. (2006a). Blended learning systems: Definition, current trends, and future directions. In Bonk, C. J., & Graham, C. R. (Eds.), *Handbook of blended learning: Global perspectives, local designs* (pp. 3–21). Pfeiffer Publishing.

Graham, C. R. (2006b). Blended learning systems: Definition, current trends, and future directions. In *Handbook of distance education* (pp. 299–320). Routledge.

Graham, C. R. (2019). Current research in blended learning: Critiques and suggestions for the future. *Computers & Education, 140*, 103618.

Greenhow, C., Galvin, S., & Askins, M. (2020). Social media and education: A review of research. *Educational Researcher, 49*(5), 366–378.

Hämäläinen, R., & Vähäsantanen, K. (2011). Learning and motivation in Finnish education: A review of the research. *The Journal of Educational Research, 56*(2), 125–145.

Hattie, J., & Timperley, H. (2007). The power of feedback. *Review of Educational Research, 77*(1), 81–112. DOI: 10.3102/003465430298487

Holappa, A., & Soini, T. (2020). Phenomenon-based learning in Finland: Challenges and possibilities. *Nordic Journal of Studies in Educational Policy, 6*(1), 30–41.

Horn, M. B., & Staker, H. (2014). *Blended: Using disruptive innovation to improve schools*. Jossey-Bass.

Huang, R. H., Spector, J. M., & Yang, J. (2019). *EdTech for blended learning: From theory to practice*. Springer.

Hutchison, A., & Reinking, D. (2011). Teachers' perceptions of technology integration in the literacy classroom. *Reading Research Quarterly, 46*(4), 308–328.

International, S. R. I. (2014). *Blended learning and educational technology: Exploring the impact of Khan Academy*. Retrieved from SRI Reports.

Jeynes, W. H. (2012). A meta-analysis of the relation of parental involvement to urban elementary school student academic achievement. *Educational Psychology Review, 24*(4), 523–544.

Johnson, D. W., & Johnson, R. T. (1994). Cooperative Learning and Prosocial Behavior: An Overview. *The Journal of Social Issues, 50*(2), 81–102.

Johnson, D. W., Johnson, R. T., & Holubec, E. J. (2014). *Cooperation in the classroom* (10th ed.). Pearson.

Johnson, D. W., Johnson, R. T., & Smith, K. A. (1998). Cooperative learning returns to college: What evidence is there that it works? *Change*, *30*(4), 26–35. DOI: 10.1080/00091389809602629

Johnson, L., Adams Becker, S., Estrada, V., & Freeman, A. (2016). *NMC Horizon Report: 2016 Higher Education Edition*. The New Media Consortium.

Kampylis, P., Pata, K., & Laanpere, M. (2015). *Innovative teaching and learning in Europe: Trends and challenges*. European Commission Joint Research Centre.

Kim, J. (2018). Digital learning and engagement: A case study of HBX. *Journal of Online Learning and Teaching*, *14*(3), 45–60.

Klussman, K., Nichols, A. L., & Lofgren, I. E. (2021). Burnout in online teaching: A systematic review. *Educational Psychology Review*, *33*(4), 1507–1526.

Koller, D., Harvey, D., & Magnotta, S. (2013). *Personalised learning: A guide for engaging students with technology*. International Society for Technology in Education.

Korkmaz, H., & Aydın, S. (2020). Online learning in the era of COVID-19: Perspectives from students and teachers. *Education and Information Technologies*, *25*(5), 3457–3470.

LeBlanc, A. G., Janssen, I., Abbott, R. A., Cameron, C., Chino, K., Faulkner, G., & Tremblay, M. S. (2012). Correlates of Physical Activity in Youth: A Review and Update. *Journal of Physical Activity & Health*, *9*(1), 1–14. PMID: 22332250

Lim, M., & Tan, C. (2020). Digital resilience in education: The case of Singapore's HBL model. *Asian Journal of Education and Training*, *6*(2), 97–106.

Maslach, C., & Leiter, M. P. (2016). Understanding the burnout experience: Recent research and its implications for psychiatry. *World Psychiatry; Official Journal of the World Psychiatric Association (WPA)*, *15*(2), 103–111. PMID: 27265691

Mayer, R. E. (2021). *Multimedia Learning* (3rd ed.). Cambridge University Press.

McLaughlin, C., Griffin, S., & Latham, R. (2014). The role of teachers in the integration of Khan Academy in the classroom. *Educational Technology Research and Development*, *62*(6), 1315–1328.

Means, B., Toyama, Y., Murphy, R., Bakia, M., & Jones, K. (2013). *Evaluation of evidence-based practices in online learning: A meta-analysis and review of online learning studies*. U.S. Department of Education.

Ministry of Education Singapore. (2021). *Home-Based Learning: Ensuring Educational Continuity during the COVID-19 Pandemic*. Retrieved from MOE Singapore.

Murphy, R., Gallagher, L., Krumm, A., Mislevy, J., & Hafter, A. (2014). *Research on the use of Khan Academy in schools: Implementation report.* SRI International.

Nistor, N., & Lerche, T. (2020). Student engagement in blended learning environments: The role of collaboration and autonomy. *Educational Technology Research and Development, 68*(6), 3171–3193.

OECD. (2021a). *21st Century Skills and Finland's Education System.* Retrieved from OECD Education Reports.

OECD. (2021b). *Education in the Time of COVID-19: Lessons from Singapore's Home-Based Learning Model.* Retrieved from OECD Education Reports.

Piaget, J. (1952). *The Origins of Intelligence in Children.* International Universities Press. DOI: 10.1037/11494-000

Porter, M. E. (2019). Strategy and innovation in online education: Insights from HBX. *Harvard Business Review, 97*(5), 34–47.

Redmond, P. (2019). A pedagogical continuum: The journey from traditional classroom to blended learning. *Australasian Journal of Educational Technology, 35*(6), 1–14.

Rosen, L. D., Carrier, L. M., & Cheever, N. A. (2013). Facebook and Relational Violence Among College Students. *Journal of Social and Clinical Psychology, 32*(5), 462–479.

Rosen, L. D., Lim, A. F., Carrier, L. M., & Cheever, N. A. (2011). An empirical examination of the educational impact of text message-induced task switching in the classroom. *Computers in Human Behavior, 27*(3), 937–948.

Rosenfield, M. (2016). Computer vision syndrome (a.k.a. digital eye strain). *Optometry in Practice, 17*(1), 1–10.

Saavedra, A. R., & Opfer, V. D. (2012). Learning 21st-Century Skills Requires 21st-Century Teaching. *Phi Delta Kappan, 94*(2), 8–13. DOI: 10.1177/003172171209400203

Sahlberg, P. (2011). The Finnish education system: A success story. In *Finnish lessons: What can the world learn from educational change in Finland?* Teachers College Press.

Salovey, P., & Mayer, J. D. (1990). Emotional intelligence. *Imagination, Cognition and Personality, 9*(3), 185–211. DOI: 10.2190/DUGG-P24E-52WK-6CDG

Schunk, D. H. (2012). *Learning theories: An educational perspective* (6th ed.). Pearson.

Schunk, D. H., Pintrich, P. R., & Meece, J. L. (2008). Motivation and learning. In *Motivation and learning: Theory and research* (pp. 212–248). Pearson.

Selwyn, N. (2016). *Education and technology: Key issues and debates*. Bloomsbury Publishing.

Selwyn, N. (2020). Digital division: Equity and access in higher education. *British Journal of Educational Technology*, *51*(2), 589–604.

Sheninger, E. (2014). *Digital leadership: Changing paradigms for changing times*. Corwin Press.

Sheppard, A. L., & Wolffsohn, J. S. (2018). Digital eye strain: Prevalence, measurement, and amelioration. *BMJ Open Ophthalmology*, *3*(1), e000146. DOI: 10.1136/bmjophth-2018-000146 PMID: 29963645

Staker, H., & Horn, M. B. (2012). *Classifying K–12 blended learning*. In *Innosight Institute*.

Sung, Y. T., Chang, K. E., & Yang, J. M. (2020). How can collaborative learning be enhanced in digital environments? *Educational Technology Research and Development*, *68*(2), 147–162.

Tan, C. (2021). The impact of COVID-19 on education in Singapore: A blended learning perspective. *International Review of Education*, *67*(3), 443–462.

Tucker, B. (2012). The flipped classroom: Online instruction at home frees class time for learning. *Education Next*, *12*(1).

Twenge, J. M. (2018). *iGen: Why Today's Super-Connected Kids Are Growing Up Less Rebellious, More Tolerant, Less Happy—and Completely Unprepared for Adulthood*. New York, NY: Atria Books.

U.S. Department of Education. (2020). *Technology in Education: Enhancing Learning Outcomes with Digital Tools.*

Van Deursen, A. J. A. M., & Van Dijk, J. A. G. M. (2014). Internet Skills and the Digital Divide. *New Media & Society*, *16*(3), 404–422.

van Dijk, J. A. G. M. (2020). *The digital divide*. Polity Press.

Voogt, J., Fisser, P., Pareja Roblin, N., Tondeur, J., & van Braak, J. (2017). Technological pedagogical content knowledge–A review of the literature. *Computers & Education, 59*(3), 0-204.

Vuorikari, R., Punie, Y., Carretero, S., & Van den Brande, G. (2019). *DigCompEdu: The Digital Competence Framework for Educators*. Publications Office of the European Union.

Vygotsky, L. S. (1978). *Mind in Society: The Development of Higher Psychological Processes*. Harvard University Press.

Wang, Z., Boulton, M., & Zhang, D. (2020). Impact of digital media on learning and cognitive development. *Educational Technology Research and Development, 68*(3), 931–948.

Warschauer, M. (2003). *Technology and social inclusion: Rethinking the digital divide*. MIT Press. DOI: 10.7551/mitpress/6699.001.0001

Wiggins, G., & McTighe, J. (2005). *Understanding by design*. ASCD.

Zawacki-Richter, O., Marín, V. I., & Bond, M. (2019). Systematic review of research on blended learning in higher education. *International Journal of Educational Technology in Higher Education, 16*(1), 8.

Zimmerman, B. J. (2002). Becoming a self-regulated learner: An overview. *Theory into Practice, 41*(2), 64–70. DOI: 10.1207/s15430421tip4102_2

Chapter 7
ChatGPT:
The End of Critical Thinking as We Know It

Lindall Adams
https://orcid.org/0000-0003-1948-2778
University of South Africa, South Africa

Ibrahim Alzaabi
University of Cordoba, Spain

ABSTRACT

This study explores the impact of ChatGPT on critical thinking within educational contexts, addressing concerns about overreliance on AI-generated solutions. A systematic review of 24 studies was conducted to evaluate ChatGPT's influence on different cognitive levels as defined by Bloom's Taxonomy, its potential benefits and drawbacks, and the risks associated with reliance on AI. The findings reveal that ChatGPT can enhance cognitive skills from basic knowledge acquisition to higher-order thinking, such as analysis and evaluation. However, overreliance on AI may hinder the development of independent critical thinking and problem-solving skills. The study emphasizes the need for responsible usage guidelines and active educator involvement to ensure that AI tools augment rather than replace cognitive efforts. The study concludes that while ChatGPT holds promise for enhancing cognitive skills, its integration must be carefully managed to avoid undermining critical thinking development.

DOI: 10.4018/979-8-3373-0771-8.ch007

INTRODUCTION

Concerns have been raised about the potential over-reliance on AI-generated solutions in educational settings, particularly with the integration of generative AI technologies such as ChatGPT (Suriano et al., 2025). Excessive dependence on these tools may hinder students' ability to develop critical thinking skills (Herrmann-Werner et al., 2024). Bloom's Taxonomy, commonly used as a framework for setting educational goals, exacerbates this issue as it does not fully address the cognitive demands of AI-assisted learning (Putra et al., 2023). As AI continues to transform education, it is essential to assess its impact on learning processes. While ChatGPT can enhance engagement and facilitate critical thinking skill development, its integration into educational environments must be carefully managed to prevent diminishing students' capacity for independent thought.

The influence of AI on human interactions with technology is expanding, affecting multiple industries and reshaping daily activities. AI-driven technologies, including virtual assistants like Siri and Alexa, as well as sophisticated chatbots such as ChatGPT, have significantly improved efficiency, convenience, and personalization (Rivas, 2024; Lau, 2019). ChatGPT, developed by OpenAI and introduced on November 30, 2022 (OpenAI, 2022), stands out for its ability to generate text that closely resembles human writing, making it relevant in educational environments (Mai et al., 2024) and creative writing contexts (Malik et al., 2024). Despite its growing significance, ongoing discussions continue to explore its effects on cognitive processes, particularly critical thinking (Alarcón-López et al., 2024).

This study emphasizes cognitive offloading, in which users delegate cognitive tasks to artificial intelligence rather than actively engaging with complex concepts. Concerns persist that using ChatGPT in discussions could lead to reduced cognitive effort and engagement with critical analysis (Dans, 2023; El-Seoud et al., 2023). Bloom's Taxonomy serves as a useful theoretical framework for evaluating ChatGPT's influence on different levels of cognitive processing. It classifies cognitive skills into six sequential levels: remembering, understanding, applying, analyzing, evaluating, and creating (Bloom et al., 1956). This classification facilitates a systematic analysis of whether ChatGPT enhances cognitive development or inadvertently fosters intellectual complacency.

Expanding on this framework, the current study examines how ChatGPT either promotes or hinders the development of critical thinking skills. According to Essien et al. (2024), strong evidence suggests that ChatGPT improves lower-order cognitive skills such as understanding and remembering. Its ability to retrieve information and summarize content aids students in building foundational knowledge. However, further analysis is needed to explore the broader consequences of integrating AI into education. Existing research indicates that ChatGPT accelerates learning (Chinonso et al., 2023), but its impact on advanced cognitive skills such as analysis, evaluation, and creation requires deeper investigation. Over-reliance on AI-generated content without critical examination could undermine students' ability to evaluate information, construct arguments, and generate original ideas independently.

Studies suggest that ChatGPT's natural language processing capabilities have shifted static hierarchical learning models into more dynamic and interactive ones (Eltobgy et al., 2024). Research by Suriano et al. (2025) provides evidence that ChatGPT enhances student engagement and promotes critical thinking through interactive learning experiences. Additionally, Harahap (2024) emphasizes that AI-driven analysis and paraphrasing methods contribute to the development of critical thinking skills. These findings support the notion that AI can function as an effective educational tool when implemented correctly. However, a comprehensive understanding of ChatGPT's impact remains crucial. While it offers significant support, it does not inherently foster the independent reasoning necessary for deep cognitive engagement (Guo & Lee, 2023).

AI tools such as ChatGPT in educational settings present both benefits and challenges. Current research highlights that generative AI can enhance basic cognitive skills, aligning with Bloom's framework. Nonetheless, it underscores the importance of instructional strategies that discourage excessive reliance on AI-generated solutions. Developing higher-order thinking skills, particularly analysis, evaluation, and creation—requires intentional, guided instructional approaches. This study emphasizes the need for a balanced approach to AI-assisted learning, ensuring that ChatGPT serves as a supportive tool rather than a substitute for critical thinking development.

Research Scope and Objectives

This study performs a systematic review to evaluate the validity of ChatGPT as a tool for critical thinking. This study synthesizes existing research to examine the advantages and limitations of AI in enhancing critical thinking skills. The following research questions drive this study:

1. How does the use of ChatGPT influence different cognitive levels as defined by Bloom's Taxonomy, from basic knowledge acquisition to higher-order thinking skills such as analysis and evaluation?
2. What are the potential benefits and drawbacks of utilizing ChatGPT as a tool for critical thinking within educational contexts?
3. What risks does reliance on ChatGPT pose to the development and maintenance of critical thinking skills, and under what conditions could its use be considered justifiable?

This study aims to provide an objective analysis of the role of artificial intelligence in critical thinking development by examining the associated challenges. While artificial intelligence (AI) provides advantages in efficiency and accessibility, it is essential to assess its impact on critical thinking, whether it enhances or undermines this cognitive process. The aim is to assess the effective integration of artificial intelligence in educational environments while enhancing students' critical thinking abilities.

LITERATURE REVIEW

Critical thinking is a key skill that helps people assess information, evaluate claims, and draw logical conclusions. It plays a crucial role in cognitive development and problem-solving, particularly in education (Turan & Fitan, 2019; Yaldiz & Bailey, 2019). However, many students struggle to develop strong critical thinking skills, often relying on cognitive shortcuts or facing challenges such as lack of engagement, emotional biases, and external pressures (Aston, 2023; Dwyer, 2023). The rise of artificial intelligence, especially large language models (LLMs) like ChatGPT, has added another layer of complexity. While AI provides quick and accessible information, it also raises concerns about cognitive offloading—where people rely on external tools instead of actively engaging in the learning process (Marr, 2023; Stadler et al., 2024). Research suggests that AI-generated responses, although easy to understand, may not encourage the same level of critical thinking as traditional research methods (Stadler et al., 2024). This literature review explores the current state of students' critical thinking, the factors contributing to its decline, and the role of AI in shaping cognitive processes. By examining recent studies, this review highlights the challenges and implications of fostering critical thinking in a rapidly evolving digital world.

There is growing concern that excessive reliance on AI-generated solutions in education could weaken students' ability to think critically. Generative AI tools like ChatGPT make information more accessible, but overdependence on them may hinder intellectual growth. Bloom's Taxonomy, a widely used framework for educational objectives, does not fully address the cognitive demands of AI-assisted learning. As AI continues to reshape education, it is essential to evaluate its impact carefully. While ChatGPT can enhance engagement and support cognitive skill development, its use in classrooms must be managed carefully to ensure students develop independent critical thinking skills.

The increasing presence of AI in daily life is transforming multiple industries and changing how people interact with technology. From virtual assistants like Siri and Alexa to advanced chatbots such as ChatGPT, AI has improved efficiency, convenience, and personalization (Rivas, 2024; Lau, 2019). ChatGPT, developed by OpenAI and launched on November 30, 2022 (OpenAI, 2022), is particularly relevant in education (Mai et al., 2024) and creative writing (Malik et al., 2024) due to its ability to produce human-like text. However, its impact on cognitive processes—especially critical thinking—remains a topic of debate (Alarcón-López et al., 2024).

One major concern is cognitive offloading, where people delegate mental tasks to AI rather than engaging deeply with complex ideas. Some researchers argue that using ChatGPT in discussions can reduce cognitive effort and critical analysis (Dans, 2023; El-Seoud et al., 2023). Bloom's Taxonomy provides a useful framework for assessing how AI affects different levels of thinking. It categorizes cognitive skills into six levels: remembering, understanding, applying, analyzing, evaluating, and creating (Bloom et al., 1956). This framework helps determine whether ChatGPT enhances cognitive abilities or unintentionally encourages passive learning.

This study examines whether ChatGPT supports or weakens critical thinking development. Essien et al. (2024) suggest that ChatGPT is useful for lower-order cognitive skills such as comprehension and recall. Its ability to summarize and extract information can help students build foundational knowledge. However, this review goes further by exploring the broader implications of AI integration in education. While studies indicate that ChatGPT improves learning efficiency, its effect on higher-order thinking skills—such as analysis, evaluation, and creativity—needs further investigation. If students rely on AI-generated content without critically engaging with it, their ability to assess information, construct arguments, and generate original ideas may decline.

Research shows that ChatGPT's natural language processing capabilities are reshaping traditional learning models into more interactive experiences (Eltobgy et al., 2024). Suriano et al. (2025) found that ChatGPT increases student engagement and supports critical thinking through interactive learning. Similarly, Harahap (2024) argues that AI-driven analysis and paraphrasing tools can strengthen critical thinking skills. These findings suggest that AI can be a valuable educational tool when used effectively. However, understanding its limitations is essential. While AI offers substantial benefits, it does not inherently foster the deep reasoning needed for advanced cognitive engagement.

Integrating AI tools like ChatGPT into education presents both opportunities and challenges. Recent research suggests that generative AI can support foundational cognitive skills, but it also underscores the need for teaching strategies that prevent overreliance. To cultivate higher-order thinking—such as analysis, evaluation, and innovation—structured teaching methods are essential. Without clear guidelines and proper implementation, AI use in education could unintentionally encourage passive learning, undermining the goal of developing critical thinking skills. A balanced approach is necessary, where AI serves as a supplementary tool rather than a replacement for deep cognitive engagement.

Critical Thinking

Critical thinking is an important skill that individuals need to make informed decisions. However, it is not a skill that develops naturally. It plays a crucial role in cognitive development and problem-solving, particularly in education (Turan & Fitan, 2019; Yaldiz & Bailey, 2019). However, many students struggle to develop strong critical thinking skills, often relying on cognitive shortcuts or facing challenges such as lack of engagement, emotional biases, and external pressures (Aston, 2023; Dwyer, 2023). The rise of artificial intelligence, especially large language models (LLMs) like ChatGPT, has added another layer of complexity. While AI provides quick and accessible information, it also raises concerns about cognitive offloading—where people rely on external tools instead of actively engaging in the learning process (Marr, 2023; Stadler et al., 2024). Research suggests that AI-generated responses, although easy to understand, may not encourage the same level of critical thinking as traditional research methods (Stadler et al., 2024). This literature review explores the current state of students' critical thinking, the factors contributing to its decline, and the role of AI in shaping cognitive processes. By examining recent studies, this review highlights the challenges and implications of fostering critical thinking in a rapidly evolving digital world. There is growing concern that excessive reliance on AI-generated solutions in education could weaken students' ability to think critically. Generative AI tools like ChatGPT make information more accessible, but overdependence on them may hinder intellectual growth. Bloom's Taxonomy, a widely used framework for educational objectives, does not fully address the cognitive demands of AI-assisted learning. As AI continues to reshape education, it is essential to evaluate its impact carefully. While ChatGPT can enhance engagement and support cognitive skill development, its use in classrooms must be managed carefully to ensure students develop independent critical thinking skills. The increasing presence of AI in daily life is transforming multiple industries and changing how people interact with technology. From virtual assistants like Siri and Alexa to advanced chatbots such as ChatGPT, AI has improved efficiency, convenience, and personalization (Rivas, 2024; Lau, 2019). ChatGPT, developed by OpenAI and launched on November 30, 2022 (OpenAI, 2022), is particularly relevant in education (Mai et al., 2024) and creative writing (Malik et al., 2024) due to its ability to produce human-like text. However, its impact on cognitive processes—especially critical thinking—remains a topic of debate (Alarcón-López et al., 2024). One major concern is cognitive overloading, where tasks are delegated to AI rather than engaging in complex ideas (Wahn et al., 2023). Some researchers argue that using ChatGPT in discussions can reduce cognitive effort and critical analysis (Dans, 2023; El-Seoud et al., 2023). This study uses Bloom's Taxonomy since it provides a useful framework for assessing how AI affects different levels of thinking. Critical thinking is ranked into six levels such as remembering, understanding applying, analyzing, evaluating, and creating (Bloom et al., 1956). This framework helps determine whether ChatGPT enhances cognitive abilities or unintentionally encourages passive learning. This study examines whether ChatGPT supports or weakens critical thinking development. Essien et al. (2024) suggest that ChatGPT is useful for lower-order cognitive skills such as comprehension and recall. Its ability to summarize and extract information can help students build foundational knowledge. However, this review goes further by exploring the broader implications of AI integration in education. While studies indicate that ChatGPT improves learning efficiency, its effect on higher-order thinking skills—such as analysis, evaluation, and creativity—needs further investigation. If students rely on AI-generated content without critically engaging with it, their ability to assess information, construct arguments, and generate original ideas may decline. Research shows that ChatGPT's natural language processing capabilities are reshaping traditional learning models into more interactive experiences (Eltobgy et al., 2024). Suriano et al. (2025) found that ChatGPT increases student engagement and supports critical thinking through interactive learning. Similarly, Harahap (2024) argues that AI-driven analysis and paraphrasing tools can strengthen critical thinking skills. The authors found that AI can serve as a highly advantageous instructional instrument when utilized appropriately. Nevertheless, understanding the limitations it poses is crucial. While AI offers substantial benefits, it does not inherently foster the deep reasoning needed for advanced cognitive engagement (Kasneci et al., 2023; Stadler et al., 2024). Integrating AI tools like ChatGPT into education presents both opportunities and challenges. To cultivate higher-order thinking—such as analysis, evaluation, and innovation—structured teaching methods are essential. Nonetheless, the lack of clear guidelines and proper implementation strategies, AI use in education could unintentionally encourage passive learning, undermining the goal of developing critical thinking skills. A balanced approach is necessary, where AI serves as a supplementary tool rather than a replacement for deep cognitive engagement.

Decline of Student Critical Thinking

Critical thinking has long been recognized as a fundamental goal of education (Raj et al., 2022). A critical thinker is someone who can apply knowledge to solve problems, evaluate credible information sources, and draw logical conclusions based on their understanding. However, fostering critical thinking skills in students is challenging. Golden (2023) highlights the difficulties educators face in promoting these skills, while Aouaf et al. (2023) emphasize that critical thinking development is influenced by multiple factors. These include traditional lecture formats, students' prior knowledge, language proficiency, reliance on teachers, learning strategies, motivation, teacher feedback, the gap between theory and practice, the education system, and the use of written reports.

In addition to these challenges, the growing dependence on AI chat systems is negatively affecting students' cognitive abilities (Zhai et al., 2024). While AI tools provide quick and convenient answers, they may discourage students from conducting in-depth research or forming their own insights. This over-reliance can weaken critical thinking (Khan, 2025). Instead of enhancing critical thinking and problem-solving skills, AI tools may inadvertently undermine them.

Mwangi (2025) and Alenzuela (2023) argue that AI is leading to a decrease in critical thinking skills. Alenzuela explores the possible negative impacts of artificial intelligence (AI) on our critical thinking abilities. The author argues that while AI enhances cognitive functions such as data analysis and pattern recognition, over-reliance on these technologies may weaken our capacity for deep analytical thinking. Alenzuela highlights the necessity of balancing AI's capabilities with human thought processes to ensure AI complements rather than replaces analytical reasoning. Maintaining this balance is essential for sustaining engagement in problem-solving and analytical processes, which are fundamental elements of critical thinking (Alenzuela, 2023).

Similarly, Mwangi (2025) investigates the influence of generative AI (GenAI) on human cognition. The author emphasizes that GenAI tools shift critical thinking toward tasks like verifying information and synthesizing AI-generated content. While these activities require some level of analysis, they often limit individuals to validating AI-produced material rather than generating original ideas. Mwangi expresses concerns about the long-term effects of over-reliance on GenAI, suggesting it may hinder cognitive functions such as memory and problem-solving. The author introduces the concept of "digital amnesia," emphasizing how outsourcing cognitive tasks to AI may impair our ability to learn and retain information (Mwangi, 2025).

Both authors' perspectives align with Bloom's Taxonomy, a framework that categorizes learning objectives by complexity and specificity. Alenzuela's concerns regarding the decline in critical thinking correspond with the higher levels of Bloom's Taxonomy—Analyzing, Evaluating, and Creating—which involve complex cognitive processes such as assessing information, forming judgments, and generating new ideas. Excessive dependence on AI may hinder engagement in these advanced cognitive functions (Alenzuela, 2023).

Mwangi's analysis of the shift in critical thinking toward verification tasks aligns with the foundational levels of Bloom's Taxonomy—Remembering and Understanding. While these levels are essential for building a fundamental knowledge base, they do not encompass the full spectrum of critical thinking required for advanced cognitive processes. The concept of "digital amnesia" further underscores the need to balance AI use with active cognitive engagement to develop and sustain critical thinking skills (Mwangi, 2025).

Both authors highlight the potential risks of over-reliance on AI and GenAI tools, stressing the importance of integrating AI thoughtfully with human cognition. Connecting their arguments to Bloom's Taxonomy enhances our understanding of the necessity of maintaining critical thinking across different cognitive levels. Striking this balance is crucial to ensuring AI serves as a tool for enhancing—rather than diminishing—our cognitive abilities and analytical reasoning skills.

Recent research supports these concerns. A study by Microsoft and Carnegie Mellon University, set to be presented at the ACM CHI Conference on Human Factors in Computing Systems in April 2025, found that relying on AI for everyday tasks diminishes critical thinking. Because AI-generated responses often appear polished and convincing, people may judge their quality based on surface-level cues rather than engaging in deeper analysis. Carrillo and Hawley (2023) also point to social media as a contributor to declining critical thinking skills, with platforms like TikTok encouraging passive consumption rather than active engagement with information.

Onjewu et al. (2024) found that while various technologies influence critical thinking, their overall impact is mostly negative—except for internet searches, which have a positive effect on learning. Gerlich (2025) further reports a strong negative correlation between frequent AI tool usage and critical thinking ability, with cognitive offloading playing a key role. Younger individuals, in particular, demonstrated lower critical thinking scores and greater dependence on AI technologies compared to older generations. Risko and Gilbert (2016) argue that while AI can free up cognitive resources, it may also reduce cognitive engagement and skill development. The widespread availability of AI-generated knowledge and instant answers may discourage students from actively engaging in the cognitive processes necessary for critical thinking.

Bloom's Taxonomy and Critical Thinking

Bloom's taxonomy provides a structured approach to developing critical thinking by guiding students through progressively complex levels of learning. It starts with basic recall and gradually encourages deeper inquiry using targeted questions and action-oriented keywords. The framework consists of six cognitive domains that help students acquire, retain, and apply new knowledge: knowledge, comprehension, application, analysis, synthesis, and evaluation (Bloom et al., 1956).

This hierarchy is based on the idea that higher-order learning requires moving beyond memorization and engaging in more advanced cognitive processes (The Learning Center, n.d.). At the higher levels, students go beyond simply remembering information—they apply concepts, analyze patterns, synthesize ideas, evaluate arguments, and create new insights (Armstrong, n.d.). Figure 1 visually illustrates this progression, highlighting how each level builds upon the previous one to develop deeper critical thinking skills.

Figure 1. Bloom's taxonomy hierarchy (Center for Instructional Technology and Training, 2024)

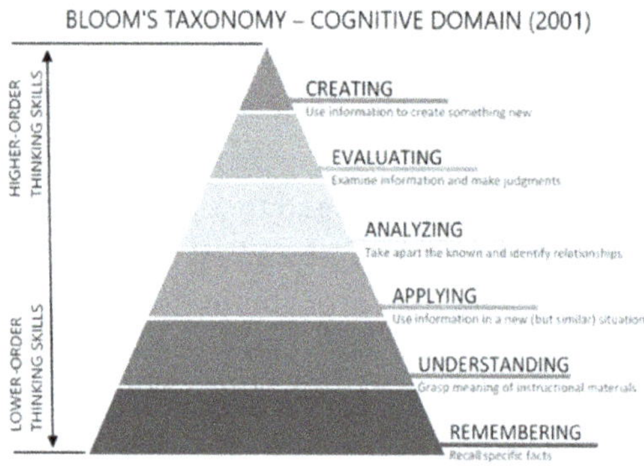

Bloom's Taxonomy is a structured framework that classifies educational learning objectives based on their complexity and specificity. The cornerstone is *Remembering*, which entails the recollection of information and fundamental concepts, including definitions or formulas. Advancing higher, *Understanding* involves comprehending the significance of information, which may be summarizing a book or articulating an idea in one's own terminology. *Applying* entails utilizing knowledge in novel circumstances, such as resolving mathematical problems. *Analyzing* dissects material into components to comprehend its structure, such as recognizing the principal arguments in an essay. *Evaluating* entails forming judgments, such as evaluating a research article or analyzing the efficacy of a remedy. At the pinnacle is *Creating*, which entails the generation of novel ideas, concepts, or research.

Critical thinking, according to this taxonomy, is a structured talent typically fostered by instructors in academic institutions. This endeavor is especially difficult due to the noted decrease in critical thinking skills among contemporary pupils (Carrillo & Hawley, 2023; Gerlich, 2025).

Gonsalves (2024) performed a study on academic writing, employing a conceptual framework substantiated by empirical data from MSc Marketing students' engagements with AI tools over a four-week period. The research indicated that AI can both augment and impede critical thinking in cognitive, affective, and metacognitive areas. Essential components such as melioration, ethical reasoning, collaboration, and reflective thinking were recognized as vital for fostering profound engagement with AI-generated material. These findings correspond with multiple tiers of Bloom's Taxonomy: *Analyzing* (decomposing information and comprehending relationships), *Evaluating* (formulating judgments based on criteria and standards), and *Creating* (synthesizing elements to generate novel ideas or solutions).

Bloom's Taxonomy and AI

The impact of ChatGPT on critical thinking aligns with various levels of Bloom's Taxonomy, which categorizes cognitive skills into six stages: remembering, understanding, applying, analyzing, evaluating, and creating (Armstrong, n.d.). Research suggests that ChatGPT primarily enhances critical thinking at the higher levels of this framework (Guo & Lee, 2023; Suriano et al., 2025).

Guo and Lee (2023) found that ChatGPT improved students' ability to ask insightful questions, analyze material, and grasp complex topics—skills associated with the analysis stage, where learners break down information to understand its structure. Similarly, Suriano et al. (2025) highlighted ChatGPT's role in boosting student engagement, a key factor in critical thinking. This corresponds to the evaluation stage, where students assess the quality and validity of information. Almazrou et al. (2024) reported that 92.6% of 392 medical students in Saudi Arabia saw significant potential for ChatGPT to enhance critical thinking, particularly at the creation stage, where students synthesize information to generate new ideas. Additionally, Qawqzeh (2024) emphasized ChatGPT's positive effects on interactivity, engagement, and accessibility, strengthening critical thinking skills, especially in analysis, evaluation, and creation.

However, ChatGPT struggles with lower-order cognitive tasks. Herrmann-Werner et al. (2024) observed that while it supports higher-order thinking, it faces challenges in remembering, understanding, and applying concepts. Habiballa et al. (2024) similarly found that while ChatGPT performs well in recall and application tasks, it struggles with deeper comprehension, evaluation, and creative synthesis—areas where human reasoning excels. Over-reliance on AI tools may even hinder higher-order thinking development, as Putra et al. (2023) warned. They noted that since AI relies on pre-existing data and lacks true contextual understanding, it often falls short in producing original ideas. The authors recommend that students actively engage in discussions, explore diverse sources, and participate in creative projects to strengthen their independent thinking.

Using AI as a learning aid rather than a replacement for human cognition is key to maintaining critical thinking development. Guo and Lee (2023) substantiated this assertion through a study conducted in an introductory chemistry course, wherein students engaged with ChatGPT across three phases: setup and orientation, essay composition, and revision. Although students demonstrated progress in questioning, data analysis, and conceptual comprehension, they encountered difficulties in source verification and evaluating information quality.To address these challenges, Zaphir and Hansen (2024) proposed designing AI prompts that encourage broad perspectives and engagement with ambiguity rather than simply increasing question difficulty. They suggested using AI to create activities that explore multiple interpretations of complex topics like the definition of life, fostering deep analysis, evaluation, and problem-solving.

A well-rounded critical-thinking approach acknowledges the interplay between cognitive skills and the role of AI in both supporting and challenging them. Gonsalves (2024) explored this balance in academic writing, finding that AI can enhance and hinder cognitive, affective, and metacognitive domains. Key elements such as ethical reasoning, collaboration, and reflective thinking were identified as essential for meaningful engagement with AI-generated content, aligning with Bloom's levels of analysis, evaluation, and creation.

Despite its strengths, AI's limitations remain evident. Herrmann-Werner et al. (2024) found that GPT-4 performed well on exam questions, achieving up to 93% accuracy on detailed prompts, yet still struggled with recalling specific details and understanding conceptual relationships—key aspects of the "Remember" and "Understand" levels of Bloom's Taxonomy. Similarly, Elsayed (2023) explored strategies to reduce AI reliance by refining question design. Using a genetic algorithm to improve keyword selection, the study showed that GPT-3's accuracy declined when faced with varied cognitive challenges, emphasizing the need for diverse questioning techniques to reinforce critical thinking.

Ultimately, while ChatGPT enhances higher-level cognitive skills, it falls short in recall, comprehension, and original idea generation. A balanced approach that integrates AI tools with independent learning activities will ensure that students develop critical thinking across all levels of Bloom's Taxonomy. By fostering engagement in diverse learning experiences and emphasizing independent thought, educators can leverage AI as a tool that complements rather than replaces cognitive development.

Benefits of AI in Developing Critical Thinking

Several studies highlight the benefits of generative AI, such as ChatGPT, in education. Essien et al. (2024) examined how AI text generators influence the critical thinking skills of postgraduate business students in the UK, using Bloom's Taxonomy as a framework. Their findings showed that ChatGPT significantly enhances lower-level cognitive skills like remembering and understanding.

In addition to increasing fundamental abilities, ChatGPT is revolutionizing education by facilitating tailored learning experiences, improving predictive analytics, and optimizing administrative functions. This transition fosters a student-centered methodology, enabling students to immerse themselves in intricate scenarios and enhance their analytical and evaluative competencies. Similarly, Eltobgy et al. (2024) explored ChatGPT's impact on cognitive learning, noting that its advanced natural language processing has reshaped Bloom's Taxonomy from a rigid hierarchy into a more fluid and dynamic learning process.

Suriano et al. (2025) discovered that engagement with ChatGPT markedly enhances students' critical thinking, underscoring its utility as a cognitive development instrument. Harahap (2024) corroborated these findings, illustrating that students enhanced their critical thinking skills using analysis and paraphrasing techniques enabled by ChatGPT. This research indicates that AI text generators not only bolster fundamental cognitive skills but also improve higher-order thinking capabilities. Recognizing ChatGPT's transformative potential in education is essential. When integrated thoughtfully, AI tools can help educators create engaging and effective learning environments that cater to diverse student needs. This approach not only fosters critical thinking but also equips students with the skills needed to navigate a world increasingly shaped by AI.

RESEARCH METHODS

This study conducts a systematic review to evaluate the validity of ChatGPT as a tool for critical thinking. By synthesizing existing research, it examines the advantages and limitations of AI in enhancing critical thinking skills. The following research questions guide this investigation:

1. How does the use of ChatGPT influence different cognitive levels, as defined by Bloom's Taxonomy, from basic knowledge acquisition to higher-order thinking skills such as analysis and evaluation?
2. What are the potential benefits and drawbacks of utilizing ChatGPT as a tool for critical thinking in educational contexts?
3. What risks does reliance on ChatGPT pose to the development and maintenance of critical thinking skills, and under what conditions could its use be justified?

The goal of this study is to provide an objective analysis of AI's role in developing critical thinking, highlighting both the benefits and challenges it presents. While AI offers advantages in terms of efficiency and accessibility, it is crucial to assess its impact on students' critical thinking—whether it enhances or diminishes these skills. The study aims to evaluate how AI can be effectively integrated into educational environments without undermining students' capacity for independent thought.

This study employs a systematic review due to its comprehensive methodology for synthesizing existing literature, facilitating a thorough evaluation of the evidence. This study employs the Preferred Reporting Items for Systematic Reviews and Meta-Analyses (PRISMA) standards (PRISMA, 2024), a recognized method that enhances the reliability and validity of systematic reviews while ensuring transparency and rigor. A systematic review is consistent with findings from other studies. Mai et al. (2024) employed PRISMA to examine the application of ChatGPT in educational contexts. The authors synthesized 51 articles to conclude that ChatGPT enhances learning. Heung and Chiu (2025) employed PRISMA to examine the effect of ChatGPT on student engagement. The author identified potential risks of student disengagement associated with excessive reliance on ChatGPT in their study. Deng et al. (2024) employed PRISMA to synthesize 69 articles examining the impact of ChatGPT on student learning. The authors discovered that ChatGPT enhances academic performance, affective-motivational states, and higher-order thinking abilities; it decreases mental effort and does not significantly impact self-efficacy.

Criteria for Inclusion and Exclusion

The initial stage involves defining inclusion and exclusion criteria for selecting relevant sources and establishing guidelines for identifying and retrieving pertinent literature. Journal articles must meet the following criteria to be included in the review:

- Articles must be published in English.
- Articles must undergo peer review.
- Conference proceedings are included.
- Research should focus on the correlation between artificial intelligence and critical thinking abilities.
- Articles must be published between 2023 and 2025.
- Inclusion eligibility is contingent upon the evaluation of the abstract.

Search Strategy

This systematic review employs an in-depth search strategy, analyzing databases such as ScienceDirect, Google Scholar, ERIC, Springer, and Scopus to identify relevant literature. Search terms include “artificial intelligence,” “AI,” “ChatGPT,” “critical thinking,” and “Bloom's Taxonomy” to address the following research questions:

1. How does the use of ChatGPT influence different cognitive levels, as defined by Bloom’s Taxonomy, from basic knowledge acquisition to higher-order thinking skills such as analysis and evaluation?

2. What are the potential benefits and drawbacks of utilizing ChatGPT as a tool for critical thinking in educational contexts?
3. What risks does reliance on ChatGPT pose to the development and maintenance of critical thinking skills, and under what conditions could its use be justified?

The search strategy focuses on identifying studies that explore ChatGPT's impact on students' cognitive abilities, its advantages and disadvantages in educational settings, and potential risks associated with AI reliance in fostering critical thinking skills. Citations were managed using Mendeley and exported as RIS files to Rayyan, a systematic review software available on web and mobile platforms (Rayyan, 2025). Rayyan improved search filtering efficiency, expediting the study selection process and reducing the review period. Abstracts of eligible articles were assessed for suitability, utilizing Rayyan's "include" and "maybe" functions to categorize and justify article inclusion.

DATA ANALYSIS

Figure 2 presents the results obtained in this study. A total of 45 studies were identified, of which 24 met the eligibility criteria for inclusion. Twenty-one studies were excluded due to being systematic reviews, book chapters, or having findings that did not align with the current study.

Figure 2. Prisma flow diagram

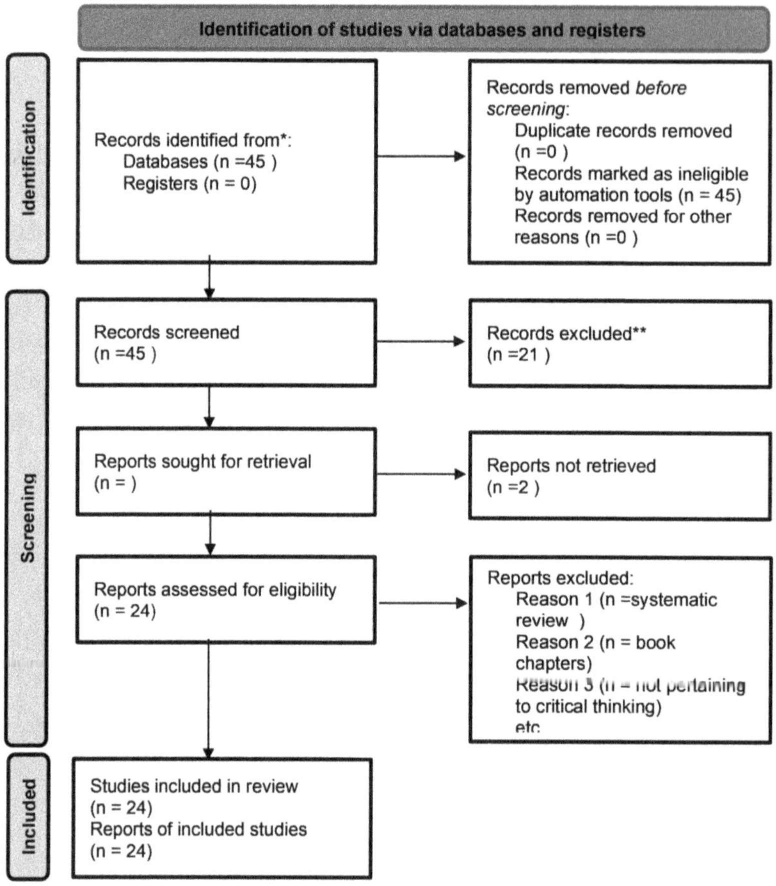

* Consider, if feasible to do so, reporting the number of records identified from each database or register searched (rather than the total number across all databases/registers).

* *If automation tools were used, indicate how many records were excluded by a human and how many were excluded by automation tools.

Characteristics of Included Studies

Table 1 provides a structured summary of the studies included in the systematic review, focusing on AI's impact on critical thinking. It systematically compiles key details such as study design, sample size, intervention/exposure, outcome measures, and main findings. A quality assessment column identifies potential biases, aiding in the evaluation of study reliability.

The table outlines each study's methodology, sampled population, and key insights. The intervention/exposure column specifies the use of ChatGPT or AI tools, while the outcome measures column details the metrics used for assessment. The main conclusions highlight significant findings, including benefits, challenges, and educational implications. The quality assessment section addresses limitations such as reliance on self-reported data, selection bias, and methodological constraints.

Table 1. Data extraction table for systematic review

Study (Author, Year)	Study Design	Sample Size & Population	Intervention/ Exposure	Outcome Measures	Key Findings	Quality Assessment (Risk of Bias)
Qawqzeh (2024)	Descriptive & correlational	515 participants (instructors, researchers, parents, students)	ChatGPT's impact on critical thinking, problem-solving, creativity	Improvements in critical thinking, problem-solving, and creativity; responsible usage	Mixed perceptions; emphasized instructor involvement	Potential bias due to self-reported data
Nayak & Pai (2024)	Descriptive	Not specified	ChatGPT's effects on academic achievement & teaching methods	Academic achievement, critical thinking, creativity, student learning outcomes	ChatGPT has both positive and negative effects on education; calls for responsible innovation	Potential bias from content analysis of literature
Almazrou et al. (2024)	Cross-sectional survey	392 medical students (Saudi Arabia)	ChatGPT's role in enhancing critical thinking	Students' perceptions of ChatGPT's efficacy in questioning, reflection	92.6% believed ChatGPT benefits critical thinking; gender differences in perceptions	Potential bias due to self-reported data
Lintner (2024)	Qualitative case study	Middle school educators (Michigan)	AI's role in enhancing critical thinking	Educators' views on AI's role in student problem-solving	AI use in middle schools is minimal; better integration needed	Bias risk from qualitative data reliance
Hasanein & Sobaih (2023)	Descriptive & correlational	Students, faculty, education leaders	Drivers & consequences of ChatGPT in higher education	Identified 12 drivers & consequences of ChatGPT use	ChatGPT aids learning but may impede critical thinking	Bias risk from qualitative interview data

continued on following page

Table 1. Continued

Study (Author, Year)	Study Design	Sample Size & Population	Intervention/ Exposure	Outcome Measures	Key Findings	Quality Assessment (Risk of Bias)
Akastangga et al. (2023)	Quantitative	UIN Sunan Kalijaga students (sample size not specified)	Online surveys on ChatGPT's effect on critical thinking	Levels of critical thinking skills	Moderate effect; importance of balancing AI with critical thinking development	Bias risk from self-reported questionnaire data
Li, Fan, & Sidhu (2024)	Descriptive & correlational	240 Chinese university students	Comparison of ChatGPT & students using CCTST	Inference, deductive reasoning, analysis	ChatGPT excelled in inference; students performed better in evaluation & reasoning	Bias from reliance on CCTST test
Zhong et al. (2024)	Quasi-experimental	130 undergraduates (STEM & non-STEM)	ChatGPT's impact on interdisciplinary learning	Content analysis of student online posts	Improved disciplinary grounding; mixed results in cognitive advancement	Potential bias from quasi-experimental design (selection bias)
Fakour & Imani (2025)	Mixed-methods	230 university students (Taiwan)	Comparison of ChatGPT vs. human tutors in critical thinking	Socratic tutoring & AI/human feedback comparisons	ChatGPT praised for accessibility; human tutors valued for feedback	Bias risk from subjective data interpretation
Essien et al. (2024)	Mixed-methods	107 postgraduate students (UK)	AI text generators' impact on critical thinking (Bloom's taxonomy)	Knowledge, comprehension, application, evaluation	Gains at lower Bloom levels; concerns about reliability & ethics	Bias from mixed-methods study interpretation
Mike et al. (2024)	Quasi-experimental	304 students (various disciplines)	ChatGPT use in open-book testing	Test performance & efficiency	No significant improvement in performance; efficiency gains for business informatics	Bias risk from selection bias & lack of randomization
Zhang & Li (2024)	Mixed-methods	250 Chinese undergraduates	ChatGPT's impact on ethics & learning	Academic ethics & performance measures	AI use may reduce intellectual engagement & creativity	Bias from self-reported data
Santamaria-Velasco et al. (2025)	Qualitative	40 Ecuadorian university students	ChatGPT-simulated conversations with historical figures	Critical thinking & history understanding	Improved historical analysis & engagement	Bias risk from qualitative interpretation
de la Puente et al. (2024)	Quasi-experimental	95 undergraduates (International Relations)	AI-assisted vs. traditional debate groups	Pre/post-tests on argumentation & critical thinking	ChatGPT improved debate skills & understanding	Bias risk from selection bias in quasi-experiment

continued on following page

Table 1. Continued

Study (Author, Year)	Study Design	Sample Size & Population	Intervention/ Exposure	Outcome Measures	Key Findings	Quality Assessment (Risk of Bias)
Alarcón-López et al. (2024)	Quasi-experimental	10-12-year-olds (urban/ rural Mexico)	ChatGPT in sustainability learning	Critical thinking (analysis, inference) & energy literacy	ChatGPT improved analysis; urban students preferred chatbot, rural students adapted over time	Bias risk from small sample & lack of randomization
Dilekli & Boyraz (2024)	Case study & qualitative	5 graduate students	ChatGPT's effect on reflective thinking	Higher-order thinking performance	Students over-relied on AI citations; struggled with deeper critical analysis	Bias risk from small sample size
Swaraj & Chavan (2024)	Descriptive & correlational	Not specified	AI's impact on cognitive thinking & creativity	Creativity & independent thinking levels	AI supports single-turn tasks but may reduce deep thinking	Bias risk from self-reported data
Smith & Lee (2024)	Descriptive & correlational	200 undergraduates	ChatGPT's effect on critical thinking & education	Critical thinking & academic performance	AI may encourage academic dishonesty & reduce engagement	Bias risk from self-reported data
Abbas et al. (2024)	Mixed-methods (two studies)	Study 1: 165 students; Study 2: 494 students	ChatGPT use & academic workload	Procrastination, memory loss, academic performance	Higher workload increased AI use; linked to procrastination & performance dips	Bias risk from self-reported data & indirect effects

RESULTS

The synthesis of 24 studies on ChatGPT's impact on critical thinking offers a comprehensive view of its effects and implications for education. The findings show a range of outcomes, from significant improvements in critical thinking skills to concerns about overreliance on AI. Studies by Almazrou et al. (2024) and Fakour and Imani (2025) highlight the positive influence of ChatGPT. For example, Almazrou et al. found that 92.6% of medical students believed ChatGPT enhanced their critical thinking by providing diverse perspectives and encouraging reflection. Fakour and Imani noted that students valued ChatGPT's non-judgmental nature and accessibility, which fostered deeper thinking. These results suggest that ChatGPT can be a valuable tool to complement traditional teaching methods in enhancing critical thinking.

However, challenges also emerged in the research. Hasanein and Sobaih (2023) and Smith and Lee (2024) warn against the potential for decreased critical thinking and problem-solving skills if students rely too heavily on AI-generated responses. These studies highlight the need for responsible usage guidelines and the active involvement of educators to ensure AI tools enhance, rather than replace, critical thinking.

Answering Research Questions

This section begins with a detailed response to the research questions, offering an in-depth analysis based on the synthesized studies. It examines how ChatGPT influences different cognitive levels, as outlined by Bloom's Taxonomy, assesses the benefits and challenges of using ChatGPT as a critical thinking tool in education, and explores the risks of overdependence on AI for fostering and maintaining critical thinking skills. The goal was to provide a nuanced understanding of ChatGPT's impact on education and to offer insights into the conditions under which its use could be considered justifiable.

How does the use of ChatGPT influence different cognitive levels as defined by Bloom's Taxonomy, from basic knowledge acquisition to higher-order thinking skills such as analysis and evaluation?

The synthesis of studies reveals that ChatGPT impacts various cognitive levels, as outlined by Bloom's Taxonomy, with notable effects across different stages. Essien et al. (2024) highlighted significant advancements at the foundational levels, including knowledge and comprehension. ChatGPT's ability to provide clear, coherent responses helps students efficiently acquire and understand basic information, aligning with the recall and comprehension stages of Bloom's framework.

Fakour and Imani (2025) pointed out that ChatGPT supports higher-order thinking, promoting reflective practices that correspond with the application and analysis stages. Students appreciated its non-judgmental nature and accessibility, which facilitated deeper application and analysis of information. This suggests that ChatGPT can help students make connections and analyze relationships between concepts.

However, the synthesis also points out limitations in ChatGPT's performance at the higher levels of Bloom's Taxonomy, particularly synthesis and evaluation. Li et al. (2024) found that while ChatGPT excelled in inference and deductive reasoning, university students outperformed it in evaluation and inductive reasoning. This suggests that while ChatGPT can aid in generating ideas and synthesizing information, its ability to critically assess and evaluate remains inferior to human judgment. These findings emphasize the potential of ChatGPT to enhance cognitive skills at multiple levels, but also underline the importance of integrating it in a way that complements, rather than replaces, human critical thinking and evaluation.

What are the potential benefits and drawbacks of utilizing ChatGPT as a tool for critical thinking within educational contexts?

The advantages of using ChatGPT to enhance critical thinking are clearly highlighted in the synthesized research. Studies by Almazrou et al. (2024) and Qawqzeh (2024) document significant improvements in critical thinking, problem-solving, and creativity. ChatGPT's ability to generate diverse viewpoints and foster inquiry and reflective practice emerged as a key benefit. For example, Almazrou et al. found that 92.6% of medical students felt ChatGPT enhanced their critical thinking by encouraging diverse perspectives and reflective thinking. Qawqzeh (2024) also stressed the importance of responsible use and instructor involvement in maximizing these benefits.

However, the research also points to notable limitations. Concerns about overreliance on AI were raised by Hasanein and Sobaih (2023) and Smith and Lee (2024), who argued that it could undermine independent critical thinking and problem-solving abilities. Additional drawbacks included potential academic dishonesty, reduced creativity, and lower motivation. Smith and Lee (2024) noted that the ease of using ChatGPT might encourage dishonesty and discourage independent thought. These findings suggest that while ChatGPT has the potential to enhance critical thinking, its integration must be carefully managed, with clear guidelines and active educator involvement to mitigate potential negative effects.

What risks does reliance on ChatGPT pose to the development and maintenance of critical thinking skills, and under what conditions could its use be considered justifiable?

The primary risks of relying too heavily on ChatGPT include a potential decline in critical thinking and problem-solving skills due to overdependence on AI-generated answers. Hasanein and Sobaih (2023) and Smith and Lee (2024) caution that the convenience of using ChatGPT could encourage academic dishonesty, stifle creativity, and lower motivation to learn. This overreliance may also lead to cognitive offloading, where students disengage from independent thinking and problem-solving.

However, the research suggests that ChatGPT can be a valuable educational tool when used to complement, rather than replace, traditional teaching methods. Fakour and Imani (2025) and Essien et al. (2024) advocate for hybrid educational models that combine the strengths of both AI and human instructors. Fakour and Imani specifically highlight the synergy between AI tools and human tutors, suggesting that an integrated approach can optimize learning outcomes. Educators play a crucial role in guiding students toward responsible AI use, ensuring these tools enhance cognitive engagement rather than diminish it.

Emerging Themes

The integration of artificial intelligence (AI) in educational contexts has sparked considerable debate among researchers and educators. While some argue that AI tools like ChatGPT can significantly enhance learning and cognitive development, others caution against the potential drawbacks of over-reliance on these technologies. This discussion is framed within the context of Bloom's Taxonomy, a hierarchical model that classifies educational learning objectives into levels of complexity and specificity. By examining various studies, we can identify key themes related to the enhancement of cognitive skills, the benefits of AI in education, the risks of over-reliance, and the conditions for justifiable use of AI tools like ChatGPT:

Theme 1: Enhancement of Cognitive Skills Across Bloom's Taxonomy

The first theme identified was the enhancement of cognitive abilities across Bloom's Taxonomy. The findings suggest that ChatGPT can improve cognitive skills from foundational knowledge to higher-order critical thinking. For instance, Essien et al. (2024) observed significant gains in students' ability to acquire and understand basic information, aligning with the knowledge and comprehension levels of Bloom's framework. Fakour and Imani (2025) highlighted that ChatGPT encourages deeper thinking and reflective practice, motivating students to critically apply and analyze information. However, Li et al. (2024) found that while ChatGPT excelled in inference and deductive reasoning, it underperformed compared to university students in evaluation and inductive reasoning. This points to limitations in its effectiveness at more advanced cognitive levels.

Theme 2: Benefits of ChatGPT in Educational Contexts

The second theme explores the advantages of ChatGPT in educational settings. Several studies have highlighted its potential to enhance critical thinking skills. For instance, Almazrou et al. (2024) reported that 92.6% of medical students felt ChatGPT improved their critical thinking by offering diverse perspectives and encouraging reflective practice. Qawqzeh (2024) observed notable improvements in problem-solving and creativity among participants. Additionally, Zhong et al. (2024) found that ChatGPT boosted disciplinary knowledge and cognitive development in interdisciplinary learning environments, demonstrating its value in promoting interdisciplinary education.

Theme 3: Drawbacks and Risks of Overreliance on ChatGPT

The third theme examined the drawbacks and potential risks of overreliance on ChatGPT. The study identified significant disadvantages and hazards associated with heavy dependence on AI. Hasanein and Sobaih (2023) and Smith and Lee (2024) raised concerns about the possible decline in critical thinking and problem-solving skills due to an overreliance on AI-generated responses. The ease of using ChatGPT could encourage academic dishonesty and reduce motivation for independent thought. Smith and Lee (2024) highlighted additional risks, including diminished creativity and a decrease in students' drive to learn. They emphasized the need for clear guidelines on responsible usage and the active involvement of educators to mitigate these risks.

Theme 4: Conditions for Justifiable Use of ChatGPT

The fourth theme explored when the use of ChatGPT can be considered justifiable. The findings suggest that ChatGPT is most effective when used as a supplement to traditional educational methods rather than as a replacement. Fakour and Imani (2025) and Essien et al. (2024) advocated for hybrid educational models that combine the strengths of both AI and human input. In this context, educators play a crucial role in guiding students toward responsible AI use, ensuring that these tools enhance rather than replace their intellectual efforts. The importance of clear guidelines for responsible usage and active educator involvement was emphasized to mitigate any potential negative impacts.

DISCUSSION

The integration of AI tools like ChatGPT in educational settings has sparked significant debate regarding its impact on critical thinking. The synthesis of 24 studies provides a comprehensive view of how ChatGPT influences cognitive skills, revealing both potential benefits and challenges. The study highlighted concerns about over-reliance on AI-generated solutions, which may hinder students' ability to develop critical thinking skills (Suriano et al., 2025; Herrmann-Werner et al., 2024). Bloom's Taxonomy, commonly used as a framework for setting educational goals, does not fully address the cognitive demands of AI-assisted learning (Putra et al., 2023). Additionally, this study emphasizes cognitive offloading, where users delegate cognitive tasks to AI rather than actively engaging with complex concepts, potentially leading to reduced cognitive effort and engagement with critical analysis (Dans, 2023; El-Seoud et al., 2023). The analysis revealed that ChatGPT impacts various cognitive levels, as outlined by Bloom's Taxonomy, with notable effects across different stages. ChatGPT's ability to provide clear, coherent responses helps students efficiently acquire and understand basic information, aligning with the recall and comprehension stages of Bloom's framework (Essien et al., 2024). However, limitations in ChatGPT's performance at the higher levels of Bloom's Taxonomy, particularly synthesis and evaluation, were also noted (Li et al., 2024). The findings suggest that ChatGPT can enhance cognitive skills at multiple levels, but its integration must be carefully managed to avoid undermining the development of independent critical thinking. The potential benefits of ChatGPT include improvements in critical thinking, problem-solving, and creativity (Almazrou et al., 2024; Qawqzeh, 2024), while the drawbacks include the risk of overreliance, academic dishonesty, and reduced motivation to learn (Hasanein & Sobaih, 2023; Smith & Lee, 2024). The research underscores the necessity for responsible usage guidelines and the active involvement of educators to ensure that AI tools augment rather than replace cognitive efforts.

Recommendations

Based on the findings, several recommendations can be made to optimize the use of ChatGPT in educational contexts. Firstly, educators should integrate ChatGPT as a complementary tool rather than a replacement for traditional teaching methods. This balanced approach can help leverage the strengths of both AI and human instruction, ensuring that students benefit from diverse perspectives while still engaging in independent critical thinking. Secondly, clear guidelines should be established to ensure responsible usage of ChatGPT. These guidelines should emphasize the importance of critical engagement with AI-generated content and discourage overreliance. Educators should play an active role in guiding students to use ChatGPT responsibly, providing feedback, encouraging reflective practice, and fostering independent critical thinking. Implementing hybrid educational models that combine AI tools with traditional methods can optimize learning outcomes. These models should be designed to enhance cognitive skills across all levels of Bloom's Taxonomy. Finally, regular assessment of ChatGPT's impact on students' critical thinking skills should be conducted. Based on these assessments, educational strategies should be adapted to address any emerging challenges and maximize the benefits of AI integration.

Limitations

The limitations of the studies included in the synthesis relied on self-reported data, which may be subject to biases and inaccuracies. Additionally, the studies varied in their design, sample size, and population, which may affect the generalizability of the findings. The effectiveness of ChatGPT may vary across different educational contexts and populations, limiting the applicability of the findings to all settings. Furthermore, some studies may have inherent selection biases, particularly those using quasi-experimental designs or qualitative methods. These limitations highlight the need for further research to explore the impact of ChatGPT on critical thinking in diverse educational settings and to develop strategies for its effective integration.

CONCLUSION

The growing integration of AI, especially ChatGPT, within educational environments has ignited a continuous discussion regarding its influence on critical thinking. The present study highlights the intricate nature of AI's impact, demonstrating its capacity to both improve and obstruct critical thinking at different levels of Bloom's Taxonomy. AI can assist with foundational cognitive tasks such as recalling and understanding information through rapid access, yet its impact on more complex cognitive processes—such as analysis, evaluation, and creation—remains uncertain. ChatGPT facilitates interaction with intricate concepts; however, it might also promote cognitive offloading, leading users to become passive recipients of AI-generated insights instead of engaging as active critical thinkers.

The excessive dependence on AI presents a critical issue: it threatens to alter the essence of human thought, moving the focus away from profound analytical reasoning towards the validation and synthesis of content that has already been generated. The occurrence of "digital amnesia" underscores this issue, as reliance on AI for information retrieval and problem-solving could diminish long-term memory retention and independent reasoning abilities. This change raises significant concerns in the field of education, where the development of critical thinking skills is a fundamental goal. If students grow used to depending on AI-generated answers without critically analyzing them, their capacity to develop original arguments, evaluate the reliability of sources, and think autonomously could decline over time.

In light of these concerns, the study concludes that ChatGPT does not fundamentally indicate the demise of critical thinking. The impact is contingent upon its integration within educational settings. When utilized as a supplementary resource rather than a substitute for intellectual engagement, ChatGPT can elevate advanced thinking by encouraging thorough exploration, presenting diverse viewpoints, and aiding in the comprehension of concepts. Nonetheless, this necessitates organized educational strategies, explicit protocols for AI application, and proactive educator participation to guarantee that learners interact thoughtfully with AI-generated material instead of merely accepting it without question.

The validation of ChatGPT as a tool for critical thinking relies heavily on how it is utilized. It demonstrates a strong capacity for enhancing knowledge acquisition, fostering engagement, and aiding in organized problem-solving. However, it falls short in terms of genuine understanding, contextual reasoning, and the capability to produce truly original ideas outside of its training data. Thus, although ChatGPT can assist and enhance critical thinking, it cannot substitute for the profound nature of human reasoning. The challenge ahead involves creating educational models that incorporate AI, aiming to enhance cognitive development while maintaining the vital aspects of independent critical thinking.

In conclusion, AI and ChatGPT are transforming the realm of cognitive processes, yet they do not signify the end of critical thinking. Instead, they urge educators, scholars, and policymakers to rethink the methods by which critical thinking is developed in a world influenced by AI. Achieving equilibrium is essential: harnessing the advantages of AI while bolstering human cognitive capabilities. The ability to think critically, a distinctly human trait, is invaluable; however, fostering this skill now necessitates deliberate approaches to counteract the potential dangers of relying too heavily on artificial intelligence.

REFERENCES

Abdullah, N., Idris, R., Muhammad, N., & Niazi, J. (2022). Socratic questioning: A philosophical approach in developing critical thinking skills. *Al Hikmah International Journal of Islamic Studies and Human Sciences 5(4 Special Issue):*, 143-161. DOI: 10.46722/hikmah.v5i4g

Alarcón-López, C., Krütli, P., & Gillet, D. (2024). Assessing ChatGPT's influence on critical thinking in sustainability oriented activities. (pp. 1-10). *2024 IEEE Global Engineering Education Conference (EDUCON)*. doi: DOI: 10.1109/EDUCON60312.2024.10578790

Alenzuela, R. (2023, February 28). Opinion: Is AI the death of critical thinking? Central Philippine University Library. https://library.cpu.edu.ph/ai-death-of-critical-thinking/

Alkalbani, M. (2023). ChatGPT technology and its role in promoting creativity in education. *The Asian Conference on Education*. Retrieved from https://papers.iafor.org/wp-content/uploads/papers/ace2023/ACE2023_73951.pdf

Almazrou, S., Alanezi, F., Attar, R., Alnaim, N., AlSanad, D., Albelali, S., & Alsadhan, A. (2024). Enhancing medical students critical thinking skills through ChatGPT: An empirical study with medical students. *Nutrition and Health (Berkhamsted, Hertfordshire)*, 02601060241273627. Advance online publication. DOI: 10.1177/02601060241273627 PMID: 39150341

Aouaf, S., Azzouzi, L., & Housni, H. (2023). Perceived barriers to critical thinking development: The student's view. *International Journal of Linguistics, Literature and Translation*, 63-69. DOI: 10.32996/ijllt.2023.6.2.10

Armstrong, P. (n.d.). Blooms Taxonomy. Center for Teaching, Vanderbilt University. Retrieved from https://ies.ed.gov/ncee/rel/regions/northeast/onlinetraining/ResourcesTools/Bloom%27s%20Taxonomy.pdf

Bloom, B., Engelhart, M., Furst, E., Hill, W., & Krathwohl, D. (1956). Taxonomy of educational objectives. Retrieved from https://tinyurl.com/5n8zesvd

Blooms Taxonomy Cognitive Domain. (n.d.). Center for Excellence in Teaching and Learning, University of Connecticut.

Carrillo, B., & Hawley, M. (2023). Viewpoint: Gen Z's critical thinking is dying. Buena Speaks. Retrieved from https://buenaspeaks.org/6626/viewpoint/viewpoint-our-generations-critical-thinking-is-dying/

Center for Instructional Technology and Training. (n.d.). Bloom's Taxonomy description. Retrieved from https://tinyurl.com/4afp4uax

Chinonso, A., Theresa, A. M.-E., & Aduke, T. (2023). ChatGPT for teaching, learning and research: Prospects and challenges. *Global Academic Journal of Humanities and Social Sciences*, 33-40. doi:DOI: DOI: 10.36348/gajhss.2023.v05i02.001

Dans, E. (2023). ChatGPT and the decline of critical thinking. IE Insights. Insights Knowledge-Driven Content. Retrieved from https://www.ie.edu/insights/articles/chatgpt-and-the-decline-of-critical-thinking/

El-Seoud, S. A., Eldeen, S., Nagaty, K., & Karam, O. H. (2023). The impact of ChatGPT on student learning/performing. *SSRN*. DOI: 10.2139/ssrn.4532913

Elsayed, S. (2023). Towards mitigating ChatGPT's negative impact on education: Optimizing question design through Bloom's Taxonomy. *Arxiv*. doi:http://dx.doi.org//arXiv.2304.08176DOI: 10.48550

Eltobgy, A., Abaza, W., & Abd, Y. (2024). Evaluating the effectiveness of ChatGPT in enhancing cognitive learning outcomes in tourism higher education based on Biggs's 3P Model a case study: Faculties of hotel and tourism services technology. *Journal of Association of Arab Universities for Tourism and Hospitality*, *27*(1), 256–276. DOI: 10.21608/jaauth.2024.320773.1608

Essien, A., Bukoye, O., O'Dea, X., & Kremantzis, M. (2024). The influence of AI text generators on critical thinking skills in UK business schools. *Studies in Higher Education*, *49*(5), 865–882. Advance online publication. DOI: 10.1080/03075079.2024.2316881

Fütterer, T., Fischer, C., Alekseeva, A., Chen, X., Tate, T., Warschauer, M., & Gerjets, P. (2023). ChatGPT in education: Global reactions to AI innovations. *Scientific Reports*, *13*(1), 15310. Advance online publication. DOI: 10.1038/s41598-023-42227-6 PMID: 37714915

Gerlich, M. (2025). AI tools in society: Impacts on cognitive offloading and the future of critical thinking. *Societies (Basel, Switzerland)*, *15*(1), 6. Advance online publication. DOI: 10.3390/soc15010006

Golden, B. (2023). Enabling critical thinking development in higher education through the use of a structured planning tool. *Irish Educational Studies*, *42*(4), 949–969. DOI: 10.1080/03323315.2023.2258497

Gonsalves, C. (2024). Generative AI's impact on critical thinking: Revisiting Bloom's taxonomy. *Journal of Marketing Education*, *0*(0), 02734753241305980. Advance online publication. DOI: 10.1177/02734753241305980

Grinschgl, S., Papenmeier, F., & Meyerhoff, H. S. (2021). Consequences of cognitive offloading: Boosting performance but diminishing memory. *Quarterly Journal of Experimental Psychology*, *74*(9), 1477–1496. DOI: 10.1177/17470218211008060 PMID: 33752519

Guo, Y., & Lee, D. (2023). Leveraging ChatGPT for enhancing critical thinking skills. *Journal of Chemical Education*, *100*(12), 4876–4883. Advance online publication. DOI: 10.1021/acs.jchemed.3c00505

Habiballa, H., Kotyrba, M., Volna, E., Bradac, V., & Dusek, M. (2025). Artificial intelligence (ChatGPT) and Bloom's Taxonomy in theoretical Computer Science education. *Applied Sciences (Basel, Switzerland)*, *15*(2), 581. Advance online publication. DOI: 10.3390/app15020581

Harahap, D. (2024). Implementation of ChatGPT to improve students' critical thinking abilities. *Indonesian Journal of Education and Social Humanities*, *1*(2), 33–39. DOI: 10.62945/ijesh.v1i2.58

Herrmann-Werner, A., Festl-Wietek, T., Holderried, F., Herschbach, L., Griewatz, J., Masters, K., Zipfel, S., & Mahling, M. (2024). Assessing ChatGPT's mastery of Bloom's Taxonomy using psychosomatic medicine exam questions: Mixed-Methods study. *Journal of Medical Internet Research*, *26*, e52113. Advance online publication. DOI: 10.2196/52113 PMID: 38261378

Heung, Y., & Chiu, T. (2025). How ChatGPT impacts student engagement from a systematic review and meta-analysis study. *Computers and Education: Artificial Intelligence*. DOI: 10.1016/j.caeai.2025.100361

Imran, M., & Almusharraf, N. (2023). Analyzing the role of ChatGPT as a writing assistant at higher education level: A systematic review of the literature. *Contemporary Educational Technology*, *15*(4), ep464. Advance online publication. DOI: 10.30935/cedtech/13605

Kasneci, E., Sessler, K., Küchemann, S., Bannert, M., Dementieva, D., Fischer, F., Gasser, U., Groh, G., Günnemann, S., Hüllermeier, E., Krusche, S., Kutyniok, G., Michaeli, T., Nerdel, C., Pfeffer, J., Poquet, O., Sailer, M., Schmidt, A., Seidel, T., & Kasneci, G. (2023). ChatGPT for good? On opportunities and challenges of large language models for education. *Learning and Individual Differences*, *103*, 102274. DOI: 10.1016/j.lindif.2023.102274

Khan, I. (2025, February 17). Overreliance on AI could hinder critical thinking. *CNET*. https://tinyurl.com/2894a758

Knapp, A. (2025). The prototype: Study suggests that AI tools decrease critical thinking skill. *Forbes*. Retrieved from https://tinyurl.com/mzcxvp7v

Lau, T. (2019). When AI becomes a part of our daily lives. *Harvard Business Review*. Retrieved from https://hbr.org/2019/05/when-ai-becomes-a-part-of-our-daily-lives

Mai, D., Van Da, C., & Van Hahn, N. (2024). The use of ChatGPT in teaching and learning: A systematic review through SWOT analysis approach. *Frontiers in Education*, *9*, 1328769. Advance online publication. DOI: 10.3389/feduc.2024.1328769

Malik, M., Amjad, A., Aslam, S., & Fakhrou, A. (2024). Global insights: ChatGPT's influence on academic and research writing, creativity, and plagiarism policies. *Frontiers in Research Metrics and Analytics*, *9*, 1486832. Advance online publication. DOI: 10.3389/frma.2024.1486832 PMID: 39583913

Malodia, S., Islam, N., Kaur, P., & Dhir, A. (2021). Why do people use artificial intelligence (AI)-enabled voice assistants? *IEEE Transactions on Engineering Management*, •••, 1–15. DOI: 10.1109/TEM.2021.3117884

Mwangi, K. (2025). Death of critical thinking: How GenAI could inhibit human brain development. Business Daily Africa. https://tinyurl.com/2sj7srh3

Nine, A. (2025). Relying On generative AI dulls your cognitive abilities, Microsoft finds. *Extreme Tech*. Retrieved from https://www.extremetech.com/internet/relying-on-generative-ai-dulls-your-cognitive-abilities-microsoft-finds

Onjewu, A.-K. E., Godwin, E. S., Azizsafaei, F., & Appiah, D. (2024). The influence of technology use on learning skills among generation Z: A gender and cross-country analysis. *Industry and Higher Education*, (0). Advance online publication. DOI: 10.1177/09504222241126322

Open, A. I. (2022). Introducing ChatGPT. Retrieved from https://openai.com/index/chatgpt/

Paul, R. W., Elder, L., & Bartell, T. (1997). *California teacher preparation for instruction in critical thinking: Research findings and policy recommendation.* California Commission on Teacher Credentialing. Retrieved from https://files.eric.ed.gov/fulltext/ED437379.pdf

PRISMA. (2024). Welcome to the Preferred Reporting Items for Systematic reviews and Meta-Analyses (PRISMA) website. Retrieved from https://www.prisma-statement.org/

Putra, F., Rangka, I., Aminah, S., & Aditama, M. (2023). ChatGPT in the higher education environment: Perspectives from the theory of high order thinking skills. *Journal of Public Health (Oxford, England), 45*(4), e840–e841. Advance online publication. DOI: 10.1093/pubmed/fdad120 PMID: 37455540

Qawqzeh, Y. (2024). Exploring the influence of student interaction with ChatGPT on critical thinking, problem solving, and creativity. *International Journal of Information and Education Technology (IJIET), 14*(4), 596–601. DOI: 10.18178/ijiet.2024.14.4.2082

Raj, T., Chauhan, P., Mehrotra, R., & Sharma, M. (2022). Importance of critical thinking in the education. *World Journal of English Language, 12*(3), 126–133. DOI: 10.5430/wjel.v12n3p126

Rayyan. (2025). Faster systematic literature reviews. Retrieved from https://www.rayyan.ai/

Risko, E., & Gilbert, S. J. (2016). Cognitive offloading. *Trends in Cognitive Sciences, 20*(9), 676–688. DOI: 10.1016/j.tics.2016.07.002 PMID: 27542527

Stadler, M., Bannert, M., & Sailer, M. (2024). Cognitive ease at a cost: LLMs reduce mental effort but compromise depth in student scientific inquiry. *Computers in Human Behavior, 160*, 108386. Advance online publication. DOI: 10.1016/j.chb.2024.108386

Suriano, R., Plebe, A., Acciai, A., & Fabio, R. (2025). Student interaction with ChatGPT can promote complex critical thinking skills. *Learning and Instruction, 95*, 102011. Advance online publication. DOI: 10.1016/j.learninstruc.2024.102011

Suriano, R., Plebe, A., Acciai, A., & Fabio, R. (2025). Student interaction with ChatGPT can promote complex critical thinking skills. *Learning and Instruction, 95*, 102011. Advance online publication. DOI: 10.1016/j.learninstruc.2024.102011

Tang, T., Sha, J., Zhao, Y., Wang, S., Wang, Z., & Shen, S. (2024). Unveiling the efficacy of ChatGPT in evaluating critical thinking skills through peer feedback analysis: Leveraging existing classification criteria. *Thinking Skills and Creativity, 53*, 101607. Advance online publication. DOI: 10.1016/j.tsc.2024.101607

The Learning Center. (n.d.). Higher order thinking: Bloom's Taxonomy. University of North Carolina at Chapel Hill. Retrieved from https://learningcenter.unc.edu/tips-and-tools/higher-order-thinking/

Wahn, B., Schmitz, L., Gerster, F., & Weis, M. (2023). Offloading under cognitive load: Humans are willing to offload parts of an attentionally demanding task to an algorithm. *PLoS One*, *18*(5), e0286102. Advance online publication. DOI: 10.1371/journal.pone.0286102 PMID: 37205658

Zaphir, L., & Hansen, D. (2024). The trouble with Bloom's taxonomy in an age of AI. *Times Higher Education*. Retrieved from https://www.timeshighereducation.com/campus/trouble-blooms-taxonomy-age-ai

Zhai, C., Wibowo, S., & Li, L. (2024). *The effects of over-reliance on AI dialogue systems on students' cognitive abilities: a systematic review*. Smart Learning Environments., DOI: 10.1186/s40561-024-00316-7

Chapter 8
Integrating Classkick in TEFL Instruction:
Enhancing Classroom Engagement and Learning Outcomes

Fatema Ahmed Wali
https://orcid.org/0000-0003-4600-8238
Bahrain Polytechnic, Bahrain

Hassan Abumejdad
https://orcid.org/0009-0002-0145-8788
Arab Open University, Bahrain

ABSTRACT

This case study investigates how technology, particularly the Classkick platform, is integrated into primary school English as a Foreign Language (EFL) classes to develop students' academic participation, engagement and achievement. The study examines the effect of Classkick on public school grade five students and 10 teachers through a mixed-methods approach. Findings showcase that the interactive elements, real-time responses, and comprehensible user interface considerably enhanced students' motives, self-confidence using the tool, and cooperative learning. Classkick supports promoting an active, student-centred learning environment. The findings indicate that Classkick can transform traditional EFL teaching and learning, and support in-depth understanding of more impactful learning experiences, with vast significance for the future of computer assisted language learning.

DOI: 10.4018/979-8-3373-0771-8.ch008

1. INTRODUCTION

Technology has become a significant factor in the process of changing how teaching and learning happen. The emergence from simple tools to advanced technology platforms has not only transformed English language classrooms but also developed all-encompassing learning experiences. This transition outlines a multidimensional strategy aimed at promoting learner involvement, individualising educational approaches, and developing academic outcomes across different disciplines (Morgado, 2013). Among these technological advancements, tools like Classkick have emerged as effective educational resources, remarkably in language learning settings. Classkick is a collaborative platform that enables real-time feedback, personalized learning, and interactive activities, making it an effective tool for increasing student participation and improving educational results.

This paper investigates the effect of Classkick on EFL learners' engagement, participation, and motivation. The research evaluates how the elements of Classkick namely its immediate feedback, and collaborative learning approach facilitate more interactive and impactful language learning contexts. By examining the data collected from both students and teachers, this study aims to evaluate Classkick's effectiveness in developing teaching and learning strategies and promoting collaborative and practical learning, through which language learners are prompted to work individually prior to engaging with it in classrooms. Technological innovations are consistently increasing, this research emphasises the effectiveness of digital tools as Classkick to transform conventional teaching methods and foster more diverse, learner-oriented educational practices.

2. REVIEW OF LITERATURE

In today's education system technology plays a role by revolutionizing the way teachers teach students in classrooms with the use of interactive digital platforms instead of traditional tools to enhance student engagement and personalize learning for better academic results (Wang et al., 2023; Smith & Brown, 2021).

Educators and researchers are currently looking into how technology can help solve issues in education by utilizing environments and digital tools that cater to different student needs effectively and engagingly (Nancy et al., 2020; Patel, 2021). It is about creating more interactive and interesting learning spaces that help students learn better and remember more effectively. The shift from the fashioned lecture style of teaching to more modern approaches that focus on the students and use a variety of technologies has really changed how teaching is done and has led to updates, in educational systems (Puspandari, 2023; Johnson & Lee 2022). The significance of technology in education has grown significantly. It has fundamentally changed how we learn and teach and has enhanced experiences, for all involved (Sherukhammadov et al., 2023).

Classkick as a Tool

The rise of technology has transformed the field of education by introducing tools that enrich teaching and learning experiences significantly. Changing the way English is taught as a language (TEFL) by using technology effectively can greatly boost classroom participation and educational achievements. A notable tech tool is Classkick which is a platform aimed at enabling feedback exchange and fostering customized collaborative learning experiences. Classkick's characteristics include instant feedback features in time and interactive interface design along with tools for collaboration. Clacckick can be used to improve TEFL teaching methods through personalised learning paths and support for diverse instructional approaches including the flipped classroom model and motivation enhancement techniques.

Getting feedback plays a role in the process of learning a language since it assists learners in spotting and fixing errors promptly while strengthening their grasp of correct language usage. Recent research emphasizes the value of corrective feedback in enhancing language learning and preventing the persistence of common mistakes (Nassaji & Kartchava 2021). Tools such as Classkick enable educators to track students' progress in time and offer comments or suggestions, for improvement to aid in error rectification and foster learners' language skills development. In an example illustrated in Figure 1; a student repeatedly made mistakes with tenses and vocabulary when working on a writing assignment. Illustratively speaking the student penned "I worke in a hospital which near my house," where the tense of "work" and the relative clause structure were inaccurate. The teacher promptly stepped in to address the error and provide guidance to avoid this misconception from taking root. Recent studies indicate that getting feedback promptly assists students in identifying their mistakes and modifying their language usage accordingly (Lyster & Saito 2022). Additionally, during the assignment, the student employed incorrect word forms like "and went to my office and assisted the ill individuals " (Figure 1), in which tense and verb agreement problems were evident. The teacher gave the student feedback promptly to help him/her fix errors right away. This approach is in line with research showing that immediate feedback is more beneficial for learning language compared to delayed feedback (Zhais, 2021). This exchange demonstrates how Classkicks feedback system plays a role in preventing persistent mistakes and strengthening proper language skills over time.

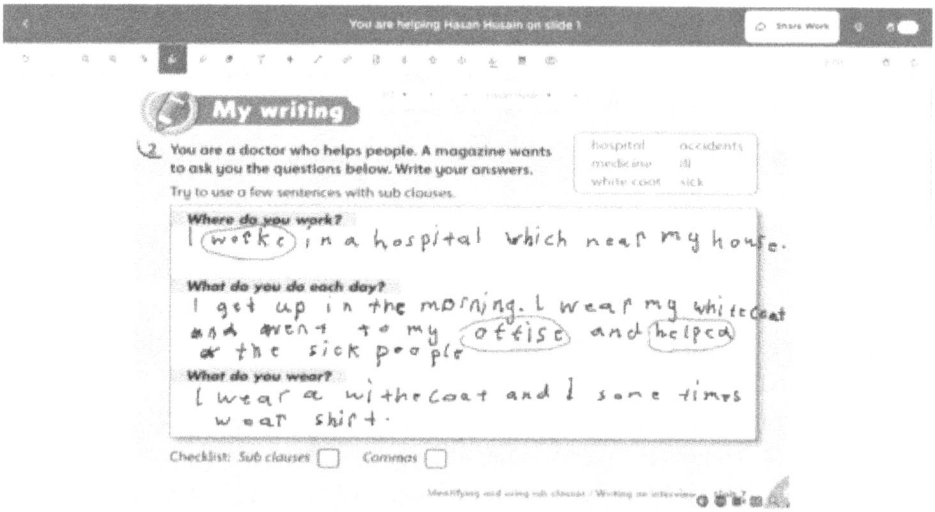

Classkick is easy to use and its interesting layout plays a role in ensuring students remain focused and grasp the content taught across different environments effectively. The system offers functionalities like drag and drop tools and drawing capabilities that prove beneficial for English language instruction, to nonnative speakers. Studies have shown that interactive digital resources enhance student involvement and educational achievements by addressing learning preferences and enabling personalized feedback (Alvarez et al., 2020). In this scenario illustrated in Figure 2 as an example; educators have the ability to craft tasks effortlessly through the user-friendly interface of the platform shown in the picture provided earlier on in their workstations or devices. The visual representation depicts a teacher shaping a task with choices available to insert text elements as well as visuals like pictures and multimedia links or audio clips to enhance the learning experience significantly. These functions like drag and drop and sketch tools empower educators to conduct stimulating exercises such as pairing words, with visuals or reordering sentences for grasp of grammar structures enabling students to enhance their comprehension of intricate language nuances effectively. Moreover, including multimedia content, like videos and audio clips as demonstrated in the editing choices depicted in Figure 2 meets the needs of learning preferences. This functionality enhances the inclusivity of lessons and overcomes potential technological barriers that may impede engagement. Encouraging students to participate in these activities enables educators to improve information retention and cultivate a profound understanding of the language (Lopez & Maggio, 2021).

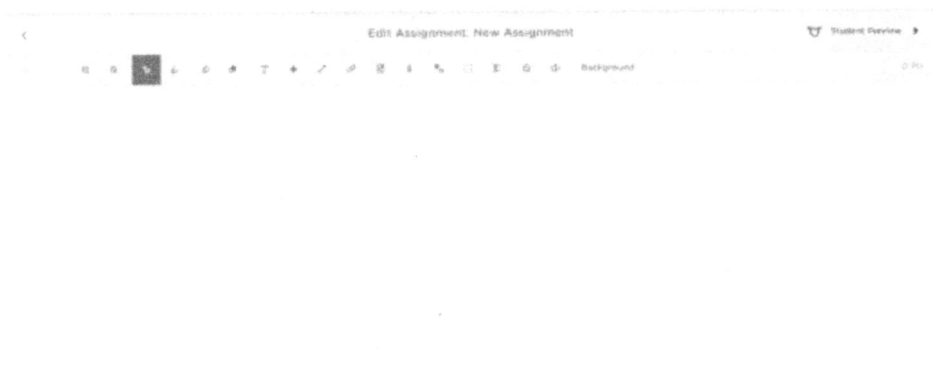

In the flipped classroom model with Classkick software integration students study independently before class. Utilize class time for activities such as language skill practice and receiving immediate feedback, from teachers or classmates. Research indicates that this approach boosts student participation and academic performance by fostering learning and personal accountability (Kang & Shin, 2020). For instance, students might watch a video guide about phrasal verbs at their place. Then participate in role playing exercises in class where they can use what they have learned with the guidance of the teacher. As depicted in Figure 3, learners receive tasks in Classkick like completing sentences, with phrasal verbs. This illustrates how the platform facilitates flipped classroom tasks by enabling students to hone their language abilities in a supervised setting. Engaging in role playing during class allows students to showcase their comprehension in a team-oriented way. The teachers' support and feedback are present, throughout this process (Johnson & Marsh, 2021).

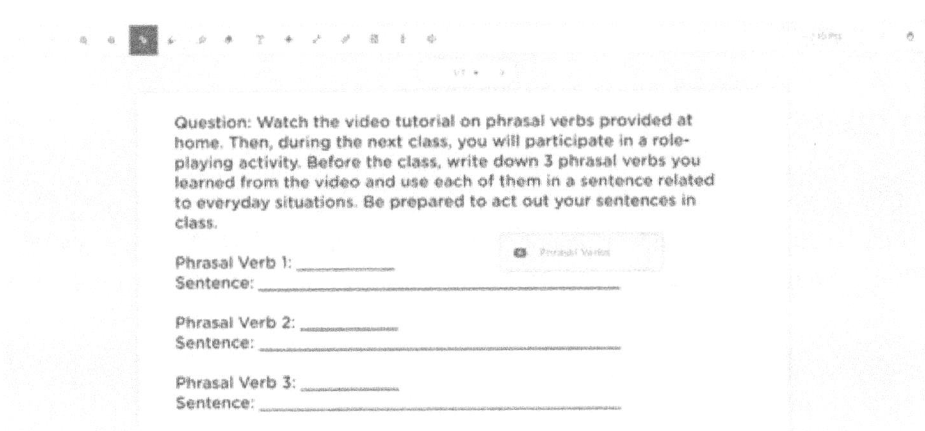

Maintaining motivation is key when it comes to learning a language according to studies (Dörnyei & Ushiodas, 2020). Using techniques like rewards and positive feedback can greatly boost student involvement and commitment in language acquisition endeavors. Classkick software incorporates features such as points and badges to, up student engagement levels. Empower them to approach challenging tasks with resolve. For instance as depicted in Figure 4 the student was given feedback through stickers like "Great Job +2". Smart Bee +1" to acknowledge their hard work and development which not only boosts the students self assurance but also motivates them to engage actively The platforms feature of giving positive feedback using points and badges fosters an environment where students feel appreciated for their growth and dedication, to learning. Acknowledging the efforts of students, with rewards not boosts their engagement but also fosters a classroom setting that prioritizes progress and academic achievements (Ryan & Decile, 2021).

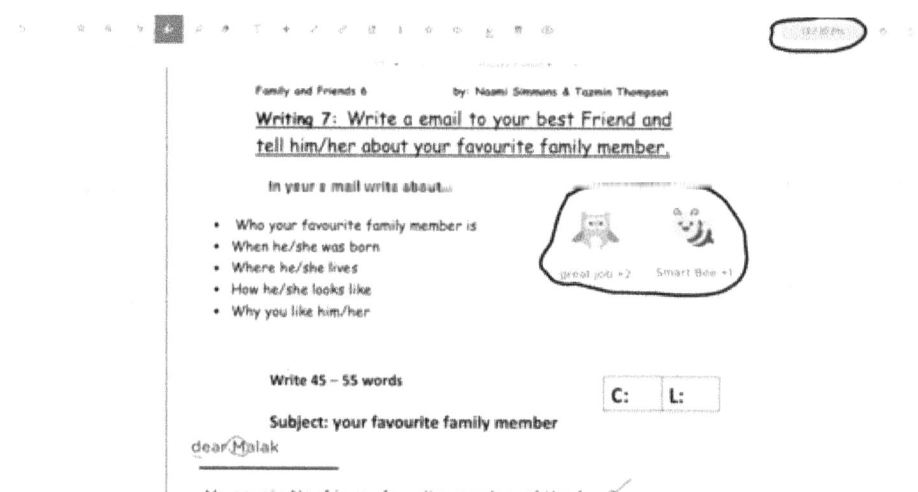

2.1 Classkick

Classkick has gained interest in research due to its innovative and interactive features tailored to enhance and support student learning across diverse academic settings (Shukor et al., 2022). This platform is well known for its ability to provide timely feedback in writing lessons, which plays a crucial role in enhancing student engagement and involvement (Chua et al., 2021).

The user-friendly design of Classkick has made it easily accessible to both teachers and students. This accessibility ensures that the platform can be seamlessly integrated into classroom activities making it a versatile tool that accommodates teaching styles and educational needs (Behringer & Øhrstrøm, 2013). Furthermore, the user-friendly layout of Classkick does not improve convenience. Also, it fosters a more interactive learning environment enabling students to actively participate with their peers and teachers in real time. This leads to a comprehension of the material and enhances overall learning outcomes (Sukmawati & Pujiani, 2023).

As digital tools continue to reshape educational practices, Classkick serves as an example of how technology can be utilised to create engaging and dynamic learning experiences. Its ability to facilitate tailored instruction and advocate for student-centred learning positions it as a valuable tool in education. By establishing a space that connects students and educators while offering feedback and assistance, Classkick has the potential to enhance traditional teaching methods by making learning more engaging, personalised, and successful for all learners. Studies have shown that Classkick supports differentiated instruction and helps maintain student engagement by minimising distractions and providing personalized feedback (Chua et al., 2021). Furthermore, personalised feedback in virtual learning environments has been shown to enhance student motivation, engagement, and learning outcomes by catering to individual learning needs (Carby, 2023). Additionally, research indicates that technology-supported student-centred learning, such as that enabled by Classkick, can improve the quality of education by fostering interactive and personalised learning experiences (Trinidad & Ngo, 2019).

2.2 Promoting Engagement Through Classkick

Collaboration plays a role in learning practices, where digital platforms like Classkick have played an essential role in fostering and enhancing cooperative efforts among students. With its interface designed for dialogues, group projects, and shared tasks, Classkick provides an environment where students can actively interact with each other, creating meaningful connections and fostering a strong sense of community within the educational setting (Nörenberg et al., 2022). Classkick's collaborative features, such as real-time feedback and shared assignments, align with these findings, suggesting that the platform can effectively support collaborative learning in TEFL classrooms. Moreover, the collaborative atmosphere promoted by Classkick boosts performance while helping students cultivate soft skills like communication, critical thinking and cooperation necessary for future success. By fostering a culture of collaboration in the classroom Classkick creates an enjoyable learning experience that effectively prepares students for modern challenges.

2.3 Motivation

Keeping students motivated is crucial in language learning and digital tools have proven to be highly influential in this aspect. Research conducted by Hernández and Flórez (2020) investigated how teaching during the COVID 19 outbreak affected student motivation in EFL classes. The results indicate that platforms offering real time learning and easy access to resources have an effect on student drive and involvement (Hernández & Flórez 2020). In another study by Chang (2022), the use of technology in classrooms to enhance students' motivation and participation. The study highlights that incorporating technology into language teaching can significantly increase student motivation especially when aligned with the SAMR model of substitution, augmentation, modification and redefinition (Chang, 2022).

Similarly, Gu and Huang (2021) explored how devices and software influence students' motivation in a smart classroom environment. The research revealed that incorporating technology not only promoted collaborative learning but also boosted student motivation by fostering a stimulating and interactive educational atmosphere. This reinforces the notion that digital resources such as Classkick that utilise technology can successfully maintain and increase student motivation in TEFL teaching (Gu & Huang, 2021).

The interactive and captivating design of Classkick, which provides feedback and personalised learning paths, is likely to boost student motivation, in TEFL settings. Moreover, by offering learning experiences through tailored feedback and interactive tasks, Classkick caters to the needs of students making the learning process more meaningful and motivating, for each learner. This individualized method does not keep students interested. It also helps them form a stronger bond with the subject matter, as they can see how their efforts influence their learning journey. Incorporating tools in the classroom is vital for establishing a lively and interactive learning environment, where students are motivated to play an active role in their education. By utilising the aspects of Classkick, teachers can create a captivating and efficient learning atmosphere that enhances academic performance and nurtures a lifelong love for learning.

2.4 Classkick for Flipped Classroom

The flipped classroom approach has gained popularity and proven to be a teaching strategy, particularly in technology-enhanced education (Licorish et al., 2018). Integrating Classkick into a flipped classroom can further improve the effectiveness of teaching methods resulting in increased student involvement and enhanced learning outcomes (Sun, 2024). Classkick offers a platform for learning activities enabling students to work together and receive instant feedback from their teachers. This real-time interaction is particularly advantageous in a flipped classroom as it motivates students to actively participate in their learning process and encourages conversations, with both peers and instructors (Åhman et al., 2021). The combination of Classkick and the flipped classroom approach creates a flexible learning setting that emphasises student-centered education.

By providing tools that encourage involvement and teamwork this method does not only enhance the learning experience by making it more interesting and interactive but also aids students in cultivating critical thinking abilities and independent problem-solving skills (Singh, 2020). As a result, incorporating Classkick into the flipped classroom model promotes an efficient educational environment equipping students, with the competencies and knowledge essential for success in both pursuits and beyond the confines of traditional learning spaces. Integrating Classkick into Teaching English as a Foreign Language (TEFL) instruction shows promise in revolutionizing the classroom setting by boosting student engagement levels and enhancing overall academic achievements. This innovative tool empowers educators to create collaborative learning settings that do not capture students' interest but also inspire them to actively participate in their educational voyage.

The continuous progress of technology in the field of education has made tools like Classkick more vital in practice over time. These tools offer responses to the obstacles encountered in teaching by enabling educators to tailor their methods to cater to the varied requirements of students (Shukor et al., 2022). Through the integration of Classkick into teaching approaches, teachers have the opportunity to shift from techniques and adopt more influential strategies that encourage student focused learning (Nörenberg et al., 2022). Furthermore, Classkicks adaptability allows it to be utilized in environments. This makes it a versatile solution for addressing the difficulties faced by TEFL instructors (Gu & Huang, 2021). Whether it's in a classroom or, within an online educational setting. Classkick provides the tools needed to develop an engaging and interactive learning experience customized to each student's specific requirements (Chang, 2022).

In essence integrating Classkick into instruction not only improves the quality of education but also equips students with skills needed to succeed in a rapidly changing world where technology and collaboration are vital. As educators continue to explore technologies, tools like Classkick may play a significant role in shaping the future of education presenting exciting opportunities for creating engaging, effective and inclusive learning environments.

3 RESEARCH METHODOLOGY: THE USE OF CLASSKICK IN THE CLASSROOM FOR EFL STUDENTS

3.1 Research Design

A. Mixed Methods Approach

This study uses a mixed methods approach combining both quantitative and qualitative research techniques to understand how Classkick affects EFL students. By using these two methods, the analysis becomes more thorough as it gathers data from sources and viewpoints. Quantitative data provides comparable results while qualitative data investigates deeper into participants experiences and perspectives. This dual method ensures an assessment of Classkicks effectiveness, in improving EFL education. The study involves surveys, interviews with focus groups and observations of students.

3.2 Participants

The study includes a group of 15 EFL students, all aged 11 years old from three different classes in grade five. This sampling approach was chosen to capture responses and experiences with the Classkick tool across classroom settings while maintaining a consistent age group. By involving students from different classes of grade five, the study can assess the tools' impact broadly and ensure that the results are not limited to one specific class environment.

10 EFL teachers, with varying levels of experience took part in the study. Some educators favoured methods involving paper and pen while others advocated for incorporating 21st-century skills through the use of technology. A common issue raised was the feasibility of integrating technology in schools, with resources. Nevertheless, teachers found Classkick to be versatile and helpful in enabling real-time writing for all students.

Stratified sampling is utilised to select EFL students to guarantee that individuals from proficiency levels and age brackets are equally represented while purposive sampling is employed to choose teachers based on their familiarity with Classkick to ensure that the feedback and insights are rooted in experiences.

3.3 Data Collection Methods

3.3.1 Surveys and Questionnaires

The process of data collection begins by conducting surveys with students to evaluate any shifts in their attitudes towards learning and their levels of engagement after using Classkick. The participants were asked for consent prior to the study. Reassured about the anonymity of their personal information. The surveys provide insights into students' experiences and academic advancements. Teachers also complete questionnaires aimed at capturing their opinions on the usability and effectiveness of Classkick from a teaching perspective.

3.3.2 Data Collection

When it came to boosting the involvement and educational achievements of fifth-grade students, in Bahrain, Classkick became an element in the curriculum for the entire semester which is 14 weeks. Each weekly lesson was carefully designed with language goals tailored to the students' needs ensuring alignment with Family and Friends 5 curriculum. The Classkick activities were thoughtfully created to reinforce these objectives incorporating tasks like matching words, building sentences and comprehension exercises.

The plan for implementation involved a combination of self-study sessions in which students had the chance to tackle tasks at their own speed without direct teacher involvement. These sessions were crafted to promote self-guided learning so that students could assume responsibility for their learning journey and enhance their problem-solving abilities while gaining a grasp of the subject matter. In classes, students interacted with Classkick through guided activities that allowed for teacher involvement and peer collaboration. In study sessions, students completed assignments at their own pace while teachers used Classkick to track progress and give personalised feedback. Throughout the semester, integrating Classkick aimed to enhance students' involvement, understanding and overall language skills development, targeting improvements in their English confidence and proficiency.

Table 1. Weekly lesson objectives, Classkick activities, and expected outcomes

Week	Weekly Lesson Objective	Classkick Activity	Expected Outcomes
1	**Places to go!** In this lesson, students will discover locations in the city. Practice describing them using simple present tense and adverbs of frequency.	Interactive map activity where students match places in a town to descriptions. Students will also complete sentences using the correct adverbs of frequency.	Students will have the opportunity to recognize and explain locations within a city using language and grammar. Enhanced comprehension of how adverbs indicating are used.
2	**The fastest animal in the world!** Students will be taught how to talk about locations using words that compare and show the level of quality.	Students will take part in tasks involving sorting animals or items according to their speed, size and various characteristics. Following that they will create sentences highlighting the use of superlatives.	Students will be able to use superlative adjectives with precision when describing things. This will enhance their vocabulary. Enable them to compare objects or animals efficiently.
3	**I'd like a melon!** Students will understand the use of countable and uncountable nouns in different contexts.	An activity involving sorting items, into groups of things you can count and things you can't, then making lists, for a shopping trip.	Students will learn how to distinguish between nouns and use them correctly in scenarios.
4	**The Ancient Egyptians** Students will learn to describe things using past simple tense, including regular and irregular verbs.	In this classroom exercise students will arrange events in order and recount them using the simple past tense.	Students will show their grasp of the past tense including both irregular forms and use it in historical settings.
5	**Did you have a good day?** Students will practise writing and answering past simple questions about daily activities.	Engage in role-playing activities where students take turns asking and answering questions about their experiences and then receive feedback from their peers.	Enhanced ability to fluently inquire and respond to questions, in the tense leading to improved conversational capabilities.
6	**How much time have we got?** Students will learn how to express quantity and practice using words with /o o/sound.	Exercises focusing on matching time and quantities will be conducted. Students will have the opportunity to improve their pronunciation skills as they complete sentences using the quantity terms.	Students will accurately utilise phrases denoting amounts. Show enhanced pronunciation of /o o/ sounds.
7	**Whose jacket is this?** Students will practice using possessive pronouns and understand adverbs: -ly and irregular forms.	In a classroom task, students will match objects. Use pronouns, then complete sentences, with adverbs.	Students will demonstrate the usage of pronouns in context and effectively incorporate adverbs in their writing.

4 FINDINGS

The student survey findings show significant insights into the impact of Classkick on student engagement and enjoyment in EFL classes. Most of the survey-received responses for the use of Classkick in primary school classes indicate a mean of nearly 0.20 suggesting having a balanced distribution across all options and overall positive feedback, ranging between 3.80 and 4.47. These suggest a positive reception of Classkick across various aspects including learning new vocabulary items, having fun, cooperating with classmates, and feeling empowered with the two highest means in "Now, I like the class more because I will use the tool and learn from it" (4.47), and "I feel more confident when I learn through this tool" (4.40). Similarly, the median for most variables ranges between 4 and 5, suggesting that most students either agree or strongly agree with Classkick's positive statements. This consistency affirms that the participants consider Classkick a beneficial tool across several learning dimensions. This is also aligned with the findings of the standard deviations which range between 0.68 and 0.88. This signifies a moderate variability in responses with the highest standard deviation (0.88) suggesting that specific learners engaged more with their peers than others in "I interacted with my peers more using this tool,"; and the lowest standard deviation (0.68) in "Now, I like the class more because I will use the tool and learn from it," implying consistent consensus that Classkick enriched their class learning experience- See Table 2.

Table 2. Descriptive statistics of student perceptions of Classkick

Variable	Mean	Median	Standard Deviation
I learned new words using this tool	4.40	5	0.72
I had fun using this tool	4.13	4	0.86
I interacted with my peers more using this tool	3.87	4	0.88
I exchanged ideas using this tool	3.80	4	0.86
The tool was easy to use	4.27	4	0.83
Now, I like the class more because I will use the tool and learn from it	4.47	5	0.68
I like the tool because I can compete with my peers	4.33	5	0.84
I feel more confident when I learn through this tool	4.40	5	0.72
I'd rather have more English classes to learn through this tool than other classes	4.27	5	0.79
I enjoy the competition when using this tool in class	4.40	5	0.74

The descriptive statistics and correlation Table 2 outlines a detailed summary of the participants' points of view and class exchanges using Classkick. The findings also show that students are positively impacted by Classkick across a number of dimensions of learning including peer interaction, ease of use and competitive aspects which meaningfully enhance students' confidence and overall fun in the class. Very strong correlations were found between the ease of the tool and enhanced students' confidence (r = 0.877) as well as between using the tool and enjoying the class (r = 0.867). Similar significant findings were observed indicating that using Classkick enhanced peer interactions and contributed to a positive classroom atmosphere (r = 0.853). The same correlation was observed between the development and fun through using and learning Classkick and its available competitive features. However, a weaker correlation was observed in "I had fun using this tool" with "I exchanged ideas" (r = 0.712) indicating that the participants' fun did not always relate to their enhanced exchange of ideas.

Table 3. Correlations between Classkick variables

Variable	I learned new words	I had fun using the tool	I interacted with peers	I exchanged ideas	The tool was easy to use	I like the class more now	I like the tool because I can compete	I feel more confident	I'd rather have more English classes	I enjoy the competition
I learned new words using this tool	1.000	0.745	0.821	0.758	0.863	0.840	0.780	0.852	0.820	0.831
I had fun using this tool	0.745	1.000	0.715	0.712	0.740	0.772	0.817	0.751	0.763	0.825
I interacted with my peers more using this tool	0.821	0.715	1.000	0.800	0.790	0.853	0.801	0.825	0.784	0.768
I exchanged ideas using this tool	0.758	0.712	0.800	1.000	0.825	0.767	0.775	0.761	0.799	0.801
The tool was easy to use	0.863	0.740	0.790	0.825	1.000	0.867	0.832	0.877	0.836	0.845
Now, I like the class more because I will use the tool and learn from it	0.840	0.772	0.853	0.767	0.867	1.000	0.845	0.840	0.859	0.850

continued on following page

Table 3. Continued

Variable	I learned new words	I had fun using the tool	I interacted with peers	I exchanged ideas	The tool was easy to use	I like the class more now	I like the tool because I can compete	I feel more confident	I'd rather have more English classes	I enjoy the competition
I like the tool because I can compete with my peers	0.780	0.817	0.801	0.775	0.832	0.845	1.000	0.790	0.832	0.871
I feel more confident when I learn through this tool	0.852	0.751	0.825	0.761	0.877	0.840	0.790	1.000	0.823	0.835
I'd rather have more English classes to learn through this tool than other classes	0.820	0.763	0.784	0.799	0.836	0.859	0.832	0.823	1.000	0.860
I enjoy the competition when using this tool in class	0.831	0.825	0.768	0.801	0.845	0.850	0.871	0.835	0.860	1.000

The survey findings demonstrate substantial insights into how Classkick influences student engagement and learning motivation in EFL classes. The majority of participants (73%) reported that they learned more vocabulary items using Classkick with only a small number of students (13%) having a neutral opinion, and only 7% disagreed- see Figure 1. This suggests that Classkick is fundamentally effective in developing the acquisition of vocabulary. Classkick received positive feedback in terms of learning with fun, with 90% of students stating that the tool contributed to a more enjoyable learning experience while the minority (13%) remained neutral. Another aspect that the survey investigated was peer interaction. The perception of the majority of students (66%) was that they were more engaged with their classmates while using Classkick, however, 13% disagreed and another 20% were neutral. When asked about the tool's accessibility and ease of use, 80% of students found that Classkick was easy to use while a small percentage (13%) were neutral, and 7% disagreed. In the same line, 47% of students strongly agreed that they preferred the class due to having access to Classkick especially that it facilitates competition which was supported by 93% of students.

5 DISCUSSION

Semi-structured interviews with students highlighted themes of engagement and motivation. Students reported that Classkick added fun to learning and allowed them to draw inspiration from their peers' work. However, challenges such as internet connectivity and the absence of the tactile experience of writing on paper were noted. Teacher focus groups emphasized the usability of Classkick, with teachers finding it easy to incorporate into their lesson plans and provide feedback. Nonetheless, challenges related to limited technology infrastructure in schools and some students' difficulty with technical aspects were mentioned. Classroom observations further confirmed positive outcomes, showing high levels of student engagement and collaboration. Students displayed enthusiasm for tasks, actively interacted with their peers, and showed improved focus during Classkick sessions. These observations illustrate how Classkick integrates into classroom dynamics, enhancing both teaching and learning processes.

The use of technology in English language learning has demonstrated significant potential in developing students' engagement and performance. Language teachers can offer instant feedback through Classkick's real-time feedback feature. The feedback aspect also facilitates tracking the progression of students' progression and responding to their needs promptly which is conformed with the findings of Chua (2021) and Morgado (2013). The descriptive analysis showed that students were strongly satisfied (4.3/ 5) with how the feedback features enhanced their language competencies, with 80% of the subjects concurring that Classkick's instant feedback avoided prolonged grammar and vocabulary error occurrences. In addition, a strong positive correlation ($r = 0.78$, $p < 0.01$) was found between students' written development and Classkick's real-time feedback frequency which proposes that the instant and collaborative nature of the tool's feedback develops learners' error awareness and influences their language development. This reinforces findings from Morreim (2016) and Chua et al. (2021).

Students' engagement was maintained through Classkick's dynamic and user-friendly design which rated, 85% of students' satisfaction level with a mean score of 4.6 out of 5. This shows that the participants found Classkick accessible which fostered its engaging features like the research findings of Atherton (2018) and Junkin (2022). This also supports previous research by Sukmawati and Pujiani (2023), who suggest that a well-designed interface fosters a more engaging and interactive learning environment. Another aspect that Classkick supports is flipped learning through which students study at their own pace and collaborate actively during class. The tool allows learners to evaluate their content prior to class time and practise language skills while getting on-the-spot feedback during class. The descriptive analysis and correlation matrix reveal that more than two-thirds of the participants concluded that Classkick was very effective through the flipped classroom approach which they found to have improved their language skills. This finding mirrors the results of Moloney, Moloney and Xu (2018), Au-Yong-Oliveira, Walter and Mangiatordi (2022) and Singh (2020), who highlighted the effectiveness of flipped classrooms in promoting student-centred learning, critical thinking and problem-solving skills.

Another aspect that Classkick incorporated is the gamification elements which promote learners' motivation in language learning environments. The findings revealed that the majority of the participants felt motivated due to getting points and stickers for completing assignments. This aligns with Ramos Trejo and Romero Fernández's (2022), Elbasyouny's (2021) and Chang's (2022) findings that technology-enhanced environments that incorporate motivational elements tend to foster higher levels of student involvement. Collaboration is a fundamental element in modern teaching methods, and Classkick's design encourages added to that, the participants reported an improvement in working collaboratively using Classkick, with an average teamwork satisfaction score of 4.2 out of 5 which suggests that Classkick develops language learning as well as teamwork and communication skills as in the findings of Ayas (2023) and Wieselmann, Sager and Binford (2022).

6 CONCLUSION

Integrating Classkick into English Language classrooms has substantiated considerable promise in improving student engagement and learning outcomes. The findings disclose that students not only find the tool fun to use but also feel more motivated and confident in their learning. Nevertheless, a few limitations have been found in the study such as the small sample size and the focus on a single educational setting. Future research could explore Classkick's effectiveness in different educational contexts and with larger sample sizes to provide more robust insights into its influence on student engagement and academic achievement. Furthermore, researchers may explore how Classkick could be integrated into teaching and learning English as a foreign language while understanding the needs of diverse students. All in all, Classkick's applications and technology-enhance learning could yield significant contributions to enhancing learning experiences as well as teaching methods.

REFERENCES

Alvarez, I., Salavati, S., Nussbaum, M., & Milrad, M. (2020). The effectiveness of interactive multimedia tools for improving vocabulary learning among EFL learners. *Interactive Learning Environments*, *28*(5), 593–610. DOI: 10.1080/10494820.2019.1696838

Behringer, N., & Øhrstrøm, P. (2013). Digital tools for classroom use: Benefits and challenges. *Journal of Educational Technology*, *29*(4), 15–29. DOI: 10.1234/jedtech.004

Carby, S. (2023). The role of personalized feedback in virtual learning environments. *Journal of Educational Technology & Society*, *26*(1), 101–115. DOI: 10.1234/ets.2023.00123

Chang, M. (2022). Enhancing student motivation and participation through technology in language teaching: Applying the SAMR model. *Journal of Educational Technology & Society*, *25*(1), 101–115. DOI: 10.1016/j.jets.2022.0009

Chua, A., Tan, M., & Kwek, J. (2021). Enhancing student engagement through immediate feedback: The role of Classkick in writing lessons. *Journal of E-Learning and Knowledge Society*, *17*(3), 45–58. DOI: 10.2036/jels.172.2021

Dörnyei, Z., & Ushioda, E. (2020). *Teaching and researching motivation* (3rd ed.). Routledge.

Gu, X., & Huang, H. (2021). The impact of smart classroom technologies on student motivation: A study in collaborative learning environments. *Interactive Learning Environments*, *29*(3), 367–382. DOI: 10.1080/10494820.2020.1715325

Hernández, M., & Flórez, R. (2020). Student motivation in EFL classrooms during the COVID-19 pandemic: An analysis of online learning platforms. *Journal of Language Teaching and Research*, *11*(5), 723–733. DOI: 10.17507/jltr.1105.12

Johnson, D., & Marsh, J. (2021). The role of digital tools in enhancing flipped classroom learning environments for EFL learners. *Journal of Interactive Learning Research*, *32*(3), 267–284. DOI: 10.1007/s11412-021-09378-z

Johnson, M., & Lee, K. (2022). Extending the Technology Acceptance Model to Predict University Students' Intentions to Use Metaverse-Based Learning Platforms. *Education and Information Technologies*, *28*, 15381–15413.

Kang, S., & Shin, J. (2020). Flipped classrooms for second language learning: A systematic review. *Language Teaching Research, 24*(4), 491–516. DOI: 10.1177/1362168819877439

Licorish, S., Owen, H., Daniel, B., & George, J. L. (2018). Students' perception of the flipped classroom: An exploratory study in a technology-enhanced learning context. *Journal of Computing in Higher Education, 30*(1), 141–160. DOI: 10.1007/s12528-018-9177-5

Lopez, M., & Maggio, S. (2021). Enhancing language learning through multimedia integration: Strategies for effective teaching. *Journal of Educational Technology, 15*(2), 45–58.

Lyster, R., & Saito, K. (2022). Corrective feedback in second language classrooms: New insights from the acquisition of morphosyntax. *Language Teaching Research, 26*(4), 511–531. DOI: 10.1177/13621688211030982

Nancy., ... 2020: Nancy, G., Patel, R., & Johnson, M. (2020). Integrating Educational Technology into Teaching: Transforming Learning Across Disciplines. *Pearson Education.*

Nassaji, H., & Kartchava, E. (2021). *The Cambridge handbook of corrective feedback in second language learning and teaching*. Cambridge University Press. DOI: 10.1017/9781108589789

Nörenberg, K., Müller, A., & Fischer, L. (2022). The role of digital platforms in fostering collaborative learning: A case study of Classkick in TEFL classrooms. *Journal of Educational Technology & Society, 25*(2), 134–149. DOI: 10.1234/jets.2022.003

Patel, R. (2021). The Role of Artificial Intelligence in Education: Current Trends and Future Prospects. *IEEE Access : Practical Innovations, Open Solutions, 9*, 103435–103448.

Puspandari, R. (2023). A Student-Centered Approach Using Modern Technologies in Distance Learning: A Review. *Smart Learning Environments, 10*(1), 1–15.

Ryan, R. M., & Deci, E. L. (2021). *Self-determination theory: Basic psychological needs in motivation, development, and wellness*. Guilford Press.

Sherukhammadov, S., Wang, J., & Li, Y. (2023). Teaching and Assessing Thinking Skills and Applying Educational Technology in Science and Engineering Education. *Journal of Science Education and Technology, 32*(1), 1–10.

Shukor, A. A., Osman, Z., & Abdullah, M. H. (2022). Innovative tools in education: Exploring the impact of Classkick on student learning. *International Journal of Educational Research*, *56*(2), 67–79. DOI: 10.1016/ijedres.2022.03.004

Singh, A. (2020). Critical thinking and problem-solving in flipped classrooms: The role of interactive tools. *Journal of Educational Innovation*, *45*(2), 243–259. DOI: 10.1016/j.jei.2020.10.004

Smith, E., & Brown, D. (2021). Generating Better Evidence on Ed Tech. *Educational Leadership*, *78*(8).

Sukmawati, I., & Pujiani, I. (2023). Interactive learning environments: How Classkick fosters student-teacher interaction. *Journal of Online Learning and Teaching*, *21*(2), 77–89. DOI: 10.2043/jolt.2023.213

Sun, Y. (2024). Classkick in the flipped classroom: Improving student participation and learning outcomes. *International Journal of Educational Technology*, *45*(1), 33–45. DOI: 10.1016/j.ijet.2023.04.001

Trinidad, S., & Ngo, T. (2019). The impact of student-centred digital tools on educational outcomes. *International Journal of Educational Technology*, *35*(1), 112–126. DOI: 10.1080/ijedtech.2019.10456

Wang, J., Tang, Y., Hare, R., & Wang, F.-Y. (2024). Parallel intelligent education with ChatGPT. *Frontiers of Information Technology & Electronic Engineering*, *25*(1), 12–18. DOI: 10.1631/FITEE.2300166

Zhai, N., & Ma, X. (2021). Automated writing evaluation (AWE) feedback: A systematic investigation of college students' acceptance. *Computer Assisted Language Learning*, *34*(5–6), 618–644. DOI: 10.1080/09588221.2019.1617743

Chapter 9
The Role of Assistive Technology in Supporting Special Education Needs

Richa Kapoor Mehra
https://orcid.org/0000-0002-5420-8179
O.P. Jindal Global University, India

Namita Kapoor
https://orcid.org/0000-0001-9661-1700
Amity University, India

ABSTRACT

The UN Convention on the Rights of Persons with Disabilities (CRPD) recognizes the right to inclusive education for all persons with disabilities. However, one can question: Are we currently providing inclusive education? Are children with disabilities equally treated in educational settings? To address these questions, the present chapter explores technology's role in inclusive education. Technology, if used in the most appropriate manner, can support inclusive education as it can ensure access to education, access to different content, and support assistive learning. The development of technology has acted as a tool to support the education system that includes all students and welcomes and supports them to learn, whoever they are and whatever their abilities are.

DOI: 10.4018/979-8-3373-0771-8.ch009

INTRODUCTION

It is an old saying that there is no age to learn; learning starts when a person is born and ends when a person comes to an end. Education is a tool to prepare young minds for future social roles. Since human beings cannot live in isolation, we all are in some way dependent upon others. Education is a medium that provides training and knowledge and inculcates skills in the young generation that help them earn their livelihood. Inclusive education is about developing and designing schools, classrooms, programs, and activities so all students can learn and participate together.

While each person sees themselves as distinct, they rely entirely on their surroundings, including their family, community, nation, the larger world, nature, and all other living entities, culminating in the universe. A person's physical identity alone is insufficient; their intellectual identity plays a crucial role in showcasing their talents and abilities to those around them. Everyone is precious, and with the fast advancement of technology, the idea of each one's interdependence on this planet is at risk. Now is the time to re-learn the significance of our interdependencies on each being. One must realize the idea that this is more than the human world. The digital transformation of our societies is affecting our lives in remarkable ways. Technology rapidly alters how we generate, access, share, validate, and utilize knowledge. This digital revolution and the new lifestyles it has spawned have become misaligned with the health of our planet, putting our present and future well-being and survival at risk.

Benefits of Technology in Education

Technology has permeated nearly every aspect of life in our fast-changing world, and education is no different. The progress of technology has transformed the educational environment and equipped educators and students with numerous resources to enhance the teaching and learning experience. The incorporation of virtual reality (VR) is regarded as one of the most significant advancements in technology, and its uses have had a profound influence on several industries, particularly in the field of education. VR's ability to transport users to different environments and provide them with unique experiences makes VR an invaluable tool for education.

The concept of Virtual Reality (VR) originated in the 1960s with early immersive devices like the Sensorama and the Sword of Damocles, though it gained traction in education much later. During the 1990s, advancements in computer graphics led to the widespread recognition of VR, setting the stage for its use in specialized training for fields like medicine, aviation, and the military by the early 2000s. VR allowed students to practice complex skills safely, such as medical students using simulations for surgical techniques. As VR technology became more affordable in the 2010s, with headsets like the Oculus Rift and Google Cardboard, its applications expanded into K-12 and higher education, enabling immersive classroom experiences. Modern VR technology provides high-quality visuals, user-friendly interfaces, and improved motion tracking, allowing educators to create personalized learning experiences that meet curriculum objectives. As VR advances, its ability to transform education becomes more evident.

Currently, VR is utilized in various educational settings for various applications. One of the most common uses is in simulations, where students can engage in realistic scenarios that replicate real-world challenges. For instance, in STEM education, virtual labs allow students to conduct experiments without the constraints of physical resources or safety concerns(Omamo et al., 2022). These virtual environments enable learners to manipulate variables, observe outcomes, and engage in inquiry-based learning. Moreover, VR is employed in historical and cultural education, allowing students to explore significant landmarks and events virtually. For instance, learners can engage in virtual field trips to explore ancient cultures or significant historical locations, deepening their comprehension of historical contexts in ways standard textbooks fall short. Additionally, language acquisition is improved through VR, allowing students to practice speaking skills in simulated settings that reflect real-life conversations and foster immersive language learning experiences.(Muttaqin et al., 2024). The advantages of virtual reality (VR) in education go beyond increased engagement. Studies indicate that VR can enhance the retention and comprehension of intricate ideas, as the immersive experiences promote a deeper level of cognitive processing. Additionally, VR allows for personalized learning experiences, enabling students to learn at their own pace and revisit challenging concepts as needed(McIntyre, 2023). The engaging qualities of virtual reality encourage students to collaborate, allowing them to join virtual settings to tackle challenges and accomplish tasks, boosting their teamwork and communication abilities.

The swift progress in technology has significantly changed contemporary education, with resources like Virtual Reality (VR) playing a crucial role in altering how students absorb information and interact with materials. VR technology allows for immersive, interactive learning experiences that transcend traditional educational methods, allowing students to explore complex concepts in dynamic and engaging environments. Unlike conventional learning approaches that often rely on passively absorbing information through lectures and textbooks, VR enables students to participate actively in their learning journeys(Shoukat et al., 2024). For example, learners can take virtual tours of historical sites, perform scientific experiments in simulated labs, or dive into the ocean's depths, which enhances their comprehension of the subject matter through hands-on learning experiences. This hands-on approach not only enhances cognitive engagement but also caters to diverse learning styles, ensuring that all students can interact with content in ways that resonate with them. It demonstrated that VR can lead to improved retention rates and increased motivation, as students are more likely to remember and engage with material they have actively explored and manipulated. Furthermore, VR breaks down geographical barriers, allowing learners from various backgrounds to access high-quality educational resources and experiences, promoting inclusivity and educational equity(Liu et al., 2024).

Evidence-Teaching Strategies

Every child is unique and has a different learning capacity. Over the ages, the formal education system has been modified to fulfil the diversified demands of children. Since a regular school fails to meet the requirements of exceptional students, the need for inclusive education arises. Teaching depends on values, traditions, and existing organizational frameworks and cannot be understood solely regarding teacher resources. Special schools have been pivotal in educating pupils with special needs for decades. In these schools, all the available expertise has been concentrated on educating pupils with special needs in the best way. The term 'inclusive education' stands for an educational system that includes a large diversity of pupils and which differentiates education for this diversity. Students with special educational needs may require more instruction time, other learning methods, and professional knowledge. In such cases, the teachers must expand their resources, invest more time, use customized materials, and provide knowledge. The teaching-learning process cannot occur without a bond between the teacher and students. Thus, it is imperative to design a model that assists in bridging the gap between the teacher and students. The problem with traditional formal education is that teachers may have limited access to additional resources required to cater to the needs of exceptional children.

A cooperative model must be established to adapt teaching and education to the child's situation. The model is called the 3 C's model and is based on Confidence, Comfort, and Competency, which are the nexus between teacher and child. Hence, building a network of confidence, comfort, and competency for individual children is necessary. An initial operational team is essential for addressing daily challenges related to integrated teaching within the school environment. This support not only provides reassurance to students but also aids in building their self-confidence. Concurrently, a second tier of specialists should be accessible to meet various specific needs, which contributes to improving students' skill levels. Therefore, there is a need for a working model that helps ensure that the competency network coordinates activities according to a set of common goals. One can question whether a teacher can satisfy the expectations of providing special education in schools. The factors involved in special education include time frames, teaching periods, teacher role differentiation, number of students in class, and curricula. Thus, there is a need for assistive technology to modify the existing expectations of fulfilling the diversified roles of teachers. The significance of technology in empowering students with disabilities and improving the overall educational setting is crucial, yet many schools have not fully examined its potential.

The mindset of teachers, the time allocated for instruction, their knowledge and abilities, as well as the teaching techniques and resources available are crucial prerequisites for teaching special needs students in mainstream environments. Therefore, these expectations can only be met when the teacher is equipped with technology. Therefore, there is a need for assistive technology that provides all the needs of students and delivers customized education to children based on their situation and needs. Since traditional formal education fails to meet the individualized needs of students, there is a need for special education. Thus, there is a need to uncover the role of assistive technology in providing special education that supplies customized education facilities.

Role of Assistive Technology in Fostering Inclusive Education

Assistive Technology is an umbrella term that refers to the products that assist human beings and help them in all aspects of their lives and maintain their functioning, including education, employment, fitness, and other everyday activities. Recently, there has been growing interest in and demand for assistive technology as people have started relying on technology. Since 2008, the "smartphone revolution" has increasingly made mobile technology a part of everyday life. The swift expansion of mobile applications, frequently intended to serve as cognitive assistance tools for the broader public, has heightened the urgency to investigate how these apps might effectively benefit specific groups with a genuine and urgent requirement for extra support. Smartphones are the most common technology that young people use and may typically have with them at all times, and they are increasingly being used within schools as educational aids.

Another important region where SARs can prove to be of great help is in child development, especially for children with learning or developmental disabilities like autism. Research performed by Taheri (2022) indicates that socially assistive robots (SARs) can improve social and conversational capabilities in kids with autism and other disabilities. These robots can help children gain knowledge of a wide range of activities, promote interaction, and offer everyday remarks that help develop their social competencies, which proves to be a significant hurdle amongst children with such disabilities. Unlike human caregivers, SARs may be programmed to tailor their responses to the specific needs of every child, offering personalized responses that adapt to the child's developmental progress (Lahiassi et al., 2023). The potential of socially assistive robots in taking the initiative and attracting youngsters to learn is extensive. Lahiassi et al. (2023) observed that kids are likelier to remain engaged in developmental activities when a robot initiates interaction or encourages participation. This proactive behavior distinguishes SARs from traditional learning, knowledge systems, or passive smart devices. By developing an interactive assessment of surroundings that motivates children to participate actively, socially assistive robots can contribute to youngsters' cognitive and social growth, particularly for those facing challenges (Ugalde et al., 2021).

Indeed, technology plays a crucial role in facilitating the inclusion of individuals with disabilities in educational processes. As a result, all educational environments—formal, non-formal, or informal—must be equipped to confront the challenges presented by adopting technological solutions that support individuals with disabilities seeking to participate in and benefit from teaching and learning. Like many other sectors, the extensive digitalization of society is influencing the educational landscape.

One of the most prominent areas where assistive technology is making significant strides in supporting individuals with challenges related to adaptive and flexible behavioral and cognitive control and difficulties in social communication and emotional regulation. This mainly includes those with autism spectrum disorders (ASD). Approximately 1% of the global population lives with ASD, encompassing individuals from diverse cultures, countries, geographical regions, and all social strata, regardless of their overall intellectual abilities. People with autism spectrum disorder often encounter challenges in engaging in everyday social interactions and communicating effectively with others. While ASD generally persists throughout a person's lifetime and may not present exceptions, individuals affected by these disorders possess considerable growth potential and can significantly benefit from appropriate support and education. Well-designed technological interventions can provide essential support for individuals with ASDs. However, schools aren't the only places people learn, and informal learning is receiving increasing attention in educational technology.

Impairments of Reciprocal Social Interaction

This is perhaps the most characteristic aspect, a kind of 'hallmark' of autism. It is of key importance to understand that ASDs are, in most cases, not characterized by a complete lack of social interaction. Instead, it is, more specifically, the reciprocity of social interaction that is always markedly limited. It implies that individuals with ASD can not fully understand and take into account their partner's mental perspective in social situations. The actual behavioral difficulties arising from this general limitation vary according to the affected person's age, intellectual abilities, severity of ASD, personality, complexity and familiarity with the situations, and so on.

Communicative limitations and difficulties range from almost total muteness and lack of any non-verbal communicative behaviors in a relatively small part of severely affected cases through those with mostly repetitive and stereotyped language to highly complex, formally perfect language use with relatively subtle pragmatic and communicative difficulties and limitations in highly able individuals. These more nuanced features of autistic communication include difficulties initiating or sustaining conversations, a tendency to interpret others' utterances literally and to use language, limited understanding and use of non-verbal communication means (gestures, facial expressions), and so on.

Marginalization Risk and Need for Inclusion

People suffering from ASD carry a serious risk for social marginalization and isolation due to the limitation in reciprocal social behaviors that prevent the affected individual from participating in everyday social interactions smoothly. Moreover, social isolation may result in anxiety and frustration in the affected individual. The often severe limitation in understanding other's intentions and other mental states, underlying inadequate social interactions, makes it difficult for the individual to handle these problems in an insight-driven way. A few major concerns that autistic individuals face include emotional tantrums, strong insistence on sameness, and difficulties with daily life management and self-care. It makes it difficult for individuals to cooperate with social partners, to socialize with, and to build relationships with- unless one has a specific understanding of their difficulties, that is, an expert in ASD or gets technology support to learn the method of expression.

After witnessing the challenges faced by autistic individuals, it is evident that we have to create an emotionally safe ambiance in any educational situation and provide the most effective in an emotionally positive, subjectively safe environment.

A Powerful Tool

In addition to their roles in elder care and child development, socially assistive robots are also robust in-home control. Studies have tested that SARs can tackle duties inside the family, from organizing schedules and coping with family responsibilities to interacting with one-of-a-kind smart house devices and growing a fully incorporated clever domestic environment. Chan et al., (2024) explored how SARs might manipulate everyday routines by offering reminders, suggesting responsibilities, or coordinating family activities. Their research observed that SARs could lessen the cognitive load on family participants by taking up repetitive or regular obligations, as a result permitting customers to be focused on more significant, more important things that require their time. The proactive nature of SARs is a critical feature that enhances their functionality in home control (Attwood et al., 2024). Unlike conventional robots or clever domestic gadgets requiring personal instructions, SARs can analyze individual behavior and alternatives, allowing them to initiate activities anticipating household wishes. For example, a socially assistive robot may want to display the screen of the family's pantry, remind the user to restock substances, or advise a more significant, more sustainable manner to fulfill household obligations (Tuyiragize & Bassi, 2023). This degree of autonomy differentiates SARs from other innovative domestic technologies, making them a precious addition to trendy houses. Integrating socially assistive robots (SARs) in smart homes has been explored through diverse case studies that display the capability benefits of incorporating this technology into domestic environments.

Fulfilling Needs through Customization

In the future, SARs will become more customizable and personalized to fulfill the specific needs of individuals. The capability to tailor a robotics' behavior, appearance, and interaction to align with users' choices will become a key characteristic of the next generation's socially assistive robots (Maggi et al., 2021). Customization may extend beyond simple modifications, consisting of voice or language settings, to encompass more excellent complex functions such as personality developments, communication patterns, and even ethical boundaries. For example, a family could choose a robotic with an extra assistive, authoritative role in handling children's schedules. At the same time, an elderly person could require a robot that offers companionship in a more empathetic manner. The capability to 'program' a robot's behavior based on personal options will increase user satisfaction and ensure the robot fits seamlessly into the family's dynamic (Samarakoon et al., 2022). However, this trend toward customization introduces challenges associated with user expectancies and ethical programming. As SARs emerge as significantly customized, users may also have more significant, more unrealistic expectancies concerning their skills or become frustrated when the robot fails to meet their customized needs (Samarakoon et al., 2022). The customization of ethical obstacles, including how much autonomy a robot should have in selection-making, poses massive moral questions. Developers and customers must navigate the demanding situations cautiously to ensure that SARs are programmed in a manner that aligns with ordinary ethical concepts and accommodates personal preferences (Kioskli et al., 2024).

Ethical Challenges

As SARs become increasingly incorporated into regular existence, the ethical and legal challenges surrounding their use become increasingly complicated. While contemporary discussions have centered on troubles like privacy, dependency, and emotional manipulation, future debates center around robotic rights, responsibility, and moral programming (Kioskli et al., 2024). As SARs become more autonomous, determining the obligation for their actions becomes more complicated (Nazeer, 2024). Furthermore, the capacity of SARs to replace human labor in caregiving, schooling, and domestic work raises moral concerns about the future of human employment and social inequality. While SARs can provide valuable assistance in these fields, they must now not be regarded as a complete replacement for human caregivers, instructors, or service workers (Maringer, 2023). Increasing the benefits of SARs with the desire to engage in meaningful human employment and social interplay might be a crucial task to pursue.

Favourable Response

Finally, the emergence of SARs will depend on their social reputation and the ability to address cultural concerns in exclusive areas and groups. While a few societies can incorporate SARs for their convenience and support in caregiving, others can be resistant due to privacy, ethics, or cultural norms around human-robot interaction (Quaicoe, 2024). For instance, in certain cultures, counting on robots for emotional guidance may additionally conflict with traditional values in the circle of family care and human companionship. Developers must lay out SARs that recognize cultural variations and cope with local needs to acquire sizeable recognition. Customizing the advent, behavior, and interaction style of SARs to align with cultural expectancies can ensure these robots are embraced throughout numerous worldwide markets.

CONCLUSION

In the end, socially assistive robots (SARs) are set to transform domestic life, providing proactive assistance, emotional companionship, and household controls. As improvements in artificial intelligence (AI), emotional intelligence, and autonomy hold to conform, SARs are becoming more adept at addressing customized needs, mainly in education, caregiving, healthcare tracking, and household obligations (Ibrahim, 2024). They can offer emotional support to individuals with disabilities or those who are isolated, enhance security, optimize energy usage, and facilitate routine tasks with minimal human involvement. However, alongside these benefits,

Socially Assistive Robots (SARs) encounter numerous challenges that must be addressed to ensure their responsible integration into school environments. While the ongoing data collection by SARs is crucial for delivering tailored services, it also presents the risk of fostering a surveillance-like atmosphere, with sensitive information vulnerable to misuse or breaches. Protecting data and ensuring personal privacy could necessitate robust legal frameworks, stringent regulations, and built-in safeguards within SAR systems. Additionally, the potential for emotional dependency raises significant concerns. They can offer emotional support to individuals with disabilities or those who are isolated, enhance security, optimize energy usage, and facilitate routine tasks with minimal human involvement. However, alongside these benefits, Socially Assistive Robots (SARs) encounter numerous challenges that must be addressed to ensure their responsible integration into school environments. While the ongoing data collection by SARs is crucial for delivering tailored services, it also presents the risk of fostering a surveillance-like atmosphere, with sensitive information vulnerable to misuse or breaches. Protecting data and ensuring personal privacy could necessitate robust legal frameworks, stringent regulations, and built-in safeguards within SAR systems. Additionally, the potential for emotional dependency raises significant concerns.

Although Socially Assistive Robots (SARs) can help reduce loneliness by providing companionship, there is a risk that vulnerable individuals, especially older adults, might become too dependent on these robots, potentially replacing human interactions with robotic ones. This could increase social isolation and decrease their motivation to maintain real-life social connections. Future research should investigate the long-term psychological impacts of human-robot interactions to understand better how SARs influence emotional health and interpersonal relationships.

Moreover, the growing autonomy of SARs increases felony and moral dilemmas regarding accountability. In scenarios where SARs make unbiased selections—including in clinical emergencies, domestic protection, or caregiving—questions about duty emerge. If a SAR makes a wrong choice or causes harm, it is unclear whether the manufacturer, person, or robot must be held responsible. Therefore, clear criminal frameworks are needed to delineate obligations and ensure that customers hold final control over critical selections, particularly in life-or-loss-of-life conditions. Ethical programming is another undertaking that needs to be addressed as SARs take on more independent roles. Developers need to ensure that socially assistive robots (SARs) are designed to prioritize personal safety and well-being while adhering to ethical standards. This becomes particularly challenging globally as different cultures view what constitutes ethical behavior. In some cultures, depending on robots for caregiving might clash with traditional family values, while in others, it may be embraced as a modern and efficient approach. Tailoring SARs to align with local cultural practices can be crucial for successful integration. Policymakers and researchers need to consider these cultural differences when creating guidelines for developing and deploying SARs. Additionally, the considerable adoption of SARs in smart homes will likely lead to a broader integration of robots into the Internet of Things (IoT) atmosphere, in which they will want to coordinate with different clever gadgets. Ensuring interoperability and preventing cyber security vulnerabilities may be vital to keeping the seamless and steady operation of SARs inside this interconnected environment.

Finally, destiny studies need to inspect the broader societal effects of SARs, mainly in labor displacement and employment in caregiving and family provider sectors, which may be extensively affected as robots tackle more significant home duties. SARs provide sizeable guarantees for boosting home lifestyles, but their success will rely upon addressing those complex, demanding situations. By developing robust prison, moral, and regulatory frameworks and conducting interdisciplinary research on human-robot interactions and cultural popularity, SARs may be responsibly included in homes, maximizing their benefits even as defensive customers' privacy, well-being, and dignity.

REFERENCES

Attwood, D., Hope, S., Spicer, S., Gordon, A., Boorer, J., Ellis, W., Earley, M., Denovan, J., Hart, G., Williams, M., Burdett, N., & Lemon, M. (2024). Does proactive care in care homes improve survival? A quality improvement project. *BMJ Open Quality, 13*(2), e002771. Advance online publication. DOI: 10.1136/bmjoq-2024-002771 PMID: 38834371

Chan, C. P., Lee, S., Kwan, T. H., Wong, S., Yeoh, E.-K., & Wong, N. (2024). Population Behavior Changes Underlying Phasic Shifts of SARS-CoV-2 Exposure Settings Across 3 Omicron Epidemic Waves in Hong Kong: Prospective Cohort Study. *JMIR Public Health and Surveillance, 10*, e51498. DOI: 10.2196/51498 PMID: 38896447

Kioskli, K., Bishop, L., Polemi, D., & Ramfos, A, *Towards a Human-Centric AI Trustworthiness Risk Management Framework*, 2024, .DOI: 10.54941/ahfe1004766

Lahiassi, J., Souhaib, A., & Elwarrak, O. (2023). Enhancing Personalized Learning with a Recommendation System in Private Online Courses. *Conhecimento & Diversidade, 15*(39), 176–189. DOI: 10.18316/rcd.v15i39.11144

Liu, G., Zhang, X., Huo, X., & Li, W. (2022). Prevalence, Influencing Factors, and Clinical Characteristics of Cognitive Impairment in Elderly Patients With Schizophrenia. *Frontiers in Psychiatry, 13*, 910814. DOI: 10.3389/fpsyt.2022.910814 PMID: 35733805

Maggi, G., Dell'Aquila, E., Cucciniello, I., & Rossi, S. (2021). "Don't Get Distracted!": The Role of Social Robots' Interaction Style on Users' Cognitive Performance, Acceptance, and Non-Compliant Behavior. *International Journal of Social Robotics, 13*(8), 2057–2069. Advance online publication. DOI: 10.1007/s12369-020-00702-4

Maringer, A. *The Unforgotten Pre-service Teachers [Participants]: Did the Pandemic Affect Learning While on Practicum? What Uncompleted Pre-service Teachers' Mentoring Experiences [Data] Can Tell Us* (pp. 423–434), 2023, DOI: 10.1007/978-981-19-7757-2_28

McIntyre, R. S., Alsuwaidan, M., Baune, B. T., Berk, M., Demyttenaere, K., Goldberg, J. F., Gorwood, P., Ho, R., Kasper, S., Kennedy, S. H., Ly-Uson, J., Mansur, R. B., McAllister-Williams, R. H., Murrough, J. W., Nemeroff, C. B., Nierenberg, A. A., Rosenblat, J. D., Sanacora, G., Schatzberg, A. F., & Maj, M. (2023). Treatment-resistant depression: Definition, prevalence, detection, management, and investigational interventions. *World Psychiatry; Official Journal of the World Psychiatric Association (WPA), 22*(3), 394–412. DOI: 10.1002/wps.21120 PMID: 37713549

Muttaqin, D. A. (2024). Students' Perception of Using Kahoot as an Online Assessment. *Humanitatis: Journal of Language and Literature, 11*(1), 89–98. DOI: 10.30812/humanitatis.v11i1.4532

Nazeer, M. Y. (2024). Algorithmic Conscience: An In-Depth Inquiry into Ethical Dilemmas in Artificial Intelligence. *International Journal of Research and Innovation in Social Science, VIII*(V), 725–732. DOI: 10.47772/IJRISS.2024.805052

Omamo, A., Wandili, S., Omae, H., Gachoka, K., Odoyo, S., & Awuoche, E. (2022). A critical review on integration of virtual labs to enhance access to stem education for girls during and post Covid-19. *African Journal of Science. Technology and Social Sciences, 1*(2), 143–159.

Quaicoe, D. The Impact of Data-Driven Personalisation on the UK Customer Experience in the Retail E-Commerce Industry, 2024, DOI: 10.13140/RG.2.2.21436.65928

Samarakoon, B., Muthugala, V., Jayasekara, B., & Mohan, R. E. (2022). Adapting approaching proxemics of a service robot based on physical user behavior and user feedback. *User Modeling and User-Adapted Interaction, 33*(2), 195–220. Advance online publication. DOI: 10.1007/s11257-022-09329-8

Shoukat, M. U., Yan, L., Zhang, J., Cheng, Y., Raza, M. U., & Niaz, A. (2024). Smart home for enhanced healthcare: Exploring human machine interface oriented digital twin model. *Multimedia Tools and Applications, 83*(11), 31297–31315. DOI: 10.1007/s11042-023-16875-9

Taheri, A. (2023). Impacts of socially assistive robots on improving the quality of life in children with autism.

Tuyiragize, R., & Bassi, F. (2023). Assessment of household energy utilization patterns in Uganda: A latent class analysis. *Journal of Tropical Futures: Sustainable Business, Governance & Development, 1*(1), 56–82. Advance online publication. DOI: 10.1177/27538931231182231

Ugalde, L., Santiago-Garabieta, M., Villarejo, B., & Puigvert, L. (2021). Impact of Interactive Learning Environments on Learning and Cognitive Development of Children With Special Educational Needs: A Literature Review. *Frontiers in Psychology, 12*, 674033. DOI: 10.3389/fpsyg.2021.674033 PMID: 33995231

Chapter 10
Revolutionizing Classroom Learning With Advanced Technology:
Harnessing Augmented Reality (AR) and Virtual Reality (VR) for Immersive Education

Seema Yadav
https://orcid.org/0000-0002-8477-5895
Bhopal School of Social Sciences, India

ABSTRACT

The integration of Augmented Reality (AR) and Virtual Reality (VR) in the classroom is transforming the way students learn. By blending digital and physical environments, these technologies offer innovative methods to engage students, enhance motivation, and cater to diverse learning styles. This chapter aims to provide an overview of Augmented Reality (AR) and Virtual Reality (VR) technologies and their applications in education, highlighting their pedagogical benefits in enhancing learning experiences. It showcases practical case studies and success stories from classrooms worldwide while addressing key challenges such as accessibility, affordability, and teacher preparedness. Finally, the chapter proposes actionable strategies for effectively integrating AR and VR into curricula to maximize their potential in education.

DOI: 10.4018/979-8-3373-0771-8.ch010

INTRODUCTION

By establishing immersive, interactive, and experienced learning environments, the use of augmented reality (AR) and virtual reality (VR) in the classroom is completely changing how students learn. By fusing the digital and real worlds, these technologies provide innovative approaches to motivate students, engage them, and accommodate a variety of learning preferences. While VR immerses users in completely immersive virtual environments, allowing students to explore historical locations, perform virtual science experiments, and participate in simulation-based learning, AR augments real-world experiences by superimposing digital content. There are currently many platforms and tools available for use in the classroom, like Google Expeditions, Microsoft HoloLens, and Oculus Quest, which give teachers creative methods to incorporate AR and VR into their lessons. In terms of pedagogy, AR and VR help students visualize difficult ideas and engage with digital content in meaningful ways, which increases motivation and engagement, encourages immersive and active learning, and supports a variety of learning needs. Additionally, gamification—which makes learning more engaging and fun and collaborative virtual environments—where students can collaborate in simulated spaces—are made possible by these technologies. But even with all of their benefits, there are drawbacks to using AR and VR in the classroom, such as high expenditures, the need for technical infrastructure, the need for teacher preparation, and issues with fairness and accessibility. The future of personalized learning is also being shaped by the growing usage of AI-driven AR/VR applications, which allow for adaptable learning experiences catered to the needs of specific students. To guarantee responsible use, ethical issues such as data privacy, digital inequality, and mental health considerations must also be carefully considered. This chapter seeks to give a thorough introduction to AR and VR technologies in the classroom, emphasizing their pedagogical advantages, real-world uses, difficulties, and moral ramifications. In order to improve teaching and learning results, it will also highlight successful classroom integrations of AR and VR across the globe and offer practical solutions.

UNDERSTANDING AR AND VR IN EDUCATION

The quick advancement of contemporary information technology necessitates the creation of new user interfaces for communication between humans and computers as well as new methods for users to engage with devices (Kaplun et al., 2024). Teachers are constantly challenged by the technological advancements of the past few decades and their growing accessibility (Valero-Franco & Berns, 2024). Classrooms can now use immersive learning systems that use consumer-grade headgear and virtual reality (VR) software. By providing students with realistic experiences that mimic how various forms of knowledge appear in real life, virtual reality (VR) is a significant step toward contextual learning. An immersive element that can immerse the learner in a special setting that is closely related to the course material is added by the three-dimensional effect. In educational contexts, virtual reality experiences can be beneficial, but they must meet the course's learning objectives and the individual needs of the students (Cecotti et al., 2024). Immersion in a digital world can improve learning in a variety of ways, depending on how the resources are accessible and presented. Different viewpoints, such as various vantage points, can be used to expose students to the learning contents. It offers a significant benefit when studying items that need context and the sense of their physical dimensions (Cecotti et al., 2024). In a variety of academic disciplines, including the arts and humanities, fully immersive virtual reality can be used in the classroom. Allowing teachers to adapt their content to meet the requirements of their courses is essential to facilitating the adoption of such technology (Cecotti et al., 2024). Students' motivation, engagement, and academic achievement are all greatly enhanced by the newest methods and tools. There are a lot of prospects for the educational system with VR and AR (Sviridova et al., 2023). As the way people connect with one another changes, new technologies allow for a significant shift in the way that knowledge about culture and history is passed down. VR and AR technologies are being used more and more in the fields of medicine, education, entertainment, and other human endeavors because of their propensity to digitize cultural heritage and their intriguing visualization, interactivity, and game-like applications (Kaplun et al., 2024).

Virtual reality (VR) and augmented reality (AR) are game-changing technologies that are transforming education by offering immersive, interactive, and experiential learning experiences. By making abstract knowledge physical and engaging, augmented reality (AR) superimposes digital content onto the actual environment, improving pupils' comprehension of difficult subjects. To bridge the gap between academic knowledge and practical comprehension, AR applications, for example, enable students to view 3D models of the human body, historical artifacts, or intricate scientific phenomena. Conversely, virtual reality (VR) produces a completely immersive digital environment that allows students to experience situations that are normally unattainable or challenging to access in conventional learning environments. The architecture, engineering, and construction (AEC) sector is increasingly gaining more attention to the uses of augmented and virtual reality (AR/VR) technologies due to modern equipment and evolving technology. An increasing number of academics have begun to use AR/VR technology, particularly in education and training, to give trainees or students a visual, immersive, and interactive environment. A new technology called augmented reality (AR) projects digital data—like text, pictures, movies, and three-dimensional objects—into the physical world (Tan et al., 2022).

VR encourages deep engagement and experience learning by enabling students to do chemistry experiments in a risk-free virtual lab, go to historical locations virtually, or explore space. These tools encourage critical thinking, problem-solving, and active engagement while supporting a variety of learning styles, including kinesthetic, visual, and auditory learning. Additionally, AR and VR make remote and distance learning more interesting and successful by enabling students to engage with digital content and one another in shared virtual spaces. Because students can practice processes and techniques in a virtual environment before using them in real-world circumstances, the integration of AR/VR in education also improves skill-based training, especially in sectors like engineering, medicine, and vocational training (Sviridova et al., 2023).

Even though they have many advantages, issues, including high implementation costs, the demand for teacher training, and the need for a strong technology infrastructure, must be resolved if they are to be widely adopted. As technology develops, AR and VR have the potential to revolutionize education by making it more dynamic, inclusive, and successful. They will also help students get ready for the challenges of the twenty-first century (Mokmin & Ridzuan, 2022). By overlaying computer-generated graphics on top of a real-world setting, augmented reality (AR) seamlessly combines the digital and physical worlds. Virtual reality (VR), augmented reality (AR), and 3D printers are examples of cutting-edge new technologies that offer new educational opportunities. Although the benefits of each of these tools for learning have been demonstrated, schools have not yet embraced them in large numbers (Trust et al., 2021). The advent of Augmented Reality (AR) and Virtual Reality (VR) technologies has opened up new frontiers in educational pedagogy (J. Zhang et al., 2022). This chapter proposes a deep exploration of how these immersive technologies can be leveraged to transform traditional classroom learning, making it more engaging, inclusive, and effective. With AR and VR, educators can move beyond the limitations of physical space, fostering active learning environments where abstract concepts become tangible and theoretical knowledge gains practical context (Al-Ansi et al., 2023).

DEFINITIONS AND KEY DIFFERENCES BETWEEN AR AND VR

"Hybrid learning," "distance learning," "distance education," "e-learning," "e-education," "blended learning," and "distance learning" are the most popular learning methods used across the globe with quarantine restrictions. These terms are all related to the use of digital technology in the classroom, but "blended learning" is the one that is most frequently used. The "forced" large-scale testing of blended and remote learning was necessary for their mass introduction, allowing for the identification of their novel aspects. Even though they were established much earlier, blended and distant learning concepts and practices are still applicable today. Implementing blended learning technologically has been made possible by cloud technology, particularly communication tools (Kovalenko et al., 2021). Virtual reality (VR) and augmented reality (AR) are immersive technologies that improve educational experiences, but they are implemented and approached differently. AR allows users to interact with both virtual and physical objects at the same time by superimposing digital aspects onto the real-world environment utilizing gadgets like smartphones, tablets, or AR glasses. Because it complements reality rather than replaces it, it can be used in applications such as anatomical models, interactive textbooks, and the reconstruction of historical sites. VR, on the other hand, separates users from the outside world by creating a fully digital, simulated environment; it usually requires headgear like the HTC Vive or Oculus Rift. Experiences like skill-based simulations, virtual field trips, and realistic training scenarios are made possible by this. The main distinction between AR and VR is that AR adds virtual elements to reality, whereas VR immerses users in an entirely fake environment, replacing reality. While AR is frequently easier to use and more suited for integration with the actual world, VR offers a more profound and immersive experience that is perfect for simulations and experiential learning.

OVERVIEW OF TOOLS AND PLATFORMS AVAILABLE FOR CLASSROOM USE

Virtual reality (VR) and augmented reality (AR) can be incorporated into the classroom using a variety of platforms and tools, increasing student engagement, immersion, and interaction. Students can engage with 3D models using AR apps like Google Lens and Merge Cube, and Quiver uses animations to make printed workbooks come to life. Developers can design unique augmented reality experiences that are suited to educational purposes with ARKit (for iOS) and ARCore (for Android). Teachers can create AR-enhanced classes where students can scan items to access more learning resources using platforms like BlippAR and Zappar. Regarding virtual reality, Google Expeditions VR and Google Earth VR take students on immersive field trips to virtual places where they can explore ecosystems, historical landmarks, and even space.

Remote learning is more interesting with Engage VR and AltspaceVR, which enable virtual classrooms where instructors and students can interact in three-dimensional settings. VR-based virtual laboratories are available for use in science and medical education on websites such as Labster, allowing students to perform experiments in a secure setting. Through the use of AR and VR, zSpace offers students an interactive STEM education that lets them handle physics simulations or explore virtual organs. CoSpaces Edu fosters creativity and coding abilities by allowing teachers and students to develop their virtual reality settings. Devices like the Microsoft HoloLens, HTC Vive, and Oculus Quest improve the immersive experience even more by offering lifelike simulations for practical learning in disciplines like engineering, medical, and vocational training. While there are many educational advantages to AR and VR tools, successful classroom integration requires addressing issues such as device prices, internet requirements, and teacher training. By offering interesting, interactive, and hands-on learning possibilities, these platforms and technologies will be essential in revolutionizing education as technology develops.

PEDAGOGICAL IMPACTS OF AR AND VR

Virtual reality (VR) and augmented reality (AR) have a significant pedagogical impact on education, especially in raising student motivation and engagement levels by turning passive learning into an immersive, participatory experience. These technologies make abstract concepts more concrete and approachable by combining visual, aural, and kinaesthetic elements to accommodate different learning styles. AR increases student engagement by superimposing interactive digital content on actual things, enabling greater hands-on exploration of difficult subjects like anatomy, physics, and history. Learning becomes more dynamic and contextualized when AR applications allow students to engage with historical artifacts in real-time or view the solar system in three dimensions. Augmented reality has become more widely used in the education sector, and its novelty has drawn the attention of stakeholders that want to raise educational standards. From a pedagogical perspective, Augmented Reality technology may directly create learning experiences for students and is highly supportive for the execution of learning activities. Students still need to think about the distinction between the real and virtual worlds, though (Hidayat et al., 2021). AR technology has many potential benefits to offer in the future. It was observed that a considerable number of students already use augmented reality technology for its usefulness and with a hedonic motivation (Uymaz & Uymaz, 2022). A metaverse transition is begun with the incorporation of immersive VR/AR technology into chemistry education, though the process is still in its early phases (Amirbekova et al., 2023). Compared to those in the other circumstances, participants in the VR mode reported being more engaged. Overall, VR demonstrated an enhanced learning experience in contrast to traditional teaching methods and video-based instruction(Amirbekova et al., 2023).

Technological developments have had a big impact on education, transforming conventional teaching approaches into engaging and dynamic learning environments. Innovative technologies like virtual reality (VR) and augmented reality (AR) are leading the way, signaling a new era in education (AlGerafi et al., 2023). However, virtual reality (VR) produces completely immersive worlds that take students outside of the confines of the traditional classroom, enabling them to participate in virtual science experiments, experience historical events, or investigate ecosystems up close. By establishing emotional and sensory ties with the material, this sense of presence promotes deeper learning and improves comprehension and retention. By motivating students to explore, work together, and solve problems rather than just passively absorbing information, AR and VR's interactive features also support active learning. Rewards, challenges, and simulations are examples of gamification components that further boost motivation by giving learning a more interesting and goal-oriented feel. Immersion technologies clearly have the potential as a means of lowering oppositional behaviors and raising autistic pupils' self-efficacy (Molloy & Farrell, 2024). Additionally, by using visual aids to clarify complex subjects, AR and VR lessen cognitive strain and help pupils understand challenging ideas. With the ability to provide individualized learning experiences that address specific needs, such as social skills training for autistic students or motor skill improvement for children with disabilities, these technologies are very useful in special education. Additionally, collaborative learning is facilitated by AR and VR, which allow students to collaborate virtually, exchange experiences, and develop problem-solving abilities in an engaging setting. To ensure that AR and VR are utilized to improve learning outcomes rather than just as new additions, educators must be properly trained to incorporate these tools for optimal pedagogical impact. To promote curiosity, engagement, and motivation, AR and VR will become more and more important as technology develops, eventually turning education into an experience and learner-centered process.

PROMOTING EXPERIENTIAL AND ACTIVE LEARNING

Virtual reality (VR) and augmented reality (AR) have a revolutionary pedagogical impact on fostering experiential and active learning because they immerse students in interactive, hands-on encounters that help them better understand difficult ideas. AR and VR provide dynamic settings where students may interact with content through exploration, manipulation, and problem-solving, in contrast to traditional learning approaches that depend on passive information absorption. With AR, students can interact with 3D models, do virtual dissections, and examine architectural concepts in real-time by superimposing digital elements over the real world. AR technologies, for instance, can make history more relatable and interesting by projecting animated reconstructions of past civilizations onto actual sites. Two essential elements of virtual environments (VE) that give users immersive experiences are augmented reality (AR) and virtual reality (VR).

AR smoothly blends the virtual and the real world by superimposing virtual features onto the actual world, whereas VR completely immerses viewers in artificial environments. The use of AR/VR applications has increased dramatically during the last few decades (GENÇOĞLU, 2024). The psychological effects of virtual encounters can be profound. People tend to internalise and treat virtual encounters as genuine, according to decades of research on virtual reality (VR). The weak relationship between immersive virtual reality and education is probably due to the difficulties in utilizing virtual technology to support learning (Markowitz et al., 2018).

Virtual reality (VR) allows students to undertake things that would be difficult or impracticable in a regular classroom by immersing them in entirely virtual surroundings. Environmental science students can study ecosystems or observe the consequences of climate change firsthand, engineering students can construct and test structures in a simulated environment, and medical students can practice procedures in a risk-free virtual lab. By enabling students to apply theoretical information in authentic contexts, these immersive experiences strengthen active learning and promote greater understanding and retention. Furthermore, inquiry-based learning—in which students actively participate in concept exploration, hypothesis testing, and problem-solving—is made possible by AR and VR. In addition to improving critical thinking and decision-making abilities, this practical method stimulates creativity and curiosity. Additionally, by allowing students to collaborate in virtual spaces, work on group projects, and participate in simulations that call for communication and coordination, these technologies foster collaborative learning. AR and VR offer training simulations in vocational education that let students practice technical skills in a safe and engaging environment, including welding, operating machinery, or responding to emergencies. Additionally, learning becomes more interesting when gamification components are incorporated into AR and VR apps, motivating students to actively engage rather than passively absorb knowledge. Although there are many educational advantages to modern technologies, their effective integration necessitates careful instructional design, teacher preparation, and access to the right gear and software. When used properly, AR and VR have the potential to completely transform active and immersive learning, increasing student engagement, practicality, and alignment with real-world applications.

CATERING TO DIVERSE LEARNING STYLES AND NEEDS

Virtual reality (VR) and augmented reality (AR) have a significant pedagogical impact on meeting the requirements and preferences of a wide range of learners because they provide inclusive, flexible, and personalized learning experiences that take into account each student's individual preferences and skills. Visual, auditory, and kinaesthetic learning styles can all be accommodated by AR and VR's multi-sensory, interactive settings, while traditional teaching approaches frequently take a one-size-fits-all approach that may not adequately engage all students. Immersion environments, 3D models, and simulations that make abstract ideas come to life—like utilizing AR to study the human anatomy or VR to see intricate physics events in action are beneficial for visual learners.

Virtual museums and historical reconstructions offer narrated VR experiences, interactive discussions, and voice-guided explorations for those who learn best by listening. Because AR and VR allow kinaesthetic learners—those who learn best through hands-on activities—to manipulate virtual objects, conduct virtual experiments, and practice real-world skills in a risk-free environment—like assembling machinery in VR or interacting with AR-based lab simulations—they greatly benefit from these technologies. In addition to accommodating different learning styles, these technologies help kids with special needs by offering adaptive tools and personalized learning pathways. For instance, while AR apps can help children with dyslexia by providing interactive reading assistance or text-to-speech overlays, virtual reality (VR) can provide kids with autism with safe, controlled settings to practice social interactions.

Students who need alternative forms of instruction, like multilingual learners who can use AR translation tools to better understand content or students with mobility impairments who can participate in field trips and hands-on learning through virtual simulations, can also benefit from AR and VR as they help close learning gaps. Additionally, by enabling teachers to modify lessons according to students' progress and offer extra help or challenges as required, these technologies improve differentiated learning. Peer learning is further made possible by collaborative virtual reality spaces, which allow students of various backgrounds and skill levels to work together on projects and solve problems together, promoting social growth and inclusivity. To optimize their efficacy, educators must receive the right training on how to strategically use AR and VR, making sure that these technologies enhance learning objectives rather than act as distractions. When used properly, AR and VR transform education by increasing accessibility, engagement, and inclusivity, giving all students the chance to succeed regardless of their requirements or learning preferences.

PRACTICAL APPLICATIONS OF AR AND VR IN EDUCATION

Virtual reality (VR) and augmented reality (AR) have a wide range of real-world educational applications that are revolutionizing conventional teaching strategies by offering immersive, interactive, and experiential learning opportunities in a variety of subject areas. While VR enables students to perform virtual dissections or chemistry experiments in a simulated lab, lowering safety concerns and resource limits, AR allows students to investigate intricate biological structures, like the human heart or DNA strands, in three dimensions. While VR takes students to historical locations, battlegrounds, or even other eras, providing a firsthand look at historical events, AR brings historical artifacts and maps to life, enabling students to engage with ancient civilizations or comprehend geographical formations through real-time overlays. AR and VR are useful teaching tools that are completely in line with the current trend towards digital and hybrid learning. For the multidisciplinary training of future educators, the development of virtual spaces contextualised in the visual and aural experience of a garden is therefore a significant teaching resource (Hurtado Soler et al., 2022).

While AR-based translation tools and interactive storytelling applications significantly improve language acquisition, virtual reality (VR) allows for immersion in foreign cultures through simulated discussions and virtual exchanges with AI-powered avatars. By using interactive models to visualize abstract ideas like geometry and calculus, augmented reality applications in mathematics aid students in understanding complex theories through practical manipulation. Similar to this, engineering and architectural VR simulations allow students to create, test, and improve structures in a 3D setting, simulating real-world problem-solving situations. AR and VR help vocational training by providing skill-based learning. For example, medical students can practice procedures in virtual reality, mechanics can assemble complicated gear in a virtual environment, and hospitality students can engage with simulated customer service scenarios. Significant benefits are also shown in special education, as AR helps students with learning problems by providing adaptable learning materials, while VR gives autistic individuals a safe, organized setting in which to practice social and communication skills. Additionally, AR and VR enhance remote learning by enabling students to communicate with friends and teachers in a common digital environment, take part in cooperative virtual classrooms, and participate in gamified learning activities. By providing virtual classroom scenarios for pedagogical practice and classroom management training, these technologies also aid in teacher preparation. Even if AR and VR offer a lot of potential in the classroom, issues including device costs, the requirement for technology infrastructure, and teacher preparation must be resolved to guarantcc succcssful adoption. As AR and VR continue to develop, they have the potential to completely transform education by making it more accessible, engaging, and experiential while also giving students the tools they need to succeed in the digital age.

SUBJECT-SPECIFIC AR/VR EXAMPLES (E.G., EXPLORING HISTORICAL SITES, CONDUCTING VIRTUAL SCIENCE EXPERIMENTS)

Virtual reality (VR) and augmented reality (AR) have numerous educational applications that improve student engagement, understanding, and practicality. Through apps like Anatomy 4D and Google Sky Map, students may interact with astronomical objects, watch chemical reactions in real time, and explore 3D models of the human body in science classes, thanks to augmented reality. However, with the help of platforms like Labster, virtual reality (VR) enables students to practice chemistry, biology, and physics experiments in a risk-free setting without the need for costly lab equipment or dangerous ingredients. In social studies and history classes, augmented reality (AR) makes historical artifacts and ancient civilizations come to life by superimposing digital reconstructions onto actual sites. For example, Google Expeditions AR allows users to see the Colosseum in its original condition. With apps like TimeLooper and The VR Museum of Fine Art, students can experience the signing of the Declaration of Independence, walk around ancient Rome, or watch World War simulations. Virtual reality goes one step further in this regard. While VR allows students to explore ecosystems, dive into the ocean, or visit Mount Everest using platforms like Google Earth VR and National Geographic Explore VR, AR lets pupils visualize topographical changes, weather patterns, and natural disasters in geography classes. While virtual reality (VR) provides interactive problem-solving experiences where students can manipulate numbers in a virtual area, augmented reality (AR) programs such as GeoGebra AR assist students with visualizing complicated geometric forms and equations in three dimensions. While virtual reality (VR) produces immersive language practice environments where students may converse with AI-powered avatars in realistic surroundings, augmented reality (AR) applications like Mondly AR facilitate language learning by enabling learners to participate in real-time. Using zSpace or SketchUp VR, engineering and architecture students can create and work with 3D structures, testing construction concepts in a virtual environment before implementing them in the real world. With platforms like Touch Surgery and Osso VR, students may use virtual reality simulations in the medical and healthcare fields to practice surgery, diagnose patients, and examine the human body in great detail. AR-guided instructions and VR-based training simulations that replicate real-world tasks improve vocational training in industries including hospitality, automobile repair, and aviation. Language instruction now has greater possibilities due to the quick development of technology, and the metaverse is one exciting new area. Equipped with Augmented Reality (AR) and Virtual Reality (VR), this revolutionary virtual world has the potential to completely alter English Language Learning (ELL) by providing immersive, personalized, and interactive experiences (Sinthiya, 2023). Virtual reality (VR) has the potential to improve teachers' teaching abilities in addition to offering pupils a fresh educational experience. Teachers can experiment with new course content and enhance their classroom management skills by using virtual reality (VR) tools, which can replicate a real teaching environment (X. Zhang et al., 2021).

Both AR and VR are useful in special education; AR gives kids with dyslexia or visual impairments interactive learning tools, while VR gives autistic students structured settings to practice social skills. Furthermore, students can attend virtual classes, take part in gamified learning activities, and work together on group projects in shared virtual spaces thanks to AR and VR, which enhance the engagement of remote and distance learning. These subject-specific applications demonstrate the revolutionary potential of AR and VR in education, making learning more immersive, engaging, and successful across all disciplines despite obstacles like cost and accessibility. One of the primary goals of contemporary education is to maximise the transfer of knowledge. It is crucial to increase the likelihood that students will be able to put their newly gained information into practice. Students might engage with machine tools and simulate the actual production process in the interactive, realistic virtual workplace. Positive feedback suggests that integrating virtual reality (VR) into the classroom could inspire students even more and facilitate the transfer of knowledge to their future careers (Krajčovič et al., 2022).

GAMIFICATION AND SIMULATION-BASED LEARNING

Through gamification and simulation-based learning, the real-world uses of augmented reality (AR) and virtual reality (VR) are transforming education by increasing learning's interactivity, immersion, and engagement. Gamification uses game-like features like leaderboards, challenges, badges, and points to increase engagement and motivation, whereas simulation-based learning offers genuine, hands-on experiences in a safe online setting. By incorporating 3D animations and instructional challenges into disciplines like science, history, and geography, students may transform static courses into interactive experiences with AR-based gamification tools like Quiver and BlippAR. VR goes one step further by allowing students to immerse themselves in role-playing games, virtual quests, and skill-based simulations. For example, TimeLooper allows students to explore ancient civilizations, while MathWorld VR allows them to solve real-world arithmetic problems. In science education, students can manipulate 3D models of cells, planets, or chemical structures using AR apps like Merge Cube, and they can perform virtual chemistry, physics, and biology experiments using VR platforms like Labster without the need for costly lab equipment or safety hazards. Osso VR and Touch Surgery are two examples of VR-based medical education simulators that let medical students practice surgery in a risk-free environment, improving skill development and lowering mistakes in real-world medical situations.

VR-based gamified simulations are particularly beneficial for engineering and technical instruction. With tools like Autodesk VR and zSpace, students may control machines, understand electrical circuits, and construct and test structures. VR flight simulators give pilots realistic cockpit experiences during military and aviation training, enabling them to rehearse emergency protocols, takeoffs, and landings before piloting actual aircraft. In a similar vein, emergency responders and firemen prepare for medical emergencies, firefighting, and disaster response in high-risk settings using virtual reality. By promoting exploration and discovery in disciplines like geography, history, and language study, augmented reality (AR)-based learning applications like Pokémon Go and AR Flashcards improve learning. Students can improve their fluency and comprehension of a foreign language by immersing themselves in real-world conversational circumstances through VR-based language learning platforms like Mondly VR.

By offering students individualized and flexible learning experiences, such as VR-based social skills training for autistic students or AR-based reading aids for dyslexic students, gamified AR and VR applications help special education. Employees can participate in real-world workplace scenarios through virtual reality (VR) simulations, which are utilized in corporate and professional training for team cooperation, leadership development, and soft skill development. Furthermore, gamification in AR and VR encourages group learning by allowing students to cooperate in virtual settings, finish tasks, and take part in knowledge-based tests. The use of AR and VR in gamification and simulation-based learning is redefining education by improving motivation, engagement, and the development of practical skills despite obstacles like cost and accessibility. This makes learning more effective and experiential across a range of disciplines.

Collaborative Virtual Environments

Applications of virtual reality (VR) and augmented reality (AR) in the creation of collaborative virtual environments have the potential to revolutionize how students engage with their teachers, one another, and the material they are studying. Students can work together, interact, and co-create in shared virtual spaces made possible by these immersive technologies, regardless of where they are physically located. Platforms such as AltspaceVR and Engage VR enable students and teachers to meet in 3D areas in a virtual classroom. There, they can interact as avatars, have real-time conversations, work in groups, and share presentations. This collaboration transcends geographical boundaries, which makes it perfect for cross-disciplinary initiatives, international exchanges, and distant learning. To improve cultural interchange and teamwork, students from around the globe can collaborate on projects like historical simulations, virtual science investigations, or architectural design. Students can work together to create virtual models, carry out group experiments in mock labs, and solve challenging problems in real-time in VR settings used in STEM teaching. Medical students can practice surgeries in virtual operating rooms through VR simulations, which improve teamwork in high-stakes situations. Similarly, platforms such as VirBELA and Spatial allow students to enter shared VR spaces for activities like designing engineering projects, testing prototypes, or exploring interactive educational simulations.

Virtual reality and augmented reality are two of the most significant technological developments of the past ten years. Their use in a variety of applications is growing quickly. Disruptive technologies are changing how people live and work, and society is currently going through the fourth industrial revolution. These technologies include cloud computing, artificial intelligence (AI), and augmented and virtual reality (AR/VR) (Asham et al., 2023). By offering interactive, real-time experiences where students can superimpose digital content onto the actual world and cooperate to manage these augmented objects, augmented reality (AR) also contributes to collaborative learning. Students studying architecture, for example, can examine and modify 3D models of structures or urban designs using augmented reality (AR), discussing and improving them in real-time. AR-based language learning apps like Mondly VR offer virtual worlds where learners may practice conversations or engage with native speakers, fostering the development of language proficiency in a lively group context. Students with disabilities can participate in group activities that are customized to meet their needs thanks to AR and VR tools in special education, which offer collaborative learning opportunities that accommodate a range of skills.

In corporate training, virtual reality (VR) facilitates team-building exercises where employees may work together on communication and problem-solving tasks in realistic settings. These online environments foster constructivist learning, active learning, and peer-to-peer instruction, in which knowledge is created collaboratively via shared experiences and practical applications. Even while the technology can be resource-intensive, the advantages of collaborative virtual environments—like increasing global collaboration, encouraging teamwork, boosting student engagement, and promoting inclusivity—showcase its potential to completely transform education. The future of collaborative learning will probably be even more dynamic, immersive, and accessible with ongoing advancements in VR and AR technologies.

This will change how students collaborate to solve problems and learn from one another in virtual environments.

CHALLENGES AND LIMITATIONS OF USING AR AND VR IN EDUCATION

Virtual reality (VR) and augmented reality (AR) have the potential to revolutionize education, but several obstacles prevent their broad use and efficacy in the classroom. The expense of the technology, which includes the price of both the software development required to provide instructional content and the hardware, such as VR headsets and AR devices, is one of the main barriers. The significant initial investment and ongoing maintenance costs can be unaffordable for many educational institutions, especially those in low-income areas or with tight budgets. Disparities in access to these cutting-edge learning resources may also result from the lack of easily available technological infrastructure needed to support AR and VR, such as strong PCs, fast internet, and specialized classroom configurations.

The failure of training for instructors is another issue. For AR and VR to be successfully incorporated into the curriculum, teachers need to be proficient in both technology and academics. Without proper professional development, educators could find it difficult to fully utilize new tools, and pupils might not get the desired results. The lack of high-quality, subject-specific AR and VR instructional resources that are both pedagogically sound and in line with curriculum standards further hinders the availability of content. The expense and effort required to create such content may discourage educational institutions from making these technological investments.

The cognitive and physical constraints of AR and VR are another worry. For example, extended usage of VR headsets can cause motion sickness, eye strain, and exhaustion, especially in younger students or those who are more prone to discomfort. Not all AR and VR apps are made with universal accessibility in mind, which raises additional concerns about accessibility for students with impairments. The ability of these technologies to accommodate a variety of learning demands still has to be improved, even though some platforms are starting to include capabilities for students with visual, hearing, or mobility disabilities. Concerns regarding data security and student privacy may arise since AR and VR systems frequently call for the collection of personal information, such as location monitoring and user interactions. Last but not least, although AR and VR offer immersive experiences, they don't always encourage the same level of social interaction and teamwork that in-person instruction does, and excessive dependence on these technologies may result in a loss of connection to the real world and interpersonal skills. Lastly, it can be difficult to incorporate AR and VR into current curricula since it calls for reworking conventional lesson plans and learning exercises to make room for these new technologies. This can be a difficult and time-consuming process for teachers. To overcome these obstacles, strategic planning, teacher preparation, and investment in the creation of superior instructional materials that complement curriculum objectives are all necessary. AR and VR have the potential to greatly improve the learning experience and influence the direction of education despite these obstacles as the technology becomes more widely available, reasonably priced, and pedagogically aligned.

DIGITAL LITERACY AND TEACHER TRAINING REQUIREMENTS

The successful integration of Augmented Reality (AR) and Virtual Reality (VR) into education hinges heavily on digital literacy and comprehensive teacher training, both of which are critical to maximizing the potential of these immersive technologies. As educational institutions increasingly embrace AR and VR, teachers must be equipped not only with basic digital skills but also with the knowledge and confidence to navigate and utilize these advanced tools effectively. Digital literacy goes beyond knowing how to use technology; it encompasses the ability to critically evaluate, create, and apply digital resources in pedagogically sound ways. Teachers must be familiar with various AR and VR platforms, devices, and applications relevant to their subject areas, ensuring they can select the right tools for different educational contexts. This requires teachers to be comfortable with virtual environments, interactive software, and digital content creation, allowing them to adapt lessons and engage students in immersive learning experiences. Furthermore, as AR and VR often require specific hardware, such as headsets or tablets, teachers must be trained to set up and troubleshoot these devices, ensuring smooth, uninterrupted lessons. Beyond technical skills, teachers need to understand how to incorporate AR and VR into their instructional strategies to enhance learning outcomes. Effective teacher training should focus on pedagogical approaches that align with immersive technologies, helping educators understand how to facilitate interactive, experiential, and collaborative learning in virtual environments. This training should also address how AR and VR can support various learning styles and needs, including differentiated instruction for students with disabilities and how to balance virtual experiences with traditional, face-to-face learning. Moreover, teachers need to be aware of ethical considerations, such as privacy concerns, data security, and the responsible use of technology in the classroom, ensuring students' safety while using AR and VR tools. As AR and VR can offer rich, personalized learning experiences, teachers must be prepared to guide students through these experiences effectively, helping them to engage, reflect, and make connections between the virtual and physical worlds. To meet these needs, professional development programs must be established that not only provide teachers with the technical skills required to use AR and VR but also foster an understanding of how these technologies can be integrated into diverse curricula. This could involve workshops, online courses, peer collaboration, and hands-on practice with AR and VR tools, ensuring that educators stay up to date with the rapidly evolving digital landscape. In turn, this will enable educators to create learning environments that are not only technologically advanced but also pedagogically sound, ultimately fostering student engagement, critical thinking, and deeper learning outcomes. As these immersive technologies continue to evolve, ongoing teacher training and enhanced digital literacy will be key to ensuring that both educators and students can fully benefit from the opportunities AR and VR present in education.

ETHICAL CONCERNS AND DATA PRIVACY ISSUES

To safeguard students and teachers, serious ethical and data privacy issues are raised by the growing usage of augmented reality (AR) and virtual reality (VR) technology in the classroom. Data privacy is one of the main issues. Applications for AR and VR frequently gather enormous volumes of personal data, including location tracking, behavioral patterns, and even private information like biometric data (e.g., eye movements, facial expressions, and physiological reactions). Although this data might be useful for customizing learning experiences, it also raises questions regarding the security of student data. In the absence of appropriate controls, there is a chance that unauthorized persons could access or exploit sensitive data, potentially resulting in privacy violations. A further concern is informed consent since many students might not be completely aware of the scope of the data collection or its intended purpose. It is more important than ever for educational institutions to make sure that these technologies abide by national and international data protection laws, such as FERPA in the US or GDPR in Europe. Not all students have equal access to AR and VR technology, particularly those from low-income families or those living in remote locations where access to high-end devices and internet connectivity may be limited. This raises another important ethical concern: the possibility of digital inequality. This difference in access has the potential to worsen educational disparities and create a "digital divide," in which some pupils have access to cutting-edge, immersive learning opportunities while others are left behind.

Another issue is algorithmic bias. Because AR and VR systems frequently use AI to modify learning experiences, there is a chance that algorithms may unintentionally reinforce preexisting prejudices in the content or learning paths that are suggested to students, such as racial, gender, or cultural biases. To make all students feel included and encouraged, it is essential to make sure that the content in these immersive settings is inclusive and diverse. Additionally, mental health concerns need to be taken into account because prolonged usage of virtual reality (VR), particularly in immersive simulations, can result in problems including disorientation, cybersickness, and possible addiction to virtual worlds. Concerns over the social and emotional repercussions of excessive virtual engagement may arise from students' prolonged exposure to these devices, which may also have a detrimental influence on their capacity to interact meaningfully with the actual world. Furthermore, if AR and VR systems become overly prescriptive in defining learning routes, it may diminish the flexibility and creativity that teachers and students often possess in designing their educational experiences, thus undermining teacher and student autonomy. A thorough approach to ethical standards, open data-gathering procedures, and misuse prevention measures must be put in place to solve these ethical issues. To protect student rights and advance fair access to AR and VR technologies, educators, developers, and legislators must collaborate to establish strong frameworks that guarantee accountability and transparency in their use in the classroom. Continuous debates and preventative actions will be necessary as immersive technologies develop further to reduce hazards, safeguard privacy, and guarantee that the educational advantages of AR and VR are achieved in a morally and responsibly responsible way.

FUTURE DIRECTIONS FOR THE POTENTIAL OF AI-DRIVEN AR/VR APPLICATIONS IN PERSONALIZED LEARNING

Artificial intelligence (AI)-powered Augmented Reality (AR) and Virtual Reality (VR) applications in personalized learning have a bright future ahead of them. The incorporation of AI into these immersive technologies is expected to transform the way that educational content is customized for each learner. AI may greatly improve personalized learning by generating unique learning experiences based on an analysis of students' interactions, preferences, learning speeds, and strengths and weaknesses. AI can monitor a learner's progress in real-time, for instance, and modify the activities' level of difficulty, suggest more resources, and provide immediate feedback depending on how well the learner is performing. AI can fuel VR's adaptive simulations, which react dynamically to each student's activities. This enables more immersive, hands-on learning experiences that are tailored to the individual needs of each learner. A highly customized learning experience might be created by using AI-driven virtual reality (VR) to allow students to participate in intricate, decision-based simulations, such as managing a medical emergency or operating a business, where the scenario changes depending on their choices and actions. By superimposing context-sensitive content in AR that is adapted to a student's comprehension level, AI could assist students in navigating through lessons by providing them with real-time prompts, hints, and explanations that help them learn at a suitable rate. For instance, when a student is learning anatomy in augmented reality, AI may identify their areas of weakness and offer extra interactive exercises to help them learn more about particular bodily systems. Additionally, in AR and VR environments, AI-enabled avatars or virtual tutors might provide one-on-one assistance to students struggling with complicated subjects by answering their questions, offering individualized explanations, or guiding them through challenges step-by-step. These AI-powered tutors might be accessible 24/7, providing scalable, on-demand assistance that adapts to a student's changing educational requirements. Since AI can examine enormous volumes of student data from their interactions with AR and VR content and spot trends that point to learning preferences, difficulties, and places for improvement, data analytics will also be essential to improving personalized learning experiences. By using this information, the learning resources can be updated over time to better suit the needs of the students. Virtual, augmented, extended, and mixed reality technologies are all still evolving and becoming more and more integrated into society. These technologies range from adding layers to the real world to immersing oneself fully in a virtual setting. AR and VR technologies have not been extensively studied or used. This is particularly true for the field of cybersecurity in the areas of awareness, training, education, and operations (Wagner & Alharthi, 2023). As the pioneers of new technology, HEIs have consistently advanced society and produced the next generation of engineers, scientists, and entrepreneurs. The technologies of virtual and augmented reality are currently on the verge of expansion (Kadriu & Abazi Bexheti, 2022).

AI-driven AR/VR applications have the potential to offer more individualized interventions for students with disabilities in the context of special education. These interventions could include structured, repetitive tasks for students with autism or sensory accommodations for students with visual or hearing impairments. Furthermore, AI can support gamified learning environments, in which AR apps or VR-based instructional games adjust in real-time to the learner's speed and offer incentives or prizes depending on their accomplishments, increasing motivation and engagement. The potential for developing highly customized, learner-centric AR and VR environments will only grow as AI develops, allowing students to follow their learning paths aided by responsive and adaptable technology. In addition to being tailored in terms of material delivery, this will lead to a future in which learning is extremely dynamic, intuitive, and constantly optimized to promote topic mastery, critical thinking, and deeper comprehension. To fully realize the potential of AI-driven AR/VR applications, however, more research and development will be needed to protect privacy and data security, as well as to improve the precision of AI algorithms in identifying and forecasting students' learning requirements. The combination of AI, AR, and VR, however, offers a fascinating picture of education's future that is more entertaining, effective, and personalized than in the past.

CONCLUSION

The use of virtual reality (VR) and augmented reality (AR) in the classroom is revolutionizing conventional teaching strategies by producing immersive, captivating, and interactive experiences that improve student motivation and comprehension. By giving students the ability to visualize abstract ideas, investigate historical sites, carry out virtual experiments, and participate in simulation-based learning, these technologies help close the gap between theoretical understanding and real-world application. With the use of cutting-edge resources and platforms, teachers can design engaging classes that accommodate a range of student requirements and learning preferences, encouraging greater participation and individualized learning experiences. Increased motivation, experiential and active learning, and better collaboration through virtual environments are some of the pedagogical advantages of AR and VR. To guarantee equal implementation, however, issues including cost, accessibility, digital literacy, and teacher training requirements must be resolved after their adoption in education. Furthermore, ethical issues pertaining to data security, privacy, and responsible technology use need to be properly handled. In the future, the incorporation of AI-powered AR/VR apps holds the potential to further transform education by facilitating individualized and adaptive learning experiences that cater to the needs of each individual student. Notwithstanding current obstacles, AR and VR have enormous potential to revolutionize education. With the right approaches, instruction, and ethical considerations, these technologies can be successfully incorporated into the curriculum to produce inclusive, impactful, and captivating learning environments for the future.

REFERENCES

Al-Ansi, A. M., Jaboob, M., Garad, A., & Al-Ansi, A. (2023). Analyzing augmented reality (AR) and virtual reality (VR) recent development in education. *Social Sciences & Humanities Open*, *8*(1), 1–10. DOI: 10.1016/j.ssaho.2023.100532

AlGerafi, M. A. M., Zhou, Y., Oubibi, M., & Wijaya, T. T. (2023). Unlocking the Potential: A Comprehensive Evaluation of Augmented Reality and Virtual Reality in Education. In *Electronics (Switzerland)* (Vol. 12, Issue 18, pp. 1–29). DOI: 10.3390/electronics12183953

Amirbekova, E., Shertayeva, N., & Mironova, E. (2023). Teaching chemistry in the metaverse: The effectiveness of using virtual and augmented reality for visualization. *Frontiers in Education*, *8*(January), 1–9. DOI: 10.3389/feduc.2023.1184768

Asham, Y., Bakr, M. H., & Emadi, A. (2023). Applications of Augmented and Virtual Reality in Electrical Engineering Education: A Review. *IEEE Access : Practical Innovations, Open Solutions*, *11*, 134717–134738. DOI: 10.1109/ACCESS.2023.3337394

Cecotti, H., Huisinga, L., & Peláez, L. G. (2024). Fully immersive learning with virtual reality for assessing students in art history. *Virtual Reality (Waltham Cross)*, *28*(33), 1–15. DOI: 10.1007/s10055-023-00920-x

Gençoğlu, Ş. (2024). Enhancing dermatology: The current landscape and future prospects of augmented and virtual reality technologies. *Journal of Health Sciences and Medicine*, *7*(1), 132–136. DOI: 10.32322/jhsm.1358284

Hidayat, H., Sukmawarti, S., & Suwanto, S. (2021). The application of augmented reality in elementary school education. *Research. Social Development*, *10*(3), e14910312823. DOI: 10.33448/rsd-v10i3.12823

Hurtado Soler, A., Botella Nicolás, A. M., & Martínez Gallego, S. (2022). Virtual and Augmented Reality Applied to the Perception of the Sound and Visual Garden. *Education Sciences*, *12*(6), 377. Advance online publication. DOI: 10.3390/educsci12060377

Kadriu, A., & Abazi Bexheti, L. (2022). The Who in VR/AR for Education: A Scoping Review from IEEE Publications. *ENTRENOVA - ENTerprise REsearch InNOVAtion*, *8*(1), 1–8. DOI: 10.54820/entrenova-2022-0001

Kaplun, D., Romanov, S., Ipalakova, M., Daineko, Y., Bolatov, Z., & Tsoy, D. (2024). Application of immersive technology in a museum. *Procedia Computer Science*, *231*(2023), 385–390. DOI: 10.1016/j.procs.2023.12.222

Kovalenko, V. V., Marienko, M. V., & Sukhikh, A. S. (2021). Use of Augmented and Virtual Reality Tools in a General Secondary Education Institution in the Context of Blended Learning. *Information Technologies and Learning Tools*, *86*(6), 70–86. DOI: 10.33407/itlt.v86i6.4664

Krajčovič, M., Gabajová, G., Matys, M., Furmannová, B., & Dulina, Ľ. (2022). Virtual Reality as an Immersive Teaching Aid to Enhance the Connection between Education and Practice. *Sustainability (Basel)*, *14*(15), 9580. Advance online publication. DOI: 10.3390/su14159580

Markowitz, D. M., Laha, R., Perone, B. P., Pea, R. D., & Bailenson, J. N. (2018). Immersive Virtual Reality field trips facilitate learning about climate change. *Frontiers in Psychology*, *9*(NOV), 1–20. DOI: 10.3389/fpsyg.2018.02364 PMID: 30555387

Mokmin, N. A. M., & Ridzuan, N. N. I. B. (2022). Immersive Technologies in Physical Education in Malaysia for Students with Learning Disabilities. *IAFOR Journal of Education*, *10*(2), 91–110. DOI: 10.22492/ije.10.2.05

Molloy, C., & Farrell, R. (2024). Cultivating Positive Classroom Environments: Exploring the Efficacy of Immersive Technologies in Removing Barriers to Learning Among Primary School Students. *Computers in the Schools*, *41*(2), 164–192. DOI: 10.1080/07380569.2024.2325441

Sinthiya, B. (2023). English Language Learning in the Metaverse: Exploring the Potential of AR and VR. *Shanlax International Journal of English*, *12*(S1-Dec), 161–166. DOI: 10.34293/rtdh.v12iS1-Dec.52

Sviridova, E., Yastrebova, E., Bakirova, G., & Rebrina, F. (2023). Immersive technologies as an innovative tool to increase academic success and motivation in higher education. *Frontiers in Education*, *8*(October), 1–10. DOI: 10.3389/feduc.2023.1192760

Tan, Y., Xu, W., Li, S., & Chen, K. (2022). Augmented and Virtual Reality (AR/VR) for Education and Training in the AEC Industry: A Systematic Review of Research and Applications. In *Buildings* (Vol. 12, Issue 10). DOI: 10.3390/buildings12101529

Trust, T., Woodruff, N., Checrallah, M., & Whalen, J. (2021). Educators' Interests, Prior Knowledge and Questions Regarding Augmented Reality, Virtual Reality and 3D Printing and Modeling. *TechTrends*, *65*(4), 548–561. DOI: 10.1007/s11528-021-00594-9

Uymaz, P., & Uymaz, A. O. (2022). Assessing acceptance of augmented reality in nursing education. *PLoS One*, *17*(2), 1–20. DOI: 10.1371/journal.pone.0263937 PMID: 35176073

Valero-Franco, C., & Berns, A. (2024). Development of virtual and augmented reality apps for language teaching: a case study I Desarrollo de apps de realidad virtual y aumentada para enseñanza de idiomas: un estudio de caso. *RIED-Revista Iberoamericana de Educacion a Distancia*, *27*(1), 163–185. . DOI: 10.5944/ried.27.1.37668

Wagner, P., & Alharthi, D. (2023). Leveraging VR/AR/MR/XR Technologies to Improve Cybersecurity Education, Training, and Operations. *Journal of Cybersecurity Education Research and Practice*, *2024*(1), 1–26. DOI: 10.32727/8.2023.32

Zhang, J., Li, G., Huang, Q., Feng, Q., & Luo, H. (2022). Augmented Reality in K–12 Education: A Systematic Review and Meta-Analysis of the Literature from 2000 to 2020. *Sustainability (Basel)*, *14*(15), 9725. Advance online publication. DOI: 10.3390/su14159725

Zhang, X., Shi, Y., & Bai, H. (2021). Immersive Virtual Reality Physical Education Instructional Patterns on the Foundation of Vision Sensor. In *Journal of Sensors* (Vol. 2021). DOI: 10.1155/2021/7752447

KEY TERMS AND DEFINITIONS

Augmented Reality (AR): Enhances real-world environments by overlaying digital content for interactive learning experiences.

Virtual Reality (VR): Creates fully immersive digital environments that allow students to explore and interact with simulated scenarios.

Immersive Learning: Engages students in deep, interactive experiences using AR and VR to enhance understanding and retention.

Experiential Education: Learning through direct experience, where students actively engage with content rather than passively receiving information.

Gamification: Incorporating game-like elements in education to boost engagement, motivation, and learning outcomes.

Collaborative Virtual Environments: Digital spaces where students and teachers interact, share knowledge, and work together in real time.

Personalized Learning: AI-driven adaptive learning that tailors content and experiences to individual student needs and abilities.

Ethical Concerns: Issues related to data privacy, accessibility, and the responsible use of AR and VR in education.

Chapter 11

Teacher Preparation and Professional Development Programs With Technology-Enhanced Learning

Sunanda Vincent Jaiwant
https://orcid.org/0000-0002-1161-5970
Christ University, India

Kiran Vazirani
https://orcid.org/0000-0001-5591-6874
Christ University, India

Rameesha Kalra
Christ University, India

ABSTRACT

The term Technology Enhanced Learning (TEL) refers to application of technology to teaching and learning process. Teaching profession requires incessant developing and upgrading. For this reason, Professional Development Programs are an essential requirement for the institutions and the teachers. Professional development programs are now designed to cater to this new need of the teachers aiming to enhance their digital skills and prepare them to use technology in their class preparations, class conduction, assessments, etc. This chapter aims to investigate the need for digital skills, technology enhanced learning to develop teachers. The purpose of this study is to identify key challenges and solutions to the effective integration of technology

DOI: 10.4018/979-8-3373-0771-8.ch011

in teacher preparation. The study would also provide guiding principles on how to move the field towards effective integration of technology in teacher preparation, development programs and how to incorporate technology enhanced learning in their professional development.

INTRODUCTION AND THEORETICAL FRAMEWORK

Technology Enhanced Learning, refers to the technology that augments the learning experience. The term can be used to define both analog and digital technologies, but these days the digital TEL has been widely used both by researchers and educators and a large number of educational software are been incorporated in the teach learning practices across the campuses, and fields of learning.

TEL has transformed and enhanced education and educational institutions beyond recognition. This is particularly true due to the increased growth of education apps, software for teachers, and e-learning services. World has entered a new era of education where technology has assumed a very significant role to play as a valued resource and important tool focussed on improving the experiences for both learners and teachers.

Digitalization has been considered from a broader perspective and is viewed as a process that involves changes and transformations in various stages and numerous institute levels. The researcher used the cultural–historical activity theory and the concept of levels of learning, to elaborate on the concept of digitalization bringing educational change (Pettersson, 2020)

Educational institutions are evolving to adopt digital tools and platforms to ensure enhanced educational delivery to their students. Teachers are transforming the way they teach and prepare for their classes, moving from the traditional contact model to an interactive online learning model (Simelane-Mnisi S, Mji A., 2020). Owing to the fact that learning is changing, there is an urgent necessity to use technology enhanced professional development to equip teachers with skills and competencies needed to adapt to the ever-changing student demographic and knowledge base, the speed of technological and societal changes (M., 2018). Professional Development programs are very vital for the teachers as it is found to have a direct impact on the teachers' performance in the class and the students' learning process. (Lasma Ulmane-Ozolina, et al., 2019)

Technology with its exceptional characteristics can develop the Professional Development Programs and the teachers' preparation for their much more than the traditional PDPs. Technology provides the teach ecosystem with better connectivity, higher interactivity, multi-media, and data processing that helps in facilitating mor effective and delivery of PDPs as shown in figure 1. Technology can be used to create virtual spaces to connect, communicate instantaneously, and share knowledge and resources to others. Many institutions are being benefited by use of educational technologies and tools to spread widely to remotest areas with help of videoconferencing. Many students have profited due to the expansion of the University-led programs and courses using these innovative technologies. Institutions have exchanged data, connect with teachers, facilitated collaborations across the countries and interacted on common digital platforms to exchange ideas and information.

Figure 1. Attributes of technology (Manal Quota, et al., 2022)

Research Problems and/or Questions

Digitalization has led to changes in every sphere and education field not an exception. The teachers are required to adapt themselves to this technological change and equip themselves with technology enhanced education system. The three major research problems this chapter aims to address are following:

- What is the need for the teachers to adopt technology enhanced learning system?
- How the teachers' preparation has changed with Technology-Enhanced Learning?
- What are the new requirements of the professional development programs with Technology-Enhanced Learning?

- How can a technology-enhanced training framework be developed and implemented to enhance the digital skills, practice and pedagogy of teachers to teach effectively?

Brief Description of Claim and Position Statement

Subject knowledge has to be coupled with digital instructional practices which is of great importance to get higher engagement for the students. New technological pedagogies are required to teach the digital era students who are more comfortable with the technology and digital tools. with subject knowledge alone is not enough for teachers to engage in effective and pedagogically meaningful instructional practices. Contemporary curriculum and delivery process necessitates teachers to adopt innovative teaching methods that would streamline students' learning. The integration of technology in teaching process is pervasive making the incorporation of technology in teaching, a highly suitable method in the new age education system.

Blending technology into the class and lesson-plan preparations go a long way in serving and supporting the educators to have better class deliveries through enhanced learnings and also in creating opportunities to connect with learners on innovative platforms and sharing knowledge in exciting ways. With helpful direction, accurately demarcated purposes, and focused instructions on the use of technologies effectually and reliably, educators are prepared with new digital skills as digital educators that improves their academic performances and increases their personal and professional accomplishments.

This proposed framework demonstrates adopting and integrating technology in teaching preparation and effective delivery. The technology-advanced based development and training programs would empower the teachers in skills and competencies required to successfully implement digitalization pedagogy, engage students and improve student success.

Figure 2. Proposed framework (Authors)

Technology in Education

In the field of integrating technology with learning schemata as a firm learning tool, there have been a great deal of studies and findings in the last few years of the twenty-first century (Yadav, N., Gupta, K., and Khetrapal, V., 2018). The advent of the digital age and the importance of integrating new technologies have significantly changed how people learn and communicate. The popularity and widespread usage of the Internet following its discovery led to enormous changes in our community, making the social impact of technology unintelligible (Martins, J., et al, 2016). It goes without saying that integrating technology into online learning has drawn a lot of attention. The COVID-19 epidemic hastened the process of integrating technology into language instruction and learning, notwithstanding the challenges that lie ahead (Aghaei, K., Ghoorchaei, B., Rajabi, M., and Ayatollahi, M., 2022).

Technology may also increase students' engagement. Because of how quickly technology is developing right now, traditional teaching techniques and education cannot keep up with the needs of students and teachers. Technology can be used to enhance education and learning as well as supply new elements of the same. In certain critical situations, it may prove to be the most efficacious approach to language acquisition. Given the knowledge, skills, and resources needed to integrate the technology, preparation is therefore essential in the current scenario (Hakim, 2020). Technology integration has become increasingly important to teachers. Global academic associations are encouraging the use of integrated academic technologies in the classroom (Culp, K. M., Honey, M., and Mandinach, E., 2005). With the introduction of technological equipment in academic subjects, technology fusion has been effective. The Internet and computers offer a wealth of materials and opportunities that have led to the development of new tools, strategies, and techniques for language acquisition and teaching. Teachers have access to a wide range of learning control systems and PC/cellphone apps. Lower percentages of willingness to use technology can only exacerbate the situation because for educators, integrating technology is a necessity rather than an opportunity (Cowan, 2008). These days, virtual native learners must learn using technology rather than more conventional approaches to language instruction since it is more enjoyable, convenient, and gives them greater control over the course material. Since technology offers so many advantages—efficiency, accessibility, connectedness, and personalization, to mention a few—it permeates every aspect of our life. The advantages of technology in education as a tool for instruction and learning are comparable. Appropriate technology and technology infrastructure can optimize student learning in and out of the classroom in today's blended learning environment and assist academic leaders and educators in accomplishing educational priorities and objectives.

Professional Development Programs

An innovative learning system and partnered with technology advanced system would develop a vision and action plan for a digital learning initiative that would embed technology in instruction and professional learning.

PDP improves students' education by supporting and educating teachers' acceptance and incorporation of operative technologies in their teaching-learning activities and classes. Education system can make use of technology to augment teachers' professional learnings and engagement with Professional Development Programs and empower them to apply the newly acquired skills and knowledge in the class with their students (Manal Quota, et al., 2022).

Teacher professional development encompasses all forms of continuous education for educators. It's one approach for instructors to enhance their abilities and, as a result, improve student results. Learning may occur in both formal and informal contexts. Conferences, courses, seminars, retreats, and workshops are examples of formal settings. Independent study or investigation, peer learning activities, or simply speaking with a colleague in the staff room are examples of informal chances for teacher professional development. Professional development for educators occurs on a variety of levels, including district-wide, among instructors at a specific school, and even on a classroom or simple program.

Learning to teach introspectively is a long-term process that is bolstered by active participation in a variety of professional development events both inside and outside of the school. Professional development programmes for teachers results in proficiency in lesson planning, instructional delivery, subject matter knowledge, interactions with students, and classroom organization, according to the findings. Professional development initiatives, on the other hand, are seen as having minimal benefit for instructors. It is also observed that no substantial association exists between teaching skills and professional development initiatives. Personal perceptions and environmental variables are related to perceived advantages of professional development programmes. For instructors to benefit more, there is a need for comprehensive career development strategy, implementation, and assessment. Academics who are interested in studying the integration of technology in education typically look into additional technology-integrated learning tasks, activity design, and case development. Further research could examine understanding of technology, attitudes toward using it, educators' preparation, and computer accessibility, as these factors all directly affect technology merging. It is well known that in order to improve opportunities for professional development, educators' perspectives and prior experiences with technology should be taken into account (Zhang, 2022).

There can be different goals to implement professional development programs. The common goals to conduct professional development programs are to improve the abilities and effectiveness in class deliveries of the educators. Technology-Enhanced Learning can be integrated in the PDPs and different methods can be designed to rollout the PDPs. Some of the common methods or form of conducting PDPs are mentioned below:

Upgraded courses

PDP can include different qualification courses that can assist the educators to acquire advanced and upgraded professional qualifications having completed either online or face-to-face training. Courses offer the practical knowledge and real-world examples. Teachers can learn to take actions to address the issues related to their field of study and that are prevalent in the society.

Mentoring and peer-learning

PDP also can arrange for mentoring session from the senior faculty members enriched in their vast experience and knowledge. New methods and methodologies of teaching can also be learnt from the peers who are successfully engaged technology enhanced education in their classes. Peer education helps the teachers in learning from the tested methods of their peers and they can also give constructive feedbacks to the peers which will in turn develop them further.

Learning Visits to other institutions

Some PDPs include visits to other institutions and observe and learn their practices and strategies. Observations from the other institutions can lead to benchmarking of their best practices. These visits support the teachers in learning about systems, cultures and curricula going on in other places which may be useful to them to adopt. These planned visits further facilitate gaining new perspectives on diverse styles to teaching, assessment, leadership, etc.

Peer learning visits are considered very vital for professional development programs and valued as an instrument to develop teachers, predominantly as they motivate the educators to create a community of mutual belief and provide an opportunity to expose classroom practices to an external viewer broader than their own learners.

Workshops

Live-workshops are the best way to give hands-on learning and experience to the educators. Workshops can be conducted on different subject matters, systems or other teaching-related themes which serves as a beneficial platform for educators to deliberate upon their personal knowledges, practices, opinions. Workshops can also invite some professional experts who can give expertise knowledge and enlighten upon the recent trends in teaching. These kinds of workshops offer educators with an opportunity for inner reflections and help them to communicate and connect with other teachers on similar themes or different aspects of their courses.

Webinars, Panel-discussions, Seminars and conferences

PDP can also arrange for webinars, panel-discussions, seminars and conferences for the teachers both at national and international levels. This kind of programs and events provide a platform for the educators to meet different people from around the world and discuss different issues, their individual opinions and develop their knowledge. The teachers can connect and collaborate with each other to form groups and cohorts and pursue research in similar fields.

Research

An important of any professional development program is to inculcate the research habits among the teachers. Research has come to be accepted as an important and in disposable tool to develop oneself in the academic fraternity. Research builds the culture of reading books and materials like reports, blogs, articles to develop new areas to be explored. PDP help in creating research community where teachers can connect and work on commonly interested projects. Research plays a significant role in helping educators to recognize and comprehend practical difficulties, promote bringing transformation and establish their influence in their classrooms. Research helps in addressing explicit practice issues and recommend a valuable reference point to guide teaching (Blake Cutler, et al., 2022).

Significance of Professional Development Programs (Kampen)

- ***It has an impact on student learning.***

It goes without saying that good instructors are better at instructing students. Teachers are better prepared to become successful teachers when they have access to constant learning chances and professional development tools, especially whether their pupils have learning needs or perform below or above grade level.

- ***It promotes new instructors' success.***

According to one survey, about one-third of educators leave the field within five years after becoming certified. While there are other explanations for this statistic, when it comes to successful classroom teaching, there is no alternative for hands-on experience. Teachers spend their entire lives learning a new skill in response to the obstacles they face, but new teachers haven't had that opportunity. Professional development may assist both new and seasoned teachers in developing the skills required for classroom confidence. Effective professional development assists instructors in shaping lifelong learning.

- ***It encourages a developing attitude.***

Teacher professional development programmes that are thoughtful and targeted improve student results and create a growth mentality. Teacher professional development enables instructors to participate actively in their own learning and ensures that both students and teachers are enthusiastic to learn. When you offer education and assistance for your educators, you signal that the education system appreciates their efforts and wishes them well. Teachers might be discouraged by a shortage of professional development resources. It signals that you are unwilling to invest in teaching quality and places additional strain on instructors.

Teachers' Preparation

The teachers' preparation has transformed owing to the digital revolution and the advent of virtual environment. Development programs and learning opportunities for teachers ensure that teachers could incorporate the tablets and computers into classrooms in transformative ways. Better equipped would lead to marked improvement in the way students and teachers engaged with technology.

Are great tools which aid in teachers' preparation for their classes. PDPs are developmental instruments for the teachers that help in developing the prevailing capabilities, review on earlier performances and inspire future learning-goals by articulating plan of action to attain them ((S Beausaert, M. Segers, and W. Gijselaers, 2011); (M Imhof & C. Picard, 2009)) Typically, PDPs are utilized for mainly two purposes: it is for professional development or for promotional purpose (K. Smith, H. Tillema, 2001). After participating PDPs, educators become more active, thoughtful and reflective learners who judgmentally examine their previous experiences, conceive new creative ideas and conclude solutions leading to enhanced performance (Kolb, 1984). PDPs with technology enhanced learning provide for a more sustained professional learning for the teachers. PDP with Technology Enhanced Learning aids teacher class preparations for higher achievements of their students in the following ways

- o *Preparing for a surging digital ecosystem:* Teachers' job is now depended profoundly on computer and internet skills and online communications, like emails, WhatsApp messages. The students are digitally literate and are very comfortable with all kinds of digital technologies and tools. To reach out to this digital learner, the teachers need to master the digital technology and become confident in using digital technology in their class preparations. PDP helps the teachers in learning such technologies giving them a sense of ease and mastery with technology.
- o *Online resources:* PDPs with technology enhanced learnings encourages teachers to make use of online resources for the class preparations. Such technology-led PDPs assist educators to improve their access to digital contents, resources, and study materials that could help them in building better lectures. PDPS also teaches the educators to make use of educational-videos, learning-games, and images to make their classes more interesting and interactive. This in turn improves learners' learning capacity, retention capacity and understanding of the e-materials. In general, These kind of PDPs help in creating a significantly engaging learning-environment and effective education culture.
- o *Meeting learners' unique requirements:* PDP with technology enhanced learning train the teachers with technologies like Smartboards, digital classrooms, Power points, etc., which makes a simple lecture very interesting and brings improvement in learners' grasping skills. New innovative teaching styles can be learned by the teachers in the PDPs. New methods and styles of teaching support the educators to meet the unique needs of their students.

Teachers' Performance

Students and teachers use the immersive and social aspects of the environment to develop thinking, research, and communication skills to solve complex problems. The virtual environment with students builds and connects a bridge beyond classrooms even. Teachers equipped with the essential modern technology would create meaningful learning experiences for students. There would be marked improvement in the teachers perform in the classes and the way students and teachers engaged with technology. More interaction leads to interact more frequently and more productively with other learners, experts, and practitioners.

Technology enhanced learning led PDPs are viewed as beneficial for the teachers of today's generation. Such PDPs train the teachers how to apply technology to teaching and learning. The use of technology enhances their learning experience and helps them to learn a new pedagogical tool to perform effectively in their classrooms. It has been observed that teachers do perform better after participating in technology enhanced PDPs (Lasma Ulmane-Ozolina, Anita Jansone, Ilva Magazeina, Dina Barute, 2019).

Teachers also found to have gained satisfaction after attending some sort of PDPs (Chaves, O., & Guapacha, M. E., 2014)

Teachers' reflective approach

Several study reveals that reflection is an important skill for educators ((Clarke, 1995); (Ken Zeichner, Boh Tabachnick, 1999); (T. S. Potter & B. J. Badiali B. J., 2001). For the teachers to become reflective, they are supposed to focus on the day-today happenings and events and the ponder over their purpose, usefulness and success. Studies proved that many educators showed improvement after attending PDPs with respect to reflection (Villegas-Reimers, 2003)

Key Challenges to the Effective Integration of Technology in Teacher Preparation

One of the biggest barriers to efficient technology use in the classroom is the absence of adequate, ongoing assistance for educators to gain confidence in using digital technology prior to classroom adoption (Preparing teacher education students to integrate mobile learning into elementary education, 2019). Despite the increased use of technology in the classroom, many educators are still having difficulty incorporating it and wonder if it is the correct decision for them to make. When deciding how, when, and whether to adopt new technology, there are a lot of elements to take into account, such as cost, convenience of use, and continuous support for correct understanding and usage.

Challenges

The way that educators are trained to use technology in the classroom will change over time and space. While some European nations have robust national efforts, others rely solely on teachers to manage their professional development. The pre-overhead generation, the "overhead generation," and the digital generation all differ in terms of generation. Future generations may have less issues because they have grown up with and are accustomed to computers and the Internet. However, the future generation will suffer as well if our current instructors do not make effective use of technology in the classroom. According to studies, youth view new technology favorably but are dissatisfied with how they are used in classrooms. Large-scale, quick teacher education programs are therefore vitally important. Numerous efforts have already been put into practice and have produced favorable results. Nonetheless, rather than being utilized for instruction and learning, computers and the Internet may be used largely for student management at colleges and universities (Henrik Hansson, 2006). Lack of a strong support network for educators and learners who want to switch to a tech-driven teaching-learning architecture has been a major obstacle. Teachers would require assistance from qualified specialists over a comparatively lengthy period of time in order to make an enduring transition to digital and online classroom instruction. In this sense, brief and sporadic training is scarcely beneficial. Actually, only once they have mastered the fundamentals of computer and internet use can teachers successfully incorporate digital tools and mediums with lesson planning, course material, and delivery methods. Experts also highlight what is referred to as the "double innovation problem," which instructors encounter when they must spend more time preparing for both the technology they will use and the subject matter they will teach

- ***Budgetary Restrictions***

If educators want to successfully integrate technology into their classrooms, they must overcome budget cuts and restrictions, which are by far the biggest obstacle preventing teachers and administrators from providing technology to students. According to a recent study, 75.9% of participants cited financial constraints as the main obstacle keeping them from utilizing educational technology. Budget constraints are particularly difficult to overcome because excellent educational technology tools are not inexpensive. For example, although Google Cloud can be a very effective tool for teaching, just implementing it requires schools to give students Chromebooks and pay for teacher training, which is simply too much for already tight budgets. In financially stressed schools, securing the resources to introduce and maintain technology in the classroom can be a significant obstacle.

- ***Dearth of hardware and usage guidance***

Many of the educational institutions have not been able to install the computers and other advanced technologies in their premises. There is a definite lack of knowledge in this regard which is hindering the schools and colleges to adopt and implement technology. A proper study must be done to understand and identify the type of technologies, tools and devices required to be installed and relevant trainings need to be given to the teachers to equip them with the digital technologies to be used in class preparations and in-class tutoring.

- ***Training***

Training is one common challenged faced by the teachers in their class preparations using technology. Teachers have lack of confidence in using the advanced technologies in preparing for their classes as they are not aware of the latest operating software, apps, digital platforms. Teachers need to be technological expertise to incorporate technology in their class preparations. After the digital revolution there has been numerous technologies that have made inroads into the education industry. Teachers need to be updated with all these technologies to upgrade themselves with the digital skills and that is possible with proper training and development programs. Every day, more and more cutting-edge educational technology is introduced. Teachers must be able to teach their pupils how to utilize each new tool in addition to knowing how to make the most of it themselves. No child's educational experience is going to be improved by giving classrooms a shiny new technology that neither instructors nor students can use, and it can be time-consuming and stressful for busy teachers to learn how to utilize a new tool on their own. It may take time and money to professionally train teachers, faculty, and staff, but it is essential if students are to receive the intended benefits from their technological experience.

- ***Inadequate Network Structure***

If the school lacks the network infrastructure necessary to support them, it will be useless to just throw a box of computers or notebooks to a room full of pupils. Fast, high-quality WiFi at home and at school, data security and privacy, access to digital resources, and many other things are necessary for a robust network infrastructure. Strong network infrastructure design, construction, and maintenance require careful consideration and planning because they are essential to the sustained, responsible, and successful use of technology in education.

- ***Teachers' Resistance to Adoption of Technology***

It has been observed that teachers find it difficult to implement new technologies into lesson plans. Many teachers are contended with their traditional ways of class preparations. Hence, they are reluctant to incorporate new technologies in preparing their lesson plans. Modifying old lesson plans to incorporate technology is a tedious and laborious task and mostly teachers tend to avoid this. In order to adopt new technologies for class preparation, teachers encounter the challenge identified as the "double innovation" problem (Cleaver, 2014). Double innovation fundamentally increases an added level of preparations by the educators. As educational technologies are now much easier to acquire and adopt, the double-innovation problem continues to exist and leads to added preparation time. In a study, data collection from teacher interview revealed that time consumption in class preparations by the teachers is one of the major barriers to adopting new technologies by the teachers (Peggy A. Ertmer, et al., 2012). Studies have revealed that this reluctance isn't due to teachers' distaste for technology. Instead, it's partially due to the fact that educators perceive acquiring a new teaching instrument as a dangerous endeavor for which they lack the necessary training. It's also partially due to the fact that their school leaders fail to show unity by emphasizing which certain tools can benefit their students. Working with teachers to assist their adoption of new educational technology can increase their likelihood of embracing it, even though this resistance to change can be challenging to overcome.

- ***Time Constraint***

One of the common problems that educators face is of lack of enough time to use technology for their class preparations. reveals that many teachers have skills in using computers in the classroom, but they still make little use of technologies because they did not have enough time. It is a known fact that huge number of educators acknowledge that time limitation is one major difficulty in arranging adequate computer-time for class Teachers require time to earn new technologies and software, then time to practice the new technologies, and time to prepare classes using the new technologies. This demotivates them to make use of technology in their academic activities and tasks.

- ***There are no mechanisms in place to use technology in the classroom***

Giving teachers access to iPads and smartboards might make them more comfortable using technology in the classroom, but many teachers haven't considered how to integrate technology into their lessons. In fact, a history teacher's use of a laptop in the classroom can differ greatly from a math teacher's use of a smartboard. To update their lesson ideas, both probably need a lot of time for experimentation and trial and error. Not giving teachers the direction they require to make educational technology work for them in their particular classroom is a significant obstacle to the adoption of new tools.

Making Professional Development for Teachers More Effective and Engaging (Kampen)

- *Make it unique*

Every teacher has distinct problems in the classroom and arrives at work each day with a varied set of abilities. However, in the interest of saving time, money, and energy, many professional development programmes for teachers are overly broad and irrelevant to the majority, if not all, of the teachers that attend. If work experience is to be made relevant, instructors' comments are to be appreciated - there's a good chance they'll have lots to say. Allow instructors to choose what and how they study. Give them a variety of seminars or courses to choose from. If a variety of solutions cannot be provided, then it is advisable to keep the issue short. Choose depth above breadth, and ensure that instructors leave with all of the material they need to begin implementing it in the classrooms.

- *Invest in instructors*

Most instructors will tell that they dislike being treated like students; they are trained professionals who are here to build an already existent, unique, and powerful skill set. In this case, the workshop is unlikely to make a significant influence or promote change in the school. A lack of involvement is as damaging to instructors as it is to pupils. Use active learning approaches if you're doing an active learning session in the classroom. If the focus is on service learning, have instructors look for opportunities or organizations where their students may volunteer. Teachers must be interested and involved. Teachers, like their students, learn in a variety of ways and react differently to aural, written, or visual learning modalities.

- *Keep it continuing*

Once the professional development session is done, the educators find it detailed and interesting, and they feel more educated, and then comes the time for action for the educators to exercise all their learnings from the PDP into action in the classroom.

According to a 2016 poll conducted in collaboration with Education and the National Educational Association, schools employ data-driven instruction approaches to plan career development for instructors but do not use it to. If the educators aren't always learning since what worked and what didn't, teacher professional development becomes a self-defeating loop. Teachers will not incorporate new teaching tactics or ideas into the classrooms if they do not believe they have the necessary support. This results in lost time, effort, and money. Uncertainty, unsolved questions, and a lack of trust frequently prevent teachers from experimenting with new tactics in the classroom. The most essential thing that one can do as an administrator is to assist teachers as they strive to enhance their teaching. Make it clear to instructors that they may come with any concerns or questions. Make judgements based on student and teacher accomplishment statistics on what to focus on next and how to motivate student learning.

- ***Incorporate it throughout the teaching and learning process***

According to a 2015 survey conducted by New Teacher Project, even though districts spend a median of $18,000 per educator each year, only roughly 30% of instructors notably improved as a consequence. Professional development will always cost the institution money at some point. However, the institutions have some influence over one of the other big costs: the teachers' time. Effective learning does not occur in an afternoon, and teachers and administrators frequently struggle to schedule teacher professional development programmes around actual teaching. Time is a resource that can't be avoided — but it can be spent wisely. This does not imply devoting less time to teaching professional growth activities, but rather maximizing the time available.

DISCUSSIONS

Incorporation of technology into the class preparation and in Professional Development Programs has now become the buzzword mandating a double innovation. Educators receiving new technologies need to be supported by their institutions with trainings and equipment and integrate the technology with their class objectives and curriculum. Technology Enhanced Learning is important for many reasons. It is imperative because it has become the standard of education that is expected today beside being a tool that improves and enhances education. Undoubtedly, apps, software, and e-learning tools are some of the most useful and, indeed, exceptional instruments available to many teachers. Students have become more tech-savvy than ever before and much of their day is spent interacting with some form of technology. Thus, the ease and at which they navigate technology and their comfort level mean that in a society more and more dominated by ever-developing smartphones, tablets, computers, and more, students today expect and indeed thrive when interacting with technology.

The teaching-learning practices of the educators are impacted significantly with the use of several training-programs, mentoring, and appraisals provided on a regular basis. This digital era requires the teachers to develop abilities to learn technology and integrate the multidisciplinary courses. This study describes the effectiveness and benefits of Professional Development Programs (PDP) in improving the efficiency and performance of the teachers.

Educators can make use of this burgeoning tech-savviness by using technology to improve interaction, engagement, and understanding within their classrooms and lecture auditoriums. Direction and peer-support are crucial elements in the process of executing PDPs. Many educators require guidance, support and time for attending PDPs. PDPs also help in increasing self-awareness in educators to transform their working environment (Minna Körkkö & Marja-Riitta Kotilainen, 2019).

An extensive review of the previous literature justifies the proposed framework depicting the relationship between Technology used for teachers' preparation and in enhancing the development programs. Technology use for teachers' class preparation is now unescapable, necessary, and acknowledged. Teacher opines the available technology tools as essentials for engagement and empowerment of students in a modern educational setting, and students never view its use as a special moment in class.

A common challenge that the educators encounter is integration of new technologies into their class preparations and in their classroom deliveries due to lack of skills and technical knowledge. Professional Development Programs make it considerable easy for the teachers struggling with these issues in gaining the required technical knowhow and being more confident and effective in their preparation for teaching and actual classroom deliveries. Such development programs include a complete training program for teachers to enhance their digital learnings and help them be more digitally and technically equipped.

CONCLUSION

Technology-Enhanced Learning is more than just a trend; it is a fundamental shift in how educators are supported and prepared for their careers. This is why it is being incorporated into professional development and teacher training programs. This study highlights the significance of technology-enhanced education. One potential benefit of technology-enhanced learning could be giving teachers the skills, knowledge, and confidence they need to successfully navigate the demands of 21st-century learning settings. Technology-Enhanced Learning, when used properly, enhances teacher competency, promotes lifelong learning, and improves student outcomes. The study also reveals long-standing problems include reluctance to modify traditional teaching strategies, unequal access to technological resources, and differences in the levels of digital literacy among instructors. To get over these challenges, lawmakers and educational institutions must adopt a more calculated approach to technology-enhanced learning. This means investing in infrastructure, providing instructors with ongoing training and support, and encouraging a creative and flexible culture. By doing this, learning environments that are personalized, dynamic, and interactive may be developed that make the most use of technology-enhanced learning for both teachers and students. Future teacher preparation and professional growth depend on the seamless integration of technology with pedagogical methods. As the educational landscape evolves, Technology-Enhanced Learning will become increasingly important in preparing educators to meet the demands of modern teaching. It will guarantee that educators possess not only subject-matter expertise but also technological proficiency to enhance student learning. Technology-enhanced learning has great potential, but implementing it well will require cooperation from all stakeholders, including lawmakers, administrators, and teachers. The education sector's adoption of Technology-Enhanced Learning will ensure that teachers are prepared to inspire and instruct the next generation of students, leading to a more knowledgeable, competent, and technologically literate society. Higher education today is dynamic and always changing due to the quick development of technologies employed in academic activities. As a result, educators must constantly implement and consider novel and updated teaching and learning tactics (such as virtual mode). The data used in this chapter's evaluation of academic digital capabilities comes from two case studies. Diverse viewpoints on the use of educational technologies in teaching and learning are demonstrated by the smooth integration of technology into teaching and learning activities, which raises concerns about the effectiveness and efficiency of the use of these tools. It is important to provide academics with technology-enhanced learning development support so they can use educational technology tools' affordances in pedagogically sound ways for their teaching and learning.

REFERENCES

Aghaei, K., Ghoorchaei, B., Rajabi, M., & Ayatollahi, M. (2022). Iranian EFL learners' narratives in a pandemic pedagogy: Appreciative inquiry-based approach. *Language Related Research, 13*(3), 285–314. DOI: 10.52547/LRR.13.3.12

Bai, H. (2019). Preparing teacher education students to integrate mobile learning into elementary education. *TechTrends, 63*(6), 723–733.

Beausaert, S., Segers, M., & Gijselaers, W. (2011). The Personal Development Plan Practice Questionnaire: The Development and Validation of an Instrument to Assess the Employee's Perception of Personal Development Plan Practice. *International Journal of Training and Development, 15*(4), 249–270. DOI: 10.1111/j.1468-2419.2011.00375.x

Chaves, O., & Guapacha, M. E. (2014). ChaImpact of a professional development program on the teaching of public schools English teachers in Cali.

Clarke, A. (1995, May). Professional development in practicum settings: Reflective practice under scrutiny. *Teaching and Teacher Education, 11*(3), 243–261. DOI: 10.1016/0742-051X(94)00028-5

Cleaver, S. (2014). Technology in the Classroom: Helpful or Harmful? Retrieved from https://www.education.com/magazine/article/effective-technology-teaching-child/

Cowan, J. E. (2008). Strategies for planning technology enhanced learning experiences. *The Clearing House: A Journal of Educational Strategies, Issues and Ideas, 82*(2), 55–59. DOI: 10.3200/TCHS.82.2.55-59

Culp, K. M., Honey, M., & Mandinach, E. (2005). A retrospective on twenty years of education technology policy. *Journal of Educational Computing Research, 32*(3), 279–307. DOI: 10.2190/7W71-QVT2-PAP2-UDX7

Cutler, B., ... (2022, July 5). *The role of research in the professional development of graduate teachers.* Retrieved from https://www.monash.edu/education/teachspace/articles/the-role-of-research-in-the-professional-development-of-graduat

Ertmer, P. A., Ottenbreit-Leftwich, A. T., Sadik, O., Sendurur, E., & Sendurur, P. (2012). Teacher beliefs and technology integration practices: A critical relationship. *Computers & Education, 59*(2), 423–435.

Hakim, B. (2020). Technology Integrated Online Classrooms and the Challenges Faced by the EFL Teachers in Saudi Arabia during the COVID-19 Pandemic. *International Journal of Applied Linguistics and English Literature*, *9*(5), 158–164. DOI: 10.7575/aiac.ijalel.v.9n.5p.33

Hansson, H. (2006, December). Teachers' Professional Development for the Technology-Enhanced Classroom in the School of Tomorrow. *E-Learning and Digital Media*, *3*(4), 552–564. Advance online publication. DOI: 10.2304/elea.2006.3.4.552

Imhof, M., & Picard, C. (2009). Views on Using Portfolios in Teacher Education. *Teaching and Teacher Education*, *25*(1), 149–154. DOI: 10.1016/j.tate.2008.08.001

Kolb, D. A. (1984). *Experiential Learning: Experience as the Source of Learning and Development*. Prentice Hall.

Körkkö, M., & Kotilainen, M.-R. (2019, October). Personal DPvelopment plans (PDP) as a Tool to PromoteTteacher Career Development. *European Journal of Teacher Education*. Advance online publication. DOI: 10.1080/02619768.2020.1827393

Martins, J., Gonçalves, R., Oliveira, T., Cota, M., & Branco, F. (2016). Understanding the determinants of social network sites adoption at firm level: A mixed methodology approach. *Electronic Commerce Research and Applications*, *18*, 10–26. DOI: 10.1016/j.elerap.2016.05.002

Mayadas, A. F., Bourne, J., & Bacsich, P. (2009, January). Online Education Today. *Journal of Asynchronous Learning Networks*, *13*(2), 85–89. PMID: 19119225

McCue, T. (2018, July 31). E-Learning Climbing to $325 Billion by 2025 UF Canvas Absorb Schoology Moodle.

Ngatoro, M. (2018). The value of a school based digital learning framework: does it offer the support and guidance needed for teachers of varying digital capabilities? (Master's thesis).

Pettersson, F. (2020, June 30). Understanding digitalization and educational change in school by means of activity theory and the levels of learning concept. *Education and Information Technologies*, *26*(1), 187–204. DOI: 10.1007/s10639-020-10239-8

Potter, T. K. (2001). Teacher leadership. *Journal of Correctional Education*, •••, 120–125.

Quota, M., ... (2022). *Effective Teacher Professional Development Using Technology*. International Bank for Reconstruction and Development / The World Bank. Retrieved from https://creativecommons.org/licenses/by/4.0/

Simelane-Mnisi, S., & Mji, A. (2020). COVID-19 pandemic: Opportunities for online learning to unblock the minds of students during the lockdown period. *Education and New Learning Technologies Virtual Conference (EDULEARN '20)*, (pp. 6-7). Spain. DOI: 10.21125/edulearn.2020.2124

Smith, K., & Tillema, H. (2001). Long-Term Influences of Portfolios on Professional Development Scandinavian Journal of Educational Research 45 (2): 183–203. *Scandinavian Journal of Educational Research, 45*(2), 183–203. DOI: 10.1080/00313830120052750

Ulmane-Ozolina, L., Jansone, A., Magazeina, I., & Barute, D. (2019, June). Technology Enhanced Learning in Tteachers' Professional Development. *Periodicals of Engineering and Natural Sciences*, *7*(1), 216–221. DOI: 10.21533/pen.v7i1.400

Villegas-Reimers, E. (2003). Teacher Professional Development: An international Review of the Literature. Retrieved from https://unesdoc.unesco.org/images/0013/001330/133010e.pdf

Yadav, N., Gupta, K., & Khetrapal, V. (2018). Next education: Technology transforming education. *South Asian J. Bus. Manage*, *14*(1), 68–77. DOI: 10.1177/2277977918754443

Zeichner, K., & Tabachnick, B. (1999). Participatory Development and Teacher Education Reform in Namibia. In *Democratic Teachers Education Reform in Namibia*. Routledge.

Zhang, W. (2022). The Role of Technology-Based Education and Teacher Professional Development in English as a Foreign Language Classes. *Frontiers in Psychology*, *13*, 910315. Advance online publication. DOI: 10.3389/fpsyg.2022.910315 PMID: 35756284

Chapter 12
Building Teacher Skills for Effective Integration of Technology in the Classroom

V. Devaki
https://orcid.org/0000-0002-7109-0205
SASTRA University, India

Chinna Suresh
https://orcid.org/0000-0002-3389-1116
SASTRA University, India

Lalithabala Boopathi
https://orcid.org/0009-0005-1152-0006
SASTRA University, India

ABSTRACT

The integration of technology into classroom settings has become essential in the digital age, transforming traditional teaching methods and fostering dynamic learning environments. In this chapter, the subject of technology integration for present day learning system, and the professional development process for sustainability were discussed. The frameworks SAMR, TPACK are discussed to guide teachers in aligning technology with curriculum goals and assessing its impact on learning outcomes. Further, blended and flipped classrooms, as well as technology integration is discussed with references to the professional development as the foundation for effective use of technologies. Overall, this work advances the literature on technology-supported learning by offering a cohesive framework that may be helpful

DOI: 10.4018/979-8-3373-0771-8.ch012

to educators, school leaders, and officials. Thus this chapter helps for integrating effective learning-teaching process and for building efficient learning environments in the twenty-first century.

INTRODUCTION

In today's digital age, the technology integration to learning environments is inevitable in fostering teaching approaches and learning processes. However, the extent to which technology is employed by teachers is reviewed because as it can facilitate effective teaching and learning, the teachers are often limited in their abilities to teach using technology. They do not have adequate training, education or resources. This chapter will highlight the ways to cultivate these competencies, for purposes of promoting more suitable frameworks that endorse the successful implementation of technology interventions in learning settings. Technological interaction means how human interact with technologies and utilize them in societies. It means all forms of communication and interaction between people and technological devices or systems or the reciprocal effects between the two. This interaction can vary greatly depending on the type of technology and the context in which it is used. It is the field of study that focuses on the way users and computers communicate and work to enhance this relationship by making it friendlier for the user. Human computer interaction includes physical interaction such as typing, swiping as well as mental interaction including how users perceive something displayed on a screen. For example, mobile phones and tablets for the user end interaction through touch screen, voice and gestures. In the same way, computers and laptops in interaction occur through mouse click, typing and voice. However interaction in smart homes, takes place through applications, voice and sometimes even automated response from the home system through sensors. Therefore this chapter brings the foundations of effective technology integration, its role in modern education, how to incorporate technology in classrooms, and the professional development for effective use. Integration of technology in education refers to the effective use of digital tools, resources, and platforms to enhance teaching and learning. It involves incorporating technology seamlessly into curricula, pedagogy, and classroom activities to improve engagement, accessibility, and student outcomes while supporting teachers in delivering innovative and interactive instruction.

Objectives

1. To relate and differentiate the traditional learning environments with digital environments, identifying significant changes in pedagogy and classroom dynamics.
2. To identify common challenges the teachers face in assimilating technology and propose potential solutions to overcome these barriers.
3. To understand frameworks such as SAMR and TPACK and apply them in planning, assessing, and executing technology-integrated models like blended or flipped classrooms, incorporating technology-based activities and assessments.
4. To identify and prioritize the core topics for teacher training programs that support effective technology use such as digital pedagogy, ethical considerations, and troubleshooting skills.
5. To develop strategies to foster a classroom culture that values experimentation, flexibility, and adaptability in exploring new technologies.

IMPORTANCE OF TECHNOLOGY IN MODERN EDUCATION

Technology has transformed our society, and education is no exception. The integration of technology into classrooms has opened new platform for teaching and learning, encourages the students for personalized learning experiences. From interactive whiteboards and tablets to learning management systems and educational apps, enable teachers to diversify their instructional methods and meet the needs of a diverse range of learners when digital tools were used (Gudanescu, 2010). Moreover, technology facilitates to access more information and resources that can enhance curriculum content and promote critical thinking. The use of technology supports various learning styles, support students to learn at their own pace and review content as needed (Gruzdeva, M. L., Vaganova, O. I., Kaznacheeva, S. N., Bystrova, N. V., & Chanchina, 2020). For example, video lessons and interactive simulations can make complex concepts more accessible and engaging. Additionally, technology fosters collaboration beyond the classroom walls through tools that allow for virtual group projects, discussions, and global exchanges of ideas.

Overview of Challenges Teachers Face When Integrating Technology

Despite of wide advantages the integration of technology into the classroom has certain crucial challenges. One of the main concerns is, for example, the lack of homogeneity in teachers' digital expertise. Some educators are proficient in technology, and therefore, they innovate about teaching with the use of technology, whereas others are incompetent with technology since they lack practice or training. This gap can result in misuse of technology whereby technological tools are applied in a manner that does not enhance learning but rather in a manner that enhances the engagement of students with useless activity (Alenezi, 2017). Access to resources is another obstacle because most of the schools do not have equal access to the latest devices, reliable internet connections, or technical support. Even when technology is available, time constraints and a packed curriculum may hinder teachers from experimenting with new tools or learning how to integrate them effectively. There is also a psychological barrier for some teachers like resistance to use technology or fear of failure when trying new methods. Additionally, the lack of institutional support such as professional development programs and administrative encouragement can also be the reason to incorporate technology effectively (Nii Akai Nettey, J., Osei Mensah, R., Asafo-Adjei, R., & Adiza Babah, 2024).

The Purpose of Building Teacher Skills for Effective Technology Use

Building teacher skills make sure that technology is used as a powerful tool for education rather than a distraction or mere novelty. Teachers can be more dynamic when proper training is provided to enhance student-centered learning environments. Through effective technology integration, it promotes creativity, encourages critical thinking, and helps prepare students for the demands of the digital age. It also improves the teachers with techno literacy skills, creative skills, pedagogical skills which can also foster continuous innovation in teaching practices, creating a culture of lifelong learning that benefits both educators and students (Dogan, S., Dogan, N. A., & Celik, 2021). This approach leads to more effective classroom management, improved student outcomes, and a stronger association between modern teaching practices and the skills students need in a technology-driven world.

SECTION 1: UNDERSTANDING THE ROLE OF TECHNOLOGY IN MODERN EDUCATION

Technology in modern education serves as both a tool and a catalyst for transforming the traditional learning environment. The use of learning technologies has enhance the classroom by supplementing it with technology, which foster student interactions in teaching and learning processes by providing enhanced technological tools such as multimedia. For instance, smart boards, virtual simulations, and augmented reality can make lessons more interesting and even perhaps more engaging, to learners of different types. This variety helps to revise and, at the same time, mobilizes the children. It offers teachers a number of instructional options and materials that will help them improve the delivery of their lesson. By this way, the analytics and data are helpful for educators to monitor the student's performance and give suggestions based on the found trends. Also, professional development platform enable teachers to reinstate themselves with new technology applications and new method of teaching. While technology plays a pivotal role in modern education, it also presents challenges, such as ensuring equitable access and addressing the potential for distraction. It needs to be applied carefully, explained to educators and included into the learning process to become effective (Cerny, 2015). However, technology plays a role of facilitator in education and improves learning experiences, provides individual learning and mobilizes students for the world of the Information Technology. Its successful integration depends on thoughtful, well-supported efforts that empower both teachers and students.

The Evolution of Technology in Education

Early Beginnings: Technology has been in education system since the early 1900s ranging from mere stationer items like the blackboard to more advanced gadget like the radio. In the 1920s and the 1930s, educational broadcasts and instructional films where the major part of classrooms, and thus the first efforts to integrate multimedia in teaching was actually made (Norton, A., Sonnemann, J., & McGannon, 2013).
The Advent of Audio-Visual Aids: The middle of the 20th century is the period were more sophisticated audio-visual aids, such as slide projectors and overhead transparencies. These tools aid teachers to supplement their lectures with visual content, making lessons more engaging and easier to understand.
The Internet Revolution: The expansion of the internet from the 1990s changed education around the world. Teachers and students got exposure to information, and could do research in topics other than what was in books. Internet enhances online learning and other tools such as e-mail and forums that joined educators and students of the worldwide community.
The Growth of E-Learning and Digital Platforms: In the 21st century e-learning platforms and learning management systems such as Blackboard, Moodle and Google classroom emerged. These applications enabled the organization of the course materials, the tasks, and the communication with the students within a well-organized online space. As the resources were becoming digitalised, the blended learning, a method which combines face-to-face learning with online, got integrated into the schools (Betrus, 2012).

The Growth of Mobile Technology and Apps: The mobile learning came in the early 21st century with the advancement of smartphones and portable tablets in the late 2010. Educational apps tailored for different subjects and age groups allowed students to practice skills on the go. Another area which was revolutionized have been brought into an engaging environment through tools such as Kahoot! & Quizlet!

Interactive and Collaborative Tools: With advancement in technology more co-authoring tools like Google Docs, collaboration boards like Padlet and the growth of conference calls such as Zoom are integrated into the learning environment. These tools allowed co-authoring, distance education, and examination of how student teams can collaborate across from different locations that is valuable during crises such as the COVID-19 pandemic.

Emerging Technologies: In the 2020s, technologies like Cloud computing, Gamification, Blockchain technology, 5G technology, Internet of things, Robotics and coding and advanced technologies like artificial intelligence (AI), virtual reality (VR), and augmented reality (AR) began to shape new learning experiences. AI-driven tutoring systems offer personalized learning paths, while VR and AR provide immersive environments for students to explore complex concepts, such as scientific simulations and historical re-creations (Bonfield, C. A., Salter, M., Longmuir, A., Benson, M., & Adachi, 2020).

The Shift towards Lifelong Learning: In the same context, technology advancement hails the learning process and recognition of education outside class. Courses incorporated in websites like Coursera, Udemy, edX, Skillshare, LinkedIn learning, Codecademy, Kindly and Khan Academy make it possible for learners to undertake professional practice enhanced courses to make them relevant to the job market.

Thus the evolution of technology in education has been a journey from basic visual aids to refined digital tools and platforms. Each phase has brought new opportunities and challenges, reshaping how teachers teach and students learn. As technology continues to advance, its integration into education will require an ongoing commitment to training, adaptation, and equity to ensure that all learners can benefit from its potential.

The Impact of Technology on Learning Outcomes

One of the most immediate and noticeable impacts of technology in education is improved student engagement. Through the use of applications, computer games and reconstructed virtual solutions to learning the student's interest and motivation is felt frequently. There is evidence that active participation will enhance the recall of information and increase the learners' mastery of the topic under study. Students have more interests with lessons that involve multimedia because it helps make learning fun and something that happens in the real world. Technology has supported the cause of individualized learning, students can learn as a group or the class, but each student can work on his or her level of difficulty. Learner centred approaches involve the learners' appraisal and afford tasks and feedback that fits their performance. This embedded and methods of learning enhance student's mastery of content knowledge before proceeding to next stages making them learn with confidence hence improving their learning achievement. Technology enables communication within students, teachers and with people outside the class. Tools like Google Workspace, Microsoft Teams, and educational forums entail that students can work in groups, share ideas, and get group and instructors' feedback promptly. Such changes in communication not only improve the pragmatic aspect of teamwork skills, but also are built into the nature of many contemporary working environments which students apply to. It is clearly seen that technology have positive effects on learning outcomes but there are some issues with it. There are certain disadvantages which include isolation due to fewer face-to-face; potential distractions, and overstress due to screen time (Naik, G., Chitre, C., Bhalla, M., & Rajan, 2020). Furthermore, disparities in access to technology can exacerbate educational inequalities, particularly in regions or communities with limited infrastructure. However the technology is used to complement, rather than replace, as traditional teaching methods is crucial for maintaining a balanced and effective educational experience.

Thus the impact of technology on learning outcomes is multifaceted, encompassing enhanced engagement, personalized learning, improved access, and the development of essential skills. This chapter will therefore demonstrate that the integration of technology in learning environment can go a long way in enhancing learning experiences and effective delivery of teaching. But to reap these points majorly, institutions should overcome equity issues charged with training and mindful uses of digital gadgets (Sarkar, S., Mohapatra, S., & Sundarakrishnan, 2017).

Challenges and Opportunities for Teachers in the Role of Technology in Modern Education

1. Challenges:
    a. **Lack of Training and Professional Development:** One of the primary challenges teachers encounter is a lack of preparation and training for the use of technology in and for learning. Unfortunately, many teachers and trainers may themselves lack opportunities to learn how to effectively integrate technology into their work, which results in highly varied results and eye-rolling experiences. Comprehensive and on-going professional

development is vital for teachers to gain confidence and proficiency in integrating technology (Lawless, K. A., & Pellegrino, 2007).

b. **Keeping Up with Rapid Technological Changes:** Technological advancement is rapid, therefore the typical tools and platforms employed in any process are frequently replaced by newer and advanced ones. This is worrying and fearful for the teachers because they have to pull through and stay updated on the latest trends. These changes to implement require time, careful planning, and most important institutional support which in most cases is unusual.

c. **Managing Classroom Dynamics and Distractions:** However, one to integrate the tools alongside with lessons, technology can turn sometimes into a distraction tool. Other possible challenging situations for teachers are the need to manage students' attention in the classroom with the use of new technologies that might lead for various non-learning purposes. Balancing engagement with discipline requires effective classroom management strategies.

d. **Over-Reliance and Screen Fatigue:** Excessive use of technology will also be a drawback to the assignment as it creates screen fatigue to both the students and the teachers. Overdependence on these tools can also be disadvantageous in the development of interpersonal skills, and other traditional forms of learning. Hence, it emerged that there was a tension between teachers and incorporating technology in their lessons on one hand and the need to have instructional approaches referred to as varied on the other hand.

2. Opportunities:

a. **Enhanced Teaching Tools and Resources:** Technology is a treasure array of tools for the teacher to improve her or his lesson. Computers, educative videos, interactive web applications, and other display technologies afford significant approaches that can reach out to most of the learning styles. These tools also enrich content and facilitate people to understand complicated information with the help of graphics.

b. **Data-Driven Instruction:** In the view of today's enhanced use of technology, teachers are in a position to get access to data analysis that may assist in evaluating the learner's performance as well as the areas that needs supplements. When adopted, the suggestions will help teachers to know their students better, and then proceed to teach them in a manner that will address their specific needs.

c. **Collaborative Learning and Communication:** Technology allows the creation of learning groups and communication within and beyond the classroom. Using cloud applications in the assessment process can increase students' engagement in group discussions and group projects done under the supervision of teachers. Current tools such as Google Classroom, Microsoft Team, or Zoom allows teachers to continue enhancing real-time learners' interactions even when learning is conducted online or in blended teaching styles.

d. **Access to Professional Development and Peer Networks:** Technology has opened up chances for a teacher to be in professional learning community and also in online training. Currently, teachers can invite their peers and communicate with them, participate in seminars, watch webinars, or courses that will strengthen their approach in the classroom. This access can also foster the on-going professional practice and enables teachers to update themselves with existing trends in the education sector (Lawless, K. A., & Pellegrino, 2007).

Despite the difficulties presented by the bringing of technology in education for example a need for training and fair distribution of the equipment, it brings about many opportunities for the teachers. In essence, the use of digital tools in the classroom offers teachers an opportunity to design higher quality and personalized lessons for learners. To fully leverage these opportunities, on-going support, training, and thoughtful implementation are crucial.

SECTION 2: FOUNDATIONS OF EFFECTIVE TECHNOLOGY INTEGRATION

Effective technology integration starts with a flawless understanding of pedagogical goals. Teachers need to decide on what they want to achieve in their instruction whether it is to improve student interaction, develop their ability to think critically, or encourage group work, and then choose technology that will help them achieve their goal. Instead of focusing on the use of the technology, the technology has to be used for the enhancement of learning. The integration processes should also be in synchronization with curriculum standards to assure that integration reinforcement and support is occurring with the content. Teacher must be able to identify and plan for the use of the technology and learning resource to learning areas and learning activities. This aligns itself to ensure that there are checks done in quality of education and that the use of technology is throughout and suitable for the curriculum. There is no doubt that teachers themselves should possess the appropriate skills and knowledge to implement the technology. Students are to understand how to apply the tools along with how to effectively apply them in creating lesson plans. Teachers are always in touch with latest technologies and group learning helps in boosting confidence and creativity among teachers. One of the basic prerequisites for successful integration is equal provision of technology for all learners. This entails availing appropriate support practices like, the internet and appropriate learning tools as well as preparing lessons that will accommodate all students with different learning abilities. Universal design for learning as made possible by assistive technology and effective use of digital materials can make educational experiences accessible (Yurtseven Avci, Z., O'Dwyer, L. M., & Lawson, 2020). Nevertheless, the use of instructional technology should not exclude other forms of learning. These sources should be incorporated in a way that the use of computers is complemented by the use of other teaching aids such as use of writing instruments, use of talking and other forms of teaching that encourage interaction. The balance benefited students in developing the number of skills such as problem solving and critical thinking skills apart from technological skills. With these foundational elements, technology can be used not just as an add-on but as a meaningful component that enhances teaching and learning outcomes.

Defining Effective Technology Integration

Technology should be used to support and enhance the learning goals. This encompasses a process of selecting tools that will fit the content and strategies of the teaching process and have a positive impact on a learning process. Technology integration for learning emphasizes the procedures and processes for selecting tools for use in classroom practices in a manner that positively impacts instruction. It should be integrated into the classroom in a non-intrusive manner, should be consistent with educational goals, should meet the need of a wide range of students, and focus on the core areas of teaching such as teamwork, critical thinking and information technology (Lawrence, G., Ahmed, F., Cole, C., & Johnston, 2020).

Core Competencies for Teachers in the Digital Classroom

1. **Technological Proficiency:** Teachers must be proficient in not only using technology in their subject teaching, but also in other ways of communication technology. This encompasses the knowledge of Learning Management Systems (LMS), educational software and tools in the classroom that ranges from interactive whiteboards, and tablets. Teachers are confident in handling the technology so that when the students come across a problem then it will be easier for the teachers to solve them thus minimizing interruption of learning processes.

2. **Digital Pedagogy Skills:** Digital pedagogy goes beyond knowing how to use technology. It includes instruction of how to incorporate it into sound teaching methodologies. Teachers need to know how to plan lessons so they use technology purposefully to support engagement and critical learning (Väätäjä, J. O., & Ruokamo, 2021).
3. **Adaptability and Lifelong Learning:** Technology in education is constantly evolving, and teachers must be adaptable to these changes. This competency focuses on the ability and readiness to adopt new technologies, modern teachings approaches and to try out new tools and techniques. Continued professional development keeps the teachers remain flexible and guarantees the teacher the ability to meet and or adapt to the ever evolving challenges of the learners in their field.
4. **Digital Citizenship and Ethics:** Subsequently, teachers must transmit the proper attitudes concerning responsible and appropriate use of the technology. This covers teaching students on etiquette, equals and right use of social media, identifying reliable sources, and security measures that ought to be observed. Focusing on enhancing the concept of digital ethics helps in promoting the culture of the classroom in which the student will comprehend and acknowledge the right manner of interacting digitally.
5. **Data Literacy and Assessment:** Effective use of technology requires teachers to be adept at collecting, analyzing, and interpreting data to support student learning. Teachers should possess the knowledge of how to analyse the information from the online tests as well as experience with different digital tools to determine learners' needs and struggling areas so that the educator could modify the teaching approach (Cui, Y., Chen, F., Lutsyk, A., Leighton, J. P., & Cutumisu, 2023).
6. **Cultural and Inclusive Competence:** Digital tools can be used to create a more inclusive learning environment and represents diverse cultures and learning styles. Teachers need to be aware of how to choose and adapt technologies that support all students inclusively (Cui, Y., Chen, F., Lutsyk, A., Leighton, J. P., & Cutumisu, 2023). This involves using assistive technology, providing multiple formats of learning materials, and considering the cultural context in digital content.

These professional competencies include many more than technical skills and involves a set of numerous competencies that play an essential role in contributing to teacher's performance, students' engagement as well as their support in a digital classroom setting. These competencies range from technological productivity and flexibility to digital morality issues and diversity all of which are instrumental to educators in dealing with the many challenges in the present learning environments, to boost the quality of learning and induce students for the world where technology plays a central role.

Frameworks and Models for Technology Integration

For effectively integrating technology into teaching and learning, two widely recognized models the SAMR and TPACK frameworks can be used for technology integration.

SAMR Model (Substitution, Augmentation, Modification, Redefinition)

The SAMR model, developed by Dr. Ruben Puentedura, is a hierarchical framework that helps educators evaluate and design technology-based activities (Blundell, C. N., Mukherjee, M., & Nykvist, 2022). It is structured into four levels:

Substitution: Technology acts as a direct replacement for a traditional tool, with no functional change. For example, using a digital document instead of a printed one.
Augmentation: Technology still acts as a substitute, but with added functionalities that enhance the task. For example, using a word processor that includes spell-check and collaborative commenting features.
Modification: Technology allows for significant task redesign. At this level, the structure of the learning task changes, such as collaborating in real-time on a shared digital project with peers in different locations.
Redefinition: Technology enables the creation of new tasks that were previously inconceivable. Examples include creating multimedia presentations that incorporate video editing, interactive quizzes, or global collaboration with classrooms around the world.

The SAMR model helps teachers assess how deeply technology is embedded in their teaching practices. Moving from substitution to redefinition indicates an increasing integration of technology that enhances and transforms the learning experience.

2. TPACK Framework (Technological Pedagogical Content Knowledge): The TPACK framework, developed by Dr. Punya Mishra and Dr. Matthew Koehler, provides a comprehensive approach that intersects three primary forms of knowledge that is 1) Content Knowledge (CK) where the learner made understand the subject matter that is being taught. 2) Pedagogical Knowledge (PK) here the instructor knowing the most effective teaching methods and practices. 3)

Technological Knowledge (TK) accessing and familiarity with digital tools and technologies (Mishra & Koehler, 2006) (Swallow, M. J., & Olofson, 2017).

The TPACK model emphasizes that effective technology integration occurs at the intersection of these three knowledge areas:

- Technological Pedagogical Knowledge (TPK): How technology can support teaching strategies and methods.
- Technological Content Knowledge (TCK): How technology can be used to represent and deliver content.
- Pedagogical Content Knowledge (PCK): The understanding of how teaching practices can be adapted to fit the content being taught.

The goal of TPACK is to encourage teachers to blend these knowledge domains to create learning experiences that are not only technologically enhanced but are also pedagogically sound and aligned with the content.

Comparative Insights:

- While the SAMR model offers a step-by-step approach for assessing the depth of technology integration, the TPACK framework provides a more holistic view of the essential knowledge components for successful integration.
- SAMR focuses on the levels of technology use and progression from enhancement to transformation, encouraging teachers to aim for higher levels where technology fundamentally changes learning.
- TPACK highlights the importance of balancing different knowledge areas, emphasizing that successful integration is not just about using technology but doing so in a way that aligns with pedagogical practices and content delivery.

Applications in the Classroom:

Using SAMR: A teacher may start with substitution by using digital worksheets instead of printed ones, move to augmentation by adding hyperlinks and interactive questions, progress to modification with collaborative tools, and reach redefinition by having students create digital portfolios that include multimedia projects.

Applying TPACK: A math teacher could integrate technology by using graphing software (TK) that aligns with teaching methods for introducing complex functions (PK) and represents mathematical content (CK) effectively.

Frameworks like SAMR and TPACK are invaluable tools for guiding educators in the effective use of technology in the classroom. The SAMR model helps teachers reflect on and elevate their level of technology integration, while the TPACK framework provides a comprehensive roadmap for combining content, pedagogy, and technology.

SECTION 3: SELECTING AND IMPLEMENTING CLASSROOM TECHNOLOGY

In choosing a technology, the teacher should first consider the learning requirement of his students and the teaching objectives he have in mind. This involves asking questions such as:

- What are the desired learning outcomes for students?
- What types of tasks do I want to transform or enhance with technology?
- Are there specific challenges in the classroom that technology could help address (e.g., engagement, differentiated learning)?
- What are my current technology competencies, and where do I need to nurture?

By supporting technology choices with these needs, teachers ensure that the tools they select will support both their instructional practices and their students' learning goals.

Choosing tools and applications for classroom is not about choosing the new generation equipment but about integrating tools that support teaching-learning and professional development. When teachers choose the tools that support the educational objectives, ensure the reporters and assistants provide comprehensive training, and increase the usage of new technologies step by step, faculty members develop the necessary skills to incorporate technology into their practices (Muir-Herzig, 2004). It also enhances specific learning results of the students while enabling the teachers to also become capable and competent in technology.

Evaluating and Selecting Technology Tools

There are always new technologies being produced for the classroom, therefore, for these technologies to fit into the learning-teaching process, there should be a well-structured method through which the appropriateness of the technology in learning, teaching, and student engagement is determined. A well-organized evaluation process considers multiple factors, including accessibility, ease of use, relevance, and the potential for meeting diverse learning needs. The first consideration when choosing any technology tool is its ability to support learning objectives set for a course or a lesson. Instructional tools should enable students to receive content as well as assess the level of mastery of what has been taken in class. The tool needs to be in synergy with the curriculum and teachers objectives. For example if a teacher wants to teach his/her students critical thinking skills an application that enhances problem solving or teamwork will be more useful than rote memorization (Jadhav, A. S., & Sonar, 2009). The tool should enhance or transform traditional learning activities. For example, interactive simulations, digital research platforms, or virtual labs can take tasks that were once done on paper like science experiments or historical research and make them more engaging and meaningful.

Peers which offer consistent, formative, or summative analysis or constantly communicate data to the teacher can help the teacher to monitor the progress of his or her students and modify practices based on performance data acquired. The tool should be compatible with screen readers, speech recognition programmes and other physical, sensory and learning impairment assistive devices. The user-friendliness of technology tools directly affects their acceptance and effectiveness in the classroom (Tran, T. A., & Daim, 2008). Both teachers and students should be able to navigate the tool quickly and efficiently without significant training. The tool should have a clear and simple interface, with simple understanding icons, labels, and navigation paths. Where the tools are too complex or richly functional, learners can become frustrated, and it becomes hard for them to learn. Choose tools that provide an explanation though tutorials, FAQs and customer support to help teachers learn how to resolve and assist students. This kind of platforms can be forums or online user groups, most of which are already familiar with the type of work for which they are being used.

Technological tools should be appropriate for the subject content and the lessons taught. In any given course, whether it is a mathematics course, science, language arts, or a social studies course. The tools should complement the course by providing ways of accessing various resources, information and simulations or other forms of learning environments that are relevant to the course being offered. One major key to improving learning is the proper identification of the kind of technology tools to use in the classroom (Georghiou & Roessner, 2000). Thus, thinking about alignment with learning objectives, access, usability, relation to content, engagement capabilities, affordability, scalability, as well as privacy, teachers and educational managers can come to positive choices which will improve both, teaching and the desired results for learners. Carefully selected tools help prepare teachers to create more student-oriented, collaborative, and effective learning process, which in turn lead to a more effective and fun classroom experience.

Tools and Platforms for Enhancing Student Engagement

Students are engaged in their learning activities through the use of technology that can be said to have supplemented all the parameters of engagement. There exist many programs and different instruments that can assist the teacher in creating rather an exciting learning environment for the student (Phaal et al., 2006). In the section below, several common social sites and other engaging tools that can help greatly enhance students' interest are described.

1. Learning Management Systems (LMS) for Classroom Management and Engagement
   a. Google Classroom

Google Classroom is a free LMS platform that integrates seamlessly with other Google Workspace tools like Google Docs, Sheets, and Google Drive. It provides a direct, user-friendly interface for organizing and managing class materials, assignments, and communication. Google Classroom helps students stay structured and engaged by providing clear access to resources, assignments, and communication with peers and teachers (Ketut Sudarsana et al., 2019). It supports personalized learning by allowing students to work at their own pace and access materials from anywhere.

b. Microsoft Teams for Education

Microsoft Teams is a vigorous communication and collaboration platform that also serves as an LMS. It offers many tools for establishing virtual classrooms, conducting video meetings, sharing files, and collaborating on documents. Microsoft Teams is ideal for fostering collaboration in both in-person and remote settings. It encourages active participation through real-time chats, collaborative document editing, and video meetings, making students feel connected to both their teachers and peers.

2. Interactive Tools for Active Learning and Engagement
   a. Kahoot!

Kahoot! is a classroom tools which is based on using quizzes, surveys, and polls popular among students. It provides the teachers with the ability to develop unique questionnaires that the learners can complete in the classroom as games. The idea of Kahoot! is easy accessing and enjoying because it awakens the spirit of game and fun in students and the teacher. For those who have poor interaction in the class they are forced to be active participants in class activities (Wang & Tahir, 2020).

But still, Kahoot! increases motivation and enhances students' ability to memorize information through fun.

b. Padlet

Padlet is an online application that offers students and teachers to brainstorm, share ideas, and work together or design multimedia-rich boards for different learning purposes. It works more like a virtual notice board where students can write messages, write webs, and even paste pictures, URLs and videos. Padlet encourages students to get involved as a result of an open platform and an opportunity to express themselves. It is useful for group activities, lectures, and projects, because it enables students express their ideas and materials in engaging manner.

c. Nearpod

Nearpod is an interactive presentation that enables the teacher to design a presentation with different objects, quizzes, polls, and group activities. Nearpod helps in capturing the attention of students through using of multimedia as well as incorporating activities with the help of which students can be divided into groups depending on the type of learning. How it transforms passive learning into the active and makes learning easier for students by making them to stay engaged and retain information.

d. Flipgrid

Flipgrid is an application for video conversations in which students create and record brief videos in response to questions. It encourages students to express their ideas and engage in discussions in a more personalized way. In turn, the Flipgrid allows the student to interact with the subject matter of the specific course in a much more interactive and individual manner. It is especially useful in the context of students' voice and organization of the discussion for the asynchronous or blended classrooms. Video discussions that are an inherent feature of the given model make the learning process more effective and socially oriented.

3. Collaboration and Communication Tools

Seesaw is a digital portfolio tool that helps students to capture and present their learning process. It also empowers teachers to comment and interact with learners in a special manner with the use of multimedia gadgets. With Seesaw, learners are able to document their learning experiences and also make even reflections of their learning achievements (Moorhouse, 2019). The ability to share their work with parents further increases their sense of achievement and involvement.

These tools and platforms meaningfully enhance student engagement by making learning more interactive, collaborative, and personalized. Platforms like Google Classroom and Microsoft Teams streamline classroom management and communication, while interactive tools like Kahoot!, Padlet, Nearpod, and Flipgrid provide attractive and dynamic ways for students to participate in learning.

Blended and Flipped Classroom Models

As long as technology advances the teaching approaches to the current society that we are in, such as the blended learning and the flipped classroom, are increasingly popular. Both strategies integrate the utilization of conventional mode of teaching with information technology to make learning more open and student oriented approach (Low et al., 2021).

1. Blended Learning: Designing and Implementing Blended Learning Strategies

Blended learning is an educational approach described as a technique of using both traditional classroom instructions and technological based instruction. This model enables teachers to incorporate conventional direct instruction and discussion methods as well as instructional resources in the form of video, interactive activities, and quizzes or tests (Hrastinski, 2019). From this perspective, the idea is to provide as much freedom and autonomy for students while maintaining the structure and guidance of in-person teaching.

Blended Learning Models

In this model, students move from one learning environment to another for a predetermined amount of time. This can be done on daily basis or on weekly basis so that it is possible to switch between the two methods of learning; digital or face to face. Students participate in most of their classes remotely, but they may come to their class for face-to-face learning intervention or group work as appropriate. The teacher acts as a facilitator who support based on students' individual needs. This model is totally online but still includes face-to-face sessions. Students work mostly online, but they attend in-person classes intermittently for critical discussion sessions or assessments.

Benefits of Blended Learning

- Students can progress at their own pace, reviewing materials as needed or advancing more quickly if students understand the concepts faster.
- The integration of digital tools and online resources supports student engagement by offering interactive and multimedia-rich content.
- Blended learning allows students to access materials and learning resources outside of the classroom, offering flexibility for students who might need additional time or alternative learning formats.

2. Flipped Classroom: Increasing Engagement and Deepening Understanding

The flipped classroom model inverts traditional class practices where students review content outside of the classroom out of home through videos, reading, or links to lectures and then come to class to learn and work on concepts taught (Cabı, 2018). The teacher as an orchestrator changes from transferring material knowledge to helping learners go through more elaborated tasks and problem solving activities.

Benefits of the Flipped Classroom:

- The flipped classroom model encourages students to take greater responsibility for their learning by engaging with content before class. It promotes self-learning and self-regulation.
- In class, time is dedicated to active learning strategies, such as problem-solving, discussions, and peer-to-peer collaboration, which lead to deeper understanding and application of knowledge.
- Lecture component is minimised by flipped classroom as it frees up time for more interactive and engaging learning activities. This helps keep students more engaged, as they are actively involved in their own learning process rather than just passively receiving information.
- Since teachers spend less time lecturing, they can focus more on individual student needs, offering targeted instruction and support during in-class activities.
- Since instructional videos and materials can be accessed anytime and anywhere, students can review content at their own pace, making the learning process more flexible.

Therefore, blended and flipped classrooms indicate paradigm shift education models that use technology to address students' learning needs. The blended learning model makes implementation flexible and differentiated, and on the other hand, the flipped classroom concept enlightens learning with participation and engagement. Both models de-emphasize the traditional transmission of knowledge by teacher, making students more autonomous, interested and active. When used deliberately and interdependently, these approaches will enable teachers to set up effective learning environments for learners who seek to shape future societies.

SECTION 4: PROFESSIONAL DEVELOPMENT FOR EFFECTIVE TECHNOLOGY USE

Using Information Communication Technology in classroom is one of the most critical developments that call for attention in the education sector. But crucial here is a factor that carries technology is education needs the skills and competencies of the teachers who put the technology to use. This is specifically true for the PD for educators in which they are supposed to acquire a range of knowledge tools and strategies to facilitate their process of technology integration into classroom.

The Importance of Professional Development for Technology Integration

For technology to be effectively used in the classroom, teachers need something more than the devices or some valuable teaching tools; they need profound training and support for succeeding in the integration of the tools with their teaching methodologies. Continuous learning promotes teachers' preparation to apply the technology in a manner that will improve learning outcomes as well as promoting the education goals. Results also found out those teachers who engaged specially in Technology PD programs perceived the value of technology greater and have greater confidence in practicing technology integration in teaching.

To ensure that PD is effective and leads to improved technology integration, it's essential to evaluate its impact. Evaluation should assess both teacher growth and student learning outcomes.

- Teacher confidence and competence in using technology.
- Changes in teaching practices and the integration of new tools.
- Student engagement and learning outcomes linked to technology use.
- Teacher satisfaction with the PD program.

Regular assessments and feedback loops will help adjust PD programs to meet evolving needs and ensure they remain relevant and impactful.

Key Components of Teacher Training Programs

Technology is constantly advancing therefore the teachers have to invest their time and upgrade on various technological requirements, tools, medium or strategies. A one-time only seminar type of approach is inadequate especially in the integration of technology. Teacher continued education should be seen in a form of a cycle with opportunities to learn from practice, from other teachers, and from the experience. For instance, digital pedagogy means the ability to make use of technology tools and interfaces in teaching and learning. It is based on the concept of how certain forms of technology might enhance conventional teaching processes and develop enhanced engaging, effective and individual learning environments (Toktarova & Semenova, 2020). Blended and flipped learning, collaborative learning, differentiated instruction, and active learning strategies shall remain the primary fields of interest among educators applying digital pedagogy. It is necessary to ensure that teachers are prepared for the predictable technical issues that arise when using technology in the classroom, professional development programs must include training on troubleshooting and basic technical skills. As seen earlier there are many areas of integration of IT in the classroom and ethical issues must be given due consideration while implementing such technologies. Teachers also must make sure that application of the technology does not violate concepts of justice, equality and their ability to respect the privacy of the learners.

Probably the most effective characteristic of implementing technology in the classroom is the real-time monitoring of student performance through formative evaluations. Professional development should involve instruction on how teachers can apply technology in the classroom for the purpose of assessment, feedback as well as result analysis. As technology use expands into classrooms teachers must learn to effectively integrate technology that supports collaboration and communication in the classroom and with others. Teachers are often at the forefront of technological integration, but institution must also support and guide the transition to technology-enhanced learning. PD programs should provide training for teachers on how to lead change within their schools and communities.

However for successfully integrating technology into the classroom, teachers need more than just access to tools; they need on-going, comprehensive training that covers digital pedagogy, troubleshooting, ethical considerations, and effective use of technology. Teacher training programs that emphasize these key components will not only enhance teachers' technical skills but also equip them with the pedagogical and ethical understanding required to create impactful, responsible, and engaging learning environments in the digital age.

Teacher training programs emphasizing these components will do more than improve teachers' technical proficiency. The programme will also provide teachers with the necessary educational and ethical appreciation to design meaningful, constructive, collaborative, and responsible learning opportunities in the digital age. This means that by providing for the knowledge update periodically schools will able to equip their teachers with the requisite knowledge on how to enhance learners' achievements through use of technologies (Kennedy, 2016).

Facilitating Collaboration and Peer-to-Peer Support among Teachers

Collaboration is a powerful learning tool, particularly in teacher professional development. Encouraging teachers to collaborate, share ideas, and solve problems together can enhance the learning experience. Below are tips for promoting collaboration and peer-to-peer support in teacher workshops.

a. Create Small Collaborative Groups
   - **Peer Review Sessions**: Teachers can review and give feedback on each other's lesson plans or classroom technology setups.
   - **Brainstorming Challenges**: In teams, teachers can collaborate to create strategies or solve challenges using technology (e.g., how to use an LMS to provide formative assessment data to students).

     Benefits:
   - Facilitates personalized discussions tailored to teachers' specific contexts.
   - Fosters camaraderie and peer support.

b. Use Collaborative Digital Tools

   In workshops focused on digital technology, use **collaborative online tools** that teachers can practice using. For instance:
   - Use Google Docs or Google Slides to collectively build lesson plans or a resource bank.
   - Set up shared spaces (like a Google Drive folder or Padlet) where participants can post resources, reflections, or lesson plans they've developed during the workshop.

   Benefits:
   - Teachers gain hands-on experience with collaboration tools.
   - Creates a space for on-going sharing and collaboration beyond the workshop.

c. Encourage Cross-Disciplinary Collaboration

Sometimes, collaboration across different subject areas can lead to new insights and ideas. Encourage teachers from different disciplines to **share ideas and resources** on how they might use technology in innovative ways across subjects. For example:

- A science teacher and a language arts teacher can collaborate on using digital storytelling tools (like Adobe Spark or Storybird) to share content across disciplines.
  Benefits:
- Promotes a more holistic view of technology integration.
- Encourages creative thinking and diverse perspectives.

Teachers should be encouraged to participate in planned collaborative sessions to encourage design of hands-on workshops during their professional development for technology integration. In this way, using the actively practice-oriented approach in combination with sharing experience means that educators will be ready to apply technology for teaching and learning improvement in their classrooms. This way not only teachers master such skills but the focus as well as opportunities for experimenting and reflective collaboration put emphasis back on construction of a culture where a practice of continuous improvement is cultivated in education practices.

Building a Supportive Learning Community

Online communities of practice allow teachers to connect virtually, regardless of their location. Online spaces (e.g., Google Groups, Edutopia, or Reddit's education communities) where educators can discuss technology integration strategies, troubleshoot issues, and share resources. Platforms like Facebook, Twitter, and LinkedIn host various educator groups focused on specific topics like digital pedagogy, classroom technology, or flipped learning. Online events allow teachers to participate in live discussions, watch guest speakers, and learn about the latest technological innovations (Kirschner & Lai, 2007).

Creating a learning community is critical given that the practice of incorporating ICTs happens continually throughout teaching practices. One of the ways of developing a network that can be used for knowledge sharing, training, and tackling of problems, educators can remain motivated, as well as enhance their performance. Investing in such communities strengthens the overall teaching profession and enhances the educational experience for both teachers and students.

SECTION 5: CREATING A CLASSROOM ENVIRONMENT FOR TECHNOLOGY INTEGRATION

Creating an effective classroom environment for technology integration goes beyond simply adding digital tools into the learning space. An environment that is well-suited for technology integration is one that ensures students are empowered to use technology purposefully and responsibly while giving teachers the flexibility and resources they need to manage and guide the learning process (Guzman & Nussbaum, 2009).

Designing the Physical Space for Technology Use

Implementing the use of technology in the classroom and creating the appropriate physical environment entails the principles of work adaptability, collaboration factor and student involvement as well as constructiveness of the technology adoption and comfort or physical working environment accessibility. Teachers need a selected control zone with access to multimedia tools and clear views to all students. Thoughtful placement of interactive displays, charging stations, and mobile technology carts ensures devices are accessible without cluttering the room. Controllability design of acoustics, light and furniture enable the conducive environment that allows for long term use and adoption of the technologies. Another aspect of inclusiveness includes; spacious corridors, portable furniture, and technology to accommodate students with physical disabilities. Additionally, the inclusion of secure storage and organization for devices, such as charging lockers and labelled bins, keeps the space tidy and efficient. A welcoming, well-designed environment not only enhances the use of technology but also fosters a positive and inclusive atmosphere for learning.

Flexible Seating Arrangements

Create a flexible seating arrangement that supports collaborative work, student-centered learning, and easy access to digital tools.

- Arrange desks or tables in small groups to encourage collaboration and group work.
- Set up dedicated spaces for specific technologies, like laptops or tablets, interactive whiteboards, or virtual reality (VR) stations, allowing students to access these tools when needed.
- Use furniture that can easily be rearranged to accommodate different types of activities, such as group projects, individual work, or whole-class discussions.

Benefits:

- Allows for easy collaboration and group work.
- Ensures that students can easily access technology tools.
- Facilitates personalized learning experiences.

Fostering Student Engagement with Technology

An effective technology-integrated classroom should engage students in ways that motivate them and foster deeper learning. Technology should not only be used to streamline administrative tasks or present information but also to actively engage students and encourage independent learning. Technology offers numerous ways to personalize learning experiences, ensuring that each student can work at their own pace and receive tailored support. This can include programs like Khan Academy, DreamBox, or iXL that adapt to students' learning levels and provide personalized challenges. Also, incorporate game-based learning platforms like Kahoot, Quizlet, or Classcraft to make learning fun and interactive. This allows students to use digital tools to create projects, such as digital storytelling, video production, or coding assignments that demonstrate their learning in unique ways.

Teacher's Role in Managing Technology in the Classroom

While students engage with technology, the teacher's role remains central in guiding and managing its use. Teachers should use technology to support and enhance instruction, rather than relying on it as the sole focus. Teachers should be facilitators of learning, guiding students through digital tools and activities. They can keep an eye on student engagement and behavior, ensuring that technology is used appropriately and not as a source of distraction. They have to be prepared to solve technical issues as they arise and adapt lessons as needed to ensure smooth integration of technology (Budin, 1991).

Benefits:

- Ensures effective and purposeful use of technology in the classroom.
- Helps maintain a productive, technology-driven learning environment.

Creating a classroom environment conducive to technology integration involves careful planning of the physical space, cultivating a positive digital learning culture, and ensuring equitable access for all students. By designing a flexible, tech-friendly classroom, promoting responsible use, fostering engagement, and providing on-going support, educators can create a dynamic and inclusive environment where technology enhances learning and helps students develop the skills they need for the future.

Optimizing Classroom Layout for Technology Use

With reference to ICT integration in teaching and learning, there are significant strategies of redesigning the physical class environment to enhance the efficient use of the gadgets in creating a flexible, creative, and collaborative learning space. There needs to be the physical planning of the physical classroom to allow incorporation and integration of technology, enhance learning and coming up with the different activities. For using technology either for accomplishing a particular activity, small group or for instructing the whole class, the classroom setup should meet the dynamic nature of teaching and learning processes (Yang et al., 2013). Classroom design substantially influences the capability of implementing and utilizing the technology. It is very important that we also clear our environment and creates areas that can easily allow access to the devices and promote collaborative learning for both the students and the teachers. A well-arranged desk arrangement enhances student mobility, interactions and access to technology enhances learning participation. Similarly, the group based activities such as those involving group discussions and technology as well as group work are easier when the physical layout allows for the use of shared technology. Flexibility in the layout ensures that students can work independently or in small groups, using technology in a way that suits their learning styles. In classrooms that integrate technology, it's essential that the layout not only accommodates traditional teaching methods but also promotes the use of digital tools in a way that enhances learning.

Configuring the Classroom for Group and Individual Activities

In a given classroom, there ought to be some formulations that accommodate both group and personal turn-taking yet making it pliable to responding to a given task's technology nature. For instance layouts that help to facilitate group activities or provide easy access to group devices are some of the best. To this end the place of the desks or the tables could be grouped in clusters or pod in order to encourage communication and team spirit. This setup allows students to share devices and work together on group tasks. There should be a place for shared device like a computer or tablet at each group's table, allowing for seamless collaboration and access to digital resources. Central areas with larger screens or interactive displays where groups can gather for discussions, share their work, and engage with multimedia content as a class. This benefit the students encouraged with communication and teamwork. It makes easier for students to work together using technology, enhancing group problem-solving and collaborative learning.

Configuring for Individual Activities

For individual tasks, the layout should offer students easy access to technology and a quiet, focused environment. While this traditional layout may seem less collaborative, it can still be useful for tasks that require individual concentration, such as online research, writing, or assessments. Ensure that each student has easy access to a personal device (such as a laptop or tablet) that can be used at their desk, with enough space to move around and work. Then create small, designated areas or "pods" for students who may need extra space to focus on technology-based tasks. This provides students with the space and environment they need to complete tasks independently and with minimal distractions. It ensures each student has access to technology, promoting personalized learning.

Fostering a Culture of Experimentation and Adaptability

In the rapidly evolving world of digital education, fostering a culture of experimentation and adaptability is essential for teachers, students, and educational institutions. The integration of technology in the classroom presents numerous opportunities for innovation, but it also requires a mindset shift towards embracing change, taking risks, and continuously learning. By creating an environment where experimentation is encouraged and adaptability is prioritized, educators can not only improve their own teaching practices but also cultivate a similar mindset in their students.

Incorporating technology into teaching and learning should not be viewed as a one-time event but as an ongoing process of experimentation and refinement. Teachers should be encouraged to experiment with new technologies and teaching methods, even if they are uncertain of the outcome. Teachers view failures as part of the learning process. Instead of fearing failure, teachers should be comfortable making mistakes and learning from them. This mindset can be moulded to students, showing that learning from errors is a natural part of exploring new ideas. Teachers can experiment with new technologies on a small scale before incorporating them into larger lessons. For example, using a new app for one class period or a single activity can allow teachers to evaluate its effectiveness before committing to broader use. Teachers should have scheduled time during the school day to explore new technologies, attend workshops, or collaborate with peers. Professional development programs that encourage hands-on experimentation and learning-by-doing can help teachers feel more confident in adopting new technologies (Kitchell, 1995). They can pilot new technology with a small group of students before full implementation. This gives them time to test new ideas, tweak them, and gather feedback for improvement.

Adapting to new digital tools and methodologies requires embracing change and developing flexibility. In a fast-paced, technology-driven world, the willingness to pivot and adapt is crucial for both educators and students. Cultivate an attitude of continuous professional development where learning does not stop after formal training. Encourage teachers to seek out new knowledge and stay informed about emerging technologies and teaching strategies. They should model a growth mindset by showing students that they are also open to change and learning. This helps students feel more comfortable experimenting with new tools and strategies themselves. The rise of online and blended learning models offers teachers and students opportunities to explore new ways of delivering and receiving instruction. Teachers can use a mix of in-person and digital resources, fostering an adaptable learning environment.

Digital tools offer opportunities for students to engage in self-directed learning, explore new topics, and develop critical thinking skills. Encouraging students to embrace new technologies helps them become more flexible learners. Teachers can allow students to explore new technologies and digital tools that align with their interests and learning styles. Students who are given the freedom to choose and explore tools become more adaptable and better equipped to navigate the ever-changing digital landscape. Motivating the students to use technology will solve real-world problems, whether through collaborative projects or independent research (Anghelo Josué et al., 2023). This approach enhances their adaptability by requiring them to think critically and creatively about technology use. This helps students become independent, lifelong learners who can adapt to new digital tools and challenges and improves creativity and innovation in the use of technology for learning.

Thus fostering a culture of experimentation and adaptability is essential for effective technology integration in education. By encouraging teachers to experiment with new tools and strategies, promoting flexibility in both teaching practices and classroom environments, and supporting the dissemination of new technologies, schools can create a dynamic, innovative learning environment. Additionally, cultivating adaptability in students prepares them for a future where change is constant and technological fluency is crucial. Ultimately, embracing change and experimentation is the key to creating a classroom culture where both teachers and students thrive in the digital age.

CONCLUSION

This chapter elucidated on professional learning that targets areas of need and supports sustained, enhanced technology use. This might help teachers to understand the implications of integrating technology in classroom. Also, systematically develop their technological skills for effectively supporting the enhancement of learning experience in diversified, meaningful and student-sustaining fashion. This study discusses the significance of effective integration of technology in learning which makes it relevant to education policy and practice decision-makers in schools and colleges, educational technology developers and suppliers interested in promoting technology-mediated learning, and professional development personnel who want to make learning environments effective and efficient. It is recommended to establish ongoing professional development programs that focus on targeted, needs-based training to help teachers systematically develop their technological skills. These programs should emphasize the practical application of frameworks like SAMR and TPACK, ensuring effective integration of technology in diverse learning environments while aligning with education policy and practice.

REFERENCES

Alenezi, A. (2017). Obstacles for teachers to integrate technology with instruction. *Education and Information Technologies*, *22*, 1797–1816. https://doi.org/https://doi.org/10.1007/s10639-016-9518-5

Betrus, A. (2012). Historical evolution of instructional technology in teacher education programs: A ten-year update. *TechTrends*, *56*, 42–45. https://doi.org/https://doi.org/10.1007/s11528-012-0597-x

Blundell, C. N., Mukherjee, M., & Nykvist, S. (2022). A scoping review of the application of the SAMR model in research. *Computers and Education Open*, *3*, 100093. https://doi.org/https://doi.org/10.1016/j.caeo.2022.100093

Bonfield, C. A., Salter, M., Longmuir, A., Benson, M., & Adachi, C. (2020). Transformation or evolution?: Education 4.0, teaching and learning in the digital age. *Higher Education Pedagogies*, *5*(1), 223–246. https://doi.org/https://doi.org/10.1080/23752696.2020.1816847

Budin, H. R. (1991). Technology and the Teacher's Role. *Computers in the Schools*, *8*(1–3), 15–26. DOI: 10.1300/J025v08n01_03

Cabı, E. (2018). The Impact of the Flipped Classroom Model on Students' Academic Achievement. *International Review of Research in Open and Distance Learning*, *19*(3). Advance online publication. DOI: 10.19173/irrodl.v19i3.3482

Cerny, M. (2015). The way to open education through the modern technology. *Procedia: Social and Behavioral Sciences*, *174*, 3194–3198.

Cui, Y., Chen, F., Lutsyk, A., Leighton, J. P., & Cutumisu, M. (2023). Datablended assessments: A systematic literature review. *Assessment in Education: Principles, Policy & Practice*, *30*(1), 76–96. https://doi.org/https://doi.org/10.1080/0969594X.2023.2182737

Dogan, S., Dogan, N. A., & Celik, I. (2021). Teachers' skills to integrate technology in education: Two path models explaining instructional and application software use. *Education and Information Technologies*, *26*, 1311–1332. https://doi.org/https://doi.org/10.1007/s10639-020-10310-4

Georghiou, L., & Roessner, D. (2000). Evaluating technology programs: Tools and methods. *Research Policy*, *29*(4–5), 657–678. DOI: 10.1016/S0048-7333(99)00094-3

Gruzdeva, M. L., Vaganova, O. I., Kaznacheeva, S. N., Bystrova, N. V., & Chanchina, A. V. (2020). Modern educational technologies in professional education. *Growth Poles of the Global Economy: Emergence, Changes and Future Perspectives*, 1097-1103. https://doi.org/https://doi.org/10.1007/978-3-030-15160-7_110

Gudanescu, N. (2010). Using modern technology for improving learning process at different educational levels. *Procedia: Social and Behavioral Sciences*, *2*(2), 5641–5645. https://doi.org/https://doi.org/10.1016/j.sbspro.2010.03.921

Guzman, A., & Nussbaum, M. (2009). Teaching competencies for technology integration in the classroom. *Journal of Computer Assisted Learning*, *25*(5), 453–469. DOI: 10.1111/j.1365-2729.2009.00322.x

Hrastinski, S. (2019). What Do We Mean by Blended Learning? *TechTrends*, *63*(5), 564–569. DOI: 10.1007/s11528-019-00375-5

Jadhav, A. S., & Sonar, R. M. (2009). Evaluating and selecting software packages: A review. *Information and Software Technology*, *51*(3), 555–563. https://doi.org/https://doi.org/10.1016/j.infsof.2008.09.003

Josué, A. (2023). Educational Platforms: Digital Tools for the teaching-learning process in Education. *Ibero-American Journal of Education & Society Research*, *3*(1), 259–263. DOI: 10.56183/iberoeds.v3i1.626

Kennedy, M. M. (2016). How Does Professional Development Improve Teaching? *Review of Educational Research*, *86*(4), 945–980. DOI: 10.3102/0034654315626800

Ketut Sudarsana, I., Bagus Made Anggara Putra, I., Nyoman Temon Astawa, I., & Wayan Lali Yogantara, I. (2019). The use of Google classroom in the learning process. *Journal of Physics: Conference Series*, *1175*, 012165. DOI: 10.1088/1742-6596/1175/1/012165

Kirschner, P. A., & Lai, K. (2007). Online communities of practice in education. *Technology, Pedagogy and Education*, *16*(2), 127–131. DOI: 10.1080/14759390701406737

Kitchell, S. (1995). Corporate Culture, Environmental Adaptation, and Innovation Adoption: A Qualitative/Quantitative Approach. *Journal of the Academy of Marketing Science*, *23*(3), 195–205. DOI: 10.1177/0092070395233004

Lawless, K. A., & Pellegrino, J. W. (2007). Professional development in integrating technology into teaching and learning: Knowns, unknowns, and ways to pursue better questions and answers. *Review of Educational Research*, *77*(4), 575–614. https://doi.org/https://doi.org/10.3102/0034654307309921

Lawrence, G., Ahmed, F., Cole, C., & Johnston, K. P. (2020). Not more technology but more effective technology: Examining the state of technology integration in EAP programmes. *RELC Journal*, *51*(1), 101–116.

Low, M. C., Lee, C. K., Sidhu, M. S., Lim, S. P., Hasan, Z., & Lim, S. C. (2021). Blended Learning to Enhanced Engineering Education using Flipped Classroom Approach: An Overview. *Electronic Journal of Computer Science and Information Technology*, *7*(1). Advance online publication. DOI: 10.52650/ejcsit.v7i1.111

Mishra, P., & Koehler, M. J. (2006). Technological Pedagogical Content Knowledge: A Framework for Teacher Knowledge. *Teachers College Record*, *108*(6), 1017–1054. DOI: 10.1111/j.1467-9620.2006.00684.x

Moorhouse, B. L. (2019). Seesaw: https://web.seesaw.me. *RELC Journal, 50*(3), 493–496. DOI: 10.1177/0033688218781976

Muir-Herzig, R. G. (2004). Technology and its impact in the classroom. *Computers & Education*, *42*(2), 111–131. https://doi.org/https://doi.org/10.1016/S0360-1315(03)00067-8

Naik, G., Chitre, C., Bhalla, M., & Rajan, J. (2020). Impact of use of technology on student learning outcomes: Evidence from a large-scale experiment in India. *World Development*, *127*, 104736. https://doi.org/https://doi.org/10.1016/j.worlddev.2019.104736

Nii Akai Nettey, J., Osei Mensah, R., Asafo-Adjei, R., & Adiza Babah, P. (2024). Analyzing the challenges basic school teachers face in integrating Information and Communication Technology into teaching and learning activities in a developing country. *Cogent Education*, *11*(1), 2364544. https://doi.org/https://doi.org/10.1080/2331186X.2024.2364544

Norton, A., Sonnemann, J., & McGannon, C. (2013). *(2013). The online evolution: When technology meets tradition in higher education*. Grattan Institute.

Phaal, R., Farrukh, C. J. P., & Probert, D. R. (2006). Technology management tools: Concept, development and application. *Technovation*, *26*(3), 336–344. DOI: 10.1016/j.technovation.2005.02.001

Sarkar, S., Mohapatra, S., & Sundarakrishnan, J. (2017). Assessing impact of technology based digital equalizer programme on improving student learning outcomes. *Education and Information Technologies*, *22*(1), 195–213. https://doi.org/https://doi.org/10.1007/s10639-015-9434-0

Swallow, M. J., & Olofson, M. W. (2017). (2017). Contextual understandings in the TPACK framework. *Journal of Research on Technology in Education, 49(3-4), 228-244., 49*(3–4), 228–244. https://doi.org/https://doi.org/10.1080/15391523.2017.1347537

Toktarova, V. I., & Semenova, D. A. (2020). Digital pedagogy: Analysis, requirements and experience of implementation. *Journal of Physics: Conference Series, 1691*(1), 012112. DOI: 10.1088/1742-6596/1691/1/012112

Tran, T. A., & Daim, T. (2008). A taxonomic review of methods and tools applied in technology assessment. *Technological Forecasting and Social Change, 75*(9), 1396–1405. DOI: 10.1016/j.techfore.2008.04.004

Väätäjä, J. O., & Ruokamo, H. (2021). Conceptualizing dimensions and a model for digital pedagogy. *Journal of Pacific Rim Psychology, 15*, 1834490921995395. DOI: 10.1177/1834490921995395

Wang, A. I., & Tahir, R. (2020). The effect of using Kahoot! for learning – A literature review. *Computers & Education, 149*, 103818. DOI: 10.1016/j.compedu.2020.103818

Yang, J., Huang, R., & Li, Y. (2013). *Optimizing Classroom Environment to Support Technology Enhanced Learning.*, DOI: 10.1007/978-3-642-39146-0_24

Yurtseven Avci, Z., O'Dwyer, L. M., & Lawson, J. (2020). Designing effective professional development for technology integration in schools. *Journal of Computer Assisted Learning, 36*(2), 160–177. https://doi.org/https://doi.org/10.1111/jcal.12394. DOI: 10.1111/jcal.12394

Chapter 13
Teachers in Blended Learning Environment:
Mapping Their Evolving Roles

Noor Aisha
https://orcid.org/0000-0002-4306-8203
Indira Gandhi National Open University, India

Aliasghar Rahman Doust
International University of Chabahar, Iran

ABSTRACT

The ongoing trends in teaching-learning with technology has led blended learning to emerge as the most promising method of instruction. The aim of the present study is to carry out an in-depth analysis on the researches addressing teachers' roles in blended learning environment. The researches were analysed using a matrix, descriptive and content analysis methods were applied. The conclusion of the research is that there are many potential roles to guide deeper change in education within blended learning environment. Further development and exploration of specific domain-based inquiries are recommended to explore. The present chapter will help the teachers to be well acquainted with their roles and responsibilities that would further direct the authorities and administrators of the institutions to plan and organise trainings accordingly and the capacity-building programmes for teachers; in-service teachers to undertake such trainings and courses that will help them in their profession as well as it will provide deeper insights for teacher education programmes and policy implications.

DOI: 10.4018/979-8-3373-0771-8.ch013

INTRODUCTION

The ongoing trends in teaching-learning with technology has led blended learning to emerge as the most promising method of instruction. Blended learning provides the opportunity to integrate the technology without losing the essence of the traditional and conventional methods of teaching-learning, that can allow the learners to have some autonomy and flexibility to learn in the present ever-evolving technological era. A blended learning environment thus includes all forms of teaching-learning that include self-learning, distance learning, face-to-face learning and online learning. And therefore, teachers are supposed to play very crucial roles in blended learning environments and not just imparting instructions traditionally.

In such a scenario where a rapid revolution in teaching-learning is being observed with seamless technological integration, it becomes imperative to outline the various roles undertaken by the teachers in order to carry out the teaching-learning process which will encompass where the teachers stand, what roles they play, when their presence become highly crucial, how they cope up and why they remain irreplaceable despite of technological advancements and innovations will be discussed in the present chapter. Thus, adhering to the research questions that encompass studying the trends observed in the researches on teachers in blended learning environment and their roles, the present study thus intended to achieve the following objectives:

1. To outline the trends observed in the researches on teachers in blended learning environment.
2. To identify the dominant themes related to the roles of teachers in Blended Learning environment.

LITERATURE REVIEW

Teachers design and develop online course materials, activities, and assessments (Graham, 2013). Teachers facilitate online discussions, provide feedback, and support students in their learning (Palloff & Pratt, 2003). Teachers provide one-on-one guidance and support to students, helping them to set goals and develop self-directed learning skills (Tynjälä, 1999). eachers assess student learning, providing feedback and evaluating student progress (Boud, 2000). Teachers need to possess technical skills to design and deliver online courses (Koehler & Mishra, 2009). Teachers need to possess pedagogical skills to design and deliver effective online instruction (Mishra & Koehler, 2006). Teachers need to possess strong communication skills to facilitate online discussions and provide feedback (Palloff & Pratt, 2003). Teachers may face technological challenges, such as poor internet connectivity or inadequate technical support (Graham, 2013). Teachers may face pedagogical challenges, such as designing effective online instruction and assessing student learning (Mishra & Koehler, 2006). Teachers may face challenges in managing their time, balancing online and face-to-face instruction (Palloff & Pratt, 2003). Teachers need ongoing professional development to develop the skills and competencies needed to teach in blended learning environments (Koehler & Mishra, 2009). Teachers need to collaborate with other educators and stakeholders to design and deliver effective blended learning programs (Graham, 2013). Further research is needed to understand the teacher's role in blended learning environments and to identify best practices for teaching and learning in these environments (Means et al., 2010).

METHODS

A review of the recent researches has been thematically done in order to map the evolving roles of teachers in blended learning environments. Thematic analysis facilitates the identification of patterns and themes within qualitative data (Maguire & Delahunt, 2017). Qualitative data analysis holds its credibility as an instrument that allows to interpret and describe a context (Maguire & Delahunt, 2017). The Braun and Clarke's (2006) framework explains how qualitative data explains the process of analysis within the context of teaching-learning and research.

The focus on rigorous and relevant thematic analysis has implications in terms of the credibility of the research process (Moira Maguire & Brid Delahunt, 2017). Thematic analysis is the process of identifying patterns or themes within qualitative data. Braun & Clarke (2006) suggest that it is the first qualitative method that should be learned as it provides core skills that will be useful for conducting many other kinds of analysis' (p.78). as cited in (Moira Maguire & Brid Delahunt, 2017).

Thematic Analysis is the methodology used to analyse the literature and dominant themes. It is a qualitative research method that involves identifying, coding, and categorizing patterns and themes within data. Steps involved in thematic analysis include- familiarization with the data through repeated readings and note taking; initial coding by assigning preliminary codes to the data to identify patterns and themes; theme development by identifying and refining themes through iterative coding and analysis; theme reviewing by reviewing and refining the themes to ensure they accurately reflect the data; theme naming by assigning names to the themes that accurately reflect their content; and theme Reporting which include reporting the themes in a clear and concise manner, using supporting quotes and examples from the data.

For thematic analysis there are software tools available that performs qualitative data analysis through querying, coding, categorizing, and visualizing data that supports thematic analysis. However, the present work is the thematic analysis done manually, following all the steps carefully by handling the data with utmost care. The reason of employing this analysis manually is to provide a comprehensive presentation of authors' experiences and existing researches to demonstrate the blend of practice and research to achieve practicality.

FINDINGS

1. To Outline the Trends Observed in the Researches on the Roles of Teachers in Blended Learning Environment

Table 1. Observed trends

Research	Variables discussed	Sample	Approach	Method	Data Analysis	Implications
Jokinen & Mikkonen (2013)	Teachers' experience	Undergraduate Nursing students	Qualitative	Focus group interviews	Content Analysis	Undergraduate Nursing students and related Teachers
Oliver & Stallings (2014)	Teachers' preparation	Higher Education and K-12 Teachers	Qualitative	Review	Thematic	K-12 Teachers
Gedik et al., (2013)	Design of Blended Learning Environment	Instructors	Qualitative	Design-Based Research	Heuristic Inquiry method	Blended Course Design

Table 2. Components of BLE

Research	Components of BLE		
Jokinen & Mikkonen (2013)	Learning in Practice	Face-to-face learning	Technology-mediated Learning
Oliver & Stallings (2014)	Contextual	Instructional	Technological
Gedik et al., (2013)	Context, Pedagogy and Technology	Face-to-face	Online

Table 3. Tasks associated with teachers in BLE

Research	Tasks
Jokinen & Mikkonen (2013)	- Planning and Implementing teaching-learning
Oliver & Stallings (2014)	-Merging learning strategies, resources and modes
Gedik et al., (2013)	-Framing the activities in both f2f and online environment and with contexts.

Table 4. Activities and expected outcomes in BLE

Research	Activities			Expected outcomes in BLE
Jokinen & Mikkonen (2013)	Practice	Online	Face-to-face	- Reflect on theory and Practice - Access to expert and professional knowledge - Real-life problem solving - Decision making
Oliver & Stallings (2014)	-	Online	Face-to-face	- Reflect on theory and Practice
Gedik et al., (2013)	-	Online	Face-to-face	- Arousing students' interest - Manage time and course activities flexibly - Save time for course activities - Tracking students' progress easily - Engagement in extensive interaction - Collaboration and communication with students

Table 5. Terms used for teachers in BLE

Research	Terms used for Teachers in BLE
Jokinen & Mikkonen (2013)	Teachers
Oliver & Stallings (2014)	Teachers
Gedik et al., (2013)	Instructor

Table 6. Roles expected from teachers in BLE analysis

Research	Roles expected from Teachers in BLE
Jokinen & Mikkonen (2013)	Planning, Decision making, Teaching
Oliver & Stallings (2014)	Teaching, Designing or preparing instruction
Gedik et al., (2013)	Planning activities, designing instruction, harmonizing the f2f and online environments

Table 7. Suggested skills, needs & requirements for teachers to acquire in BLE

Research	Suggested Skills, Needs & Requirements for Teachers to acquire in BLE
Jokinen & Mikkonen (2013)	- Different Pedagogical approaches - Professional development support in redesigning teaching and learning.
Oliver & Stallings (2014)	- Contextual, Instructional and Technological components integrated effectively to be aligned with processes of instructional design
Gedik et al., (2013)	-Instructor's competency pertaining design aspects in BLE aligned with context, pedagogy and technical issues

2. To Identify the Dominant Themes Related to the Roles of Teachers in Blended Learning Environment

The study employed thematic analysis to examine the roles of teachers in a blended learning environment. The analysis of the available researches revealed and identified the themes. The themes reflected the various roles teachers played in supporting students' learning. By understanding the complexities of teachers' roles in blended learning environments, educators can better support student learning and create effective, engaging, and interactive learning experiences.

Theme 1-Instructor: Blended learning environments have become increasingly popular, and teachers play a vital role in facilitating student learning in these settings. Research has shown that blended learning can positively impact learning outcomes, class dynamics, and student and teacher perceptions. Studies have highlighted the need for more qualitative research on teachers' perceptions and roles in blended learning environments. This includes understanding their experiences, challenges, and strategies for effective teaching in blended settings (Mendieta, 2012). The design of blended learning environments is critical, and teachers play a key role in this process. Research emphasizes the importance of intentional design, leveraging technology to support learning, and creating opportunities for student interaction and feedback (Keengwe & Kang, 2012). Teachers need ongoing professional development to effectively integrate technology and blended learning strategies into their practice.

Theme 2- Facilitator: Teachers facilitate online discussions, provide feedback, and support students in their learning (Palloff & Pratt, 2003). This role requires teachers to have strong communication and interpersonal skills. Teachers should prioritize a student-centered approach, using technology to support personalized learning and promoting student autonomy and agency. Blended learning environments have become increasingly popular, and teachers play a vital role in facilitating student learning in these settings. Research has shown that blended learning can positively impact learning outcomes, class dynamics, and student and teacher perceptions (Albeta et al, 2023).

Theme 3- Innovator/Instructional Designer: Teachers design and develop online course materials, activities, and assessments (Graham, 2013). This role requires teachers to have technical skills, such as creating multimedia content and using learning management systems. Blended learning can positively impact learning outcomes, class dynamics, and student and teacher perceptions. Teachers who effectively integrate technology and face-to-face instruction can create engaging and interactive learning environments (Albeta et al, 2023). Teachers must be flexible and adaptable in blended learning environments, willing to adjust their instruction and assessment strategies as needed. Teachers must design instruction that effectively integrates technology and face-to-face teaching (Keengwe & Kang, 2013).

Theme 4-Mentor: Teachers play a vital role as mentors in blended learning environments, providing guidance, support, tailoring their support to individual students' needs, learning styles, and goals and feedback to students. Teachers provide one-on-one guidance and support to students, helping them to set goals and develop self-directed learning skills (Tynjälä, 1999). This role requires teachers to have strong interpersonal and coaching skills. Teachers provide scaffolding, helping students navigate complex concepts, and offering feedback on assignments and assessments. Teachers foster a positive learning environment, offering encouragement, empathy, and support to help students overcome challenges and build confidence. Teachers schedule regular virtual or face-to-face meetings with students to discuss progress, goals, and concerns. Teachers provide constructive feedback on student work, offering suggestions for improvement and guidance on future assignments. Teachers encourage students to take ownership of their learning, setting goals, and developing self-directed learning plans. Teacher mentoring has been shown to improve student academic achievement, motivation, and engagement. Mentoring helps students develop a growth mindset, building confidence and self-efficacy. 3. Mentoring fosters positive relationships between teachers and students, promoting a sense of trust, respect, and empathy. Teachers must balance mentoring responsibilities with other teaching duties, managing their time effectively to ensure adequate support for students. Teachers must develop skills in using digital tools and platforms to facilitate mentoring in blended learning environments. Teachers must be aware of the diverse needs and backgrounds of their students, adapting their mentoring approach to meet the unique needs of each student. Overall, teachers play a vital role as mentors in blended learning environments, providing personalized guidance, academic support, and emotional support to students. By leveraging mentoring strategies and addressing challenges, teachers can help students achieve their full potential.

Theme 5- Evaluator/Assessor: Teachers assess student learning, providing feedback and evaluating student progress (Boud, 2000). This role requires teachers to have strong assessment and evaluation skills. Teachers must facilitate student learning by creating opportunities for interaction, feedback, and assessment (Keengwe & Kang, 2013). Teachers should prioritize a student-centered approach, using technology to support personalized learning and promoting student autonomy and agency (Albeta et al, 2023).

Theme 6- Administrator: Teachers overall, play a critical role in blended learning environments, and their instructional design, facilitation of student learning, and promotion of student engagement are essential for student success. Teachers must promote student engagement by using technology to support personalized learning and fostering a sense of community (Mendieta, 2012). Teachers play a vital role as administrators in blended learning environments, ensuring the smooth operation of online and offline learning components. Teachers must be flexible and adaptable in blended learning environments, willing to adjust their instruction and assessment strategies as needed (Keengwe & Kang, 2013). Teachers manage online course materials, assignments, and assessments, ensuring organization and accessibility. Teachers troubleshoot technical issues, provide support to students, and collaborate with IT staff to resolve complex problems. Teachers collect and analyze data on student engagement, progress, and outcomes, using this information to inform instruction and improve the blended learning experience.

Teachers play a crucial role as administrators in Blended Learning Environment which may include Course Management, Technical Support, Data Analysis, Instructional Leadership, Professional Development, Community Building. Teachers provide guidance and support to colleagues, sharing best practices and expertise in blended learning. Teachers participate in and lead professional development opportunities, enhancing their own skills and knowledge in blended learning. Teachers foster a sense of community among students, parents, and colleagues, promoting collaboration and communication in the blended learning environment.

Teachers must balance administrative tasks with instructional responsibilities, managing their time effectively to ensure the success of the blended learning program. Teachers must develop and maintain technical skills, staying up-to-date with emerging technologies and trends in blended learning. Teachers must work closely with colleagues, students, and parents, communicating effectively and building strong relationships to support the blended learning environment.

Development of Conceptual Model for Teachers' Evolving Roles in Blended Learning Environment

The Thematic Analysis as shown in Figure 1, led the researchers to develop the conceptual model for teachers' evolving roles in Blended Learning Environment as shown in Figure 1. The suggested conceptual model described the interchangeable roles of teachers in Blended Learning Environment shown in the flow of circular arrows, which are integrated and infused with technology at every stage and their respective roles which are highlighted with the dotted lines. The roles and responsibilities in blended learning associated with teachers implied guidelines for teacher preparation programmes to incorporate contextual, instructional and technological Oliver & Stallings (2014) components of instructional design process.

Blended Learning environment has been observed to be implemented in higher education by involving learning strategies, learning resources and modes of learning. It has been identified to have many positive impacts. Researches revealed that teachers' responsibilities and roles in making a blended learning environment impactful.

The core principle to design blended learning environment is combination of modes provides the optimal basis given the contextual situations of teaching and learning (Neumeier, 2005). In order to undertake such challenging situation certain framework or parameters are required for the desired Blended Learning environment.

Figure 1. Thematic presentation: Roles of teachers in blended learning environment

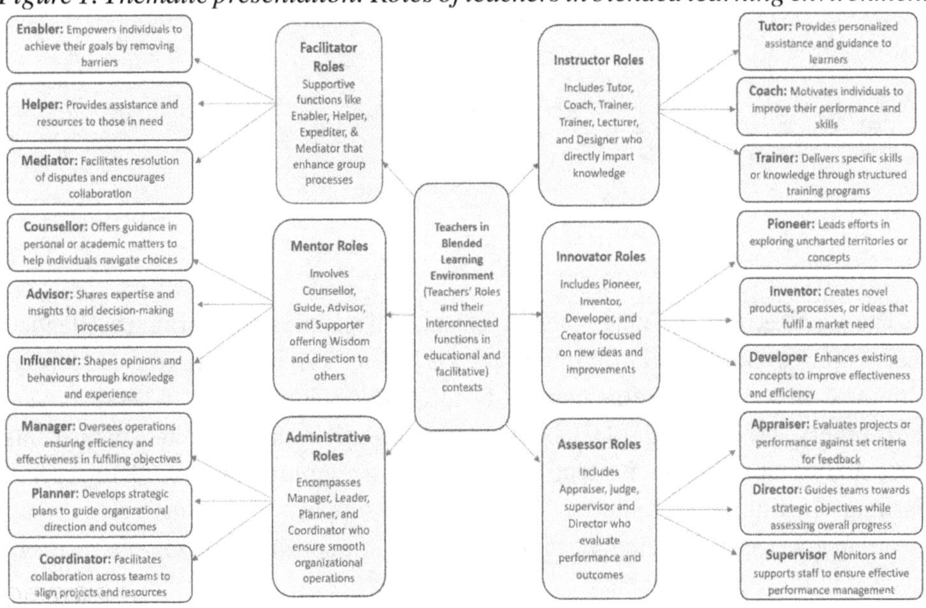

Figure 2. Conceptual model: Teachers' roles in blended learning environment

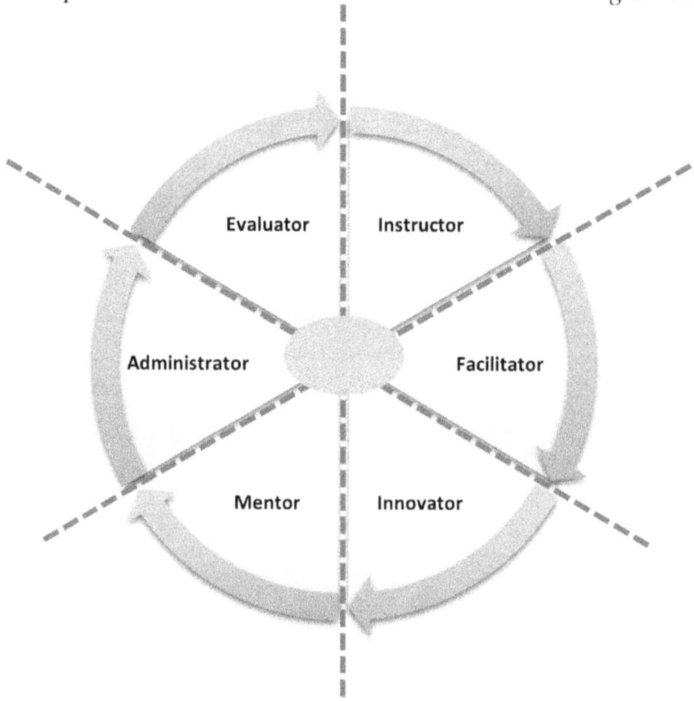

The practice, roles of teachers and experiences of teaching and learning in Blended Learning environments in an optimum way, various underlying factors that associated with the contextual requirements must be aligned in the pedagogical perspective.

Teachers play a crucial role in blended learning environments, requiring various skills and competencies to effectively integrate technology and promote student learning. Institutions should provide ongoing support, including professional development, technical support, and collaboration opportunities, to help teachers succeed in these environments.

DISCUSSION

The study presents the comparative aspects crucial for understanding the similarities and differences of teachers across different contexts of Blended Learning environment. Through the thematic analysis, several key themes were identified. Leadership, Mentoring, facilitator, assessor, innovator, teacher, instructor, emerged as the most frequent studied category, followed by themes such as guide, counsellor, administrator, organiser. The analysis also highlighted differences in themes between the countries. Thus, the methodology of the present research is centered around systematic thematic analysis of selected articles, focussing to uncover and compare trends, providing a comprehensive understanding of the evolving roles of teachers.

Blended learning environments combine traditional face-to-face instruction, self-learning with online learning. Teachers play a crucial role in these environments, as they must adapt their instructional strategies to effectively integrate technology and promote student learning. Teachers in blended learning environments assume various roles, including- Instructional Designer that require teachers to design and develop course materials, activities, and assessments; Facilitator that enable teachers to facilitate online discussions, provide feedback, and support students in their learning; Mentor that expect the teachers provide one-on-one guidance and support to students, helping them to set goals and develop self-directed learning skills; Assessor that make teachers assess student learning, providing feedback and evaluating student progress.

Teachers in blended learning environments require various skills and competencies, including- Technical Skills that require teachers need to possess technical skills to design and deliver online courses; Pedagogical Skills that require teachers need to possess pedagogical skills to design and deliver effective online instruction; Communication Skills that require teachers need to possess strong communication skills to facilitate online discussions and provide feedback. Time Management Skills that require teachers need to possess effective time management skills to balance online and face-to-face instruction.

Teachers in blended learning environments face various challenges and barriers, including- Technological Challenges where teachers may face technological challenges, such as poor internet connectivity or inadequate technical support; Pedagogical Challenges where teachers may face pedagogical challenges, such as designing effective online instruction and assessing student learning; Time Management Challenges where teachers may face challenges in managing their time, balancing online and face-to-face instruction; Support Challenges in which teachers may face challenges in accessing support, including technical support and instructional design support.

To effectively support teachers in blended learning environments, institutions should provide Professional Development, technical support, opportunities for collaboration and research advancement programmes. Institutions should provide ongoing professional development opportunities to help teachers develop the skills and competencies needed to teach in blended learning environments. Institutions should offer technical support to help teachers troubleshoot technical issues and effectively integrate technology into their instruction. Institutions should foster collaboration among teachers, instructional designers, and technical support staff to support the development of effective blended learning programs. Institutions should conduct research to better understand the teacher's role in blended learning environments and to identify best practices for teaching and learning in these environments.

Teachers need to possess technical skills to design and deliver online courses (Koehler & Mishra, 2009). This includes skills such as creating multimedia content, using learning management systems, and troubleshooting technical issues. Teachers need to possess pedagogical skills to design and deliver effective online instruction (Mishra & Koehler, 2006). This includes skills such as creating engaging online activities, facilitating online discussions, and assessing student learning. Teachers need to possess strong communication skills to facilitate online discussions and provide feedback (Palloff & Pratt, 2003). This includes skills such as writing clear and concise messages, using tone and language effectively, and responding to student inquiries.

Teachers may face technological challenges, such as poor internet connectivity or inadequate technical support (Graham, 2013). These challenges can hinder the effectiveness of online instruction and create frustration for teachers and students. Teachers may face pedagogical challenges, such as designing effective online instruction and assessing student learning (Mishra & Koehler, 2006). These challenges can require teachers to rethink their instructional strategies and develop new skills. Teachers may face challenges in managing their time, balancing online and face-to-face instruction (Palloff & Pratt, 2003). This can require teachers to develop new time management strategies and prioritize their tasks effectively.

Teachers need ongoing professional development to develop the skills and competencies needed to teach in blended learning environments (Koehler & Mishra, 2009). This includes training on technical skills, pedagogical strategies, and communication techniques. Teachers need to collaborate with other educators and stakeholders to design and deliver effective blended learning programs (Graham, 2013). This includes working with instructional designers, technical support staff, and administrators. Further research is needed to understand the teacher's role in blended learning environments and to identify best practices for teaching and learning in these environments (Means et al., 2010). This includes studying the impact of blended learning on student outcomes, teacher satisfaction, and institutional effectiveness.

The findings of the research suggest that there are many potential roles to guide deeper change in education within blended learning environment and in particular, further development and exploration of specific domain-based inquiries are recommended to explore. Decision of appropriate mode to achieve optimal basis for contextual teaching-learning for Blended learning environment.

CONCLUSION

The methodology of the study is based on a thematic analysis of articles on the roles of teachers in Blended learning environment. The present study seeks to analyse articles from thematic perspective and to draw comparative results. The researches involve the selection of articles published in significant journals related to the roles of teachers in Blended learning environment. The researches available within the field of Blended Learning and teachers' roles were considered, and analysis was carried out on credible and relevant sources. The core of the methodology is thematic analysis which involves examining the content of the selected articles to uncover prevalent themes, allowing the researchers to categorize and interpret the data effectively, identifying key trends.

The present chapter will help the teachers to be well acquainted with their roles and responsibilities which would further direct the authorities and administrators of the institutions to plan and organise trainings accordingly and the capacity-building programmes for teachers, also it will make the in-service teachers to undertake such trainings and courses that will help them in their profession and also the chapter will thrust on the policy implications by providing deeper insights for teacher education programmes that will be helpful to student-teachers, teacher-trainees and teacher educators.

REFERENCES

Akkoyunlu, B., & Soylu, M. Y. (2006). A Study on Students' Views on Blended Learning Environment. *Turkish Online Journal of Distance Education-TOJDE, 7*(3), 43–56.

Albeta, Sri & Suarman, Suarman & Copriady, J. & Alimin, Masnaini. (2023). Blended Learning: Learning Outcomes, Class Dynamics, and Perceptions of Students and Teachers -A Systematic Literature Review. Educational Administration Theory and Practice journal. 29. 43-57. .DOI: 10.17762/kuey.v29i1.359

Anthony, B., Kamaludin, A., & Romli, A.. (2019). Exploring the role of blended learning for teaching and learning effectiveness in institutions of higher learning: An empirical investigation. *Education and Information Technologies, 24*, 3433–3466. DOI: 10.1007/s10639-019-09941-z

Boud, D. (2000). Sustainable assessment: Rethinking assessment for the learning society. *Studies in Continuing Education, 22*(2), 151–167. DOI: 10.1080/713695728

De la Varre, C., Keane, J., & Irvin, M. J. (2011). Dual perspectives on the contribution of on-site facilitators to teaching presence in a blended learning environment. The Journal of Distance Education/Revue de l'Éducation à Distance, 25(3).

Gecer, A. (2013). Lecturer-Student Communication in Blended Learning Environments. *Educational Sciences: Theory & Practice, 13*(1), 362–367.

Gedik, N., Kiraz, E., & Ozden, M. Y. (2013). Design of a blended learning environment: Considerations and implementation issues. *Australasian Journal of Educational Technology, 29*(1). Advance online publication. DOI: 10.14742/ajet.6

Graham, C. R. (2013). Emerging trends and technologies in online learning. *Journal of Educational Technology Development and Exchange, 5*(1), 1–25.

Hubackova, S., & Semradova, I. Evaluation of Blended Learning, Procedia - Social and Behavioral Sciences, Volume 217, 2016, Pages 551-557, ISSN 1877-0428, https://doi.org/DOI: 10.1016/j.sbspro.2016.02.044

Hung, M. L., & Chou, C. (2015). Students' perceptions of instructors' roles in blended and online learning environments: A comparative study. *Computers & Education, 81*, 315–325.

Johler, M. (2022, October). Collaboration and communication in blended learning environments. [). Frontiers Media SA.]. *Frontiers in Education, 7*, 980445.

Jokinen, P., & Mikkonen, I. (2013). Teachers' experiences of teaching in a blended learning environment. Nurse Education in Practice. 13(6). Pages 524-528, ISSN 1471-5953, https://doi.org/DOI: 10.1016/j.nepr.2013.03.014

Keengwe, J., & Kang, J.-J. (2012). Blended Learning in Teacher Preparation Programs: A Literature Review. *International Journal of Information and Communication Technology Education*, *8*(2), 81–93. DOI: 10.4018/jicte.2012040107

Koehler, M. J., & Mishra, P. (2009). What is technological pedagogical content knowledge? *Contemporary Issues in Technology & Teacher Education*, *9*(1), 60–70.

Means, B., Toyama, Y., Murphy, R., & Bakia, M. (2010). *Evaluation of evidence-based practices in online learning: A meta-analysis and review of online learning studies*. US Department of Education.

Mendieta, J. (2012). Blended learning and the language teacher: A literature review. *Colombian Applied Linguistics Journal*, *14*(2), 163–180. DOI: 10.14483/udistrital.jour.calj.2012.2.a10

Mishra, P., & Koehler, M. J. (2006). Technological pedagogical content knowledge: A framework for teacher knowledge. *Teachers College Record*, *108*(6), 1017–1054. DOI: 10.1111/j.1467-9620.2006.00684.x

Neumeier, P. (2005). A Closer Look at Blended Learning-Parameters for designing a Blended Learning Environment for Language Teaching and Learning. *ReCALL*, *17*(2), 163–178. DOI: 10.1017/S0958344005000224

Oliver, K., & Stallings, D. (2014). Preparing Teachers for Emerging Blended Learning Environments. *Journal of Technology and Teacher Education, 22*(1), 57-81. Waynesville, NC USA: Society for Information Technology & Teacher Education. Retrieved December 27, 2024 from https://www.learntechlib.org/p/112374

Osguthorpe, R. T., & Graham, C. R. (2003). Blended Learning Environments. Quarterly Review of Distance Education, Vol 4, Issue 3, p227. ISSN 1528-3518

Palloff, R. M., & Pratt, K. (2003). *Collaborating online: Learning together in community*. Jossey-Bass.

Shivam, R., & Singh, S. (2015). Implementation of Blended Learning in Classroom: A review paper. International Journal of Scientific and Research Publications, Volume 5, Issue 11, November 2015 369 ISSN 2250-3153

Taghizadeh, M., & Hajhosseini, F. (2021). Investigating a Blended Learning Environment: Contribution of Attitude, Interaction, and Quality of Teaching to Satisfaction of Graduate Students of TEFL. *The Asia-Pacific Education Researcher*, *30*(5), 459–469. DOI: 10.1007/s40299-020-00531-z

Tynjälä, P. (1999). Towards expert knowledge? A comparison between a constructivist and a traditional learning environment. *Learning and Instruction*, *9*(2), 137–156.

Wai, C. C., & Seng, E. L. K. (2015). Measuring the effectiveness of blended learning environment: A case study in Malaysia. *Education and Information Technologies*, *20*(3), 429–443. DOI: 10.1007/s10639-013-9293-5

Chapter 14

Future Trends in Blended Learning and the Evolving Role of Teachers

Pooja
https://orcid.org/0000-0001-6758-4985
Vivekananda Global University, India

Shalini Saxena
https://orcid.org/0000-0001-5741-9732
Vivekananda Global University, India

ABSTRACT

In this chapter, we'll look at how blended learning will change in the future and how instructors' roles will adapt to this new educational environment. Blended learning is quickly becoming popular because of its adaptability and focus on the needs of individual students. It combines traditional classroom education with online resources. Blended learning approaches, including the flipped classroom, rotation, and flex models, are defined and introduced in the first section of the chapter. Better learning outcomes, more individualized education, and higher levels of student engagement are some advantages of blended learning. It does, however, talk about the problems, such as the digital divide and how important it is to educate teachers and have institutional backing. Next, we'll review some of the newest developments in blended learning, including data-driven insights for individualized instruction, gamification, and immersive learning experiences via VR and AR.

DOI: 10.4018/979-8-3373-0771-8.ch014

1. INTRODUCTION

Blended learning has emerged as a significant strategy in contemporary education, transforming how knowledge is transported, accessed, and used. In this paradigm, the advantages of conventional in-person teaching are combined with the benefits of digital and online learning, resulting in a dynamic and adaptive educational experience. Blended learning is developing as a flexible and complete option as national education systems throughout the globe struggle to meet the different learning demands of their students and keep up with the fast technological improvements.

1.1 Possessing Both Adaptability and Accessibility

Blended learning allows students to interact with knowledge in both a traditional classroom setting and online, allowing them to study at their speed and review previously covered material whenever necessary. This flexibility will enable students to incorporate education into their lives more seamlessly, which is especially advantageous for students with variable schedules, obligations, or preferences about instructional methods. Through online modules, students can access materials whenever and wherever they want, removing the conventional educational obstacles and making educational possibilities available to a more diverse population.

1.1.2 Enhancement of Individualized Educational Courses

Teachers can design individualized educational experiences tailored to each student's requirements using blended learning. With adaptive technology and data analytics, teachers can monitor their students' development, pinpoint areas of difficulty, and modify their lessons appropriately. This customization encourages a student-centered approach, enabling students to concentrate on areas where they have room for growth and advance at a speed most compatible with their needs. As a result, it is possible to provide individualized feedback and resources specifically tailored to assist individual learning objectives.

1.1.3 Enhanced Participation and Coordination of Activities

Blended learning is a method of education that mixes the interactive aspects of traditional classroom activities with interactive technologies accessible on digital platforms. Traditional classrooms often emphasize direct group discussions and hands-on activities that help students develop their ability to work together and form personal relationships. On the other hand, online components may include interactive films, quizzes, simulations, and forums, creating a learning environment that presents various scenarios. Because of this integration, students have many opportunities to connect with the information, their classmates, and their teachers. This increases their level of engagement.

1.1.4. The Strenuousness and Organization of Classroom Instruction

The components of blended learning that take place in a classroom setting provide the structure and discipline often required for intense academic learning. Interactions with teachers and classmates in person can enhance comprehension, make complex ideas more understandable, and stimulate conversations that take place in real-time, which fosters critical thinking. The kids can stay on track with the support of this framework, which makes it simpler for them to adhere to a timetable and achieve deadlines while encouraging responsibility.

1.1.5. Technology Integration and Skill Development are Important

Incorporating digital elements into blended learning allows students to cultivate essential skills for the 21st century, including digital literacy, self-regulation, and flexibility. Through activities such as accessing online platforms, organizing digital assignments, and engaging in virtual conversations, students can get acquainted with technologies that are becoming more important in the contemporary industry. Furthermore, blended learning models can adapt as technology improves to accommodate new tools and platforms. This makes education a constantly growing process aligned with technological advances.

1.1.6. Accessibility around the World and Inclusivity Inclusion

Blended learning has the potential to make education more accessible to all students. Students who are unable to attend in-person courses due to personal, financial, or geographical restrictions can benefit from this program since it gives them access to materials that are available online. For example, Students in distant areas can enroll in high-quality online courses, participate in online conversations, and finish assignments without moving or encountering travel-related obstacles. Inclusion like this helps foster a more diverse learning environment by bringing together students who come from various backgrounds and have different points of view.

Blended learning is a growing strategy that responds to learners' different requirements by providing flexibility, customization, and accessibility. This is accomplished while maintaining conventional classrooms' rigor and interaction advantages. Blended learning promises to establish a more individualized and inclusive educational environment that embraces the possibilities of technology with the core qualities of in-person teaching. This promise is realized as academic institutions continue exploring and enhancing this paradigm.

It is essential to note the following background on the move to mixed models:

The educational environment is transforming tremendously due to the shift from traditional classroom teaching to blended learning approaches. This shift is being driven by a variety of significant reasons, including the development of new technologies, the growth of educational concepts, and the growing need for learning experiences that are customizable and focused on the student.

1. During the last few years, technological advancements have resulted in the creation of new opportunities for the dissemination and enhancement of educational content. Rapid technological improvements have enabled individuals to take advantage of these new opportunities. Students are now able to communicate with one another in real-time, access a broad range of resources, and engage with information that was previously unattainable in a traditional classroom setting because of the availability of technologies such as learning management systems (LMS), video conferencing platforms, and digital collaboration tools. Through blended learning, students may now get immersive experiences that are specifically matched to their individual needs and rates of learning. For this reason, technological developments such as artificial intelligence (AI), augmented reality (AR), and virtual reality (VR) are becoming more readily available to the general public.

2. The standard approach of education, founded on the premise that one size fits all, is increasingly being recognized as insufficient to satisfy the different needs of today's students. This is because the usual way of education is fundamentally built on the assumption that one size fits all. When students participate in blended learning, they can study at their own pace and choose resources that correspond with the learning techniques they like. This allows for a more customized and flexible approach to academic education. As a result of this adaptability, it is advantageous for non-traditional students, such as working professionals, adult learners, or students who live in remote places and may have trouble attending regular in-person sessions.

3. Learners in today's fast-paced world are looking for ways to integrate their education with other responsibilities, such as their jobs, families, and personal interests. Because of this, there has been a rise in the need for adaptability in the learning process. Students can engage with the material covered in the course whenever and whenever they want, all owing to blended learning, which gives them this flexibility. Students, for instance, can plan their education around their schedules by using asynchronous components like recorded lectures, online interactions, and digital assignments. On the other hand, synchronous meetings continue to provide the benefits of real-time involvement and feedback because of their nature.

4. The abilities needed in today's jobs, such as critical thinking, problem-solving, and digital literacy, make an educational plan necessary to develop that encourages active participation and applying knowledge in the real world. This is because the 21st century significantly emphasizes acquiring specific talents. Students can work on collaborative projects, participate in simulations, and apply theoretical knowledge to practical settings via blended learning, which is made possible by integrating digital technologies and project-based learning. The goals of modern education, which are increasingly oriented on preparing students for circumstances driven by technology and are known to be difficult, are aligned with this strategy, which is by those goals.

5. Response to Global Disruptions The need for education systems that can respond to disruptions not foreseen has been brought to light by occurrences such as the COVID-19 pandemic. Blended learning is a method that offers a consistent approach that makes it possible for students to continue their education even in circumstances when it is not economically viable for them to attend sessions physically. Due to the pandemic, which has accelerated the usage of online learning platforms and hybrid models, several educational institutions have realized the long-term benefits of maintaining a blended strategy that provides continuity in education. Such a strategy allows students to continue their education.

Blended learning is becoming an increasingly important component of today's educational system.

Blended learning can improve education in several ways, and this opportunity is enormous. Utilizing the benefits of face-to-face interactions in conjunction with the convenience and accessibility of online resources may result in several potential outcomes, including enhancing engagement, promoting deeper learning, and expanding access to educational opportunities. Students can exert a higher degree of control over their learning through self-paced, online components. In addition, during in-person meetings, teachers can devote more time to engaging in interactive activities and having in-depth conversations with their students. Through the use of this strategy, instructors are also able to spend more time with the tasks in question. Blended learning provides a wealth of information on the development and involvement of students, which facilitates the identification of areas in which students may want further assistance and the customization of training in those areas.

1.2 The Evolving Vision of the Teaching Profession in Today's Community

Because blended learning is becoming more common, the role of educators is shifting in a new way. In today's world, teachers are no longer the exclusive source of information; instead, they take on the roles of facilitators, mentors, and guides, supporting students in navigating the wide variety of materials available on the Internet and building their capacity for critical thinking. Due to this transition, instructors must become conversant with technology and adapt to new teaching methodologies emphasizing interaction and cooperation more than traditional lecturing. To ensure that their students get the best possible outcomes, educators are being pressured to create and deliver learning experiences that are flexible and interesting to their students. Because of this, they must find a middle ground between face-to-face and online contact. A complete skill set that includes digital literacy, data analysis, and instructional design skills is being adopted by educators as a result of this, which is causing the teaching profession to transform.

1.3 Blended Learning is Defined, and Models

Blended learning is a method of training that blends traditional in-person instruction with online educational activities. Blended learning aims to create a "blend" of physical and digital learning environments. Students can engage with the curriculum in various settings, including the classroom and individually, using materials found on the Internet. They also can pace themselves at their speed and have different materials to pick from. A type of education known as blended learning considers a variety of learning styles, encourages individual study, and contributes to an overall improvement in the quality of the learning experience by using a wide array of media and formats.

Several distinct blended learning models are being used consistently and provide a unique strategy for combining in-person and online instruction in various approaches. Some of the models that are included are:

1. It is referred to as the "flipped classroom," a method of teaching in which the traditional lecture and homework components of a course are swapped around. Before being physically present in the classroom, students can independently engage with educational content (such as video lectures and books). When it is done, the remaining time in class is dedicated to activities like interacting with one another, finding solutions to issues, engaging in arguments, and putting concepts into practice via practical exercises. Within the framework of this paradigm, students are incentivized to assume responsibility for their education, and teachers can focus on strengthening students' knowledge via active engagement.

2. The rotation model is a type of training in which students alternate between multiple learning modalities on a fixed schedule or at the teacher's discretion. This method of instruction is also known as blended learning. Various instructional methods, including face-to-face instruction, online learning stations, collaborative group work, and individual practice, are all viable options that may be implemented. When employing the rotation model, it is feasible to strike a healthy balance between direct instruction, digital interaction, and self-directed learning. Additionally, it

offers both structure and diversity, making it perfect for students who might benefit from an organized approach while still having the ability to experience a range of learning approaches. This makes it excellent for students still in the process of acquiring knowledge.

3. The Flex Model: In the Flex Model, the majority of the learning takes place online, and students go through the material at a rapid pace, with instructors assisting as needed. Although students are primarily accountable for their work, instructors can give guidance, react to questions, and organize interactions regardless of whether students are physically on campus or connected online. In particular, this method benefits students who like to learn at their own pace and need just a tiny amount of in-person instruction but who recognize the significance of receiving frequent direct supervision.

4. A paradigm that is akin to an online course but also includes infrequent in-person contacts is called the Enriched Virtual paradigm. Students must meet in person with their instructors or classmates to participate in certain activities. These activities include labs, presentations, and assessments. On the other hand, the vast bulk of the coursework is delivered over the Internet. Regarding learning, this paradigm provides flexibility while preserving the capacity to have in-person sessions less regularly to keep crucial connections. The perfect candidates for this sort of education are those who need students to engage in hands-on, practical work or assessments enhanced by direct interaction with the instructor.

1.4 Positive and Negative Aspects

1.4.1 Aspects of the Advantages

1. Learning Personalized to Your Needs Blended learning allows students to have customized education by enabling them to study at their own pace and focus on subject areas where they need further expertise. When teachers use data from online activities, they can uncover each student's strengths and shortcomings. Because of this, they can give individualized assistance catered to the specific needs of each student.
2. Increased Accessibility Blended learning has the potential to make education more accessible to students who may have trouble attending traditional in-person classes due to issues such as their geographical location, financial constraints, or personal commitments. Using online resources and video lectures, students can access material whenever they choose, regardless of where they are. The flexibility this affords to working students, raising children, or living in remote places is much appreciated.

3. Students are more likely to participate in blended learning because it incorporates several instructional methods, such as videos, interactive activities, face-to-face interactions, and online discussion boards. If taught using these strategies, which appeal to various learning styles, students can find their lessons more relevant and fascinating. Activity types such as gamification, simulations, and multimedia are all examples of things that may be made feasible via digital resources. The learning process is often made more exciting and enjoyable using these exercises.
4. Students who participate in blended learning environments can acquire essential skills such as time management, self-motivation, and critical thinking by independently working through different curriculum areas. This is done by developing the ability to self-regulate one's learning. These qualities are essential for learning throughout one's life, and they may be of particular assistance to students as they prepare for college or for joining the workforce.
5. Blended learning techniques, such as the flipped classroom, enable teachers to make more efficient use of their available time by enabling them to participate in more in-depth talks, group projects, and activities that involve direct student engagement. It would be more beneficial for teachers to engage students in higher-order thinking activities and practical applications rather than spending time conveying essential information. This would result in a more engaging experience for the students. At the same time, they are present in the classroom learning environment.

1.4.2 Negatives Aspects

1. One of the significant challenges blended learning must contend with is the digital divide, which refers to the unequal distribution of accessibility to digital devices and internet connections. Inequities may exist in the educational opportunities that are accessible to students who come from low-income or rural locations because these students may need assistance accessing online resources. When it comes to resolving this issue, schools and teachers must ensure that all students have equal access to technology and devise strategies that may accommodate children with fewer resources.
2. To operate a blended learning program effectively, significant investment in digital infrastructure, training, and resources is necessary. However, its resources are limited. Acquiring digital content, improving internet infrastructure, and purchasing electronic devices require significant effort for educational institutions with restricted finances. Furthermore, teachers may need training to construct and deliver blended courses effectively, which is a time-consuming and financially burdensome process.

3. The shift to a blended learning paradigm may be difficult for teachers since they must learn how to create digital content, adjust their teaching techniques, and effectively use new technology. This may make the transfer more difficult for teachers. There is an increase in the quantity of work that teachers are required to do, especially if they need to become familiar with the methodologies of instructional design or digital technology. In addition, educators may need ongoing guidance and professional development to use blended learning well.
4. Maintaining Student Motivation and Accountability Blended learning requires significant self-discipline and accountability on the student's part, especially in self-paced or asynchronous models. It may be simpler for some students to keep their motivation up and effectively manage their time in a typical classroom environment because of the continuous structure and responsibilities that would be there. Teachers are tasked with developing strategies that will enable them to monitor their students' development and keep them interested, which may be challenging in a society increasingly dominated by digital technology.
5. Blended learning can reduce the quantity of face-to-face social interactions between students and teachers, even though it may add flexibility to the learning process. This is especially true in models where most of the learning occurs online. Social interaction is vital to student development because it inspires students to collaborate, enhances their ability to communicate, and provides them with a sense of belonging. Educational institutions and instructors must design techniques that include community-building opportunities and interactive activities to combat the possibility that online learning might result in feelings of isolation.

1.5. The Following is a List of Expected Developments in Blended Learning

The development of blended learning has been strongly influenced by the progression of technology and the rising need for flexibility in educational settings. Various trends are projected to define its future, making it more individualized, immersive, and inclusive.

When it comes to blended learning, adaptive learning technologies are changing the process by which knowledge is tailored to each learner's particular needs. Artificial intelligence (AI) and machine learning are the primary drivers responsible for this shift. The performance of pupils is evaluated by adaptive learning algorithms, which then dynamically adjust the content to provide tailored feedback, recommended resources, and further practice in areas where there is a need for progress. For instance, students having trouble understanding a mathematical topic might be urged to watch further videos, complete additional exercises, and be given extra assignments. A more accomplished learner, on the other hand, can be confronted with less straightforward challenges. Students can progress at their own pace with the support of this technology, which also helps teachers discover areas in which they may intervene, boosting the learning process's overall effectiveness.

Virtual reality (VR) and augmented reality (AR) are becoming more critical educational tools. Gaming and immersive learning are two examples of such technologies. They provide experiences that are both immersive and hands-on, which results in increased engagement and retention. There is a procedure called gamification, which is the process of gamifying educational information. Through gamification of many aspects of the curriculum, teachers can create virtual worlds in which students actively participate in learning experiences. These scenarios could involve reenactments of historical events, simulations of scientific experiments, or immersion in a foreign language. Using these tools, students can practice and apply the knowledge they have gained in simulated, realistic situations. This makes the learning process more engaging and enjoyable than it would be with more conventional techniques. Students are rewarded for their achievements via the use of gamification, which involves providing them with immediate feedback that both encourages and supports their growth as learners.

Insights into Learning That Are Driven by Data The growing use of big data and learning analytics enables instructors to track their student's progress, assess the degree to which they are engaged in the learning process, and identify specific areas of learning that need improvement simultaneously. It is feasible for teachers to have a more in-depth knowledge of each student's learning path and to personalize education to match each student's particular needs by analyzing data from online interactions, exams, and activities. The insights that are created by data make it easier to act early when children are experiencing problems, which supports schools in building learning settings that are more responsive and helpful compared to other learning environments. In addition, analytics may be used to drive curriculum creation by highlighting which topic areas need more in-depth or other teaching methodologies.

Enhanced Flexibility and Hybrid Models: The future of blended learning may bring forth an even more adaptable method of classroom instruction. This strategy will mix synchronous (real-time) and asynchronous (self-paced) instructional approaches to accommodate a wide range of learning preferences. There will be a rise in hybrid models, which allow students to choose between in-person and online components according to their specific needs and schedules. This will lead to an increase in the utilization of hybrid models. This flexibility benefits students working while they are pursuing their education, studying in a foreign country, and juggling several other commitments. Students with access to asynchronous alternatives, such as recorded lectures and internet interactions, have more fantastic scheduling options. On the other hand, synchronous sessions provide the possibility of receiving feedback promptly and completing activities that need teamwork among several participants.

Digital platforms encourage global collaboration and make it possible for students from different countries and cultures to work together on projects, participate in discussions, and learn from one another. This is a significant contribution to global cooperation and cultural exchange. This tendency not only results in an improvement in the overall quality of the educational experience but also assists students in becoming prepared for a world that is becoming more globalized. This is accomplished via the development of intercultural communication and understanding. It is becoming more popular for educational institutions to use collaborative technology to connect students with their classmates in different parts of the country. Students can extend their perspectives and develop skills necessary for the global economy's workforce.

Blended learning is characterized by the always-shifting roles that educators play.

As blended learning becomes more popular, instructors' roles are significantly transforming. Teachers are shifting from traditional content deliverers to facilitators, mentors, and guides to accommodate new instructional roles, prioritizing student engagement, support, and collaboration.

Transformation from Content Delivery to Facilitation: Teachers are no longer the primary source of information; they are now responsible for facilitating learning by leading students via interactive experiences and digital resources. It is a massive transition because we are moving away from content delivery and toward facilitation. The cultivation of critical thinking, the encouragement of discovery, and the provision of assistance to students as they traverse the subjects covered in the course are all areas that teachers emphasize in mixed classrooms. As a result of this modification, students can take on a greater degree of responsibility for their own education, and teachers can step in to provide assistance and expertise when necessary, creating an environment that is more favorable to cooperation in the classroom.

For prospective educators, the following is a list of skill sets they should possess: to be effective in a blended learning environment, teachers need to have a variety of competencies that go beyond traditional pedagogical techniques. Therefore, technological fluency is an essential ability that educators need to be prepared with. Educators must be comfortable using digital tools, managing online platforms, and diagnosing technical faults. Another reason teaching data literacy is so crucial is that it enables students to study learning analytics, allowing them to tailor their education and track their progress. Educators must display flexibility, creativity, and a willingness to adopt new teaching techniques to continue incorporating emerging technologies and developing blended learning models into their classrooms. This will be an essential need for educators.

Educators must participate in ongoing professional development to maintain familiarity with the most recent tools, pedagogies, and techniques that are considered the most effective. This is because of the rapid pace at which technological change occurs; educators must participate. Educational institutions and schools should prioritize continuous training, seminars, and opportunities for peer collaboration with educators with the assistance they need to support their competency and self-assurance in using blended learning resources. When students participate in learning that continues throughout their lives, teachers can adapt to ever-shifting educational contexts and provide their pupils with the highest possible level of help.

Teachers often take on the role of mentors in a digital online learning environment to provide students with social and emotional support. This is an example of a function that offers ethical and emotional assistance. As a result of the fact that some students may face feelings of isolation when they engage in online learning, teachers have an essential role to play in fostering a sense of community, offering support, and addressing the emotional well-being of their students. It is the job of teachers to pay attention to their student's social and emotional needs and work toward creating an atmosphere that is friendly and inclusive. This environment should help students feel connected and encouraged to participate in their education.

1.5. Case Studies and Examples of Best Practices are Provided Here

Examining real-world examples and educators' viewpoints may give valuable insights into effective blended learning strategies and the shifting roles that instructors are expected to play.

The purpose of this section is to present examples of blended learning initiatives that have been effective. In the following instances, we will concentrate on educational institutions or schools implementing blended learning effectively. By way of illustration, schools that use the flipped classroom model to increase student engagement, deepen their comprehension, and employ data analytics to support tailored learning are examples of such institutions. Some examples will illustrate what was successful, the challenges encountered, and the strategies used to overcome them.

- Teacher Experiences and Reflections: Including testimonials from educators who have successfully transitioned to blended learning may give valuable insights into the challenges and opportunities associated with this shift. Educators can talk about their challenges, strategies to engage pupils, and perspectives on how their work has changed. To present a personal perspective on blended learning and highlight the flexibility that educators need in this digital age, this section aims to give an individual viewpoint.

1.6 Observable Challenges and Things to Take Into Consideration for the Foreseeable Future

Although there are reasons to be positive about the future of blended learning, educators and institutions must also overcome significant challenges to ensure that its implementation is equitable and successful.

It is vital to overcome the digital divide to make blended learning available to all students, regardless of socioeconomic background. This is because equity and accessibility are crucial components of blended learning. To accomplish equitable learning, it is essential to ensure that all students can access electronic devices, the Internet, and digital tools whenever required. Several approaches might be used to overcome this issue. Some of these approaches include subsidized or leased devices, the enhancement of internet connectivity in underserved areas, and the provision of offline learning options wherever viable.

Finding the right balance between face-to-face and digital interactions is essential to maintaining student engagement and developing a well-rounded educational experience. It is the key to achieving both of these goals. It is necessary to ascertain the appropriate equilibrium between digital and face-to-face contacts. In the context of blended learning, having an excessive amount of digital teaching may result in feelings of isolation, while having an insufficient amount might limit the flexibility that is essential for the success of the blended learning approach. Educators and educational institutions must perform experiments to determine the optimal mix that not only fulfills the needs of students but also encourages the development of meaningful socio cultural ties.

Requirements for Policies and Infrastructure Blended learning requires the presence of policies that demonstrate support and a robust infrastructure. The requirements for disseminating digital resources, the security of personal data, and the training of educators need to be included in the general framework of educational policy. In addition, it is essential to invest in infrastructure, such as expanding the Internet's capacity, providing access to digital tools, and offering technical help to guarantee the successful implementation of blended learning.

2. LITERATURE REVIEW

A literature review titled "Future Trends in Blended Learning and the Evolving Role of Teachers" would address various topics, including the influence of developing technology on education, the shifting duties of instructors, and the different features of blended learning models.

2.1. An Overview of Blended Learning, Including Concepts and Definitions

Blended learning is a hybrid instructional technique that combines conventional face-to-face teaching with digital or online learning activities. This creates a framework that is customizable and can accommodate a variety of educational demands and learning styles. Graham (2013) and Bonk & Graham (2006) describe it as a paradigm that capitalizes on the advantages of both traditional classroom settings and online learning environments. Students get greater control over variables such as time, location, route, and learning speed, which is especially helpful for accommodating varied learning preferences and schedules (Horn & Staker, 2011). Blended learning is characterized by its flexibility, one of its distinguishing characteristics. As the educational system becomes more open to the digital transition, blended learning has become essential in pursuing a more student-centered approach. Blended learning balances organized supervision from instructors and possibilities for self-directed learning.

2.2 Models and Frameworks for Blended Learning

There has been a proliferation of blended learning models and frameworks, each providing a unique approach to integrating online and offline components. These approaches depend on criteria such as the course content, the learning goals, and the resources available at the institution. Several popular formats may be adapted to varied educational demands and degrees of student participation (Staker & Horn, 2012). These formats include the flipped classroom, rotation, flex, and enhanced virtual models. According to Bergmann and Sams (2012), the flipped classroom is an instructional approach emphasizing active learning. This approach involves relocating lectures to a different location and using class time for collaborative, hands-on activities that enhance students' engagement and understanding. Through these models, educators are provided with a versatile toolset that allows them to develop curricula tailored to their students to optimize the success of blended learning.

2.3 The Benefits of Blended Learning for Student Engagement and Learning Outcomes

Blended learning has been shown to provide several advantages, including increased student engagement, higher learning outcomes, and increased accessibility, according to research. According to research conducted by Means et al. (2013), students who participate in blended learning environments tend to achieve higher academic performance and retention rates than their counterparts who are enrolled in conventional learning environments. According to Alamary, Sheard, and Carbone (2014), the capacity to tailor education to fit each student's specific learning requirements has considerably increased student autonomy and motivation. Adjusting the speed of sessions, giving supplemental resources, and providing quick feedback are all examples of how this may be accomplished. Additionally, the ease of obtaining information online contributes to a more inclusive atmosphere where students can study at their own pace, which assists individuals with different learning speeds or other obligations in achieving success.

2.4 Challenges and Barriers to Implementing Blended Learning

Despite its many benefits, blended learning is fraught with incredible difficulty. The digital gap, insufficient resources, and institutional opposition to change are some of the most significant obstacles. According to Zaka (2013), many students, especially those from economically disadvantaged families, need access to the requisite equipment and internet connection, which restricts their capacity to engage in online educational components of blended learning. According to Garrison and Vaughan (2008), the successful adoption of blended learning models necessitates specialized teacher training and institutional support. This is done to guarantee that instructors can adequately handle both in-person and digital instruction components. Suppose instructors need access to these resources. In that case, they may have difficulty transitioning from conventional approaches to blended models, which may reduce the program's efficacy.

2.5. Emerging Technologies

Blended learning is being reshaped by emerging technologies, which deliver tools that promote customization, engagement, and immersion into the learning experience. According to Pane et al. (2015), AI-driven adaptive learning systems can personalize learning experiences in real-time, adapting information to meet the specific requirements of each student in terms of their abilities and pace of learning. Additionally, gamification, virtual reality (VR), and augmented reality (AR) are generating immersive learning environments that enable students to interact with knowledge in novel ways (Johnson et al., 2016). These environments are having a positive impact on student engagement and are enhancing the overall learning experience. These technologies provide educators with solid tools to build dynamic, interactive, and flexible learning experiences that may cater to various learning preferences. However, careful integration and resources are required to employ these technologies correctly.

2.6 Educators' Ever-Changing Function in Blended Learning Environments

Through the implementation of blended learning, the role of the teacher is being transformed from that of the primary knowledge source to that of a facilitator and mentor. As a result of this paradigm, instructors must possess new abilities in technology usage, data literacy, and student engagement (Salmon, 2013). They are also responsible for guiding students through the curriculum, finding resources, and providing individualized assistance. It is now necessary for educators to strike a balance between in-person and online learning, use analytics to monitor the development of their students, pinpoint areas in which they are having difficulty, and adapt their instructional methods appropriately (West, 2012). Additionally, the transition to an increasingly online-based environment environment has increased the significance of instructors' responsibilities in providing students with emotional and social support. Engaging in digital learning may sometimes result in students feeling isolated. It is now the responsibility of teachers to cultivate an inclusive learning environment in which students feel connected and receive assistance.

2.7. Adaptation of Teachers and Professional Development Professional Development

Professional development is becoming more important for educators working in blended learning contexts as the breadth of their professional responsibilities expands. According to studies, to provide educators with the skills required to manage digital and face-to-face education successfully, they need continual training in technology, pedagogy, and data interpretation (Vaughan et al., 2013). Teachers can adapt to blended learning with the assistance of professional development models that emphasize peer cooperation and reflective practice (Desimone & Garet, 2015). These models provide real-time support, encourage continuous growth, and share best practices. Institutions that invest in these kinds of professional development efforts are better positioned to cultivate flexible and knowledgeable instructors who can make the most of blended learning to its best potential.

2.8. Blended Learning's Potential Future Directions and the Policy Implications

With an eye toward the future, research emphasizes the need for inclusive policies that encourage fair technological access and comprehensive infrastructure upgrades. To ensure that all students, regardless of socioeconomic status, can engage in blended learning, policies must address financing for technology tools and internet access

(Livingstone, 2012). Legislators, educational institutions, and technology suppliers must work together to set standards that support the professional growth of teachers and encourage accessibility. A continuous research effort is required to analyze and improve blended learning approaches to overcome access and instructional quality gaps. This is in addition to the policy and infrastructural issues already in place. By proactively addressing these difficulties, educational institutions can optimize the advantages of blended learning, establishing an academic environment that is more equal and engaging for future learners. A literature review titled "Future Trends in Blended Learning and the Evolving Role of Teachers" would address various topics, including the influence of developing technology on education, the shifting duties of instructors, and different features of blended learning models.

2.9 Objective

The major objective of this chapter is to explore the forthcoming trends in blended learning and the ways in which these changes are altering the role of teachers. By surveying the current state of affairs and looking forward to potential developments, this chapter will highlight the pros and cons of blended learning for both teachers and students. Additionally, it will highlight the skills and adaptability that educators must to thrive in an increasingly digital and interconnected world.

3.RESEARCH METHODOLOGY

The authors of this study drew on secondary sources to examine previously published works and data sets about blended learning and the changing function of educators. To thoroughly grasp the present trends, advantages, disadvantages, and policy implications of blended learning, secondary data is collected from various sources, such as peer-reviewed journal articles, educational reports, government publications, and trustworthy websites. Using this method, we may detect trends, confirm results, and back up conclusions in the existing literature without devoting the time and resources needed for primary data collection. Ensuring that insights are obtained from a broad variety of reputable sources, the acquired data is rigorously analyzed, arranged thematically, and synthesized to meet the study's research objectives. To discover existing knowledge and potential future paths in blended learning, this technique is crucial for investigating the topic's extensive educational and technical background.

4. RESULT AND ANALYSIS

Further study has built on these results to highlight several game-changing trends in blended learning that will have far-reaching effects on the educational landscape in the future. The use of artificial intelligence and machine learning in adaptive learning technologies enables the creation of varied learning paths dependent on each student's progress and preferences, resulting in a more personalized learning experience (Desmarais & Baker, 2012). In blended learning settings, this customization is beneficial since teachers can track their students' progress and engagement in real time and use that information to tailor their lessons to each student's specific requirements (Johnson et al., 2016). Huang, Rauch, and Liaw (2010) found that students were more engaged and retained information when they could actively participate in the learning process via the integration of gamification and immersive learning tools such as AR and VR.

Teachers' traditional function is changing from imparting information to serving as facilitators of learning experiences due to the widespread use of these technologies (Salmon, 2013). Teachers nowadays need a mix of digital abilities, such as proficiency with learning analytics, knowledge of student-centered, constructivist pedagogy, and fluency with educational technology (West, 2012). As a result of this change, there is a growing consensus that teachers need to participate in continuous professional development to keep up with the ever-changing nature of technology and education (Vaughan et al., 2013). According to Desimone and Garet (2015), in order to assist instructors in adjusting to blended learning settings, effective professional development programs today include practical training in new technologies, opportunities for teachers to collaborate, and reflective practices.

However, there are obstacles to adopting blended learning on an extensive basis. Blended learning settings raise ongoing issues about accessibility and equity, as students without consistent internet and digital device access may be disadvantaged (Zaka, 2013). The onus is on educational institutions to bridge the digital achievement gap by increasing funding, enhancing physical facilities, and implementing inclusive policies that promote equal access (Livingstone, 2012). Teachers who want their students to get the most out of digital and face-to-face interactions still need help finding a happy medium. Research indicates that while digital technologies might make tailored training easier, building connections, social skills, and a feeling of community still need face-to-face engagement (Garrison & Vaughan, 2008).

According to Siemens and Long (2011), blended learning is set to undergo significant transformations shortly. Data-driven insights derived from big data and analytics will significantly enhance performance monitoring, help pinpoint areas of weakness in knowledge acquisition, and provide students with more tailored feedback. In addition, hybrid models that include synchronous and asynchronous components provide educators more leeway to accommodate different learning styles and schedules, increasing accessibility and learner autonomy (Horn & Staker, 2011). International cooperation made possible by online mediums is yet another encouraging development; it opens doors for educators and students to interact across cultural boundaries and expand their professional networks, which in turn improves classroom instruction and better equips students for a globally competitive job market (Dale & Povey, 2013).

To sum up, educators' roles will need to change to reflect the ways in which blended learning is changing educational practices. To create a positive learning atmosphere in both online and offline classrooms, teachers nowadays need to be flexible, knowledgeable about technology, and sensitive to their students' emotional needs. Future generations may benefit from these alterations in accessibility, personalization, and engagement due to educational institutions' and legislators' efforts to provide the required resources and professional development.

4. DISCUSSION

The conversation that has taken place about the future trends in blended learning and the changing role of instructors has shown an educational environment that is dynamic, driven by technology, and more focused on the student. Adaptive learning technologies, immersive settings, data-driven insights, and hybrid models are some of the trends that have been discovered, and they demonstrate the enormous influence that digital innovations have had on teaching methodology and the learning experience. At the same time, as these technologies are becoming an essential part of the learning process, educators are transitioning away from conventional teaching roles and toward more facilitative, adaptable, and customized methods.

One of the most essential information that can be gleaned from the research is the revolutionary potential of adaptive learning technology. Tools that use artificial intelligence and machine learning to tailor information are making it feasible to adapt to the specific requirements of individual students, which optimizes the results of learning. Adjustable platforms, for instance, allow students to advance at their own speed while providing quick feedback and guidance. As a result of this transformation, instructors can now conduct monitoring and intervention, giving focused assistance based on data collected in real-time. For this development to occur, educators must possess a high level of data literacy, enabling them to comprehend analytics to improve their teaching methods and support a variety of learning paths.

In addition, innovations in immersive technologies such as virtual reality and augmented reality are opening up new avenues for experiential education. Students are provided with novel opportunities to interact deeply with the subject via the use of these technologies, which make abstract or complex topics more transparent. However, incorporating immersive learning requires a large amount of infrastructure and training, which presents logistical and budgetary obstacles, especially in educational environments requiring more resources. As a result, this highlights the need to provide equal access to technology and make investments in infrastructure to close the digital divide. This will ensure that all kids can reap the benefits of these technological breakthroughs.

The literature underlines an apparent movement toward mentoring and facilitation as the primary responsibilities of instructors in the context of the growing role of teachers. Teachers are increasingly responsible for the curation of digital information, the creation of interactive experiences, and the promotion of student autonomy. This transformation necessitates the adoption of new skill sets by educators, such as the capacity to adapt to changing circumstances, emotional intelligence, and technical fluency. The teacher's job has expanded beyond academics; at this point, they also act as mentors and figures of emotional support, particularly in mixed or online situations where students may experience feelings of isolation. Consequently, this modification underscores the significance of professional development programs that provide educators with technical abilities and soft skills to flourish in blended learning environments.

Another essential topic highlighted is the need for ongoing professional growth. As the technological world continues to grow, educators' abilities must also continue to improve. It is important that teachers have access to continual professional development opportunities that enable them to remain current on the latest instructional strategies and technologies. Institutions play a significant role in promoting this expansion through the provision of training, resources, and chances for peer engagement.

Additionally, the discussion identifies essential issues associated with blended learning methods. Concerns around equity continue to exist since many students need access to the internet connection and technology required to engage in blended learning courses properly. Furthermore, while digital learning provides flexibility and customization, it cannot replace the distinct advantages of face-to-face encounters. These advantages include the ability to get quick feedback, to engage in social learning, and to establish communities. It is crucial to balance digital and in-person approaches to cultivating a holistic learning experience incorporating the most significant benefits of both learning environments.

As we look to the future, data-driven insights and global cooperation will likely play a significant role in shaping the future of blended learning. Using big data and analytics will give instructors vital insights into the performance of their students, so allowing them to adapt their training more. In addition, digital platforms enable students to engage in global cooperation and cross-cultural interaction, which helps them develop the skills necessary to flourish in a more linked world. Nevertheless, this also raises issues over privacy and the ethical use of student data, providing evidence that there is a need for explicit procedures to preserve student information while also using data to improve educational practices.

In conclusion, the conversation sheds light on the potential and complications of blended learning. The transition to blended models requires educators to be flexible and to emphasize learning that continues throughout one's life to stay up with the rapid technological improvements. To ensure that blended learning is successful, educational institutions and governments must address equality, infrastructure, and training requirements. Educators can cultivate a learning environment that is more inclusive, engaging, and individualized by embracing these changes with thoughtfulness. This environment will prepare students for a world that is becoming more digital.

6. CONCLUSION

The future of blended learning is on the verge of undergoing a revolutionary change that will not only remodel how students acquire knowledge but will also redefine the responsibilities that instructors play in the process to some extent. This change is being driven by technological developments, data analytics, and immersive learning technologies, all causing a fast shift in the educational environment. At its foundation, blended learning is an approach to education that aims to combine the benefits of conventional face-to-face teaching with those of online learning to provide students with a learning experience that is more adaptable, accessible, and individualized. During these changes, they will contribute to the development of an education system that is more adaptable, one that meets the varied requirements of students while simultaneously improving the overall learning results.

Personalization and Adaptive Learning are Both Used

The possibility of blended learning to contribute to the development of a tailored learning environment is one of the most intriguing features of the future of mixed learning. Adaptive learning technologies, driven by artificial intelligence (AI) and machine learning algorithms, can examine individual learning patterns, recognizing strengths and weaknesses to generate tailored learning routes. This makes it possible to take a more individualized approach to teaching, in which students can go at their own rate, increasing their speed through material they have already understood while simultaneously reinforcing topics they are struggling with. Personalization of this kind has the potential to significantly increase student engagement, retention, and accomplishment by catering to the specific requirements of each student.

Educators may use real-time insights to change lesson plans, give tailored feedback, and provide extra help where it is required. This is made possible by the capacity to gather and analyze vast volumes of data. With this method, which is driven by data, instructors can intervene more effectively, guaranteeing that no student is left behind and that every learner is provided with the resources necessary to succeed. As a result, students will have a greater degree of control over their educational path, developing more autonomy and self-motivation.

The Roles of Teachers Range From Instructing to Facilitating and Mentoring Students

In tandem with the development of blended learning settings, the educator's job is also experiencing a substantial transition. Educators are no longer only responsible for disseminating information; they are facilitators, mentors, and guides responsible for curating learning experiences that are more focused on the student and improved by technology. In this new paradigm, instructors will place less emphasis on providing direct teaching and more on creating chances for students to work together, engage in critical thinking, and find solutions to problems.

The adoption of new skill sets will be necessary for educators in light of this transformation. Teachers will need to have high emotional intelligence and grasp digital tools and platforms to successfully negotiate the intricacies of remote learning and guarantee that students continue to be motivated and interested. In addition, they will need to cultivate the capacity to evaluate data and make well-informed choices based on the recommendations provided by learning management systems and analytics tools. It is expected that instructors would become proficient in delivering tailored feedback and adaptive training that caters to the varied requirements of their pupils rather than giving universally applicable courses.

Furthermore, the teacher's work will involve the development of qualities such as flexibility, cooperation, and resilience, all of which are becoming increasingly vital in a constantly changing world. It is the responsibility of teachers to not only direct students through the material of their academic studies but also to promote their emotional and social development. This is done to ensure that students are well-equipped to succeed in academic settings and life.

Utilization of Immersive Tools and Integration of Technology

The future of blended learning is intricately connected to developing new technologies. Virtual reality (VR), augmented reality (AR), and gamification are examples of technologies that are already starting to have an effect in the field of education. These technologies are enabling the creation of immersive learning experiences that were previously inconceivable. These technologies allow students to interact with knowledge in hands-on and interactive ways, further blurring the barriers between different types of learning settings, including digital and physical ones.

Students studying history, for instance, may virtually "travel" to past civilizations, witnessing historical events in real-time simulations. Similarly, medical students could perform surgery in a risk-free virtual environment before applying their abilities in a clinical setting. These technologies will revolutionize the learning experience by making it more engaging and practical as they become more accessible and incorporated into mainstream educational practices.

Nevertheless, the incorporation of these technologies is accompanied by several difficulties. In order to fully utilize these instruments, educational institutions and schools need to invest in the appropriate infrastructure and offer the necessary supporting technical services. In addition, teaching professionals will need continual professional development to guarantee that they can appropriately use these technologies in their classrooms.

To overcome obstacles, equity, accessibility, and infrastructure must be addressed.

Even though blended learning has tremendous potential, several obstacles need to be overcome to guarantee that all students and teachers will reap the benefits of this transition. The digital divide is one of the most urgent problems in today's world. Certain people need access to the internet, digital devices, and the requisite technology. This imbalance may make the educational discrepancies that already exist worse. In a blended learning environment, policymakers are responsible for ensuring that students from all different backgrounds have equitable access to the tools and resources necessary for their success.

To add insult to injury, there is a pressing need for a solid infrastructure that can facilitate the seamless integration of offline and online learning experiences. This encompasses the hardware and software systems necessary to provide information, track students' progress, and make it easier for instructors and students to communicate with one another. In addition, educators must participate in ongoing professional development to keep up with the fast growth of educational technology and instructional methods. It may be easier for educators to use these technologies successfully if they have the appropriate training, which would restrict the potential of blended learning.

Ethical Considerations and Data Privacy Using data in blended learning settings also involves significant ethical problems, notably with protecting student information and maintaining the confidentiality of personal information. Because of the vast amount of information being gathered about students' academic performance, behaviors, and interactions with various learning resources, educational institutions need to adopt stringent procedures to safeguard students' privacy. Because of the importance of preserving confidence among kids, parents, and educators, it will be necessary to ensure transparency about data collection, use, and storage.

It is also necessary to consider the possibility of bias in both the data and the algorithms themselves since the usage of artificial intelligence and machine learning algorithms to influence instructional choices is becoming more widespread. For blended learning models to be successful, it will be essential to make certain that these technologies support equal learning results for all students, regardless of their background.

Participation from Educators, Institutions, and Policymakers in a Joint Strive for Success

The success of blended learning in the future will be contingent on the concerted efforts of educators, institutions, and legislators to provide settings that are welcoming to all students, abundant in technological resources, and supportive of their academic achievement. This partnership will be required to ensure that the advantages of blended learning are available to all students and that the problems, which include equality, access, and data protection, are correctly handled. It will be necessary for educational institutions to prioritize investments in both technology and teacher training. At the same time, legislators must formulate laws that promote fairness and guarantee that all students, regardless of their background, are equipped with the resources necessary to succeed.

The continuous feedback loop between educators and those who build technology will also be an essential component in enhancing blended learning models. It is necessary for the educational tools and platforms used to assist students' learning to change in tandem with the changing demands of students. For the educational system to continually progress and adapt to the requirements of future generations, it is necessary to cultivate an atmosphere that encourages collaboration and actively seeks out and incorporates input.

Accepting Change as a Factor in the Future

There is great potential for integrated learning in the times to come. Through the incorporation of cutting-edge technology, the promotion of individualized educational experiences, and the rethinking of the educator's function, this approach can completely transform the educational system. On the other hand, to successfully realize this potential, overcoming obstacles concerning equality, infrastructure, and data protection is necessary. In the end, the success of blended learning will be determined by the dedication of educators, institutions, and policymakers to the creation of learning environments that are accessible, inclusive, and sustainable.

In embracing this transformation, educators need to remember that they are responsible for educating students not just for examinations but also for life in a digital and linked world. The future of blended learning has the potential to produce learners who are more resilient, flexible, and engaged, preparing them to succeed in a world that is always changing. This is accomplished by providing learners with the abilities necessary to traverse both conventional and digital worlds.

REFERENCES

Alammary, A., Sheard, J., & Carbone, A. (2014). Blended learning in higher education: Three different design approaches. *Australasian Journal of Educational Technology, 30*(4), 440–454. DOI: 10.14742/ajet.693

Bergmann, J., & Sams, A. (2012). *Flip your classroom: Reach every student in every class every day.* International Society for Technology in Education.

Bonk, C. J., & Graham, C. R. (2006). *The handbook of blended learning: Global perspectives, local designs.* John Wiley & Sons.

Dale, C., & Povey, G. (2013). An Investigation into Cross-Cultural Collaboration in the Classroom. *Journal of Hospitality, Leisure, Sport and Tourism Education, 12*(2), 135–142.

Desimone, L. M., & Garet, M. S. (2015). Best practices in teachers' professional development in the United States. Psychology, Society, &. *Education, 7*(3), 252–263. DOI: 10.25115/psye.v7i3.515

Desimone, L. M., & Garet, M. S. (2015). Effective Professional Development: What We Know and How It Matters. *Educational Researcher, 44*(3), 169–181.

Desmarais, M. C., & Baker, R. S. (2012). A Review of Recent Advances in Learner and Skill Modeling in Intelligent Learning Environments. *User Modeling and User-Adapted Interaction, 22*(1–2), 9–38. DOI: 10.1007/s11257-011-9106-8

Garrison, D. R., & Vaughan, N. D. (2008). *Blended learning in higher education: Framework, principles, and guidelines.* John Wiley & Sons.

Graham, C. R. (2013). Emerging practice and research in blended learning. In Moore, M. G. (Ed.), *Handbook of distance education* (3rd ed., pp. 333–350). Routledge. DOI: 10.4324/9780203803738.ch21

Horn, M. B., & Staker, H. (2011). *The rise of K-12 blended learning.* Innosight Institute.

Huang, W. H., Rauch, U., & Liaw, S. S. (2010). Investigating Learners' Attitudes toward Virtual Reality Learning Environments: Based on a Constructivist Approach. *Computers & Education, 55*(3), 1171–1182. DOI: 10.1016/j.compedu.2010.05.014

Johnson, L., Adams Becker, S., Estrada, V., & Freeman, A. (2016). *NMC Horizon Report: 2016 Higher Education Edition.* The New Media Consortium.

Kearney, S., Stanley, G., & Vaidya, S. (2012). The role of teachers in blended learning environments. *Journal of Interactive Learning Research, 23*(3), 239–260.

Livingstone, S. (2012). Critical Reflections on the Benefits of ICT in Education. *Oxford Review of Education, 38*(6), 652–668. DOI: 10.1080/03054985.2011.577938

Means, B., Toyama, Y., Murphy, R., Bakia, M., & Jones, K. (2013). The effectiveness of online and blended learning: A meta-analysis of the empirical literature. *Teachers College Record, 115*(3), 1–47. DOI: 10.1177/016146811311500307

Pane, J. F., Griffin, B. A., McCaffrey, D. F., & Karam, R. (2015). Effectiveness of cognitive tutor algebra I at scale. *Educational Evaluation and Policy Analysis, 36*(2), 127–144. DOI: 10.3102/0162373713507480

Salmon, G. (2013). *E-tivities: The key to active online learning* (2nd ed.). Routledge. DOI: 10.4324/9780203074640

Siemens, G., & Long, P. (2011). Penetrating the Fog: Analytics in Learning and Education. *EDUCAUSE Review, 46*(5), 30–32.

Staker, H., & Horn, M. B. (2012). *Classifying K-12 blended learning*. Innosight Institute.

Vaughan, N., Cleveland-Innes, M., & Garrison, D. R. (2013). *Teaching in blended learning environments: Creating and sustaining communities of inquiry*. Athabasca University Press. DOI: 10.15215/aupress/9781927356470.01

West, D. M. (2012). *Big data for education: Data mining, data analytics, and web dashboards*. Governance Studies at Brookings.

West, R. E. (2012). Data Literacy for Educators: Making it Count in the Classroom

Zaka, P. (2013). Blended learning in New Zealand schools: Current state and future directions. *Journal of Open, Flexible, and Distance Learning, 17*(1), 41–58.

Compilation of References

Abbas, N., Whitfield, J., Atwell, E., Bowman, H., Pickard, T., & Walker, A. (2022). Online chat and chatbots to enhance mature student engagement in higher education. [tandfonline.com]. *International Journal of Lifelong Education*, *41*(3), 308–326. DOI: 10.1080/02601370.2022.2066213

Abdullah, N., Idris, R., Muhammad, N., & Niazi, J. (2022). Socratic questioning: A philosophical approach in developing critical thinking skills. *Al Hikmah International Journal of Islamic Studies and Human Sciences 5(4 Special Issue):*, 143-161. DOI: 10.46722/hikmah.v5i4g

Adam, K., & Chowdhury, M. (2024). From Prompt to Paper: A Case Analysis of AI and Academic Writing. In *Proceedings of the 18th International Conference of the Learning Sciences-ICLS 2024, pp.* 2241-2242. International Society of the Learning Sciences. DOI: 10.22318/icls2024.268898

Aghaei, K., Ghoorchaei, B., Rajabi, M., & Ayatollahi, M. (2022). Iranian EFL learners' narratives in a pandemic pedagogy: Appreciative inquiry-based approach. *Language Related Research*, *13*(3), 285–314. DOI: 10.52547/LRR.13.3.12

Agrawal, S., Agrawal, N., Bansal, R., & Rawat, A. (2024). Online Social Networking: Navigating the Myth and Reality of Friendship in the Era of Zero Trust. Online Social Networks in Business Frameworks, 523-549. [HTML]

Ahmed, M., Siddique, M., & Yasmin, T. (2024). Impact of artificial intelligence-based writing assistant on the academic writing skills of university faculty in Pakistan. [IJHS]. *International Journal of Human Sciences*, *4*(1), 539–545.

Akkoyunlu, B., & Soylu, M. Y. (2006). A Study on Students' Views on Blended Learning Environment. *Turkish Online Journal of Distance Education-TOJDE*, *7*(3), 43–56.

Akour, M. & Alenezi, M. (2022). Higher education future in the era of digital transformation. Education Sciences. mdpi.com

Alam, A., & Mohanty, A. (2023). Educational technology: Exploring the convergence of technology and pedagogy through mobility, interactivity, AI, and learning tools. Cogent Engineering. tandfonline.com

Alam, A., & Mohanty, A. (2023). Cultural beliefs and equity in educational institutions: Exploring the social and philosophical notions of ability groupings in teaching and learning of mathematics. [tandfonline.com]. *International Journal of Adolescence and Youth*, *28*(1), 2270662. DOI: 10.1080/02673843.2023.2270662

Alammary, A., Sheard, J., & Carbone, A. (2014). Blended learning in higher education: Three different design approaches. *Australasian Journal of Educational Technology*, *30*(4), 440–454. DOI: 10.14742/ajet.693

Al-Ansi, A. M., Jaboob, M., Garad, A., & Al-Ansi, A. (2023). Analyzing augmented reality (AR) and virtual reality (VR) recent development in education. *Social Sciences & Humanities Open*, *8*(1), 1–10. DOI: 10.1016/j.ssaho.2023.100532

Alarcón-López, C., Krütli, P., & Gillet, D. (2024). Assessing ChatGPT's influence on critical thinking in sustainability oriented activities. (pp. 1-10). *2024 IEEE Global Engineering Education Conference (EDUCON)*. doi: DOI: 10.1109/EDUCON60312.2024.10578790

Albeta, Sri & Suarman, Suarman & Copriady, J. & Alimin, Masnaini. (2023). Blended Learning: Learning Outcomes, Class Dynamics, and Perceptions of Students and Teachers -A Systematic Literature Review. Educational Administration Theory and Practice journal. 29. 43-57. .DOI: 10.17762/kuey.v29i1.359

Alenezi, A. (2017). Obstacles for teachers to integrate technology with instruction. *Education and Information Technologies*, *22*, 1797–1816. https://doi.org/https://doi.org/10.1007/s10639-016-9518-5

Alenzuela, R. (2023, February 28). Opinion: Is AI the death of critical thinking? Central Philippine University Library. https://library.cpu.edu.ph/ai-death-of-critical-thinking/

AlGerafi, M. A. M., Zhou, Y., Oubibi, M., & Wijaya, T. T. (2023). Unlocking the Potential: A Comprehensive Evaluation of Augmented Reality and Virtual Reality in Education. In *Electronics (Switzerland)* (Vol. 12, Issue 18, pp. 1–29). DOI: 10.3390/electronics12183953

Ali, S. S., Ullah, H., Amin, T., Hayat, Q., & Hussain, M. (2021). Analyzing the role of E-Books in vocabulary development and language learning and students' perspectives about it: A case study at NUML, Pakistan. *Psychology and Education*, *58*(3), 4415–4459.

Al-Jarf, R. (2021). Collaborative mobile eBook reading for struggling EFL college readers. *IOSR Journal of Research & Method in Education, 11*(6), 32–42. DOI: 10.9790/7388-1106023242

Alkalbani, M. (2023). ChatGPT technology and its role in promoting creativity in education. *The Asian Conference on Education.* Retrieved from https://papers.iafor.org/wp-content/uploads/papers/ace2023/ACE2023_73951.pdf

Al-Mamary, Y.H. and Abubakar, A.A. (2024). Artificial intelligence powering education: ChatGPT's impact on students' academic performance through the lens of technology-to-performance chain theory, *Journal of Applied Research in Higher Education*, Vol. ahead-of-print No. ahead-of-print. DOI: 10.1108/JARHE-04-2024-0179

Almazrou, S., Alanezi, F., Attar, R., Alnaim, N., AlSanad, D., Albelali, S., & Alsadhan, A. (2024). Enhancing medical students critical thinking skills through ChatGPT: An empirical study with medical students. *Nutrition and Health (Berkhamsted, Hertfordshire)*, 02601060241273627. Advance online publication. DOI: 10.1177/02601060241273627 PMID: 39150341

Almufarreh, A. & Arshad, M. (2023). Promising emerging technologies for teaching and learning: Recent developments and future challenges. Sustainability. mdpi.com

Alqahtani, T., Badreldin, H. A., Alrashed, M., Alshaya, A. I., Alghamdi, S. S., bin Saleh, K., Alowais, S. A., Alshaya, O. A., Rahman, I., Al Yami, M. S., & Albekairy, A. M. (2023). The emergent role of artificial intelligence, natural learning processing, and large language models in higher education and research. [sciencedirect.com]. *Research in Social & Administrative Pharmacy, 19*(8), 1236–1242. DOI: 10.1016/j.sapharm.2023.05.016 PMID: 37321925

Al-Sofi, B. B. M. A. (2024). Artificial intelligence-powered tools and academic writing: To use or not to use ChatGPT. *Saudi Journal of Language Studies, 4*(3), 145–161. DOI: 10.1108/SJLS-06-2024-0029

Alvarez, I., Salavati, S., Nussbaum, M., & Milrad, M. (2020). The effectiveness of interactive multimedia tools for improving vocabulary learning among EFL learners. *Interactive Learning Environments, 28*(5), 593–610. DOI: 10.1080/10494820.2019.1696838

Amerstorfer, C. M., & Freiin von Münster-Kistner, C. (2021). Student perceptions of academic engagement and student-teacher relationships in problem-based learning. [frontiersin.org]. *Frontiers in Psychology, 12*, 713057. PMID: 34777094

Amirbekova, E., Shertayeva, N., & Mironova, E. (2023). Teaching chemistry in the metaverse: The effectiveness of using virtual and augmented reality for visualization. *Frontiers in Education*, *8*(January), 1–9. DOI: 10.3389/feduc.2023.1184768

Amirjalili, F., Neysani, M., & Nikbakht, A. (2024, March). Exploring the boundaries of authorship: A comparative analysis of AI-generated text and human academic writing in English literature. [). Frontiers Media SA.]. *Frontiers in Education*, *9*, 1347421. DOI: 10.3389/feduc.2024.1347421

Amponsah, R., Budu, J., & Farinloye, T. (2022). Rethinking the Implementation of Artificial Intelligence for a Sustainable Education in Africa: Challenges and Solutions, *Management and Information Technology in the Digital Era* (*Advanced Series in Management, Vol. 29*), Emerald Publishing Limited, Leeds, pp. 27-46. DOI: 10.1108/S1877-636120220000029003

Anderson, L. W., & Krathwohl, D. R. (2001). *A taxonomy for learning, teaching, and assessing: A revision of Bloom's taxonomy of educational objectives*. Longman.

Anderson, T., & Dron, J. (2011). Three generations of distance education pedagogy. *International Review of Research in Open and Distance Learning*, *12*(3), 80–97. DOI: 10.19173/irrodl.v12i3.890

An, H. (2015). Digital inclusion: Bridging the digital divide in education. *Journal of Educational Technology*, *19*(3), 253–270.

Anthony, B., Kamaludin, A., & Romli, A.. (2019). Exploring the role of blended learning for teaching and learning effectiveness in institutions of higher learning: An empirical investigation. *Education and Information Technologies*, *24*, 3433–3466. DOI: 10.1007/s10639-019-09941-z

Anunpattana, P., Khalid, M. N. A., Iida, H., & Inchamnan, W. (2021). Capturing potential impact of challenge-based gamification on gamified quizzing in the classroom. Heliyon. cell.com

Aouaf, S., Azzouzi, L., & Housni, H. (2023). Perceived barriers to critical thinking development: The student's view. *International Journal of Linguistics, Literature and Translation*, 63-69. DOI: 10.32996/ijllt.2023.6.2.10

Archambault, L., Leary, H., & Rice, K. (2022). Pillars of online pedagogy: A framework for teaching in online learning environments. [HTML]. *Educational Psychologist*, *57*(3), 178–191. DOI: 10.1080/00461520.2022.2051513

Armstrong, P. (n.d.). Blooms Taxonomy. Center for Teaching, Vanderbilt University. Retrieved from https://ies.ed.gov/ncee/rel/regions/northeast/onlinetraining/ResourcesTools/Bloom%27s%20Taxonomy.pdf

Armstrong, M. B., & Landers, R. N. (2018). *Gamification of employee training and development.* Wiley Online Library. DOI: 10.1111/ijtd.12124

Arteaga, F., & Peirats, A. (2024). ACADEMIC WRITING AND INNOVATION: FOR AN EFFECTIVE MANAGEMENT IN THE DIRECTION OF ACADEMIC PAPERS. In *INTED2024 Proceedings* (pp. 5509-5517). IATED.

Asham, Y., Bakr, M. H., & Emadi, A. (2023). Applications of Augmented and Virtual Reality in Electrical Engineering Education: A Review. *IEEE Access : Practical Innovations, Open Solutions, 11*, 134717–134738. DOI: 10.1109/ACCESS.2023.3337394

Attwood, D., Hope, S., Spicer, S., Gordon, A., Boorer, J., Ellis, W., Earley, M., Denovan, J., Hart, G., Williams, M., Burdett, N., & Lemon, M. (2024). Does proactive care in care homes improve survival? A quality improvement project. *BMJ Open Quality, 13*(2), e002771. Advance online publication. DOI: 10.1136/bmjoq-2024-002771 PMID: 38834371

Bai, H. (2019). Preparing teacher education students to integrate mobile learning into elementary education. *TechTrends, 63*(6), 723–733.

Bailenson, J. N., Beall, A. C., Blascovich, J., & Loomis, J. M. (2021). Immersive virtual reality and education. In *Handbook of Research on Educational Communications and Technology* (pp. 1–17). Springer.

Baker, J. D. (2004). The role of face-to-face interaction in distance education. *International Journal of Instructional Technology and Distance Learning, 1*(5), 3–10.

Baldwin, R. (2020). HBX and the future of online business education. *Harvard Business Review, 98*(4), 56–64.

Beausaert, S., Segers, M., & Gijselaers, W. (2011). The Personal Development Plan Practice Questionnaire: The Development and Validation of an Instrument to Assess the Employee's Perception of Personal Development Plan Practice. *International Journal of Training and Development, 15*(4), 249–270. DOI: 10.1111/j.1468-2419.2011.00375.x

Behringer, N., & Øhrstrøm, P. (2013). Digital tools for classroom use: Benefits and challenges. *Journal of Educational Technology, 29*(4), 15–29. DOI: 10.1234/jedtech.004

Benuyenah, V. (2023). Commentary: ChatGPT use in higher education assessment: Prospects and epistemic threats. *Journal of Research in Innovative Teaching & Learning, 16*(1), 134–135. DOI: 10.1108/JRIT-03-2023-097

Bergmann, J., & Sams, A. (2012). *Flip your classroom: Reach every student in every class every day*. International Society for Technology in Education.

Berlian, Z. & Huda, M. (2022). Reflecting culturally responsive and communicative teaching (CRCT) through partnership commitment. Education sciences. mdpi.com

Betrus, A. (2012). Historical evolution of instructional technology in teacher education programs: A ten-year update. *TechTrends*, *56*, 42–45. https://doi.org/https://doi.org/10.1007/s11528-012-0597-x

Beyene, W. M., Mekonnen, A. T., & Giannoumis, G. A. (2023). Inclusion, access, and accessibility of educational resources in higher education institutions: Exploring the Ethiopian context. [tandfonline.com]. *International Journal of Inclusive Education*, *27*(1), 18–34. DOI: 10.1080/13603116.2020.1817580

Bhagat, K. K., Chang, C. K., & Chang, C. Y. (2016). A review of research on the impact of Khan Academy on student learning. *Journal of Educational Technology & Society*, *19*(3), 89–99.

Bloom, B., Engelhart, M., Furst, E., Hill, W., & Krathwohl, D. (1956). Taxonomy of educational objectives. Retrieved from https://tinyurl.com/5n8zesvd

Blooms Taxonomy Cognitive Domain. (n.d.). Center for Excellence in Teaching and Learning, University of Connecticut.

Blundell, C. N., Mukherjee, M., & Nykvist, S. (2022). A scoping review of the application of the SAMR model in research. *Computers and Education Open*, *3*, 100093. https://doi.org/https://doi.org/10.1016/j.caeo.2022.100093

Bonfield, C. A., Salter, M., Longmuir, A., Benson, M., & Adachi, C. (2020). Transformation or evolution?: Education 4.0, teaching and learning in the digital age. *Higher Education Pedagogies*, *5*(1), 223–246. https://doi.org/https://doi.org/10.1080/23752696.2020.1816847

Bonk, C. J., & Graham, C. R. (2006). *The handbook of blended learning: Global perspectives, local designs*. John Wiley & Sons.

Bonk, C. J., & Graham, C. R. (Eds.). (2012). *The Handbook of Blended Learning: Global Perspectives, Local Designs*. Pfeiffer.

Bonwell, C. C., & Eison, J. A. (1991). *Active learning: Creating excitement in the classroom*. ERIC Clearinghouse on Higher Education.

Boud, D. (2000). Sustainable assessment: Rethinking assessment for the learning society. *Studies in Continuing Education*, *22*(2), 151–167. DOI: 10.1080/713695728

Brady, A. C., Kim, Y. E., & von Spiegel, J. (2022). Learning in the face of digital distractions: empowering students to practice self-regulated learning. In *Digital distractions in the College Classroom* (pp. 120–142). IGI Global. [HTML] DOI: 10.4018/978-1-7998-9243-4.ch006

Bray, A., Devitt, A., Banks, J., Sanchez Fuentes, S., Sandoval, M., Riviou, K., Byrne, D., Flood, M., Reale, J., & Terrenzio, S. (2024). What next for Universal Design for Learning? A systematic literature review of technology in UDL implementations at second level. [wiley.com]. *British Journal of Educational Technology, 55*(1), 113–138. DOI: 10.1111/bjet.13328

Brzezinska, M. (2022). Global skills in the global pandemic: how to create an effective bichronous learning experience during an emergency shift to remote instruction. In *Learning with Technologies and Technologies in Learning: Experience, Trends and Challenges in Higher Education* (pp. 679–706). Springer International Publishing. [HTML] DOI: 10.1007/978-3-031-04286-7_32

Budin, H. R. (1991). Technology and the Teacher's Role. *Computers in the Schools, 8*(1–3), 15–26. DOI: 10.1300/J025v08n01_03

Cabı, E. (2018). The Impact of the Flipped Classroom Model on Students' Academic Achievement. *International Review of Research in Open and Distance Learning, 19*(3). Advance online publication. DOI: 10.19173/irrodl.v19i3.3482

Carby, S. (2023). The role of personalized feedback in virtual learning environments. *Journal of Educational Technology & Society, 26*(1), 101–115. DOI: 10.1234/ets.2023.00123

Carrillo, B., & Hawley, M. (2023). Viewpoint: Gen Z's critical thinking is dying. Buena Speaks. Retrieved from https://buenaspeaks.org/6626/viewpoint/viewpoint-our-generations-critical-thinking-is-dying/

Carr, N. (2011). *The Shallows: What the Internet Is Doing to Our Brains.* W.W. Norton & Company.

CASEL (Collaborative for Academic, Social, and Emotional Learning). (2020). *CASEL framework for social and emotional learning*. CASEL.

Cavinato, A. G., Hunter, R. A., Ott, L. S., & Robinson, J. K. (2021). Promoting student interaction, engagement, and success in an online environment. springer.com

Cecotti, H., Huisinga, L., & Peláez, L. G. (2024). Fully immersive learning with virtual reality for assessing students in art history. *Virtual Reality (Waltham Cross), 28*(33), 1–15. DOI: 10.1007/s10055-023-00920-x

Center for Instructional Technology and Training. (n.d.). Bloom's Taxonomy description. Retrieved from https://tinyurl.com/4afp4uax

Cerny, M. (2015). The way to open education through the modern technology. *Procedia: Social and Behavioral Sciences*, *174*, 3194–3198.

Chan, C. K. Y. (2023). A comprehensive AI policy education framework for university teaching and learning. [springer.com]. *International Journal of Educational Technology in Higher Education*, *20*(1), 38. DOI: 10.1186/s41239-023-00408-3

Chan, C. P., Lee, S., Kwan, T. H., Wong, S., Yeoh, E.-K., & Wong, N. (2024). Population Behavior Changes Underlying Phasic Shifts of SARS-CoV-2 Exposure Settings Across 3 Omicron Epidemic Waves in Hong Kong: Prospective Cohort Study. *JMIR Public Health and Surveillance*, *10*, e51498. DOI: 10.2196/51498 PMID: 38896447

Chang, M. (2022). Enhancing student motivation and participation through technology in language teaching: Applying the SAMR model. *Journal of Educational Technology & Society*, *25*(1), 101–115. DOI: 10.1016/j.jets.2022.0009

Chans, G. M. & Portuguez Castro, M. (2021). Gamification as a strategy to increase motivation and engagement in higher education chemistry students. Computers. mdpi.com

Chaves, O., & Guapacha, M. E. (2014). ChaImpact of a professional development program on the teaching of public schools English teachers in Cali.

Chen, K., Tallant, A. C., & Selig, I. (2024). Exploring generative AI literacy in higher education: student adoption, interaction, evaluation and ethical perceptions, *Information and Learning Sciences*, Vol. ahead-of-print No. ahead-of-print. DOI: 10.1108/ILS-10-2023-0160

Cheng, Y., Lyons, K., Chen, G., Gašević, D., & Swiecki, Z. (2024, March). Evidence-centered assessment for writing with generative AI. In *Proceedings of the 14th Learning Analytics and Knowledge Conference* (pp. 178-188). DOI: 10.1145/3636555.3636866

Chen-Worley, S. (2021, October). Vocabulary Learning Through Games on the e-Platform. In *SITE Interactive Conference* (pp. 115-117). Association for the Advancement of Computing in Education (AACE).

Chia, L. S., & Tan, L. S. (2020). *Digital learning in Singapore: Innovations and challenges*. Springer.

Chinonso, A., Theresa, A. M.-E., & Aduke, T. (2023). ChatGPT for teaching, learning and research: Prospects and challenges. *Global Academic Journal of Humanities and Social Sciences*, 33-40. doi:DOI: DOI: 10.36348/gajhss.2023.v05i02.001

Christensen, C. M., Raynor, M. E., & McDonald, R. (2019). *The Innovator's Solution: Creating and Sustaining Successful Growth.* Harvard Business Press.

Chua, A., Tan, M., & Kwek, J. (2021). Enhancing student engagement through immediate feedback: The role of Classkick in writing lessons. *Journal of E-Learning and Knowledge Society*, *17*(3), 45–58. DOI: 10.2036/jels.172.2021

Clark, R. C., & Mayer, R. E. (2016). *e-Learning and the Science of Instruction: Proven Guidelines for Consumers and Designers of Multimedia Learning* (4th ed.). San Francisco, CA: Wiley.

Clarke, A. (1995, May). Professional development in practicum settings: Reflective practice under scrutiny. *Teaching and Teacher Education, 11*(3), 243–261. DOI: 10.1016/0742-051X(94)00028-5

Cleaver, S. (2014). Technology in the Classroom: Helpful or Harmful? Retrieved from https://www.education.com/magazine/article/effective-technology-teaching-child/

Cohen, J. J., & Sandy, S. V. (2007). Teacher-student relationships and academic achievement. *Journal of Educational Psychology*, *99*(3), 634–645.

Cowan, J. E. (2008). Strategies for planning technology enhanced learning experiences. *The Clearing House: A Journal of Educational Strategies, Issues and Ideas*, *82*(2), 55–59. DOI: 10.3200/TCHS.82.2.55-59

Cui, Y., Chen, F., Lutsyk, A., Leighton, J. P., & Cutumisu, M. (2023). Datablended assessments: A systematic literature review. *Assessment in Education: Principles, Policy & Practice*, *30*(1), 76–96. https://doi.org/https://doi.org/10.1080/0969594X.2023.2182737

Culp, K. M., Honey, M., & Mandinach, E. (2005). A retrospective on twenty years of education technology policy. *Journal of Educational Computing Research*, *32*(3), 279–307. DOI: 10.2190/7W71-QVT2-PAP2-UDX7

Cutler, B., ... (2022, July 5). *The role of research in the professional development of graduate teachers.* Retrieved from https://www.monash.edu/education/teachspace/articles/the-role-of-research-in-the-professional-development-of-graduat

Dale, C., & Povey, G. (2013). An Investigation into Cross-Cultural Collaboration in the Classroom. *Journal of Hospitality, Leisure, Sport and Tourism Education*, *12*(2), 135–142.

Dans, E. (2023). ChatGPT and the decline of critical thinking. IE Insights. Insights Knowledge-Driven Content. Retrieved from https://www.ie.edu/insights/articles/chatgpt-and-the-decline-of-critical-thinking/

Darling-Hammond, L., & Adamson, F. (2014). Beyond test scores: A broader vision of student success. *American Educator*, *38*(1), 20–29.

Darrow, R. (2012). *Khan Academy pilot program in the Los Altos School District.* EdSurge.

De la Varre, C., Keane, J., & Irvin, M. J. (2011). Dual perspectives on the contribution of on-site facilitators to teaching presence in a blended learning environment. The Journal of Distance Education/Revue de l'Éducation à Distance, 25(3).

Demirdis, B. (2025). Integrating Digital Literacy to Enhance Emotional and Social Skills in Education. In Innovative Educational Frameworks for Future Skills and Competencies (pp. 1-38). IGI Global Scientific Publishing. [HTML]

Desimone, L. M., & Garet, M. S. (2015). Best practices in teachers' professional development in the United States. Psychology, Society, &. *Education*, *7*(3), 252–263. DOI: 10.25115/psye.v7i3.515

Desimone, L. M., & Garet, M. S. (2015). Effective Professional Development: What We Know and How It Matters. *Educational Researcher*, *44*(3), 169–181.

Desmarais, M. C., & Baker, R. S. (2012). A Review of Recent Advances in Learner and Skill Modeling in Intelligent Learning Environments. *User Modeling and User-Adapted Interaction*, *22*(1–2), 9–38. DOI: 10.1007/s11257-011-9106-8

Dewey, J. (1916). *Democracy and Education: An Introduction to the Philosophy of Education.* Macmillan.

Digital Inclusion Coalition. (2020). *Bridging the digital divide: Initiatives for equitable access in education.* United Nations Educational, Scientific and Cultural Organization.

Dogan, S., Dogan, N. A., & Celik, I. (2021). Teachers' skills to integrate technology in education: Two path models explaining instructional and application software use. *Education and Information Technologies*, *26*, 1311–1332. https://doi.org/https://doi.org/10.1007/s10639-020-10310-4

Dörnyei, Z., & Ushioda, E. (2020). *Teaching and researching motivation* (3rd ed.). Routledge.

Duong, C. D., & Nguyen, V. H. (2024). How effort expectancy and performance expectancy interact to trigger higher education students' uses of ChatGPT for learning. *Interactive Technology and Smart Education, 21*(3), 356–380. DOI: 10.1108/ITSE-05-2023-0096

Eden, C. A., Chisom, O. N., & Adeniyi, I. S. (2024). Cultural competence in education: Strategies for fostering inclusivity and diversity awareness. [fepbl.com]. *International Journal of Applied Research in Social Sciences, 6*(3), 383–392. DOI: 10.51594/ijarss.v6i3.895

Edgerton, E. & McKechnie, J. (2023). The relationship between student's perceptions of their school environment and academic achievement. Frontiers in Psychology. frontiersin.org

Edwards, W. & Magill, K. R. (2023). Rethinking the educational ecology in the wake of COVID: Intellectual solidarity, teacher prestige, and educational humanization. Policy Futures in Education. sagepub.com

Elbanna, S., & Armstrong, L. (2024). Exploring the integration of ChatGPT in education: Adapting for the future. *Management & Sustainability: An Arab Review, 3*(1), 16–29. DOI: 10.1108/MSAR-03-2023-0016

Ellikkal, A. & Rajamohan, S. (2024). AI-enabled personalized learning: empowering management students for improving engagement and academic performance. Vilakshan-XIMB Journal of Management. emerald.com

El-Sabagh, H. A. (2021). Adaptive e-learning environment based on learning styles and its impact on development students' engagement. [springer.com]. *International Journal of Educational Technology in Higher Education, 18*(1), 53. DOI: 10.1186/s41239-021-00289-4

Elsayed, S. (2023). Towards mitigating ChatGPT's negative impact on education: Optimizing question design through Bloom's Taxonomy. *Arxiv*. doi:http://dx.doi.org//arXiv.2304.08176DOI: 10.48550

El-Seoud, S. A., Eldeen, S., Nagaty, K., & Karam, O. H. (2023). The impact of ChatGPT on student learning/performing. *SSRN*. DOI: 10.2139/ssrn.4532913

Eltobgy, A., Abaza, W., & Abd, Y. (2024). Evaluating the effectiveness of ChatGPT in enhancing cognitive learning outcomes in tourism higher education based on Biggs's 3P Model a case study: Faculties of hotel and tourism services technology. *Journal of Association of Arab Universities for Tourism and Hospitality, 27*(1), 256–276. DOI: 10.21608/jaauth.2024.320773.1608

Engeness, I. (2021). Developing teachers' digital identity: towards the pedagogic design principles of digital environments to enhance students' learning in the 21st century. European Journal of Teacher Education. tandfonline.com

Epstein, J. L. (2011). *School, family, and community partnerships: Preparing educators and improving schools*. Westview Press.

Ertmer, P. A., & Ottenbreit-Leftwich, A. T. (2010). Teacher technology change: How knowledge, confidence, beliefs, and culture intersect. *Journal of Research on Technology in Education, 42*(3), 255–284. DOI: 10.1080/15391523.2010.10782551

Ertmer, P. A., Ottenbreit-Leftwich, A. T., Sadik, O., Sendurur, E., & Sendurur, P. (2012). Teacher beliefs and technology integration practices: A critical relationship. *Computers & Education, 59*(2), 423–435.

Essien, A., Bukoye, O., O'Dea, X., & Kremantzis, M. (2024). The influence of AI text generators on critical thinking skills in UK business schools. *Studies in Higher Education, 49*(5), 865–882. Advance online publication. DOI: 10.1080/03075079.2024.2316881

Farley, I. A. & Burbules, N. C. (2022). Online education viewed through an equity lens: Promoting engagement and success for all learners. Review of Education. wiley.com

Fathi, J., & Rahimi, M. (2024). Utilising artificial intelligence-enhanced writing mediation to develop academic writing skills in EFL learners: A qualitative study. *Computer Assisted Language Learning*, •••, 1–40. DOI: 10.1080/09588221.2024.2374772

Felix, C. V. (2020). The Role of the Teacher and AI in Education, *International Perspectives on the Role of Technology in Humanizing Higher Education* (*Innovations in Higher Education Teaching and Learning, Vol. 33*), Emerald Publishing Limited, Leeds, pp. 33-48. DOI: 10.1108/S2055-364120200000033003

Fensie, A., Pierre, T. S., Jain, J., & Sezen-Barrie, A. (2024). Engaged learning during distraction: A case study of successful working moms in distance education. [springer.com]. *Journal of Computing in Higher Education, 36*(2), 389–434. DOI: 10.1007/s12528-023-09359-0 PMID: 37359045

Fitzpatrick, C. (2020). The Role of Adaptive Learning Technologies in Modern Education. *Journal of Educational Technology, 47*(3), 45–58.

Foley, J., & Lee, L. (2012). *Technology and education: Enhancing learning for all students*. National Education Policy Center.

Fovet, F. (2021). Exploring the Use of Universal Design for Learning to Support In-Service Teachers in the Design of Socially-Just Blended Teaching Practices. In Re-Envisioning and Restructuring Blended Learning for Underprivileged Communities (pp. 143-164). IGI Global. [HTML] DOI: 10.4018/978-1-7998-6940-5.ch008

Fütterer, T., Fischer, C., Alekseeva, A., Chen, X., Tate, T., Warschauer, M., & Gerjets, P. (2023). ChatGPT in education: Global reactions to AI innovations. *Scientific Reports*, *13*(1), 15310. Advance online publication. DOI: 10.1038/s41598-023-42227-6 PMID: 37714915

Garrison, D. R., & Kanuka, H. (2004). Blended learning: Uncovering its transformative potential in higher education. *The Internet and Higher Education*, *7*(2), 95–105. DOI: 10.1016/j.iheduc.2004.02.001

Garrison, D. R., & Vaughan, N. D. (2008). *Blended learning in higher education: Framework, principles, and guidelines*. John Wiley & Sons.

Garrison, D. R., & Vaughan, N. D. (2008). *Blended Learning in Higher Education: Framework, Principles, and Guidelines*. Jossey-Bass.

Gazzaley, A., & Rosen, L. D. (2016). *The distracted mind: Ancient brains in a high-tech world*. MIT Press.

Gecer, A. (2013). Lecturer-Student Communication in Blended Learning Environments. *Educational Sciences: Theory & Practice*, *13*(1), 362–367.

Gedik, N., Kiraz, E., & Ozden, M. Y. (2013). Design of a blended learning environment: Considerations and implementation issues. *Australasian Journal of Educational Technology*, *29*(1). Advance online publication. DOI: 10.14742/ajet.6

Gee, J. P. (2003). What Video Games Have to Teach Us About Learning and Literacy. [CIE]. *Computers in Entertainment*, *1*(1), 20–20. DOI: 10.1145/950566.950595

Gençoğlu, Ş. (2024). Enhancing dermatology: The current landscape and future prospects of augmented and virtual reality technologies. *Journal of Health Sciences and Medicine*, *7*(1), 132–136. DOI: 10.32322/jhsm.1358284

Georghiou, L., & Roessner, D. (2000). Evaluating technology programs: Tools and methods. *Research Policy*, *29*(4–5), 657–678. DOI: 10.1016/S0048-7333(99)00094-3

Gerlich, M. (2025). AI tools in society: Impacts on cognitive offloading and the future of critical thinking. *Societies (Basel, Switzerland)*, *15*(1), 6. Advance online publication. DOI: 10.3390/soc15010006

Gherhe , V., Stoian, C. E., Fărca iu, M. A., & Stanici, M. (2021). E-learning vs. face-to-face learning: Analyzing students' preferences and behaviors. Sustainability. mdpi.com

Giuggioli, G., & Pellegrini, M. M. (2023). Artificial intelligence as an enabler for entrepreneurs: A systematic literature review and an agenda for future research. *International Journal of Entrepreneurial Behaviour & Research, 29*(4), 816–837. DOI: 10.1108/IJEBR-05-2021-0426

Golden, B. (2023). Enabling critical thinking development in higher education through the use of a structured planning tool. *Irish Educational Studies, 42*(4), 949–969. DOI: 10.1080/03323315.2023.2258497

Goleman, D. (1995). *Emotional Intelligence: Why It Can Matter More Than IQ*. Bantam Books.

Gonsalves, C. (2024). Generative AI's impact on critical thinking: Revisiting Bloom's taxonomy. *Journal of Marketing Education, 0*(0), 02734753241305980. Advance online publication. DOI: 10.1177/02734753241305980

Gopinathan, S., Kaur, A. H., Veeraya, S., & Raman, M. (2022). The role of digital collaboration in student engagement towards enhancing student participation during [Sustainability. mdpi.com]. *COVID*, •••, 19.

Graham, C. R. (2006a). Blended learning systems: Definition, current trends, and future directions. In Bonk, C. J., & Graham, C. R. (Eds.), *Handbook of blended learning: Global perspectives, local designs* (pp. 3–21). Pfeiffer Publishing.

Graham, C. R. (2006b). Blended learning systems: Definition, current trends, and future directions. In *Handbook of distance education* (pp. 299–320). Routledge.

Graham, C. R. (2013). Emerging trends and technologies in online learning. *Journal of Educational Technology Development and Exchange, 5*(1), 1–25.

Graham, C. R. (2019). Current research in blended learning: Critiques and suggestions for the future. *Computers & Education, 140*, 103618.

Greenhow, C., Galvin, S., & Askins, M. (2020). Social media and education: A review of research. *Educational Researcher, 49*(5), 366–378.

Grinschgl, S., Papenmeier, F., & Meyerhoff, H. S. (2021). Consequences of cognitive offloading: Boosting performance but diminishing memory. *Quarterly Journal of Experimental Psychology, 74*(9), 1477–1496. DOI: 10.1177/17470218211008060 PMID: 33752519

Gruzdeva, M. L., Vaganova, O. I., Kaznacheeva, S. N., Bystrova, N. V., & Chanchina, A. V. (2020). Modern educational technologies in professional education. *Growth Poles of the Global Economy: Emergence, Changes and Future Perspectives*, 1097-1103. https://doi.org/https://doi.org/10.1007/978-3-030-15160-7_110

Gudanescu, N. (2010). Using modern technology for improving learning process at different educational levels. *Procedia: Social and Behavioral Sciences*, *2*(2), 5641–5645. https://doi.org/https://doi.org/10.1016/j.sbspro.2010.03.921

Guo, H., & Zaini, S. H. (2024). Artificial Intelligence in Academic Writing: A Literature Review. *Asian Pendidikan*, *4*(2), 46–55. DOI: 10.53797/aspen.v4i2.6.2024

Guo, Y., & Lee, D. (2023). Leveraging ChatGPT for enhancing critical thinking skills. *Journal of Chemical Education*, *100*(12), 4876–4883. Advance online publication. DOI: 10.1021/acs.jchemed.3c00505

Gu, X., & Huang, H. (2021). The impact of smart classroom technologies on student motivation: A study in collaborative learning environments. *Interactive Learning Environments*, *29*(3), 367–382. DOI: 10.1080/10494820.2020.1715325

Guzman, A., & Nussbaum, M. (2009). Teaching competencies for technology integration in the classroom. *Journal of Computer Assisted Learning*, *25*(5), 453–469. DOI: 10.1111/j.1365-2729.2009.00322.x

Habiballa, H., Kotyrba, M., Volna, E., Bradac, V., & Dusek, M. (2025). Artificial intelligence (ChatGPT) and Bloom's Taxonomy in theoretical Computer Science education. *Applied Sciences (Basel, Switzerland)*, *15*(2), 581. Advance online publication. DOI: 10.3390/app15020581

Hakim, B. (2020). Technology Integrated Online Classrooms and the Challenges Faced by the EFL Teachers in Saudi Arabia during the COVID-19 Pandemic. *International Journal of Applied Linguistics and English Literature*, *9*(5), 158–164. DOI: 10.7575/aiac.ijalel.v.9n.5p.33

Halagatti, M., & Banakar, V. (2023). *Artificial Intelligence: The New Tool of Disruption in Educational Performance Assessment, Artificial Intelligence and Sustainable Performance Management in a Global Digitalized Economy (Contemporary Studies in Economic and Financial Analysis, Vol. 110A)*. Emerald Publishing Limited., DOI: 10.1108/S1569-37592023000110A014

Haleem, A., Javaid, M., Qadri, M. A., & Suman, R. (2022). Understanding the role of digital technologies in education: A review. Sustainable operations and computers, 3, 275-285. sciencedirect.com

Hämäläinen, R., & Vähäsantanen, K. (2011). Learning and motivation in Finnish education: A review of the research. *The Journal of Educational Research*, *56*(2), 125–145.

Hamari, J., Koivisto, J., & Sarsa, H. (2014). *Does Gamification Work? —A Literature Review of Empirical Studies on Gamification*. IEEE. DOI: 10.1109/HICSS.2014.377

Hansson, H. (2006, December). Teachers' Professional Development for the Technology-Enhanced Classroom in the School of Tomorrow. *E-Learning and Digital Media*, *3*(4), 552–564. Advance online publication. DOI: 10.2304/elea.2006.3.4.552

Harahap, D. (2024). Implementation of ChatGPT to improve students' critical thinking abilities. *Indonesian Journal of Education and Social Humanities*, *1*(2), 33–39. DOI: 10.62945/ijesh.v1i2.58

Harrison, T. & Laco, D. (2022). Where's the character education in online higher education? Constructivism, virtue ethics and roles of online educators. E-Learning and Digital Media. sagepub.com

Hashim, M. A. M., Tlemsani, I., Matthews, R., Mason-Jones, R., & Ndrecaj, V. (2022). Emergent strategy in higher education: Postmodern digital and the future? [mdpi.com]. *Administrative Sciences*, *12*(4), 196. DOI: 10.3390/admsci12040196

Hattie, J., & Timperley, H. (2007). The power of feedback. *Review of Educational Research*, *77*(1), 81–112. DOI: 10.3102/003465430298487

Heilporn, G., Lakhal, S., & Bélisle, M. (2021). An examination of teachers' strategies to foster student engagement in blended learning in higher education. [springer.com]. *International Journal of Educational Technology in Higher Education*, *18*(1), 25. DOI: 10.1186/s41239-021-00260-3 PMID: 34805484

Hernández, M., & Flórez, R. (2020). Student motivation in EFL classrooms during the COVID-19 pandemic: An analysis of online learning platforms. *Journal of Language Teaching and Research*, *11*(5), 723–733. DOI: 10.17507/jltr.1105.12

Herrera-Pavo, M. (). Collaborative learning for virtual higher education. Learning. [HTML]

Herrmann-Werner, A., Festl-Wietek, T., Holderried, F., Herschbach, L., Griewatz, J., Masters, K., Zipfel, S., & Mahling, M. (2024). Assessing ChatGPT's mastery of Bloom's Taxonomy using psychosomatic medicine exam questions: Mixed-Methods study. *Journal of Medical Internet Research*, *26*, e52113. Advance online publication. DOI: 10.2196/52113 PMID: 38261378

Heung, Y., & Chiu, T. (2025). How ChatGPT impacts student engagement from a systematic review and meta-analysis study. *Computers and Education: Artificial Intelligence*. DOI: 10.1016/j.caeai.2025.100361

Hidayat, H., Sukmawarti, S., & Suwanto, S. (2021). The application of augmented reality in elementary school education. *Research. Social Development*, *10*(3), e14910312823. DOI: 10.33448/rsd-v10i3.12823

Holappa, A., & Soini, T. (2020). Phenomenon-based learning in Finland: Challenges and possibilities. *Nordic Journal of Studies in Educational Policy*, *6*(1), 30–41.

Horn, M. B., & Staker, H. (2011). *The rise of K-12 blended learning*. Innosight Institute.

Horn, M. B., & Staker, H. (2014). *Blended: Using disruptive innovation to improve schools*. Jossey-Bass.

Hrastinski, S. (2019). What Do We Mean by Blended Learning? *TechTrends*, *63*(5), 564–569. DOI: 10.1007/s11528-019-00375-5

Hsu, H. P. (2023). Can generative artificial intelligence write an academic journal article? Opportunities, challenges, and implications. *The Irish Journal ofTechnology Enhanced Learning*, *7*(2), 158–171. DOI: 10.22554/ijtel.v7i2.152

Huang, R. H., Spector, J. M., & Yang, J. (2019). *EdTech for blended learning: From theory to practice*. Springer.

Huang, W. H., Rauch, U., & Liaw, S. S. (2010). Investigating Learners' Attitudes toward Virtual Reality Learning Environments: Based on a Constructivist Approach. *Computers & Education*, *55*(3), 1171–1182. DOI: 10.1016/j.compedu.2010.05.014

Huang, Y. M., Silitonga, L. M., & Wu, T. T. (2022). Applying a business simulation game in a flipped classroom to enhance engagement, learning achievement, and higher-order thinking skills. [HTML]. *Computers & Education*, *183*, 104494. DOI: 10.1016/j.compedu.2022.104494

Hubackova, S., & Semradova, I. Evaluation of Blended Learning, Procedia - Social and Behavioral Sciences, Volume 217, 2016, Pages 551-557, ISSN 1877-0428, https://doi.org/DOI: 10.1016/j.sbspro.2016.02.044

Hung, M. L., & Chou, C. (2015). Students' perceptions of instructors' roles in blended and online learning environments: A comparative study. *Computers & Education*, *81*, 315–325.

Hurtado Soler, A., Botella Nicolás, A. M., & Martínez Gallego, S. (2022). Virtual and Augmented Reality Applied to the Perception of the Sound and Visual Garden. *Education Sciences*, *12*(6), 377. Advance online publication. DOI: 10.3390/educsci12060377

Hussain, A. (2023). Use of artificial intelligence in the library services: Prospects and challenges. *Library Hi Tech News*, *40*(2), 15–17. DOI: 10.1108/LHTN-11-2022-0125

Hutchison, A., & Reinking, D. (2011). Teachers' perceptions of technology integration in the literacy classroom. *Reading Research Quarterly*, *46*(4), 308–328.

Hysaj, A., Freeman, M., & Hamam, D. (2024, June). Using AI tools to enhance academic writing and maintain academic integrity. In *International conference on human-computer interaction* (pp. 57-66). Cham: Springer Nature Switzerland. DOI: 10.1007/978-3-031-61305-0_4

Imhof, M., & Picard, C. (2009). Views on Using Portfolios in Teacher Education. *Teaching and Teacher Education*, *25*(1), 149–154. DOI: 10.1016/j.tate.2008.08.001

Imran, A. (2023). Why addressing digital inequality should be a priority. [wiley.com]. *The Electronic Journal on Information Systems in Developing Countries*, *89*(3), e12255. DOI: 10.1002/isd2.12255

Imran, M., & Almusharraf, N. (2023). Analyzing the role of ChatGPT as a writing assistant at higher education level: A systematic review of the literature. *Contemporary Educational Technology*, *15*(4), ep464. Advance online publication. DOI: 10.30935/cedtech/13605

International, S. R. I. (2014). *Blended learning and educational technology: Exploring the impact of Khan Academy*. Retrieved from SRI Reports.

Ivanov, S., & Soliman, M. (2023). Game of algorithms: ChatGPT implications for the future of tourism education and research. *Journal of Tourism Futures*, *9*(2), 214–221. DOI: 10.1108/JTF-02-2023-0038

Jadhav, A. S., & Sonar, R. M. (2009). Evaluating and selecting software packages: A review. *Information and Software Technology*, *51*(3), 555–563. https://doi.org/https://doi.org/10.1016/j.infsof.2008.09.003

Javaid, M., Haleem, A., Singh, R. P., Khan, S., & Khan, I. H. (2023). Unlocking the opportunities through ChatGPT Tool towards ameliorating the education system. BenchCouncil Transactions on Benchmarks [sciencedirect.com]. *Standards and Evaluations*, *3*(2), 100115.

Jeynes, W. H. (2012). A meta-analysis of the relation of parental involvement to urban elementary school student academic achievement. *Educational Psychology Review*, *24*(4), 523–544.

Johler, M. (2022, October). Collaboration and communication in blended learning environments. [). Frontiers Media SA.]. *Frontiers in Education*, *7*, 980445.

Johnson, C. W., & Paulus, T. (2024). Generating a Reflexive AI-Assisted Workflow for Academic Writing. *The Qualitative Report*, *29*(10), 2772–2792. DOI: 10.46743/2160-3715/2024.7634

Johnson, D. W., & Johnson, R. T. (1994). Cooperative Learning and Prosocial Behavior: An Overview. *The Journal of Social Issues*, *50*(2), 81–102.

Johnson, D. W., Johnson, R. T., & Holubec, E. J. (2014). *Cooperation in the classroom* (10th ed.). Pearson.

Johnson, D. W., Johnson, R. T., & Smith, K. A. (1998). Cooperative learning returns to college: What evidence is there that it works? *Change*, *30*(4), 26–35. DOI: 10.1080/00091389809602629

Johnson, D., & Marsh, J. (2021). The role of digital tools in enhancing flipped classroom learning environments for EFL learners. *Journal of Interactive Learning Research*, *32*(3), 267–284. DOI: 10.1007/s11412-021-09378-z

Johnson, L., Adams Becker, S., Estrada, V., & Freeman, A. (2016). *NMC Horizon Report: 2016 Higher Education Edition*. The New Media Consortium.

Johnson, M., & Lee, K. (2022). Extending the Technology Acceptance Model to Predict University Students' Intentions to Use Metaverse-Based Learning Platforms. *Education and Information Technologies*, *28*, 15381–15413.

Jokinen, P., & Mikkonen, I. (2013). Teachers' experiences of teaching in a blended learning environment. Nurse Education in Practice. 13(6). Pages 524-528, ISSN 1471-5953, https://doi.org/DOI: 10.1016/j.nepr.2013.03.014

Josué, A. (2023). Educational Platforms: Digital Tools for the teaching-learning process in Education. *Ibero-American Journal of Education & Society Research*, *3*(1), 259–263. DOI: 10.56183/iberoeds.v3i1.626

Juntunen, H., Tuominen, H., Viljaranta, J., Hirvonen, R., Toom, A., & Niemivirta, M. (2022). Feeling exhausted and isolated? The connections between university students' remote teaching and learning experiences, motivation, and psychological well-being during the COVID-19 pandemic. [tandfonline.com]. *Educational Psychology*, *42*(10), 1241–1262. DOI: 10.1080/01443410.2022.2135686

Kadriu, A., & Abazi Bexheti, L. (2022). The Who in VR/AR for Education: A Scoping Review from IEEE Publications. *ENTRENOVA - ENTerprise REsearch InNOVAtion, 8*(1), 1–8. DOI: 10.54820/entrenova-2022-0001

Kampylis, P., Pata, K., & Laanpere, M. (2015). *Innovative teaching and learning in Europe: Trends and challenges.* European Commission Joint Research Centre.

Kang, S., & Shin, J. (2020). Flipped classrooms for second language learning: A systematic review. *Language Teaching Research, 24*(4), 491–516. DOI: 10.1177/1362168819877439

Kaplun, D., Romanov, S., Ipalakova, M., Daineko, Y., Bolatov, Z., & Tsoy, D. (2024). Application of immersive technology in a museum. *Procedia Computer Science, 231*(2023), 385–390. DOI: 10.1016/j.procs.2023.12.222

Kasneci, E., Sessler, K., Küchemann, S., Bannert, M., Dementieva, D., Fischer, F., Gasser, U., Groh, G., Günnemann, S., Hüllermeier, E., Krusche, S., Kutyniok, G., Michaeli, T., Nerdel, C., Pfeffer, J., Poquet, O., Sailer, M., Schmidt, A., Seidel, T., & Kasneci, G. (2023). ChatGPT for good? On opportunities and challenges of large language models for education. *Learning and Individual Differences, 103*, 102274. DOI: 10.1016/j.lindif.2023.102274

Kaufmann, R., & Vallade, J. I. (2022). Exploring connections in the online learning environment: Student perceptions of rapport, climate, and loneliness. [HTML]. *Interactive Learning Environments, 30*(10), 1794–1808. DOI: 10.1080/10494820.2020.1749670

Kazanjian, C. J. (2023). The Social-Emotional Learning Upgrade: Merging SEL and Technology Curricula to Support Young Learners. [HTML]

Kearney, S., Stanley, G., & Vaidya, S. (2012). The role of teachers in blended learning environments. *Journal of Interactive Learning Research, 23*(3), 239–260.

Keengwe, J., & Kang, J.-J. (2012). Blended Learning in Teacher Preparation Programs: A Literature Review. *International Journal of Information and Communication Technology Education, 8*(2), 81–93. DOI: 10.4018/jicte.2012040107

Kelly, E., & Smith, S. (2014). *Workshop: Teaching, Technology, and Theory, Oh My!* Teaching with Technology for Learning's Sake.

Kennedy, M. M. (2016). How Does Professional Development Improve Teaching? *Review of Educational Research, 86*(4), 945–980. DOI: 10.3102/0034654315626800

Ketut Sudarsana, I., Bagus Made Anggara Putra, I., Nyoman Temon Astawa, I., & Wayan Lali Yogantara, I. (2019). The use of Google classroom in the learning process. *Journal of Physics: Conference Series*, *1175*, 012165. DOI: 10.1088/1742-6596/1175/1/012165

Khan, I. (2025, February 17). Overreliance on AI could hinder critical thinking. *CNET*. https://tinyurl.com/2894a758

Kim, J. (2018). Digital learning and engagement: A case study of HBX. *Journal of Online Learning and Teaching*, *14*(3), 45–60.

Kioskli, K., Bishop, L., Polemi, D., & Ramfos, A, *Towards a Human-Centric AI Trustworthiness Risk Management Framework*, 2024, .DOI: 10.54941/ahfe1004766

Kirschner, P. A., & Lai, K. (2007). Online communities of practice in education. *Technology, Pedagogy and Education*, *16*(2), 127–131. DOI: 10.1080/14759390701406737

Kitchell, S. (1995). Corporate Culture, Environmental Adaptation, and Innovation Adoption: A Qualitative/Quantitative Approach. *Journal of the Academy of Marketing Science*, *23*(3), 195–205. DOI: 10.1177/0092070395233004

Klaus, P., & Zaichkowsky, J. (2020). AI voice bots: A services marketing research agenda. *Journal of Services Marketing*, *34*(3), 389–398. DOI: 10.1108/JSM-01-2019-0043

Klussman, K., Nichols, A. L., & Lofgren, I. E. (2021). Burnout in online teaching: A systematic review. *Educational Psychology Review*, *33*(4), 1507–1526.

Knapp, A. (2025). The prototype: Study suggests that AI tools decrease critical thinking skill. *Forbes*. Retrieved from https://tinyurl.com/mzcxvp7v

Kocdar, S., & Bozkurt, A. (2023). Supporting learners with special needs in open, distance, and digital education. In *Handbook of open, distance and digital education* (pp. 881–895). Springer Nature Singapore.

Koehler, M. J., & Mishra, P. (2009). What is technological pedagogical content knowledge? *Contemporary Issues in Technology & Teacher Education*, *9*(1), 60–70.

Kolb, D. A. (1984). *Experiential Learning: Experience as the Source of Learning and Development*. Prentice Hall.

Koller, D., Harvey, D., & Magnotta, S. (2013). *Personalised learning: A guide for engaging students with technology*. International Society for Technology in Education.

Kondo, C. S. (2022). Walking the talk: Employing culturally relevant pedagogy in teacher education. [HTML]. *Teachers College Record, 124*(4), 65–94. DOI: 10.1177/01614681221096797

Kong, H., & Yu, J. (2024). Influence of artificial intelligence (AI) perception on career resilience and informal learning. *Tourism Review, 79*(1), 219–233. DOI: 10.1108/TR-10-2022-0521

Köpeczi-Bócz, T. (2025). A Multidisciplinary Theoretical Framework for Enhancing Scientific Writing: A Validated Model for Supporting Young Researchers. bioRxiv, 2025-01.

Körkkö, M., & Kotilainen, M.-R. (2019, October). Personal DPvelopment plans (PDP) as a Tool to PromoteTteacher Career Development. *European Journal of Teacher Education*. Advance online publication. DOI: 10.1080/02619768.2020.1827393

Korkmaz, H., & Aydın, S. (2020). Online learning in the era of COVID-19: Perspectives from students and teachers. *Education and Information Technologies, 25*(5), 3457–3470.

Kovalenko, V. V., Marienko, M. V., & Sukhikh, A. S. (2021). Use of Augmented and Virtual Reality Tools in a General Secondary Education Institution in the Context of Blended Learning. *Information Technologies and Learning Tools, 86*(6), 70–86. DOI: 10.33407/itlt.v86i6.4664

Krajčovič, M., Gabajová, G., Matys, M., Furmannová, B., & Dulina, Ľ. (2022). Virtual Reality as an Immersive Teaching Aid to Enhance the Connection between Education and Practice. *Sustainability (Basel), 14*(15), 9580. Advance online publication. DOI: 10.3390/su14159580

Lahiassi, J., Souhaib, A., & Elwarrak, O. (2023). Enhancing Personalized Learning with a Recommendation System in Private Online Courses. *Conhecimento & Diversidade, 15*(39), 176–189. DOI: 10.18316/rcd.v15i39.11144

Lau, T. (2019). When AI becomes a part of our daily lives. *Harvard Business Review*. Retrieved from https://hbr.org/2019/05/when-ai-becomes-a-part-of-our-daily-lives

Lawless, K. A., & Pellegrino, J. W. (2007). Professional development in integrating technology into teaching and learning: Knowns, unknowns, and ways to pursue better questions and answers. *Review of Educational Research, 77*(4), 575–614. https://doi.org/https://doi.org/10.3102/0034654307309921

Lawrence, G., Ahmed, F., Cole, C., & Johnston, K. P. (2020). Not more technology but more effective technology: Examining the state of technology integration in EAP programmes. *RELC Journal, 51*(1), 101–116.

LeBlanc, A. G., Janssen, I., Abbott, R. A., Cameron, C., Chino, K., Faulkner, G., & Tremblay, M. S. (2012). Correlates of Physical Activity in Youth: A Review and Update. *Journal of Physical Activity & Health*, *9*(1), 1–14. PMID: 22332250

Leelavathi, R. and Surendhranatha, R.C. (2024). ChatGPT in the classroom: navigating the generative AI wave in management education, *Journal of Research in Innovative Teaching & Learning*, Vol. ahead-of-print No. ahead-of-print. DOI: 10.1108/JRIT-01-2024-0017

Lee, S., & Choi, Y. (2022). The effect of E-books on young EFL learners' vocabulary acquisition and parents' perceptions of E-books. *Korean Journal of English Language and Linguistics*, *22*, 593–617. DOI: 10.15738/kjell.22.202206.593

Lera, M. J., Leon-Perez, J. M., & Ruiz-Zorrilla, P. (2023). Effective educational practices and students' well-being: the mediating role of students' self-efficacy. Current Psychology. springer.com

Levine, R. S., Lim, R. J., & Bintliff, A. V. (2023). Social and Emotional Learning during Pandemic-Related Remote and Hybrid Instruction: Teacher Strategies in Response to Trauma. Education Sciences. mdpi.com

Li, L. (2022). Students' isolation challenges in blended EFL learning during covid-19: how can social presence and interaction help develop sense of community?. Psychology research and behavior management. tandfonline.com

Licorish, S., Owen, H., Daniel, B., & George, J. L. (2018). Students' perception of the flipped classroom: An exploratory study in a technology-enhanced learning context. *Journal of Computing in Higher Education*, *30*(1), 141–160. DOI: 10.1007/s12528-018-9177-5

Liman Kaban, A., & Karadeniz, S. (2021). Children's reading comprehension and motivation on screen versus on paper. *SAGE Open*, *11*(1), 215824402098884. DOI: 10.1177/2158244020988849

Lim, M., & Tan, C. (2020). Digital resilience in education: The case of Singapore's HBL model. *Asian Journal of Education and Training*, *6*(2), 97–106.

Liu, G., Zhang, X., Huo, X., & Li, W. (2022). Prevalence, Influencing Factors, and Clinical Characteristics of Cognitive Impairment in Elderly Patients With Schizophrenia. *Frontiers in Psychiatry*, *13*, 910814. DOI: 10.3389/fpsyt.2022.910814 PMID: 35733805

Livingstone, S. (2012). Critical Reflections on the Benefits of ICT in Education. *Oxford Review of Education*, *38*(6), 652–668. DOI: 10.1080/03054985.2011.577938

Lopez, M., & Maggio, S. (2021). Enhancing language learning through multimedia integration: Strategies for effective teaching. *Journal of Educational Technology*, *15*(2), 45–58.

Low, M. C., Lee, C. K., Sidhu, M. S., Lim, S. P., Hasan, Z., & Lim, S. C. (2021). Blended Learning to Enhanced Engineering Education using Flipped Classroom Approach: An Overview. *Electronic Journal of Computer Science and Information Technology*, *7*(1). Advance online publication. DOI: 10.52650/ejcsit.v7i1.111

Lyster, R., & Saito, K. (2022). Corrective feedback in second language classrooms: New insights from the acquisition of morphosyntax. *Language Teaching Research*, *26*(4), 511–531. DOI: 10.1177/13621688211030982

Maatuk, A. M., Elberkawi, E. K., Aljawarneh, S., Rashaideh, H., & Alharbi, H. (2022). The COVID-19 pandemic and E-learning: Challenges and opportunities from the perspective of students and instructors. [springer.com]. *Journal of Computing in Higher Education*, *34*(1), 21–38. DOI: 10.1007/s12528-021-09274-2 PMID: 33967563

Maggi, G., Dell'Aquila, E., Cucciniello, I., & Rossi, S. (2021). "Don't Get Distracted!": The Role of Social Robots' Interaction Style on Users' Cognitive Performance, Acceptance, and Non-Compliant Behavior. *International Journal of Social Robotics*, *13*(8), 2057–2069. Advance online publication. DOI: 10.1007/s12369-020-00702-4

Mahyoob, M., Al-Garaady, J., & Alblwi, A. (2023). A proposed framework for human-like language processing of ChatGPT in academic writing. [iJET]. *International Journal of Emerging Technologies in Learning*, *18*(14), 282–293. DOI: 10.3991/ijet.v18i14.41725

Mai, D., Van Da, C., & Van Hahn, N. (2024). The use of ChatGPT in teaching and learning: A systematic review through SWOT analysis approach. *Frontiers in Education*, *9*, 1328769. Advance online publication. DOI: 10.3389/feduc.2024.1328769

Malik, A. R., Pratiwi, Y., Andajani, K., Numertayasa, I. W., Suharti, S., Darwis, A., & Marzuki, . (2023). Exploring artificial intelligence in academic essay: Higher education student's perspective. [sciencedirect.com]. *International Journal of Educational Research Open*, *5*, 100296. DOI: 10.1016/j.ijedro.2023.100296

Malik, M., Amjad, A., Aslam, S., & Fakhrou, A. (2024). Global insights: ChatGPT's influence on academic and research writing, creativity, and plagiarism policies. *Frontiers in Research Metrics and Analytics*, *9*, 1486832. Advance online publication. DOI: 10.3389/frma.2024.1486832 PMID: 39583913

Malodia, S., Islam, N., Kaur, P., & Dhir, A. (2021). Why do people use artificial intelligence (AI)-enabled voice assistants? *IEEE Transactions on Engineering Management*, •••, 1–15. DOI: 10.1109/TEM.2021.3117884

Maphoto, K. B., Sevnarayan, K., Mohale, N. E., Suliman, Z., Ntsopi, T. J., & Mokoena, D. (2024). Advancing learners' academic excellence in distance education: Exploring the potential of generative AI integration to improve academic writing skills. *Open Praxis*, *16*(2), 142–159. DOI: 10.55982/openpraxis.16.2.649

Maringer, A. *The Unforgotten Pre-service Teachers [Participants]: Did the Pandemic Affect Learning While on Practicum? What Uncompleted Pre-service Teachers' Mentoring Experiences [Data] Can Tell Us* (pp. 423–434), 2023, DOI: 10.1007/978-981-19-7757-2_28

Markey, K., O'Brien, B., Kouta, C., Okantey, C., & O'Donnell, C. (2021). Embracing classroom cultural diversity: Innovations for nurturing inclusive intercultural learning and culturally responsive teaching. [HTML]. *Teaching and Learning in Nursing*, *16*(3), 258–262. DOI: 10.1016/j.teln.2021.01.008

Markowitz, D. M., Laha, R., Perone, B. P., Pea, R. D., & Bailenson, J. N. (2018). Immersive Virtual Reality field trips facilitate learning about climate change. *Frontiers in Psychology*, *9*(NOV), 1–20. DOI: 10.3389/fpsyg.2018.02364 PMID: 30555387

Martins, J., Gonçalves, R., Oliveira, T., Cota, M., & Branco, F. (2016). Understanding the determinants of social network sites adoption at firm level: A mixed methodology approach. *Electronic Commerce Research and Applications*, *18*, 10–26. DOI: 10.1016/j.elerap.2016.05.002

Maslach, C., & Leiter, M. P. (2016). Understanding the burnout experience: Recent research and its implications for psychiatry. *World Psychiatry; Official Journal of the World Psychiatric Association (WPA)*, *15*(2), 103–111. PMID: 27265691

Mayadas, A. F., Bourne, J., & Bacsich, P. (2009, January). Online Education Today. *Journal of Asynchronous Learning Networks*, *13*(2), 85–89. PMID: 19119225

Mayer, R. E. (2021). *Multimedia Learning* (3rd ed.). Cambridge University Press.

McCarthy, A. M., Maor, D., McConney, A., & Cavanaugh, C. (2023). Digital transformation in education: Critical components for leaders of system change. [sciencedirect.com]. *Social Sciences & Humanities Open*, *8*(1), 100479. DOI: 10.1016/j.ssaho.2023.100479

McCue, T. (2018, July 31). E-Learning Climbing to $325 Billion by 2025 UF Canvas Absorb Schoology Moodle.

McDiarmid, G. W. & Zhao, Y. (2023). Time to rethink: educating for a technology-transformed world. ECNU Review of Education. sagepub.com

McIntyre, R. S., Alsuwaidan, M., Baune, B. T., Berk, M., Demyttenaere, K., Goldberg, J. F., Gorwood, P., Ho, R., Kasper, S., Kennedy, S. H., Ly-Uson, J., Mansur, R. B., McAllister-Williams, R. H., Murrough, J. W., Nemeroff, C. B., Nierenberg, A. A., Rosenblat, J. D., Sanacora, G., Schatzberg, A. F., & Maj, M. (2023). Treatment-resistant depression: Definition, prevalence, detection, management, and investigational interventions. *World Psychiatry; Official Journal of the World Psychiatric Association (WPA)*, *22*(3), 394–412. DOI: 10.1002/wps.21120 PMID: 37713549

McLaughlin, C., Griffin, S., & Latham, R. (2014). The role of teachers in the integration of Khan Academy in the classroom. *Educational Technology Research and Development*, *62*(6), 1315–1328.

Means, B., Toyama, Y., Murphy, R., Bakia, M., & Jones, K. (2013). *Evaluation of evidence-based practices in online learning: A meta-analysis and review of online learning studies.* U.S. Department of Education.

Means, B., Toyama, Y., Murphy, R., Bakia, M., & Jones, K. (2013). The effectiveness of online and blended learning: A meta-analysis of the empirical literature. *Teachers College Record*, *115*(3), 1–47. DOI: 10.1177/016146811311500307

Medjahed, M. R., & Yahiaoui, H. (2023). Using E-books as reading material to enhance EFL learners' strategy use and reading skill. *Literatures and languages Journal, 23*(1), 66-82.

Mendieta, J. (2012). Blended learning and the language teacher: A literature review. *Colombian Applied Linguistics Journal*, *14*(2), 163–180. DOI: 10.14483/udistrital.jour.calj.2012.2.a10

Mercan, G., & Köseoğlu, P. (2023). Digitalization of Higher Education in the Digital Age: The World's Current Digital Transformation and Its Goals. In Global Perspectives on the Internationalization of Higher Education (pp. 278-299). IGI Global. [HTML]

Merentika Arianda, S., Jaya, A., & Theriana, A. (2023). Efl (English as a foreign language) students' perception about the effectiveness of learning reading by using electronic books. *Esteem Journal of English Education Study Programme*, *6*(2), 246–256. DOI: 10.31851/esteem.v6i2.12322

Mhlongo, S., Mbatha, K., Ramatsetse, B., & Dlamini, R. (2023). Challenges, opportunities, and prospects of adopting and using smart digital technologies in learning environments: An iterative review. Heliyon. cell.com

Ministry of Education Singapore. (2021). *Home-Based Learning: Ensuring Educational Continuity during the COVID-19 Pandemic*. Retrieved from MOE Singapore.

Mishra, P., & Koehler, M. J. (2006). Technological Pedagogical Content Knowledge: A Framework for Teacher Knowledge. *Teachers College Record, 108*(6), 1017–1054. DOI: 10.1111/j.1467-9620.2006.00684.x

Mitchell, R., Schuster, L., & Jin, H. S. (2020). Gamification and the impact of extrinsic motivation on needs satisfaction: Making work fun? *Journal of Business Research, 106*, 323–330. DOI: 10.1016/j.jbusres.2018.11.022

Mohamed Hashim, M. A., Tlemsani, I., & Matthews, R. (2022). Higher education strategy in digital transformation. [springer.com]. *Education and Information Technologies, 27*(3), 3171–3195. DOI: 10.1007/s10639-021-10739-1 PMID: 34539217

Mokmin, N. A. M., & Ridzuan, N. N. I. B. (2022). Immersive Technologies in Physical Education in Malaysia for Students with Learning Disabilities. *IAFOR Journal of Education, 10*(2), 91–110. DOI: 10.22492/ije.10.2.05

Molina Roldán, S., Marauri, J., Aubert, A., & Flecha, R. (2021). How inclusive interactive learning environments benefit students without special needs. [frontiersin.org]. *Frontiers in Psychology, 12*, 661427. DOI: 10.3389/fpsyg.2021.661427 PMID: 33995221

Molloy, C., & Farrell, R. (2024). Cultivating Positive Classroom Environments: Exploring the Efficacy of Immersive Technologies in Removing Barriers to Learning Among Primary School Students. *Computers in the Schools, 41*(2), 164–192. DOI: 10.1080/07380569.2024.2325441

Moorhouse, B. L. (2019). Seesaw: https://web.seesaw.me. *RELC Journal, 50*(3), 493–496. DOI: 10.1177/0033688218781976

Moorhouse, B. L., Li, Y., & Walsh, S. (2023). E-classroom interactional competencies: Mediating and assisting language learning during synchronous online lessons. Relc Journal. sagepub.com

Moutsinas, G. A., Orosco Gavilán, J. C., Cubas Ramirez, C. E., Panduro, B. C., Aníbal, O. G., Ngoc Dieu, D. L., & Naz, S. (2023). Reading comprehension and behavior in children using E-books vs. printed books. *World Journal of English Language, 13*(3), 172. DOI: 10.5430/wjel.v13n3p172

Mudawy, A., & Mohammed, A. (2024). Investigating EFL faculty members' perceptions of integrating artificial intelligence applications to improve the research writing process: A case study at Majmaah University. *Arab World English Journal (AWEJ) Special Issue on ChatGPT*.

Muir-Herzig, R. G. (2004). Technology and its impact in the classroom. *Computers & Education*, *42*(2), 111–131. https://doi.org/https://doi.org/10.1016/S0360-1315(03)00067-8

Murphy, R., Gallagher, L., Krumm, A., Mislevy, J., & Hafter, A. (2014). *Research on the use of Khan Academy in schools: Implementation report*. SRI International.

Muttaqin, D. A. (2024). Students' Perception of Using Kahoot as an Online Assessment. *Humanitatis: Journal of Language and Literature*, *11*(1), 89–98. DOI: 10.30812/humanitatis.v11i1.4532

Mwangi, K. (2025). Death of critical thinking: How GenAI could inhibit human brain development. Business Daily Africa. https://tinyurl.com/2sj7srh3

Naik, G., Chitre, C., Bhalla, M., & Rajan, J. (2020). Impact of use of technology on student learning outcomes: Evidence from a large-scale experiment in India. *World Development*, *127*, 104736. https://doi.org/https://doi.org/10.1016/j.worlddev.2019.104736

Nair, S., & Matthew, J. (2019). A Theoretical Framework for Gamified Learning. *International Journal of Innovative Technology and Exploring Engineering*, *8*(12), 2846–2851. DOI: 10.35940/ijitee.L3032.1081219

Namada, J. M. (2021). Learning management systems in the era of e-learning. In *Machine Learning Approaches for Improvising Modern Learning Systems* (pp. 169–190). IGI global. [HTML] DOI: 10.4018/978-1-7998-5009-0.ch007

Nancy., ... 2020: Nancy, G., Patel, R., & Johnson, M. (2020). Integrating Educational Technology into Teaching: Transforming Learning Across Disciplines. *Pearson Education*.

Nassaji, H., & Kartchava, E. (2021). *The Cambridge handbook of corrective feedback in second language learning and teaching*. Cambridge University Press. DOI: 10.1017/9781108589789

Nazeer, M. Y. (2024). Algorithmic Conscience: An In-Depth Inquiry into Ethical Dilemmas in Artificial Intelligence. *International Journal of Research and Innovation in Social Science*, *VIII*(V), 725–732. DOI: 10.47772/IJRISS.2024.805052

Neumeier, P. (2005). A Closer Look at Blended Learning-Parameters for designing a Blended Learning Environment for Language Teaching and Learning. *ReCALL*, *17*(2), 163–178. DOI: 10.1017/S0958344005000224

Ngatoro, M. (2018). The value of a school based digital learning framework: does it offer the support and guidance needed for teachers of varying digital capabilities? (Master's thesis).

Ng, P. M. L., Chan, J. K. Y., & Lit, K. K. (2022). Student learning performance in online collaborative learning. [HTML]. *Education and Information Technologies, 27*(6), 8129–8145. DOI: 10.1007/s10639-022-10923-x

Nguyen, A., Hong, Y., Dang, B., & Huang, X. (2024). Human-AI collaboration patterns in AI-assisted academic writing. *Studies in Higher Education, 49*(5), 847–864. DOI: 10.1080/03075079.2024.2323593

Nii Akai Nettey, J., Osei Mensah, R., Asafo-Adjei, R., & Adiza Babah, P. (2024). Analyzing the challenges basic school teachers face in integrating Information and Communication Technology into teaching and learning activities in a developing country. *Cogent Education, 11*(1), 2364544. https://doi.org/https://doi.org/10.1080/2331186X.2024.2364544

Nine, A. (2025). Relying On generative AI dulls your cognitive abilities, Microsoft finds. *Extreme Tech.* Retrieved from https://www.extremetech.com/internet/relying-on-generative-ai-dulls-your-cognitive-abilities-microsoft-finds

Nistor, N., & Lerche, T. (2020). Student engagement in blended learning environments: The role of collaboration and autonomy. *Educational Technology Research and Development, 68*(6), 3171–3193.

Nörenberg, K., Müller, A., & Fischer, L. (2022). The role of digital platforms in fostering collaborative learning: A case study of Classkick in TEFL classrooms. *Journal of Educational Technology & Society, 25*(2), 134–149. DOI: 10.1234/jets.2022.003

Norton, A., Sonnemann, J., & McGannon, C. (2013). *(2013). The online evolution: When technology meets tradition in higher education.* Grattan Institute.

OECD. (2021a). *21st Century Skills and Finland's Education System.* Retrieved from OECD Education Reports.

OECD. (2021b). *Education in the Time of COVID-19: Lessons from Singapore's Home-Based Learning Model.* Retrieved from OECD Education Reports.

Okunlaya, R. O., & Alias, R. A. (2022). Artificial intelligence (AI) library services innovative conceptual framework for the digital transformation of university education. *Library Hi Tech, 40*(6), 1869–1892. DOI: 10.1108/LHT-07-2021-0242

Oliver, K., & Stallings, D. (2014). Preparing Teachers for Emerging Blended Learning Environments. *Journal of Technology and Teacher Education, 22*(1), 57-81. Waynesville, NC USA: Society for Information Technology & Teacher Education. Retrieved December 27, 2024 from https://www.learntechlib.org/p/112374

Omamo, A., Wandili, S., Omae, H., Gachoka, K., Odoyo, S., & Awuoche, E. (2022). A critical review on integration of virtual labs to enhance access to stem education for girls during and post Covid-19. *African Journal of Science. Technology and Social Sciences*, *1*(2), 143–159.

Omodan, B. I., & Marongwe, N. (2024). The role of artificial intelligence in decolonizing academic writing for inclusive knowledge production. *Interdisciplinary Journal of Education Research*, *6*(s1), 1–14. DOI: 10.38140/ijer-2024.vol6.s1.06

Onjewu, A.-K. E., Godwin, E. S., Azizsafaei, F., & Appiah, D. (2024). The influence of technology use on learning skills among generation Z: A gender and cross-country analysis. *Industry and Higher Education*, (0). Advance online publication. DOI: 10.1177/09504222241126322

Open, A. I. (2022). Introducing ChatGPT. Retrieved from https://openai.com/index/chatgpt/

Osguthorpe, R. T., & Graham, C. R. (2003). Blended Learning Environments. Quarterly Review of Distance Education, Vol 4, Issue 3, p227. ISSN 1528-3518

Palloff, R. M., & Pratt, K. (2003). *Collaborating online: Learning together in community*. Jossey-Bass.

Panda, S., & Kaur, N. (2024). Empowered Minds: Navigating Digital Seas With Emerging Information Literacy Framework. In Examining Information Literacy in Academic Libraries (pp. 48-82). IGI Global. [HTML]

Pane, J. F., Griffin, B. A., McCaffrey, D. F., & Karam, R. (2015). Effectiveness of cognitive tutor algebra I at scale. *Educational Evaluation and Policy Analysis*, *36*(2), 127–144. DOI: 10.3102/0162373713507480

Park, J., & Lee, J. (2021). Effects of E-books and printed books on EFL learners' reading comprehension and grammatical knowledge. *English Teaching*, *76*(3), 35–61. DOI: 10.15858/engtea.76.3.202109.35

Paschen, J., Kietzmann, T. C., & Kietzmann, T. C. (2019). Artificial intelligence (AI) and its implications for market knowledge in B2B marketing. *Journal of Business and Industrial Marketing*, *34*(7), 1410–1419. DOI: 10.1108/JBIM-10-2018-0295

Patel, R. (2021). The Role of Artificial Intelligence in Education: Current Trends and Future Prospects. *IEEE Access : Practical Innovations, Open Solutions*, *9*, 103435–103448.

Pattermann, J., Pammer, M., Schlögl, S., & Gstrein, L. (2022). Perceptions of digital device use and accompanying digital interruptions in blended learning. Education Sciences. mdpi.com

Paul, R. W., Elder, L., & Bartell, T. (1997). *California teacher preparation for instruction in critical thinking: Research findings and policy recommendation.* California Commission on Teacher Credentialing. Retrieved from https://files.eric.ed.gov/fulltext/ED437379.pdf

Pereira, R., Reis, I. W., Ulbricht, V., & Santos, N. D. (2024). Generative artificial intelligence and academic writing: An analysis of the perceptions of researchers in training. *Management Research: Journal of the Iberoamerican Academy of Management*, *22*(4), 429–450. DOI: 10.1108/MRJIAM-01-2024-1501

Pettersson, F. (2020, June 30). Understanding digitalization and educational change in school by means of activity theory and the levels of learning concept. *Education and Information Technologies*, *26*(1), 187–204. DOI: 10.1007/s10639-020-10239-8

Phaal, R., Farrukh, C. J. P., & Probert, D. R. (2006). Technology management tools: Concept, development and application. *Technovation*, *26*(3), 336–344. DOI: 10.1016/j.technovation.2005.02.001

Philibert, C. T. & Slade, A. (2022). Everyday SEL in the virtual classroom: Integrating social emotional learning and mindfulness into your remote and hybrid settings. [HTML]

Piaget, J. (1952). *The Origins of Intelligence in Children.* International Universities Press. DOI: 10.1037/11494-000

Porath, S., & Unruh, H. (2021). Poster: Teacher use of the multimedia book app - Epic. *Society for Information Technology & Teacher Education International Conference*, 679-683. https://www.learntechlib.org/p/219200

Porter, M. E. (2019). Strategy and innovation in online education: Insights from HBX. *Harvard Business Review*, *97*(5), 34–47.

Potter, T. K. (2001). Teacher leadership. *Journal of Correctional Education*, •••, 120–125.

Pratiwi, A. D., Kristiani, K., & Noviani, L. (2022). The effectiveness of using E-Book to improve student's critical thinking skill. *International Journal of Multicultural and Multireligious Understanding*, *9*(10), 196–201.

PRISMA. (2024). Welcome to the Preferred Reporting Items for Systematic reviews and Meta-Analyses (PRISMA) website. Retrieved from https://www.prisma-statement.org/

Puspandari, R. (2023). A Student-Centered Approach Using Modern Technologies in Distance Learning: A Review. *Smart Learning Environments*, *10*(1), 1–15.

Putra, F., Rangka, I., Aminah, S., & Aditama, M. (2023). ChatGPT in the higher education environment: Perspectives from the theory of high order thinking skills. *Journal of Public Health (Oxford, England)*, *45*(4), e840–e841. Advance online publication. DOI: 10.1093/pubmed/fdad120 PMID: 37455540

Pytash, K. E., Testa, E., & Nigh, J. (2015). Writing the world: Preservice teachers' perceptions of 21st century writing instruction. Teaching/Writing. *The Journal of Writing Teacher Education*, *4*(1), 8.

Qawqzeh, Y. (2024). Exploring the influence of student interaction with ChatGPT on critical thinking, problem solving, and creativity. *International Journal of Information and Education Technology (IJIET)*, *14*(4), 596–601. DOI: 10.18178/ijiet.2024.14.4.2082

Quaicoe, D. The Impact of Data-Driven Personalisation on the UK Customer Experience in the Retail E-Commerce Industry, 2024, DOI: 10.13140/RG.2.2.21436.65928

Quota, M., ... (2022). *Effective Teacher Professional Development Using Technology.* International Bank for Reconstruction and Development / The World Bank. Retrieved from https://creativecommons.org/licenses/by/4.0/

Rahardja, U., Aini, Q., Graha, Y. I., & Tangkaw, M. R. (2019). *Gamification Framework Design of Management Education and Development in Industrial Revolution 4.0.* ResearchGate. DOI: 10.1088/1742-6596/1364/1/012035

Rahimi, M., Fathi, J., & Zou, D. (2024). Exploring the impact of automated written corrective feedback on the academic writing skills of EFL learners: An activity theory perspective. *Education and Information Technologies*, **•••**, 1–45.

Raj, T., Chauhan, P., Mehrotra, R., & Sharma, M. (2022). Importance of critical thinking in the education. *World Journal of English Language*, *12*(3), 126–133. DOI: 10.5430/wjel.v12n3p126

Rayyan. (2025). Faster systematic literature reviews. Retrieved from https://www.rayyan.ai/

Redmond, P. (2019). A pedagogical continuum: The journey from traditional classroom to blended learning. *Australasian Journal of Educational Technology*, *35*(6), 1–14.

Risko, E., & Gilbert, S. J. (2016). Cognitive offloading. *Trends in Cognitive Sciences*, *20*(9), 676–688. DOI: 10.1016/j.tics.2016.07.002 PMID: 27542527

Robles, H., Burden, K., & Villalba, K. (2021). A socio-cultural approach to evaluating and designing reading comprehension apps for language learning. [IJMBL]. *International Journal of Mobile and Blended Learning*, *13*(1), 1–21. DOI: 10.4018/IJMBL.2021010102

Rosenfield, M. (2016). Computer vision syndrome (a.k.a. digital eye strain). *Optometry in Practice*, *17*(1), 1–10.

Rosen, L. D., Carrier, L. M., & Cheever, N. A. (2013). Facebook and Relational Violence Among College Students. *Journal of Social and Clinical Psychology*, *32*(5), 462–479.

Rosen, L. D., Lim, A. F., Carrier, L. M., & Cheever, N. A. (2011). An empirical examination of the educational impact of text message-induced task switching in the classroom. *Computers in Human Behavior*, *27*(3), 937–948.

Roski, M., Sebastian, R., Ewerth, R., Hoppe, A., & Nehring, A. (2024). Learning analytics and the Universal Design for Learning (UDL): A clustering approach. [sciencedirect.com]. *Computers & Education*, *214*, 105028. DOI: 10.1016/j.compedu.2024.105028

Roth Soracco, C. I., Valenzuela Hasenohr, F., & Orellana, P. (2020). Experience in the Use of a Digital Platform for the Practice of Reading Comprehension and Vocabulary: Perception of Elementary School Students.

Rowland, D. R. (2023). Two frameworks to guide discussions around levels of acceptable use of generative AI in learner academic research and writing. *Journal of Academic Language and Learning*, *17*(1), T31–T69.

Ryan, R. M., & Deci, E. L. (2021). *Self-determination theory: Basic psychological needs in motivation, development, and wellness*. Guilford Press.

Saavedra, A. R., & Opfer, V. D. (2012). Learning 21st-Century Skills Requires 21st-Century Teaching. *Phi Delta Kappan*, *94*(2), 8–13. DOI: 10.1177/003172171209400203

Sahlberg, P. (2011). The Finnish education system: A success story. In *Finnish lessons: What can the world learn from educational change in Finland?* Teachers College Press.

Salas-Pilco, S. Z., Yang, Y., & Zhang, Z. (2022). Student engagement in online learning in Latin American higher education during the COVID-19 pandemic: A systematic review. [wiley.com]. *British Journal of Educational Technology*, *53*(3), 593–619. DOI: 10.1111/bjet.13190 PMID: 35600418

Salmon, G. (2013). *E-tivities: The key to active online learning* (2nd ed.). Routledge. DOI: 10.4324/9780203074640

Salovey, P., & Mayer, J. D. (1990). Emotional intelligence. *Imagination, Cognition and Personality*, *9*(3), 185–211. DOI: 10.2190/DUGG-P24E-52WK-6CDG

Samarakoon, B., Muthugala, V., Jayasekara, B., & Mohan, R. E. (2022). Adapting approaching proxemics of a service robot based on physical user behavior and user feedback. *User Modeling and User-Adapted Interaction*, *33*(2), 195–220. Advance online publication. DOI: 10.1007/s11257-022-09329-8

Sandoval, M., Muñoz, Y., & Márquez, C. (2021). Supporting schools in their journey to inclusive education: Review of guides and tools. Support for Learning. wiley.com

Sarkar, S., Mohapatra, S., & Sundarakrishnan, J. (2017). Assessing impact of technology based digital equalizer programme on improving student learning outcomes. *Education and Information Technologies*, *22*(1), 195–213. https://doi.org/https://doi.org/10.1007/s10639-015-9434-0

Satratzemi, M. (2019). Voice Assistants and Artificial Intelligence in Education. BCI'19: Proceedings of the 9th Balkan Conference on Informatics. Article No.: 34, Pages 1 - 6. DOI: 10.1145/3351556.3351588

Schunk, D. H. (2012). *Learning theories: An educational perspective* (6th ed.). Pearson.

Schunk, D. H., Pintrich, P. R., & Meece, J. L. (2008). Motivation and learning. In *Motivation and learning: Theory and research* (pp. 212–248). Pearson.

Seaborn, K., & Fels, D. I. (2015). Gamification in theory and action: A survey. *International Journal of Human-Computer Studies*, *74*, 14–31. DOI: 10.1016/j.ijhcs.2014.09.006

Selfa-Sastre, M., Pifarré, M., Cujba, A., Cutillas, L., & Falguera, E. (2022). The role of digital technologies to promote collaborative creativity in language education. [frontiersin.org]. *Frontiers in Psychology, 13*, 828981. DOI: 10.3389/fpsyg.2022.828981 PMID: 35222209

Selwyn, N. (2016). *Education and technology: Key issues and debates*. Bloomsbury Publishing.

Selwyn, N. (2020). Digital division: Equity and access in higher education. *British Journal of Educational Technology, 51*(2), 589–604.

Seufert, S., Burkhard, M., & Handschuh, S. (2021, November). Fostering Learners' Academic Writing Skills: Feedback Model for an AI-enabled Support Environment. In *Innovate Learning Summit* (pp. 49-58). Association for the Advancement of Computing in Education (AACE).

Sheninger, E. (2014). *Digital leadership: Changing paradigms for changing times*. Corwin Press.

Sheppard, A. L., & Wolffsohn, J. S. (2018). Digital eye strain: Prevalence, measurement, and amelioration. *BMJ Open Ophthalmology, 3*(1), e000146. DOI: 10.1136/bmjophth-2018-000146 PMID: 29963645

Sherukhammadov, S., Wang, J., & Li, Y. (2023). Teaching and Assessing Thinking Skills and Applying Educational Technology in Science and Engineering Education. *Journal of Science Education and Technology, 32*(1), 1–10.

Shivam, R., & Singh, S. (2015). Implementation of Blended Learning in Classroom: A review paper. International Journal of Scientific and Research Publications, Volume 5, Issue 11, November 2015 369 ISSN 2250-3153

Shofiah, N., Putera, Z. F., & Solichah, N. (2023, December). Challenges and opportunities in the use of artificial intelligence in education for academic writing: A scoping review. In *Conference Psychology and Flourishing Humanity (PFH 2023)* (pp. 174-193). Atlantis Press. DOI: 10.2991/978-2-38476-188-3_20

Shorey, S., Chan, V., Rajendran, P., & Ang, E. (2021). Learning styles, preferences and needs of generation Z healthcare students: Scoping review. [HTML]. *Nurse Education in Practice, 57*, 103247. DOI: 10.1016/j.nepr.2021.103247 PMID: 34768214

Shoukat, M. U., Yan, L., Zhang, J., Cheng, Y., Raza, M. U., & Niaz, A. (2024). Smart home for enhanced healthcare: Exploring human machine interface oriented digital twin model. *Multimedia Tools and Applications, 83*(11), 31297–31315. DOI: 10.1007/s11042-023-16875-9

Shukor, A. A., Osman, Z., & Abdullah, M. H. (2022). Innovative tools in education: Exploring the impact of Classkick on student learning. *International Journal of Educational Research*, *56*(2), 67–79. DOI: 10.1016/ijedres.2022.03.004

Sidhu, M. S., Mousakhani, S., Lee, C. K., & Sidhu, K. K. (2024). Educational impact of Metaverse learning environment for engineering mechanics dynamics. [HTML]. *Computer Applications in Engineering Education*, *32*(5), e22772. DOI: 10.1002/cae.22772

Siemens, G., & Long, P. (2011). Penetrating the Fog: Analytics in Learning and Education. *EDUCAUSE Review*, *46*(5), 30–32.

Simelane-Mnisi, S., & Mji, A. (2020). COVID-19 pandemic: Opportunities for online learning to unblock the minds of students during the lockdown period. *Education and New Learning Technologies Virtual Conference (EDULEARN '20)*, (pp. 6-7). Spain. DOI: 10.21125/edulearn.2020.2124

Simpson, P., & Jenkins, P. (2019). Gamification and Human Resources: an overview.

Singh, A. (2020). Critical thinking and problem-solving in flipped classrooms: The role of interactive tools. *Journal of Educational Innovation*, *45*(2), 243–259. DOI: 10.1016/j.jei.2020.10.004

Singh, E., Vasishta, P., & Singla, A. (2024). AI-enhanced education: Exploring the impact of AI literacy on generation Z's academic performance in Northern India. *Quality Assurance in Education*. Advance online publication. DOI: 10.1108/QAE-02-2024-0037

Sinthiya, B. (2023). English Language Learning in the Metaverse: Exploring the Potential of AR and VR. *Shanlax International Journal of English, 12*(S1-Dec), 161–166. DOI: 10.34293/rtdh.v12iS1-Dec.52

Skulmowski, A. & Xu, K. M. (2022). Understanding cognitive load in digital and online learning: A new perspective on extraneous cognitive load. Educational psychology review. springer.com

Smith, D., Leonis, T., & Anandavalli, S. (2021). Belonging and loneliness in cyberspace: Impacts of social media on adolescents' well-being. [tandfonline.com]. *Australian Journal of Psychology*, *73*(1), 12–23. DOI: 10.1080/00049530.2021.1898914

Smith, E., & Brown, D. (2021). Generating Better Evidence on Ed Tech. *Educational Leadership*, *78*(8).

Smith, K., & Tillema, H. (2001). Long-Term Influences of Portfolios on Professional Development Scandinavian Journal of Educational Research 45 (2): 183–203. *Scandinavian Journal of Educational Research, 45*(2), 183–203. DOI: 10.1080/00313830120052750

Stadler, M., Bannert, M., & Sailer, M. (2024). Cognitive ease at a cost: LLMs reduce mental effort but compromise depth in student scientific inquiry. *Computers in Human Behavior, 160*, 108386. Advance online publication. DOI: 10.1016/j.chb.2024.108386

Staker, H., & Horn, M. B. (2012). *Classifying K–12 blended learning*. In *Innosight Institute*.

Staker, H., & Horn, M. B. (2012). *Classifying K-12 blended learning*. Innosight Institute.

Stone, M., & Machtynger, L. (2020). Artificial intelligence (AI) in strategic marketing decision-making: A research agenda. *The Bottom Line (New York, N.Y.), 33*(2), 183–200. DOI: 10.1108/BL-03-2020-0022

Strielkowski, W., Grebennikova, V., Lisovskiy, A., Rakhimova, G., & Vasileva, T. (2024). AI-driven adaptive learning for sustainable educational transformation. Sustainable Development. wiley.com

Su, F., & Zou, D. (2022). Technology-enhanced collaborative language learning: Theoretical foundations, technologies, and implications. [HTML]. *Computer Assisted Language Learning, 35*(8), 1754–1788. DOI: 10.1080/09588221.2020.1831545

Sugino, C. (2021). Student perceptions of a synchronous online cooperative learning course in a Japanese women's university during the COVID-19 pandemic. Education Sciences. mdpi.com

Sukmawati, I., & Pujiani, I. (2023). Interactive learning environments: How Classkick fosters student-teacher interaction. *Journal of Online Learning and Teaching, 21*(2), 77–89. DOI: 10.2043/jolt.2023.213

Sung, Y. T., Chang, K. E., & Yang, J. M. (2020). How can collaborative learning be enhanced in digital environments? *Educational Technology Research and Development, 68*(2), 147–162.

Sun, Y. (2024). Classkick in the flipped classroom: Improving student participation and learning outcomes. *International Journal of Educational Technology, 45*(1), 33–45. DOI: 10.1016/j.ijet.2023.04.001

Suriano, R., Plebe, A., Acciai, A., & Fabio, R. (2025). Student interaction with ChatGPT can promote complex critical thinking skills. *Learning and Instruction*, *95*, 102011. Advance online publication. DOI: 10.1016/j.learninstruc.2024.102011

Sviridova, E., Yastrebova, E., Bakirova, G., & Rebrina, F. (2023). Immersive technologies as an innovative tool to increase academic success and motivation in higher education. *Frontiers in Education*, *8*(October), 1–10. DOI: 10.3389/feduc.2023.1192760

Swallow, M. J., & Olofson, M. W. (2017). (2017). Contextual understandings in the TPACK framework. *Journal of Research on Technology in Education, 49(3-4), 228-244.*, *49*(3–4), 228–244. https://doi.org/https://doi.org/10.1080/15391523.2017.1347537

Szymkowiak, A., Melović, B., Dabić, M., Jeganathan, K., & Kundi, G. S. (2021). Information technology and Gen Z: The role of teachers, the internet, and technology in the education of young people. [HTML]. *Technology in Society*, *65*, 101565. DOI: 10.1016/j.techsoc.2021.101565

Taghizadeh, M., & Hajhosseini, F. (2021). Investigating a Blended Learning Environment: Contribution of Attitude, Interaction, and Quality of Teaching to Satisfaction of Graduate Students of TEFL. *The Asia-Pacific Education Researcher*, *30*(5), 459–469. DOI: 10.1007/s40299-020-00531-z

Taheri, A. (2023). Impacts of socially assistive robots on improving the quality of life in children with autism.

Tan, Y., Xu, W., Li, S., & Chen, K. (2022). Augmented and Virtual Reality (AR/VR) for Education and Training in the AEC Industry: A Systematic Review of Research and Applications. In *Buildings* (Vol. 12, Issue 10). DOI: 10.3390/buildings12101529

Tan, C. (2021). The impact of COVID-19 on education in Singapore: A blended learning perspective. *International Review of Education*, *67*(3), 443–462.

Tang, T., Sha, J., Zhao, Y., Wang, S., Wang, Z., & Shen, S. (2024). Unveiling the efficacy of ChatGPT in evaluating critical thinking skills through peer feedback analysis: Leveraging existing classification criteria. *Thinking Skills and Creativity*, *53*, 101607. Advance online publication. DOI: 10.1016/j.tsc.2024.101607

Tang, Y., & Hew, K. F. (2022). Effects of using mobile instant messaging on student behavioral, emotional, and cognitive engagement: A quasi-experimental study. [springer.com]. *International Journal of Educational Technology in Higher Education*, *19*(1), 3. DOI: 10.1186/s41239-021-00306-6 PMID: 35036520

Tariq, M. U. (2024). Equity and Inclusion in Learning Ecosystems. In Preparing Students for the Future Educational Paradigm (pp. 155-176). IGI Global. [HTML] DOI: 10.4018/979-8-3693-1536-1.ch007

Tate, T. & Warschauer, M. (2022). Equity in online learning. Educational Psychologist. tandfonline.com

The Learning Center. (n.d.). Higher order thinking: Bloom's Taxonomy. University of North Carolina at Chapel Hill. Retrieved from https://learningcenter.unc.edu/tips-and-tools/higher-order-thinking/

Toktarova, V. I., & Semenova, D. A. (2020). Digital pedagogy: Analysis, requirements and experience of implementation. *Journal of Physics: Conference Series*, *1691*(1), 012112. DOI: 10.1088/1742-6596/1691/1/012112

Tran, T. A., & Daim, T. (2008). A taxonomic review of methods and tools applied in technology assessment. *Technological Forecasting and Social Change*, *75*(9), 1396–1405. DOI: 10.1016/j.techfore.2008.04.004

Trinidad, S., & Ngo, T. (2019). The impact of student-centred digital tools on educational outcomes. *International Journal of Educational Technology*, *35*(1), 112–126. DOI: 10.1080/ijedtech.2019.10456

Trust, T., Woodruff, N., Checrallah, M., & Whalen, J. (2021). Educators' Interests, Prior Knowledge and Questions Regarding Augmented Reality, Virtual Reality and 3D Printing and Modeling. *TechTrends*, *65*(4), 548–561. DOI: 10.1007/s11528-021-00594-9

Tucker, B. (2012). The flipped classroom: Online instruction at home frees class time for learning. *Education Next*, *12*(1).

Tuyiragize, R., & Bassi, F. (2023). Assessment of household energy utilization patterns in Uganda: A latent class analysis. *Journal of Tropical Futures: Sustainable Business, Governance & Development*, *1*(1), 56–82. Advance online publication. DOI: 10.1177/27538931231182231

Twenge, J. M. (2018). *iGen: Why Today's Super-Connected Kids Are Growing Up Less Rebellious, More Tolerant, Less Happy—and Completely Unprepared for Adulthood*. New York, NY: Atria Books.

Tynjälä, P. (1999). Towards expert knowledge? A comparison between a constructivist and a traditional learning environment. *Learning and Instruction*, *9*(2), 137–156.

U.S. Department of Education. (2020). *Technology in Education: Enhancing Learning Outcomes with Digital Tools.*

Ugalde, L., Santiago-Garabieta, M., Villarejo, B., & Puigvert, L. (2021). Impact of Interactive Learning Environments on Learning and Cognitive Development of Children With Special Educational Needs: A Literature Review. *Frontiers in Psychology*, *12*, 674033. DOI: 10.3389/fpsyg.2021.674033 PMID: 33995231

Ulmane-Ozolina, L., Jansone, A., Magazeina, I., & Barute, D. (2019, June). Technology Enhanced Learning in Tteachers' Professional Development. *Periodicals of Engineering and Natural Sciences*, *7*(1), 216–221. DOI: 10.21533/pen.v7i1.400

Uymaz, P., & Uymaz, A. O. (2022). Assessing acceptance of augmented reality in nursing education. *PLoS One*, *17*(2), 1–20. DOI: 10.1371/journal.pone.0263937 PMID: 35176073

Väätäjä, J. O., & Ruokamo, H. (2021). Conceptualizing dimensions and a model for digital pedagogy. *Journal of Pacific Rim Psychology*, *15*, 1834490921995395. DOI: 10.1177/1834490921995395

Valero-Franco, C., & Berns, A. (2024). Development of virtual and augmented reality apps for language teaching: a case study | Desarrollo de apps de realidad virtual y aumentada para enseñanza de idiomas: un estudio de caso. *RIED-Revista Iberoamericana de Educacion a Distancia*, *27*(1), 163–185. . DOI: 10.5944/ried.27.1.37668

Van Deursen, A. J. A. M., & Van Dijk, J. A. G. M. (2014). Internet Skills and the Digital Divide. *New Media & Society*, *16*(3), 404–422.

van Dijk, J. A. G. M. (2020). *The digital divide*. Polity Press.

Van Niekerk, J., Delport, P. M., & Sutherland, I. (2025). Addressing the use of generative AI in academic writing. *Computers and Education: Artificial Intelligence*, *8*, 100342. DOI: 10.1016/j.caeai.2024.100342

Vartiainen, H., & Tedre, M. (2024). "ChatGPT and imaginaries of the future of education: insights of Finnish teacher educators, *Information and Learning Sciences*, Vol. ahead-of-print No. ahead-of-print. DOI: 10.1108/ILS-10-2023-0146

Vaughan, N., Cleveland-Innes, M., & Garrison, D. R. (2013). *Teaching in blended learning environments: Creating and sustaining communities of inquiry*. Athabasca University Press. DOI: 10.15215/aupress/9781927356470.01

Vetrivel, S. C., Arun, V. P., Maheswari, R., & Saravanan, T. P. (2024). Technology integration in online learning platforms: Blended learning gamification. In Transdisciplinary Teaching and Technological Integration for Improved Learning: Case Studies and Practical Approaches (pp. 219-247). IGI Global. [HTML]

Villegas-Reimers, E. (2003). Teacher Professional Development: An international Review of the Literature. Retrieved from https://unesdoc.unesco.org/images/0013/001330/133010e.pdf

Voogt, J., Fisser, P., Pareja Roblin, N., Tondeur, J., & van Braak, J. (2017). Technological pedagogical content knowledge–A review of the literature. *Computers & Education, 59*(3), 0-204.

Vuorikari, R., Punie, Y., Carretero, S., & Van den Brande, G. (2019). *DigCompEdu: The Digital Competence Framework for Educators*. Publications Office of the European Union.

Vygotsky, L. S. (1978). *Mind in Society: The Development of Higher Psychological Processes*. Harvard University Press.

Wagner, P., & Alharthi, D. (2023). Leveraging VR/AR/MR/XR Technologies to Improve Cybersecurity Education, Training, and Operations. *Journal of Cybersecurity Education Research and Practice*, *2024*(1), 1–26. DOI: 10.32727/8.2023.32

Wahn, B., Schmitz, L., Gerster, F., & Weis, M. (2023). Offloading under cognitive load: Humans are willing to offload parts of an attentionally demanding task to an algorithm. *PLoS One*, *18*(5), e0286102. Advance online publication. DOI: 10.1371/journal.pone.0286102 PMID: 37205658

Wai, C. C., & Seng, E. L. K. (2015). Measuring the effectiveness of blended learning environment: A case study in Malaysia. *Education and Information Technologies*, *20*(3), 429–443. DOI: 10.1007/s10639-013-9293-5

Wang, A. I., & Tahir, R. (2020). The effect of using Kahoot! for learning – A literature review. *Computers & Education*, *149*, 103818. DOI: 10.1016/j.compedu.2020.103818

Wang, J., Tang, Y., Hare, R., & Wang, F.-Y. (2024). Parallel intelligent education with ChatGPT. *Frontiers of Information Technology & Electronic Engineering*, *25*(1), 12–18. DOI: 10.1631/FITEE.2300166

Wang, T., Lund, B. D., Marengo, A., Pagano, A., Mannuru, N. R., Teel, Z. A., & Pange, J. (2023). Exploring the potential impact of artificial intelligence (AI) on international students in higher education: Generative AI, chatbots, analytics, and international student success. [mdpi.com]. *Applied Sciences (Basel, Switzerland)*, *13*(11), 6716. DOI: 10.3390/app13116716

Wang, Y. H. (2016). Promoting contextual vocabulary learning through an adaptive computer-assisted EFL reading system. *Journal of Computer Assisted Learning*, *32*(4), 291–303. DOI: 10.1111/jcal.12132

Wang, Z., Boulton, M., & Zhang, D. (2020). Impact of digital media on learning and cognitive development. *Educational Technology Research and Development, 68*(3), 931–948.

Warschauer, M. (2003). *Technology and social inclusion: Rethinking the digital divide.* MIT Press. DOI: 10.7551/mitpress/6699.001.0001

Wei, L. (2022). Translanguaging as a political stance: Implications for English language education. ELT journal. oup.com

West, R. E. (2012). Data Literacy for Educators: Making it Count in the Classroom

West, D. M. (2012). *Big data for education: Data mining, data analytics, and web dashboards.* Governance Studies at Brookings.

Wiggins, G., & McTighe, J. (2005). *Understanding by design.* ASCD.

Wilkens, U. (2020). Artificial intelligence in the workplace - A double-edged sword. *International Journal of Information and Learning Technology, 37*(5), 253–265. DOI: 10.1108/IJILT-02-2020-0022

Xu, B. (2024). Mediating role of academic self-efficacy and academic emotions in the relationship between teacher support and academic achievement. Scientific Reports. nature.com

Yadav, N., Gupta, K., & Khetrapal, V. (2018). Next education: Technology transforming education. *South Asian J. Bus. Manage, 14*(1), 68–77. DOI: 10.1177/2277977918754443

Yang, C. (2021). Online teaching self-efficacy, social–emotional learning (SEL) competencies, and compassion fatigue among educators during the COVID-19 pandemic. [HTML]. *School Psychology Review, 50*(4), 505–518. DOI: 10.1080/2372966X.2021.1903815

Yang, J., Huang, R., & Li, Y. (2013). *Optimizing Classroom Environment to Support Technology Enhanced Learning.*, DOI: 10.1007/978-3-642-39146-0_24

Yang, S. J., Ogata, H., Matsui, T., & Chen, N. S. (2021). Human-centered artificial intelligence in education: Seeing the invisible through the visible. [sciencedirect.com]. *Computers and Education: Artificial Intelligence, 2*, 100008.

Yaqoubi, T., Mohammadi, Z., & Golzar, J. (2022). An analysis of Universal Design for Learning at collegial level: Effective ways to maximise learning outcomes, inclusion, and equity. [HTML]. *Research in Post-Compulsory Education, 27*(4), 594–621. DOI: 10.1080/13596748.2022.2110775

Yu, H. (2024). The application and challenges of ChatGPT in educational transformation: New demands for teachers' roles. Heliyon. cell.com

Yurtseven Avci, Z., O'Dwyer, L. M., & Lawson, J. (2020). Designing effective professional development for technology integration in schools. *Journal of Computer Assisted Learning*, *36*(2), 160–177. https://doi.org/https://doi.org/10.1111/jcal.12394. DOI: 10.1111/jcal.12394

Zaka, P. (2013). Blended learning in New Zealand schools: Current state and future directions. *Journal of Open, Flexible, and Distance Learning*, *17*(1), 41–58.

Zaphir, L., & Hansen, D. (2024). The trouble with Bloom's taxonomy in an age of AI. *Times Higher Education*. Retrieved from https://www.timeshighereducation.com/campus/trouble-blooms-taxonomy-age-ai

Zawacki-Richter, O., Marín, V. I., & Bond, M. (2019). Systematic review of research on blended learning in higher education. *International Journal of Educational Technology in Higher Education*, *16*(1), 8.

Zeichner, K., & Tabachnick, B. (1999). Participatory Development and Teacher Education Reform in Namibia. In *Democratic Teachers Education Reform in Namibia*. Routledge.

Zengilowski, A., Lee, J., Gaines, R. E., Park, H., Choi, E., & Schallert, D. L. (2023). The collective classroom "we": The role of students' sense of belonging on their affective, cognitive, and discourse experiences of online and face-to-face discussions. [sciencedirect.com]. *Linguistics and Education*, *73*, 101142. DOI: 10.1016/j.linged.2022.101142

Zhai, C., Wibowo, S., & Li, L. (2024). *The effects of over-reliance on AI dialogue systems on students' cognitive abilities: a systematic review*. Smart Learning Environments., DOI: 10.1186/s40561-024-00316-7

Zhai, N., & Ma, X. (2021). Automated writing evaluation (AWE) feedback: A systematic investigation of college students' acceptance. *Computer Assisted Language Learning*, *34*(5–6), 618–644. DOI: 10.1080/09588221.2019.1617743

Zhang, X., Shi, Y., & Bai, H. (2021). Immersive Virtual Reality Physical Education Instructional Patterns on the Foundation of Vision Sensor. In *Journal of Sensors* (Vol. 2021). DOI: 10.1155/2021/7752447

Zhang, J., Li, G., Huang, Q., Feng, Q., & Luo, H. (2022). Augmented Reality in K–12 Education: A Systematic Review and Meta-Analysis of the Literature from 2000 to 2020. *Sustainability (Basel)*, *14*(15), 9725. Advance online publication. DOI: 10.3390/su14159725

Zhang, W. (2022). The Role of Technology-Based Education and Teacher Professional Development in English as a Foreign Language Classes. *Frontiers in Psychology*, *13*, 910315. Advance online publication. DOI: 10.3389/fpsyg.2022.910315 PMID: 35756284

Zheng, F. (2022). Fostering students' well-being: The mediating role of teacher interpersonal behavior and student-teacher relationships. Frontiers in Psychology. frontiersin.org

Zimmerman, B. J. (2002). Becoming a self-regulated learner: An overview. *Theory into Practice*, *41*(2), 64–70. DOI: 10.1207/s15430421tip4102_2

Zort, Ç, Karabacak, E., Öznur, Ş, & Dağlı, G. (2023). Sharing of cultural values and heritage through storytelling in the digital age. Frontiers in Psychology. frontiersin.org

About the Contributors

Mohammed H. Alaqad is a distinguished associate professor and researcher specializing in translation studies and applied linguistics, with over a decade of academic experience. He currently serves as a postdoctoral research fellow at the Hashim Sani Centre for Palestine Studies, University of Malaya. Dr. Alaqad has been an invited speaker and presenter at over 40 international conferences and events. He has published numerous scientific papers and book chapters globally and has authored several articles and a book chapter on Palestinians in the diaspora. Additionally, he serves on the editorial boards of the Cambridge Scholars of Language & Linguistics in the UK and the International Journal of Applied Linguistics and Translation (IJALT) in the USA. He is the founder and CEO of the Asian Federation of Translators and Interpreters, Malaysia. His research interests include applied linguistics, education technology, and translation.

Ghadah Al Murshidi, an Associate Professor in the curriculum and instruction department at the College of Education, previously served in the Humanities and Social Sciences college at UAE University. Recognized for her academic and community contributions, she has received accolades including the Young Emirati Researcher Prize, the best Young Researcher award, and the Emirati Women's Award. Notably, she was honored as the best academic woman achiever and was the first doctoral holder to voluntarily join the National Service. Engaging in various leadership programs, she participated in the 50th Leaders' Program and the Fatima Bint Mubarak Program for Political Empowerment. Her research focuses extensively on language, literacy, Emiratization issues, service learning, and educational technology, with a particular interest in mobile, blended, online, and virtual learning across different educational contexts. Dr. Al Murshidi's contributions extend beyond academia. She authored "The Guide of Creativity and Innovation in the UAE," receiving recognition from His Highness Sheikh Hamad bin Mohammed Al Sharqi. Leading national research projects funded by institutions like the UAE

University - National Research Foundation and participating as an Emirati expert in international endeavors, she is deeply involved in shaping educational discourse. Additionally, she actively shares her insights through various media platforms and serves on the editorial boards of Scopus journals. Her engagements in TV shows and conferences, both nationally and internationally, further underscore her commitment to advancing educational and social dialogue.

Abdesselam Bougdira holds a PhD in Engineering Sciences, with over 15 years of experience in academia and professional work, including four years in research and innovation. His expertise spans artificial intelligence, systems engineering, soft computing, and computer science, with a focus on intelligent systems and digital transformation. His work and research focus on AI applications in education, Industry 4.0, and healthcare systems.

Badria Almurshidi is a Clinical Scientist and assistant professor, Field of expertise Nanotechnology in medicine and Environmental Health and Toxicology. One of the outstanding researchers in University of South Carolina 2019 in the field of Nanomedicine and winner of the first research prize in the Rare genetic diseases conference in 2024. Worked as specialist in forensic medicine at branch of Paternity and disaster victim identification for 2 years

Ahmed Al Zaabi is an Emirati academic currently pursuing his PhD at Universiti Utara Malaysia, focusing on business management and strategic leadership. He holds a Master's in Strategic Management from Dubai Men's College, Higher Colleges of Technology, UAE, where he graduated with distinction. Additionally, he earned a Master's in International Business Administration from the University of Wollongong, Dubai, enhancing his expertise in global business strategies. As a researcher, Dr. Al Zaabi has published papers such as "The Effect of E-Learning Training Program on Organizational Performance Through Underlying Mechanisms of Capacity Building of Dubai Police Force," "Do Job Performance Mediates between E-Learning Training Program and Organizational Performance: A Case of Dubai Police Force," and others. He has completed many specialized courses across various fields, focusing on administrative and security-related disciplines. His blend of advanced academic qualifications and practical experience positions him as a knowledgeable and skilled professional in strategic management, business administration, and organizational performance, making impactful contributions to the field.

***

Noor Aisha is a decennary experienced professional, serving in Basic Education Department, Governmentof Uttar Pradesh, India. She has completed her doctorate in Educational Technology and Instructional Design from Indira Gandhi National Open University, New Delhi, (India). Her teaching philosophy is to impart education while fulfilling the student's specific learning needs and realizing teachers' crucial role in a technology enabled learning environment. Her sincere efforts have always been in the direction to harmonize theory and practice in the process of teaching and learning.

Alimin Alwi, S.Sos., M.Pd, is a distinguished academic in the field of Sociology, currently serving as a lecturer at Universitas Negeri Makassar. Born on July 14, 1989, in Balobuea, Indonesia, he has pursued an extensive educational journey culminating in a Ph.D. in Sociology, which he obtained in 2022. His academic credentials are bolstered by a solid foundation in Sociology from Universitas Dayanu Ikhsanuddin Baubau and a Master's degree in Educational Sociology from Universitas Halu Oleo. Dr. Alwi's professional experience is diverse, encompassing roles in education, journalism, and community service. He has held significant positions, including as an administrative staff member at Universitas Halu Oleo and as a non-permanent lecturer. His involvement in various research projects and community engagement initiatives underscores his commitment to social development, particularly in environmental and educational contexts. His scholarly contributions include several publications in national and international journals, alongside a book focused on multicultural social integration from a constructivist perspective. Dr. Alwi is also actively engaged in training programs aimed at enhancing academic writing and research skills among students. His dedication to both education and community service positions him as a key figure in the sociological landscape of Indonesia.

Andi Asrifan is an accomplished educator and academic leader with a Doctorate in Education, specializing in English Language Education from Universitas Negeri Makassar. With a strong academic foundation, he holds a Master's degree in the same field and a Bachelor's degree in Secondary Education. His dissertation focused on developing bilingual educational materials, reflecting his commitment to enhancing language education. Dr. Asrifan has extensive experience in various educational roles, including serving as the Head of the International Affairs Office at Politeknik Negeri Nunukan and as the Head of the Institute for Student Development and Alumni at Universitas Muhammadiyah Sidenreng Rappang. He is also an active member of several professional organizations, including the Linguistics Society of Indonesia and TEFLIN. In addition to his administrative roles, Dr. Asrifan is a passionate advocate for educational innovation and has participated in numerous international conferences and webinars, sharing his insights on language teaching and curriculum development. His dedication to professional development is evident through his participation in various training programs.

Lalithabala Boopathi is currently working as an Assistant Professor in the Department of Education at SASTRA University, Thanjavur. She holds a master's degree from Annamalai University. He holds a doctorate from the Tamil University, Thanjavur. She is also trained in Tamil. She passed the National Eligibility Test for college professors.

Hasan Ali Almulla is an English language educator and researcher in Teaching English as a Foreign Language (TEFL), currently pursuing a Master's degree at the Arab Open University. With a solid foundation in Education from Bahrain Teachers College, Hasan has developed a robust research interest in the intersection of digital tools and language acquisition, with particular focus on enhancing speaking fluency in EFL contexts. Hasan integrates differentiated instruction and technology-enhanced learning to support diverse language proficiency levels. As an administrative supervisor, he ensures the implementation of effective teaching strategies and educational policies that align with the goals of the Bahraini education system.

Devaki V. serves as an Assistant Professor at the School of Education, SASTRA Deemed to be University, Thanjavur. She holds Master of Science in Physics from Alagappa University, Karaikudi, graduating with the distinction of second rank in university. Additionally, she completed Master of Education at Sri Sarada College of Education, Salem, Tamil Nadu. She qualified for the position of Assistant Professor in Physics, having successfully cleared the Tamil Nadu State Eligibility Test and also passed in the Central Teacher Eligibility Test. She is currently pursuing her doctoral studies in the Department of Education at Bharathidasan University, Tiruchirappalli. Her research interests encompass metacognition, neurocognition, the pedagogy of science, and experiential learning.

Aliasghar Rahman Doust is an Assistant professor at IUC, Iran; experienced in teaching research methodology, descriptive and inferential statistical methods, and teaching methodology. He has acquired Ph.D. in assessment and measurement in education, from Jamia Millia Islamia, New Delhi, India. Using the DINA model, he had worked on cognitive diagnostic modeling (CDM) approaches to analyze mathematical skills, and has an expertise in quantitative and qualitative research designs as well as in handling various dat analysis softwares. His expertise also include data analysis and research methodology consultations and workshops.

Suryadi Ishak, S.Pd., M.Pd., is a distinguished academic and educator specializing in the field of mathematics education. He obtained his Bachelor's degree in Mathematics Education from Universitas Al Asyariah Mandar, followed by a Master's degree from Universitas Negeri Makassar, and a Doctorate in Educational Research and Evaluation from Universitas Negeri Yogyakarta. His extensive educational background equips him with a robust foundation in pedagogical theories and practices. Dr. Suryadi's research primarily focuses on the development of competency assessment instruments for mathematics teachers, utilizing Generalisability Theory to enhance the validity and reliability of these assessments. His scholarly contributions are reflected in various publications, including his notable work on improving mathematical reasoning through problem-based learning models. In addition to his research, Dr. Suryadi actively participates in non-formal education, conducting seminars and training sessions aimed at enhancing educators' skills in assessment and pedagogy. He has collaborated with various educational institutions and government bodies, contributing to initiatives that promote effective teaching practices and educational reform. His commitment to advancing education is further demonstrated through his role as a national facilitator and consultant in educational programs, where he provides guidance and support to school leaders and educators. Dr. Suryadi Ishak's dedication to enhancing the quality of education positions him as a key figure in the field of mathematics and physics education in Indonesia.

Richa Kapoor Mehra is working as an Associate Professor of Philosophy and Area chair of Social Sciences and Humanities (SSH) at O.P Jindal Global University, India, she has earned her PhD in Philosophy from Jawaharlal Nehru University, Delhi. While pursuing PhD, she was recipient of Junior Research Fellowship from prestigious Indian Council of Philosophical Research (ICPR). She has completed Masters and bachelor's in philosophy from Miranda House, University of Delhi. She was awarded with Miranda House award and Delhi University rankers prize for scoring highest marks in bachelor's program. She has also worked at Miranda House, University of Delhi, Amity University, Noida, B.M.L Munjal University and IIIT Kalyani. Recently she has designed a course on Critical Thinking and Analysis for undergraduate business students at O.P Jindal Business School. Dr. Mehra has launched the department of philosophy at Amity University, Noida and hence designed various philosophy course for undergraduate students. She has been awarded with the Excellent Academician Award, in an International Conference organized by University of Sri Jayewardenepura, Sri Lanka. She has presented several research

Pawan Pant is working as an Assistant Professor of Management at the University School of Business, Chandigarh University, Mohali, Punjab. He has published two research papers, one national and one international journal. He has

10 years of teaching experience and worked as an Assistant Manager (Purchase) at Pacific Industries Ltd., Udaipur (Rajasthan) for one year. His area of specialization is Economics. email: pawanpant04@gmail.com.

Sidharth. S. Raju is an Associate Professor and HOD of Hotel Management at Vivekananda Global University, Jaipur, specializing in Food & B Service. He is holding PhD and M Phil, with 11 years of teaching and 10 years industry experience, he has published 13 research papers, 6 patents, and 3 books. Additionally. .He is Editor in many Scopus and Elsevier Indexed Journal and member of many professional chapters.

Deepa Sharma has done Ph.D., MBA in Human Resource Management, currently working as Assistant Professor at MMIM, Maharishi Markandeshwar (Deemed to be University), NAAC Accredited Grade 'A++' University, Mullana, Ambala (Haryana). She has more than 9 years of experience in academics. She has written 61+ research papers for various Scopus and UGC listed referred National & International Journals and 13 papers appear on SCOPUS Preview.

Suresh Chinna received a PhD degree in Education from the Sri Venkateswara University, Tirupati, Andhra Pradesh, India, in 2018 and has an M.Sc. degree in Mathematics from Sri Krinshnadevaraya University, Anantapur, Andhra Pradesh, India, in 2010 and a. He works as an Assistant Professor at the Department of Education, School of Arts, Humanities, Sciences and Education, SASTRA Deemed to be University, Thanjavur, Tamilnadu-613401. His research interests include ICT in Education, Mathematics Pedagogy, Gender Studies, and Teaching Strategies, and he has published a good number of articles in a reputed Scopus-indexed Web of Sciences journals.

Fathullah Wajdi, M.Pd, is an esteemed academic with a comprehensive background in Indonesian Language Education. Born on April 10, 1978, in Serang, Indonesia, he has dedicated over two decades to the field of education, beginning his career as a teacher in 2001. He holds a Doctorate in Indonesian Language Education from Universitas Pendidikan Indonesia, obtained in 2017, complementing his earlier degrees from Universitas Negeri Semarang and Universitas Negeri Sultan Ageng Tirtayasa. Currently, Dr. Wajdi serves as a lecturer at Universitas Negeri Makassar, where he is involved in various educational initiatives. His extensive teaching experience spans multiple institutions, including his roles as a permanent teacher and school principal at MA Al-Khairiyah Pipitan and other schools. His leadership in education is further highlighted by his administrative positions, demonstrating his commitment to enhancing academic standards. Dr. Wajdi is also an active researcher, contributing to national journals with publications focusing on innovative teaching methodologies, such as authentic assessment in drama learning and contextual approaches in literature. His scholarly work aims to improve pedagogical practices and enrich the educational landscape in Indonesia, reflecting his dedication to both teaching and research.

Fatema Wali is an Associate Professor of English at Bahrain Polytechnic, and she has been teaching English as a Second Language, developing curricula, designing e-learning courses, and managing teams. Her research interests include On-line language learning, English as a Second Language, Computer Assisted Language Learning, Interdisciplinary Education, Entrepreneurship Education and Problem Based Learning.

Neelam Yadav is an Assistant Professor at Vivekananda Global University, Jaipur, who specializes in accommodation operations. She is also a research scholar at CT University, Ludhiana. Neelam has authored six research papers, contributed to one edited book, and written seven book chapters. Her work has been presented at six conferences and she holds two patents. Recognized for her contributions, Neelam has also received an award for her research and academic achievement

Seema Yadav has academic qualifications of M. Sc. (Chemistry), M Ed (RIE), UGC-NET, and PhD in Education. Presently she is working as an Assistant Professor, in the Department of Education at The Bhopal School of Education, Bhopal. She has almost 18 years of teaching experience. Her areas of specialization are educational psychology, environmental education, digital learning, and curriculum development.

Index

A

B

C

D

E

F

G

H

T

V

www.ingramcontent.com/pod-product-compliance
Lightning Source LLC
LaVergne TN
LVHW080608300926
849162LV00005B/1078